CANADIAN POLITICS

Fourth Edition

Editors

Gregory S. Mahler
Kalamazoo College

Gregory S. Mahler is provost of Kalamazoo College. He received a B.A. from Oberlin College in 1972, an M.A. in 1974, and a Ph.D. in 1976 from Duke University. His publications in the field of Canadian politics include many articles and two books: *New Dimensions of Canadian Federalism: Canada in a Comparative Perspective* (1987) and *Contemporary Canadian Politics: An Annotated Bibliography* (1988). He is a member of the Association for Canadian Studies in the United States.

Roman R. March
McMaster University

Roman March is an associate professor in the Department of Political Science at McMaster University, Canada. He received a B.A. in 1957 from the University of Winnipeg, an M.A. from Carleton University (Ottawa) in 1958, and a Ph.D. in 1968 from Indiana University. He is the author of two books on Canadian politics and other published articles.

Annual Editions
A Library of Information from the Public Press
Dushkin/McGraw·Hill
Sluice Dock, Guilford, Connecticut 06437

Visit us on the Internet—http://www.dushkin.com/

The Annual Editions Series

ANNUAL EDITIONS, including GLOBAL STUDIES, consist of over 70 volumes designed to provide the reader with convenient, low-cost access to a wide range of current, carefully selected articles from some of the most important magazines, newspapers, and journals published today. ANNUAL EDITIONS are updated on an annual basis through a continuous monitoring of over 300 periodical sources. All ANNUAL EDITIONS have a number of features that are designed to make them particularly useful, including topic guides, annotated tables of contents, unit overviews, and indexes. For the teacher using ANNUAL EDITIONS in the classroom, an Instructor's Resource Guide with test questions is available for each volume. GLOBAL STUDIES titles provide comprehensive background information and selected world press articles on the regions and countries of the world.

VOLUMES AVAILABLE

ANNUAL EDITIONS
Abnormal Psychology
Accounting
Adolescent Psychology
Aging
American Foreign Policy
American Government
American History, Pre-Civil War
American History, Post-Civil War
American Public Policy
Anthropology
Archaeology
Astronomy
Biopsychology
Business Ethics
Child Growth and Development
Comparative Politics
Computers in Education
Computers in Society
Criminal Justice
Criminology
Developing World
Deviant Behavior
Drugs, Society, and Behavior
Dying, Death, and Bereavement
Early Childhood Education

Economics
Educating Exceptional Children
Education
Educational Psychology
Environment
Geography
Geology
Global Issues
Health
Human Development
Human Resources
Human Sexuality
International Business
Macroeconomics
Management
Marketing
Marriage and Family
Mass Media
Microeconomics
Multicultural Education
Nutrition
Personal Growth and Behavior
Physical Anthropology
Psychology
Public Administration
Race and Ethnic Relations

Social Problems
Social Psychology
Sociology
State and Local Government
Teaching English as a Second
   Language
Urban Society
Violence and Terrorism
Western Civilization,
   Pre-Reformation
Western Civilization,
   Post-Reformation
Women's Health
World History, Pre-Modern
World History, Modern
World Politics

GLOBAL STUDIES
Africa
China
India and South Asia
Japan and the Pacific Rim
Latin America
Middle East
Russia, the Eurasian Republics,
   and Central/Eastern Europe
Western Europe

Cataloging in Publication Data
Main entry under title: Annual Editions: Canadian Politics 4/E.
       1. Canada—Politics and Government—1945— —Periodicals. I. Mahler, Gregory S., and March, Roman R., comp. II. Title: Canadian Politics.
350'.0005   ISBN 0-07-292513-2   ISSN 1052-0678

Fourth Edition

Cover image © 1998 PhotoDisc, Inc.

Printed on Recycled Paper

Printed in the United States of America

Editors/Advisory Board

Staff

To the Reader

In publishing ANNUAL EDITIONS we recognize the enormous role played by the magazines, newspapers, and journals of the *public press* in providing current, first-rate educational information in a broad spectrum of interest areas. Many of these articles are appropriate for students, researchers, and professionals seeking accurate, current material to help bridge the gap between principles and theories and the real world. These articles, however, become more useful for study when those of lasting value are carefully *collected, organized, indexed,* and *reproduced* in a *low-cost format,* which provides easy and permanent access when the material is needed. That is the role played by ANNUAL EDITIONS. Under the direction of each volume's *academic editor,* who is an expert in the subject area, and with the guidance of an *Advisory Board,* each year we seek to provide in each ANNUAL EDITION a current, well-balanced, carefully selected collection of the best of the public press for your study and enjoyment. We think that you will find this volume useful, and we hope that you will take a moment to let us know what you think.

We are very pleased to see the fourth edition of *Annual Editions: Canadian Politics* appear, because we feel that it makes a useful contribution to materials available for students of Canadian politics. As Canada continues to face fundamental challenges to its constitutional system, substantial discussion dealing with its role as an international military actor, important questions about transborder economic and cultural relations, and continuing debate over Quebec's role in the Canadian federation and the nature of federal-provincial relations in Canada, we believe that it is especially important for students to have a wide range of materials before them in their studies.

Our goal in assembling this collection has been to include discussion and debate about many contemporary issues that are important in the study of Canadian politics but that, because of their timeliness, may not have received adequate coverage in textbooks and other reference material. The *Annual Editions* concept allows us to include very timely material and allows us to revise and update the contents of this volume periodically. Indeed, *all* of the material in this edition of this volume is new since the last edition. Although the amount of material published in the study of Canadian politics has vastly increased in recent years, we are not aware of any collections of readable, up-to-date articles similar to those found in this volume.

The selections in this collection come from a wide range of publications, including daily newspapers, weekly and monthly newsmagazines, and less frequently published sources that deal with discussion and analysis related to news of a political nature, as well as to cultural, social, and defense issues. In making our selections we have sought to include a variety of issues and perspectives that cover what we perceive to be important themes in contemporary Canadian politics. Some topics have dominated the political landscape in the last year or two—for example, the issue of Ottawa's relations with Quebec, and cultural protectionism—and they are very well represented here. Other subjects may have been less visible in national headlines but are no less important to an understanding of the dynamics of contemporary Canadian politics—for example, the question of the type of parliamentary representation system that would serve Canada best, or the developing backlog threatening Canada's judicial system.

Annual Editions: Canadian Politics is organized into 10 sections, each dealing with a broad dimension of current political interest in Canada, including (a) the constitution and Canadian federalism, (b) the parliamentary system, (c) the Supreme Court and its role in Canadian politics, (d) Quebec, (e) the provinces in the Canadian federation, (f) political parties and elections, (g) the politics of culture, (h) aboriginal issues, (I) foreign policy and the military, and (j) international trade. Within each section we have endeavored to include material touching upon a wide range of subjects from a variety of perspectives. It is, unfortunately, inevitable that subjects about which some readers will feel very strongly will have been omitted from this volume. We again invite you to contact us with your reactions to this collection and with suggestions for the next volume by completing and returning the article rating form in the back of this book.

Gregory Mahler

Gregory Mahler

Roman March

Roman March
Editors

Contents

UNIT 1

The Constitution and Canadian Federalism

Five articles discuss the challenges that Canada faces after the 1995 Quebec Referendum and the subsequent inability to resolve fundamental questions of Canadian unity.

UNIT 2

The Parliamentary System

Eight selections examine fundamental changes in the Canadian parliamentary system and the results of the 1997 parliamentary election.

The concepts in bold italics are developed in the article. For further expansion please refer to the Topic Guide and the Index.

UNIT 3

The Supreme Court and Its Role in Canadian Politics

Five essays examine the structure of Canada's Supreme Court and its role in the Canadian political system.

The concepts in bold italics are developed in the article. For further expansion please refer to the Topic Guide and the Index.

vi

UNIT 4

Quebec

Six articles discuss current debate over the nature of contemporary Quebec and its place in a Canadian union.

UNIT 5

The Provinces in the Canadian Federation

Six selections discuss the vast differences among Canada's provinces and the relationship between the provinces and Ottawa in making policy decisions.

The concepts in bold italics are developed in the article. For further expansion please refer to the Topic Guide and the Index.

UNIT 6

Political Parties and Elections

Seven articles discuss the dynamics of elections in Canada and consider the impact of the electoral system on the results of elections.

UNIT 7

The Politics of Culture

Eight essays consider how the unique political culture of Canada has developed in recent years and the role of cultural industries in Canada's future.

The concepts in bold italics are developed in the article. For further expansion please refer to the Topic Guide and the Index.

UNIT 8

Aboriginal Issues

Seven articles examine the ever-increasingly visible issue of aboriginal rights and how this important social problem is being addressed.

UNIT 9

Foreign Policy and the Military

Five selections examine the current and future choices Canada must make with regard to its foreign and military policy.

The concepts in bold italics are developed in the article. For further expansion please refer to the Topic Guide and the Index.

x

The concepts in bold italics are developed in the article. For further expansion please refer to the Topic Guide and the Index.

Topic Guide

This topic guide suggests how the selections in this book relate to topics of traditional concern to students and professionals involved with the study of Canadian politics. It is useful for locating articles that relate to each other for reading and research. The guide is arranged alphabetically according to topic. Articles may, of course, treat topics that do not appear in the topic guide. In turn, entries in the topic guide do not necessarily constitute a comprehensive listing of all the contents of each selection. **In addition, relevant Web sites, which are annotated on pages 4 and 5, are noted in bold italics under the topic articles.**

TOPIC AREA	TREATED IN	TOPIC AREA	TREATED IN
Aboriginals	47. Apartheid Has Its Attractions 48. Royal Omission 49. Writing on the Wall 50. Unworkable Vision of Self-Government 51. Aboriginal Government: Alternative Outcomes 52. Not a Word about Natives *(3, 12, 27, 28, 29, 30, 31)*	**Elections and Voting (cont.)**	34. Fickle Finger of Folk 35. Distinct Societies 36. Sovereignty's Stumbling Bloc 37. Unheeded Warnings *(3, 8, 9, 13, 14, 15, 16, 17, 18)*
		Ethnic Groups	9. Minority women in the 35th Parliament *(8, 9, 26)*
Alberta	28. Alberta Reopens the Big Spending Tap 31. Suppose Your Vote Counted *(1, 3, 12)*	**Federalism**	1. How Meech Changed History 2. Canada's Challenge 3. Separate Sovereignty—Quebec and Canada 4. Constitutional Solution 5. Case for Strengthening Federal Posers 19. Fiscal Federalism and Quebec Separatism 20. Interprovincial Role 22. Stéphane Dion: 'These Grave Questions' 26. Provinces Muscling in on Federal Territory 27. Ottawa Plays Tough Guys with Provinces *(4, 5, 7, 8, 9, 10, 11, 12, 14)*
Atlantic Provinces	30. Renewing the Case for Maritime Union *(1, 3, 12)*		
Constitution	1. How Meech Changed History 4. Constitutional Solution *(1, 2, 3, 4, 5, 29)*		
Culture	25. Not "Distinct Society" but "Distinctive Societies" 40. CRTC Abandons Cultural Red Flag 42. Culture between Commercials 43. Seven Myths about Canadian Culture 44. Exporting Canadian Culture 45. Canadian Culture Policies Pique U.S. Interest 61. Yikes! They're Tipping the Cultural Balance *(1, 3, 19, 20, 21, 22, 25, 26)*		
		Fisheries Policy	59. Darn Yankees! *(31, 33, 34)*
		Foreign Policy	53. Neighbourhood Watch 54. Canadian Strategic Policy 57. Warriors *(32)*
Decentralized Government	2. Canada's Challenge 5. Case for Strengthening Federal Powers *(1, 2, 3, 4, 5, 6, 7, 8, 9, 21)*	**Grain Policy**	62. Against the Grain *(33, 34)*
Distinct Society	25. Not "Distinct Society" but "Distinctive Societies" *(1, 2, 3, 12)*	**Health Policy**	28. Alberta Reopens the Big Spending Tap 58. Doctoring to NAFTA *(3, 24, 33, 34)*
Economy	19. Fiscal Federalism and Quebec Separatism 30. Renewing the Case for Maritime Union 43. Seven Myths about Canadian Culture 44. Exporting Canadian Culture 46. Apron-String Sovereignty 49. Writing on the Wall 58. Doctoring to NAFTA 59. Darn Yankees! *(1, 3, 12, 33, 34)*	**Indians**	46. Apron-String Sovereignty *(3, 12, 27, 28, 29, 30, 31)*
		Language and Bilingualism	21. Arrêt! You are Entering a French-Speaking Area 38. Canada Talks the Talk 39. Open to Interpretation *(1, 11, 19, 22, 25)*
		Maritime Union	30. Renewing the Case for Maritime Union *(5, 34)*
Elections and Voting	11. Lines in the Political Sand 13. Is He Up to the Job? 31. Suppose Your Vote Counted 32. Counting the Votes so All Votes Count 33. Elections Bring Polls and the Question	**Media**	40. CRTC Abandons Cultural Red Flag 41. Juneau Report and the Gordian Knot

Selected World Wide Web Sites for
Annual Editions: Canadian Politics

All of these Web sites are hot-linked through the *Annual Editions* home page:
http://www.dushkin.com/annualeditions (just click on a book). In addition, these sites are referenced
by number and appear where relevant in the Topic Guide on the previous two pages.

Some Web sites are continually changing their structure and content, so the information listed may not always be available.

General Sources

1. Canada Site/Site du Canada—*http://canada.gc.ca/*—This is the government of Canada's primary Internet site through which Internet users around the world can obtain information about Canada in both English or French.

2. Political Resources on the Net—*http://www.agora.stm.it/politic/*—Here is a listing of political sites on the Internet sorted by country. There are links to Parties, Organizations, Governments, and Media.

3. Yahoo! Canada—*http://www.yahoo.ca/*—This large search engine for Canadian Internet sites includes Arts and Humanities, Business and Economy, Education, Government, Health, Society and Culture, and many other subjects.

The Constitution and Canadian Federalism

4. Canadian Federal Organizations—*http://canada.gc.ca/depts/major/depind_e.html*—This site provides a listing of all Canadian federal organizations and their Internet sites. They cover every aspect of Canadian life.

5. 1987 Constitutional Accord—Meech Lake Accord—*http://www.cpac.ca/frame/english/resources/meech.html*—The complete text of the Meech Lake Accord is available at this site.

6. The Prime Minister's Web Site—*http://pm.gc.ca/*—This is the Web site for Canadian prime minister Jean Chretien.

7. Unity Link—*http://www.uni.ca/*—Unity Link is the Web site of a federalist group that is dedicated to maintaining a united Canada.

The Parliamentary System

8. Digital Democrat: Capital Watch—*http://www.canoe.ca/DemocratCapital/home.html*—An in-depth guide to the Canadian Parliamentary system is available at this site.

9. Parliamentary/Parlementaire Internet—*http://www.parl.gc.ca/index.html*—This Web site, created jointly by the Senate and House of Commons, offers information on the Canadian Parliament. This is the official Web site of the 36th Parliament.

The Supreme Court and Its Role in Canadian Politics

10. Department of Justice—Canada—*http://canada.justice.gc.ca/*—Information originating with the Canadian federal Department of Justice on subjects as varied as recent justice legislation, crime prevention, law reform, and the secession of Quebec is provided at this site, which also accesses all Supreme Court of Canada decisions since January 1993.

Quebec

11. National du Bloc Québécois—*http://blocquebecois.org/*—The Canadian political party Bloc Québécois can be found at this Internet site.

The Provinces in the Canadian Federation

12. Canadian Politics Page—*http://tor-pw1.netcom.ca/~storms/politics.html*—This large index was set up to help students with research and to inform the public regarding Canadian politics. There is a section linking visitors to the Web sites for all Canadian Provinces. Subjects covered include aboriginal issues, federal parties, the Canadian North, Canadian unity, the media, and much more.

Political Parties and Elections

13. Canada's New Democratic Party—*http://websmith.ca/fndp/*—This is the home page for the New Democratic Party.

14. Elections Canada—*http://www.elections.ca/*—This link takes you to Elections Canada, a nonpartisan agency that is responsible for the conduct of federal elections and referendums in Canada.

15. Marxist-Leninist Party of Canada—*http://Fox.nstn.ca:80/~cpc-ml/*—This is the home page for the Marxist-Leninist Party of Canada.

16. Liberal Party—*http://www.liberal.ca/cgi-win/core.exe*—The home page for the Liberal Party of Canada can be found here.

17. Progressive Conservative Party—*http://www.pcparty.ca/*—This is the home page for the Progressive Conservative Party of Canada.

18. Reform Party of Canada—*http://www.reform.ca/*—The home page for the Reform Party of Canada is available at this site.

The Politics of Culture

19. Alliance Quebec—*http://www.aq.qc.ca/mainengl.htm*— Founded in 1982, Alliance Quebec is a volunteer-based community organization committed to the preservation and enhancement of the English-speaking communities and institutions within Quebec.

20. Canadian Museum of Civilization—*http://www.cmcc.muse. digital.ca/cmc/cmceng/welcmeng.html*—The Canadian Museum of Civilization is the national museum of human history dedicated to promoting understanding between the various cultural groups that make up Canadian society.

21. The Council for Canadian Unity—*http://www.ccu-cuc.ca/ lien3.html*—The Council for Canadian Unity was founded in 1964 to provide information to Canadians regarding legal, fiscal, cultural, and political issues.

22. Department of Canadian Heritage—*http://www.pch.gc.ca/*— The Department of Canadian Heritage promotes Canada's distinctive identity and its cultural and natural heritage. Official Languages, Multiculturalism, Broadcasting Policy, Arts Policy, and Cultural Industries are just a few of the subjects covered.

23. Environment Canada's Green Lane—*http://www.doe.ca/*— According to this Web site, Environment Canada is a science-based government department whose business is helping Canadians live and prosper in an environment that is properly protected and conserved.

24. Health Canada—*http://www.hwc.ca/*—This government site is dedicated to helping the people of Canada maintain and improve their health. It contains links to many other health-related sites.

25. National Library of Canada—*http://www.nlc-bnc.ca/ehome. htm*—This is the link to the National Library of Canada, whose main role is to acquire, preserve, and promote the published heritage of Canada for all Canadians.

26. Status of Women Canada—*http://www.swc-cfc.gc.ca/*—The federal government agency that promotes gender equality throughout all areas of Canadian culture is at this site. It is called Status of Women Canada.

Aboriginal Issues

27. Aboriginal Super Information Highway—*http://www. abinfohwy.ca/*—This site is dedicated to providing information for aboriginal people throughout Canada.

28. Assembly of First Nations—*http://afn.ca/*—The AFN exists to promote the restoration of the nation-to-nation relationship among the 633 First Nations communities in Canada.

29. Canadian Aboriginal Law—*http://fox.nstn.ca/~nstn1439/ abolaw.html*—This site is dedicated to providing detailed information regarding aboriginal law. There is a wealth of material regarding treaties, the Constitution, and court rulings.

30. Indian and Northern Affairs Canada—*http://www.inac. gc.ca/index.html*—According to its Mission Statement, this government agency is dedicated to working together to make Canada a better place for First Nation and Northern people.

31. Innu Nation/Mamit Innuat—*http://www.web.net/~innu/ header.html*—This is the official Web site of the Innu Nation/Mamit Innuat.

Foreign Policy and the Military

32. Canadian Foreign Policy—*http://www.carleton.ca/npsia/ cfpj/cfpj.html*—*Canadian Foreign Policy* is one of the leading Canadian journals of international affairs. Abstracts of articles, essays, research articles, and workshop papers are available online.

International Trade

33. NAFTA Secretariat—*http://www.nafta-sec-alena.org/*—This site is dedicated to the study of NAFTA and the NAFTA documents provided by the NAFTA Secretariat.

34. The North American Institute—*http://www.santafe.edu/ ~naminet/index.html*—The NAMI is a trinational public affairs organization that studies the emerging regional space of North America. The group focuses especially on trade and the environment.

We highly recommend that you review our Web site for expanded information and our other product lines. We are continually updating and adding links to our Web site in order to offer you the most usable and useful information that will support and expand the value of your Annual Editions. You can reach us at: *http://www.dushkin.com/annualeditions/.*

The Constitution and Canadian Federalism

Canada has tried for most of its political history as an independent nation to resolve the question of Quebec's role in the Canadian federation. Over the years Canada has gradually evolved from a very decentralized federal system to a more centralized federal system and back to a more decentralized federal system. The question of the relationship between the federal government in Ottawa and the provincial governments in the rest of Canada has been one of the major dimensions of constitutional debate over the years. In this section five articles discuss the

challenges that Canada faces after the 1995 Quebec Referendum and the subsequent inability to resolve fundamental questions of Canadian unity. The Quebec government threatens that another referendum will be held soon and that if it is not successful another will be held after that, and another after that, until eventually a majority of voters there support independence. The federal government is concerned by, and opposes, this approach. What is to be done?

The article by Graham Fraser interprets the impact that the unsuccessful Meech Lake Agreement had on Canadian politics. The agreement, perceived by some as a dramatic success at the time, has had a lasting effect upon the language of federalism in Canadian political debates. Meech Lake identified several key issues in the debate, it highlighted contentious principles, and it offered alternatives to conflict. If not a true crossroads in Canadian political history, it was at least a milestone in the evolution of a truly Canadian approach to the question of federal constitutionalism.

The question of how Canadian federalism could have evolved to the point at which a near majority in Quebec would support secession and independence is the subject of the second article here. Stéphane Dion, Canada's federal minister of intergovernmental affairs, addresses the challenge of reversing the tendency of Quebeckers to support Quebec sovereignty and how the federal government can work toward greater Canadian unity. He suggests that a uniquely Canadian approach to "flexible federalism" and decentralized government will convince Quebeckers to stay within the federal framework.

A drastically different perspective is that Quebec should overtly move toward sovereignty and independence. Senator Jacques Brassard of Quebec argues, in our third article, that the federal government needs to recognize that a true partnership between Quebec and Ottawa is the only outcome that is viable in the long run. The government of Quebec is a democrati-

cally elected government, and it is the legitimate voice of the Quebec people. Ultimately, we are told, the only solution to the conflict is true Quebec sovereignty and independence.

A different perspective is offered by Senator Gérald-A. Beaudoin, also from Quebec, who suggests that Quebec's role in the federation must be an appropriate one that recognizes its importance in the federation. In brief, political powers of contemporary Canada must reflect the reality of the present. He suggests that it is not at all inevitable that Quebec voters will opt for sovereignty and independence, but they must be guaranteed appropriate power for their provincial government in the federal government.

The final essay of this section, by Andrew Coyne, takes a different perspective, arguing that a real understanding of federal government suggests that Canada has permitted powers to become too "decentralized" over time and that it is now appropriate for an increasingly "centralized" approach to Canadian federalism. The author suggests that too much power has shifted to the provinces and out of the control of Ottawa and that it is time for Ottawa to regain some of this power. The major reason that power continues to flow *away* from Ottawa is to permit Quebec to expand its power base, but it is time for this pattern to be reversed.

Looking Ahead: Challenge Questions

How has the balance of power between Ottawa and the provincial governments changed over the years? How does the balance today compare with 20 years ago? A hundred years ago?

What was Meech Lake's long-term legacy for Canadian politics? Would the debate be easier to address today if Meech had not taken place? Explain.

Are Quebec's demands reasonable? What would be the effect on Canada's federation if Quebec received more power?

CONSTITUTION

How Meech changed history

Ten years ago 11 premiers met on the shores of a lake north of Ottawa to hammer out an accord they thought would unify Canada. Instead, its failure has cast a lingering shadow over the country.

BY GRAHAM FRASER

The Globe and Mail

MEECH Lake. Ten years after the prime minister invited the 10 premiers to the federal government retreat north of Ottawa to discuss the Constitution, the phrase still evokes a painful bundle of emotions and memories, resentments and regrets.

For some, the phrase is inextricably linked to former prime minister Brian Mulroney, and the passions he still kindles in many English-speaking Canadians. For others, it is a symbol of English-speaking Canada's distrust and rejection of Quebec.

From its conception until its death three years later, when it failed to achieve ratification in the legislatures of Manitoba and Newfoundland, the agreement was much more than just a constitutional amendment.

Its crafted ambiguity enraged some of those who had embraced the Charter of Rights and Freedoms as a sacred text. As an icon of reconciliation, it was cherished by those who had wept to see the Constitution patriated over Quebec's objections. It helped re- elect Brian Mulroney in 1988 and Robert Bourassa in 1989. It tore apart the Liberal Party of Canada. And its collapse in 1990 changed the shape of Canadian politics.

"My view is that it is one of the seminal events of Canadian history, not unlike the death of Louis Riel,"

says former Ontario premier David Peterson, referring to the failure of the agreement. "It has fundamentally realigned the political landscape in Canada. It is responsible for the rise of the Bloc and the resurrection of the Parti Québécois. It contributed to the success of Reform."

For if the agreement at Meech Lake in 1987 seemed to contribute to the demoralization of the separatist movement in Quebec and a period of harmony in Canada as a whole, its unravelling and collapse in 1990 also led to Lucien Bouchard's departure from the federal cabinet, the surge of support in English-speaking Canada for Newfoundland premier Clyde Wells and the spectacular growth in support for sovereignty in Quebec.

The signators have no regrets. "My feeling now is the same as it was then," says former Newfoundland premier Brian Peckford. "It was an honourable compromise."

Neither do most of the opponents.

If Meech Lake had passed, "I think we would have put the country on the road to medium and long-term constitutional turmoil," says Michael Bliss, a University of Toronto historian. "We would have privileged Quebec, and given it special status. There would have been more rancour about the privileging of Quebec—and the separatists

would have had some other set of grievances. If Meech solved one problem, it would have opened up a whole bunch of others."

None of the men who were at Meech Lake that day are still in elected politics. Brian Mulroney is practicing law in Montreal, Mr. Peckford is working with a mining company in Vancouver and living on Vancouver Island, Nova Scotia's John Buchanan is in the Senate, Mr. Peterson is practicing law in Toronto, Manitoba's Howard Pawley is teaching law in Windsor and Saskatchewan's Grant Devine, Alberta's Don Getty and British Columbia's Bill Vander Zalm are all in private business. Three have died: Robert Bourassa of Quebec, Richard Hatfield of New Brunswick and Joe Ghiz of Prince Edward Island.

A decade later, the symbolism remains more important than the substance—partly because the substance of the accord has been adopted.

"If you look at the 'distinct decision' that [Prime Minister Jean] Chrétien has passed into law, the veto he has given Quebec, the statement in the budget that the spending power will never be used—Meech is all there," Mr. Mulroney says. "We got none of the benefits and all of the anguish."

What has not been achieved is the Liberal government's attempt to keep the promise that Mr. Chrétien made on the eve of the 1995 Quebec referendum—the symbolic gesture of inclusion toward Quebec that Meech Lake was intended, and largely perceived, to be.

What drove the constitutional process a decade ago was the fact that the 1982 Constitution had been amended over the objections of the Quebec National Assembly, and no Quebec government— separatist or federalist—since has been prepared to accept the Constitution without amendment.

In August 1984, at his nomination meeting in Sept-Iles, Mr. Mulroney promised that if he were elected he would make it possible for the Quebec National Assembly to sign the Constitution "with honour and enthusiasm." After the Quebec Liberals were elected in 1985, he named Senator Lowell Murray as the minister responsible—a non-Quebecker who was familiar with Quebec, and was outside the House of Commons, and thus not required to face Question Period.

In the spring of 1986, at a conference at Mont Gabriel, Quebec reiterated its five conditions and, in the ensuing sessions, the constitutional veterans present agreed that the timing was right (with a federalist government in Quebec and one in Ottawa that was sympathetic to a provincial agenda) for an agreement.

But even then, there was an awareness that there must be a good chance of success—to try and fail would be worse than not trying.

Almost a year later, after Mr. Murray had shuttled across the country to every capital, he found a greater degree of consensus than was generally recognized. Despite overwhelmingly low expectations, all 10 premiers and the prime minister agreed on a draft that long day at Meech Lake, and, after a marathon session in June, they agreed on the legal text.

After some initial reservations, Liberal leader John Turner and New Democratic Party leader Ed Broadbent endorsed the accord. And on June 23, the Quebec National Assembly became the first legislature to ratify it. The other provinces had three years to follow suit.

How did it unravel?

How did the unanimity come apart?

"In fairness to us all, nobody fully understood the implications of Section 38," Mr. Mulroney says, referring to the section in the 1982 Constitution that allowed a three-year period for ratification of constitutional amendments by provincial legislatures. During that period, it was almost inevitable that governments would change.

If the prime minister and the premiers miscalculated that, they also misjudged the depth and passion of the commitment to the Charter of Rights and Freedoms outside Quebec.

In only a few years, the Charter had acquired huge symbolic importance; a large number of groups and individuals had become what British Columbia political scientist Alan Cairns called "Charter Canadians"—people who saw the Charter as the central defining document of the country's identity and a critical tool in achieving social justice. Any suggestion that provisions of the Charter might be reinterpreted, let alone questioned or weakened, in the interests of Quebec being defined as a distinct society was unacceptable.

Pierre Trudeau accentuated that concern, and began the wave of opinion against the accord with a letter published in La Presse and The Toronto Star at the end of May, 1987, in which he argued that Meech would mean the end of "a single Canada, bilingual and multicultural . . . we are henceforth to have two Canadas, each defined in terms of language."

Paradoxically, one of the Meech Lake accord's perceived strengths was actually its greatest weakness. The fact that all three federal parties and all 10 premiers endorsed the agreement meant there was no parliamentary forum for opposition. The free-trade agreement, one of the other cornerstones of the Mulroney government, was the subject of a

---

REMEMBERING THE ACCORD

On April 30, 1987, at Meech Lake, Prime Minister Brian Mulroney and the 10 provincial premiers agreed in principle to the following five points.

1. Quebec's Distinct Society: recognizing the linguistic duality of Canada and that Quebec constitutes "a distinct society" within Canada.

2. Immigration: agreeing to increase the power of the provinces. In particular, Quebec would receive a number of immigrants proportional to its share of the population.

3. Supreme Court: entrenching the Supreme Court in the Constitution with at least three of the nine judges appointed from the civil bar. The federal government agreed to appoint judges from lists of candidates proposed by the provinces.

4. Spending Power: giving the provinces the right to opt-out with compensation from federal shared-cost programs in provincial jurisdictions if that province undertook its own program "compatible with national objectives."

5. Amending Formula: The existing amending formula was maintained with the agreement that the unanimity rule be extended so that all provinces including Quebec would have a veto over changes to the Senate, the Supreme Court and the addition of new provinces.

The 11 ministers also agreed to hold a Conference on the Constitution before the end of 1988 to discuss Senate reform and the fisheries, and to hold subsequent conferences "not less than once a year." In addition, there would be a constitutional obligation to hold an annual first ministers' conference on the economy.

On June 3, the legal text was agreed to and, after committee hearings in Quebec City, the Quebec National Assembly became the first legislature to ratify the accord on June 23, 1987, starting the clock on the three-year deadline for ratification. The time expired without the accord having been ratified by Manitoba or Newfoundland on June 23, 1990.

lengthy, passionate parliamentary debate. The fact that there was no political party in Ottawa that represented the opposition to Meech meant that antagonism built up, both inside the Liberal Party and among various interest groups.

The antagonism was all the greater because the signators agreed that the terms of deal would not be reopened. Once it had been ratified by Quebec, it could not be modified without being introduced and voted on again. The accord was "a seamless web," in Mr. Murray's words, and would only be amended if "egregious errors" were found.

Then, a number of key events occurred.

"I wish that Richard Hatfield had proceeded to have it ratified immediately," recalls Mr. Mulroney. He did not. In the election that followed in the fall of 1987, Mr. Hatfield was overwhelmingly defeated, and Frank McKenna, who had expressed serious reservations about Meech Lake was elected. Those reservations started a process of pulling back.

For Norman Spector, who was the senior federal civil servant at the talks, one of the critical moves was made by Manitoba's Mr. Pawley, who, in protest of the federal government's commitment to free trade, withdrew the Meech Lake resolution from the legislature. "Had he proceeded, McKenna would have been alone," Mr. Spector says, and this would have made the dynamic very different.

When Liberal Clyde Wells became premier of Newfoundland, its House of Assembly revoked Newfoundland's prior ratification of Meech Lake.

Finally, in 1988, the Quebec National Assembly passed Bill 178, which used the "notwithstanding" clause in the 1982 Constitution to ensure that the Charter could not be used to challenge legislation permitting the use of English on signs inside Quebec stores, but not outside.

This had nothing to do with Meech Lake directly; it was an amendment to the language law that allowed more use of English and not less; it was not the only use of the notwithstanding clause, either by Quebec or by other provinces, or on the tricky question of language rights.

No matter. The resentment toward Quebec intensified.

The unravelling and collapse of Meech Lake is also a story that involves Jean Chrétien's campaign for the Liberal leadership, which was built on the visceral opposition to Meech in large parts of the party, and explains the lack of support for him in Quebec.

It is a chronicle that explains both the anger and adulation that is felt toward Lucien Bouchard, who quit the Mulroney cabinet over his rage at the process intended to save the accord.

It is an event that includes the political earthquake that created the Bloc Québécois and the explosive growth of support for separatism in Quebec in the summer of 1990, as well as the reinforced populist support for Preston Manning and the Reform Party.

Now, 10 years after 11 first ministers prepared to go for a meeting at a retreat beside a lake north of Ottawa, a shadow remains. Intended as an icon of unity, Meech Lake remains a symbol of what divides the country.

Canada's Challenge

Uniting hearts and minds for a federal future

Hon. Stéphane Dion, MP, *in Ottawa*

In October 1995, one of Canada's largest provinces, Quebec, came within a percentage point of voting to become a sovereign nation. How could one of the world's most successful countries have created such a confrontation for itself and can it pull back from the brink of fragmentation? Canada's Minister responsible for intergovernmental relations argues that flexible federalism and a renewed appreciation of the benefits of decentralized government are the keys to maintaining a united Canada.

"The federal system was created with the intention of combining the advantages which result from the magnitude and the littleness of nations." The founders of the Canadian federal state were no doubt inspired by that principle, expressed by a champion of democracy, Alexis de Tocqueville, when in 1867 they decided to take on the formidable challenge of reconciling solidarity and local autonomy within a single federation. Did they suspect that, a centry and a quarter later, Canada would achieve a level of democracy, freedom, fairness and prosperity that would make it a model on the international scene? No less a Parliamentarian than Sir

Hon. Stéphane Dion.

M. Dion, a professor of political science at the Université de Montréal since 1984, was appointed President of the Queen's Privy Council for Canada and Minister of Intergovernmental Affairs in January 1996. Two months later he won a by-election for the governing Liberal Party in a Quebec seat in Canadian House of Commons. He has held several prestigious academic positions in Canada, Washington and Paris.

Winston Churchill described Canada as "an example to every country and a pattern for the future of the world".

Up to the task

That success is certainly not the result of happenstance. For 129 years, Canadians have striven to develop an original, flexible fed-

eral system. Canada has evolved by respecting the fundamental values shared by its citizens, while taking account of the specific needs and priorities of each region. The Canadian federal system can certainly be improved, but it has served well as a way of functioning and an instrument for economic, political and social partnership. Unlike other systems of government, it has withstood the test of time.

Canada's achievements in many areas speak for themselves: the Organization for Economic Co-operation and Development (OECD) ranks Canada among the top six countries in the world in terms of per capita income. Canada also had the second highest rate of economic growth in the past 30 years.

Canada has also won international recognition for its commitment to peacekeeping, humanitarian assistance and international co-operation, and for its technological expertise in a number of large-scale sectors, including: communications, hydroelectricity, nuclear energy, transportation, civil engineering, agro-food, biotechnology and

Reprinted with permission from *The Parliamentarian*, July 1996, pp. 217-221. © 1996 by The Parliamentarian.

aerospace.

Reconciling solidarity, local autonomy, diversity and linguistic duality within a country which occupies almost half the continent is an exceptional achievement of hearts and minds, and is the key to Canadian federalism's originality. It is to be seen not only as a reflection of Canadians' desire for and pride in uniting together in action in the name of their shared values and heritage but as a need for and a pride in belonging to their respective communities. No system can fulfil such ambitions better than federalism.

Quebec within the federation

Quebecers have every reason to be proud of what Quebec has become today. The original institutions that it has created have allowed it to prosper and to develop its unique spirit and culture within North America. Quebec is more French today than it has been since the beginnings of the federation in 1867: 94 per cent of its population speaks French. In addition to language guarantees in the Canadian constitution, Quebec has its own language laws which make French the language of work in Quebec and ensure that the vast majority of young Quebecers attend French schools.

As a Canadian province, Quebec enjoys autonomy not found in any member state of the OECD. Specific provisions distinguish Quebec from the other provinces in matters as varied as civil law, representation on the Supreme Court and the Federal Court, taxation, international relations, the provincial pension plan, social policy, post-secondary education, and immigration.

Moreover, Quebecers have always made an original and essential contribution to the success and evolution of the Canadian federation. Exactly 100 years ago, Wilfrid Laurier became the first French-speaking Quebecer to serve as Prime Minister of Canada. For 26 of the past 28 years, our country has been led by Prime Ministers from Quebec.

Quebecers also hold strategic posts in the federal cabinet and the top echelons of the federal public service. That influence can be felt in all Canadian institutions.

On 30 October 1995, Quebecers rejected, by a plurality of 50.6 per cent, the option which the secessionists were proposing for the second time in 15 years. Quebec and all of Canada came very close to being plunged into a crisis the outcome of which would be very uncertain.

Seeds of crisis

To outsiders, the threat to Canadian unity is difficult to understand. Given the sterling record of the Canadian federation as a whole and of Quebec in particular, we must ask how almost 50 per cent of Quebecers voted for an option which challenged Canada's very existence.

There is no single explanation; but if it must boil down to one, it is a question of identity. The vast majority of Quebecers want to stay Canadian, as opinion polls constantly show. Too many of them, however, have bought into the false argument that their Canadian identity threatens their identity as Quebecers. Recent failed attempts to have Quebec recognized in the Canadian constitution as a distinct society convinced many Quebecers that Canadians in the other provinces do not accept them as they are.

On the contrary, their identity as Quebecers and their Canadian identity are eminently complementary.

Another element that worked in favour of the "yes" side in the 30 October referendum was the ambiguous nature of the referendum question. Secessionists did their best to sow confusion about what was at stake in the referendum: a definitive break-up.

Their tactics proved to be effective. That was demonstrated by a poll conducted at the end of the referendum campaign which revealed that 80 per cent of Quebecers who were planning to vote "yes" believed that Quebec would automatically continue to use the Canadian dollar; 90 per cent felt that Quebec's economic ties with Canada would remain unchanged, and 50 per cent felt they would continue to use the Canadian passport. More than 25 per cent of "yes" voters believed that Quebec would continue to elect federal Members of Parliament.

In my opinion, neither the tactics nor the arguments of the Quebec secessionists, who want to break the ties of solidarity and citizenship between Quebecers and other Canadians, are justified. I know of no other well-established democracy with at least 10 consecutive years of universal suffrage that has experienced secession. Such a rupture of solidarity seems difficult to justify in a democracy, especially in Canada, which has such high, vibrant human ideals.

Canada is the last place in the world where identity-based fragmentation should be allowed to triumph. Our country symbolizes better than any other the ideal of harmonious co-existence of different communities within a single state. As long ago as the 1950s, U.S. President Harry Truman described our country in the following terms: "Canada's eminent position today is a tribute to the patience, tolerance and strength of character of her people. Canada's notable achievement of national unity and progress through accommodation, moderation and forbearance can be studied with profit by sister nations."

French facts

Nevertheless, I do not cast any doubt on the legitimacy of Quebec's quest for cultural affirmation within Canada. The minority status of French in North America is a source of concern for Quebecers — a fear that is justified by the fact that only 2.5 per cent of the North American population, or one out of every 25 people, is French-speaking. Canada has just over 7 million francophones, or one out of four Canadians, more than 6 million of whom live in Quebec.

The French language and culture in Canada are so proud and vibrant, especially in Quebec, because they have succeeded in flourishing against all expectations, partly because of the determination of French-language communities in resisting assimilation, partly because of the constitutional protection that they enjoy and partly because of Canada's Official Languages Act, which prescribes linguistic duality in all federal institutions.

Our French language and culture resonate throughout the country and around the world, supported by, among other things, Canada's cultural institutions, such as the Canadian Broadcasting Corporation, the National Film Board, Telefilm Canada and the Canada Council.

That exceptional meeting of cultures expresses Canada's true national identity. Indeed, then Prime Minister Lester B. Pearson remarked on that in 1967: "If any Canadian at any time wishes to point out how different he is from an American, and naturally how superior he is, all he has to do is address him in French."

Canada is recognized as an open country, a warm, welcoming land and a society that respects diversity. We have earned that reputation by dint of the values we advocate, and the efforts we have put into building this wonderful country, year after year, together, from the Atlantic to the Arctic to the Pacific. That is why we shall continue to shape Canada with and for all the communities that it comprises. We have chosen to take a pragmatic approach to modernize the federation, to prepare it to take on the challenges of the 21st century and to meet the aspirations of all Canadians.

Advantages unappreciated

I am not convinced that those who believe in Canadian federalism have always seen the need, in the past two decades, to make the effort to promote the advantages of our federation to Canadians. Our natural attachment to Canada leads us to take our country for granted and not highlight its assets. Canadian pride must be celebrated and fostered. By leaving the field open to secessionist arguments, we have let a number of myths and misperceptions about our federation take root in public opinion.

Canadian federalism is far from being a failure. The contention that the federation is a system which is incapable of evolving, is increasingly centralizing and offers no autonomy or advantages to its partners does not stand up to an objective and factual analysis of reality. The federal system gives citizens in each province something extra that makes the provinces stronger collectively than they could ever be individually. It gives them a strong social solidarity, an economic union which benefits every province and is eminently appropriate in a context of globalization and a leverage, presence and influence on the international scene which is now indispensable.

We have put in place a network of social programmes to ensure that all citizens enjoy an equitable level of well-being.

Canada has implemented an equalization programme, which has been incorporated into the constitution, under which the federal government provides unconditional funding to provinces whose revenues are below the Canadian average. This programme allows all provinces to provide public services of comparable quality.

That commitment to social solidarity is unequalled anywhere in the world, and it has yielded impressive results. The gap between have and have-not provinces has narrowed considerably in the past 30 years and per-capita GDP in the seven provinces that received equalization payments grew more quickly than in the three richest provinces.

Provinces' extensive autonomy over social policy enables them to find innovative solutions tailored to their specific needs. No matter what region of the country they live in, Canadians have access to equitable and comparable services. That is what Canadian social solidarity — one of the great unifying strengths of our federation — is all about.

Canada-wide economic integration is undeniably a major asset that ensures extensive mobility of goods, services, labour and capital, as well as a common currency and a uniform legislative framework. The interprovincial trade agreement that came into effect in July 1995 has almost eliminated the last obstacles to interprovincial trade, which is worth $150 billion — almost as much as trade between Canada and other countries. Some provinces' interprovincial trade is greater than their exports abroad.

The Canadian common market is a strong, diversified economic bloc in which each region can develop its own opportunities, in accordance with its natural and human resources, while benefiting from a free domestic market. That economic union also makes us more competitive internationally.

It is noteworthy that Canada is one of the largest trading nations in the world in per capita terms. Its exports account for almost 40 per cent of its gross domestic product. International trade is a major source of jobs for all Canadian provinces; every $1 billion in exports represents 11,000 jobs. In other words, one out of three jobs depends directly on our exports.

As an influential and respected member of major international organizations and institutions such as the G7, North American Free Trade Agreement (NAFTA), the Commonwealth, the Francophonie, the Organization of American States, the Asia-Pacific Economic Co-operation Council, the European Bank for Reconstruction and Development and, of course, the United Nations, Canada opens up avenues of influence to all provinces and all Canadians which enable them to develop economic and cultural ties and networks in every corner of the globe.

Quebec and New Brunswick, for example, sit on bodies of the Francophonie as participating governments, with Canada's support. The provinces have extensive rights with regard to negotiating treaties. In areas of exclusive provincial or shared jurisdiction, they can participate in negotiating a Canadian treaty and sign agreements of international scope.

A decentralized federation

Over the past four decades, Canada has seen a gradual and

substantial redistribution of the federal government's taxing and spending power to the provincial governments, which has made our country one of the most decentralized federations. In 1950, the federal government collected $3.30 for every $1 of revenue collected by the provinces; in 1993 the figure had dropped to $1.20. Federal programme spending, which was one and a half times the size of provincial and municipal spending in the 1950s, was only three quarters their size in 1990, and that proportion will drop to two-thirds by 1996.

It has often been claimed that the federal government's spending power is a powerful centralizing instrument. According to a study by Professor Ronald Watts of Queen's University in Kingston, Ontario, however, conditional transfers by the federal government account for a less substantial share of the revenues of Canada's provinces than is the case with the member states of other major OECD federations. In 1994, such conditional transfers accounted for 17 per cent of the revenues of member states in the U.S. and Australia, 16 per cent for Germany and 14 per cent for Switzerland, but only 10 per cent for Canada.

Furthermore, the numerous bilateral agreements between the federal government and the provinces create an impetus for decentralization that yields more efficient delivery of services to Canadians.

A new era in Canadian federalism

The main lesson to be learned from the referendum result is the message that Quebecers are sending their leaders, which has been echoed by other Canadians: that Canadians want the two levels of government to clarify their roles and responsibilities, to work to create a favourable economic and social climate that generates jobs and to demonstrate enlightened leadership as they take Canada and its 30 million citizens into the 21st century.

The government of Canada has shown that it is very receptive to that message for change

which was sent by Quebecers and other Canadians during the Quebec referendum. It immediately took action by passing a law that effectively gave five regions of the country, including Quebec, a veto over any constitutional change that may affect them.

Both Chambers of the Parliament of Canada have passed a resolution in favour of recognizing Quebec as a distinct society within Canada. Specifically, the resolution proclaims Quebec's distinctiveness by virtue of its unique culture, civil law tradition and French-speaking majority, and guarantees Quebecers that Parliament and all departments and agencies of the government of Canada will be guided by the resolution in their decisions and legislation. The government of Canada will continue to build a consensus to ensure that these changes are entrenched in the constitution.

The federal government has also responded to the call by Quebec and the other provinces for greater autonomy. It has thus undertaken to withdraw from certain jurisdictions — notably labour market training, some aspects of transport, forestry and mining development and recreation.

The federal government is exploring new opportunities for partnership with the provinces — notably with regard to employment measures, food inspection, social housing, tourism and environmental management. It has also proposed appropriate harmonization mechanisms to the provinces to simplify the lives of citizens and investors.

In the same vein, and for the first time in the history of the Canadian federation, the government of Canada has made a commitment no longer to use its spending power to establish new shared-cost programmes in areas of exclusive provincial jurisdiction without the consent of the majority of the provinces.

These initiatives, coupled with administrative reforms to reduce overlap and duplication between the two levels of government, are part of an appropriate, gradual, systemic process

to clarify the roles and responsibilities of the federal government and to make the Canadian federation even more efficient and better adapted to new realities. By renewing and revitalizing the Canadian federation, we have reason to believe that a clear majority of Quebecers will find what they are looking for within Canada, and will feel that another referendum on secession is unnecessary.

Clear vision

It is not and never will be the government of Canada's intention to deny Quebecers the right to express themselves on their future. Nevertheless, if there is another separation referendum in Quebec, the federal government will ensure, in the interest of Quebecers and other Canadians, that the question and the consequences of secession are clear to everyone. It would be shirking its responsibility to protect the rights of all Canadians, including Quebecers, if it let the secessionist leaders impose their own ground rules and perpetuate confusion about their real objective.

It is essential to establish mutually acceptable rules, and to do so calmly and by respecting the rule of law. The debates that have marked Canada's history have always led to consultation and compromise.

Canada is a young country which was founded on and has grown through its rich, multifaceted heritage, in historical, cultural and human terms. The key to its past, present and future lies in the tremendous complementarity of our identities, which are both dissimilar and indissoluble, and in a necessary convergence of wills to find and accept a realignment of the federation that is acceptable to all its partners and all Canadians.

The mission I have taken on, as a Minister and on behalf of the government of Canada, and also as a Quebecer and a proud Canadian, is to revitalize all Canadians' desire for and pride in being together, to renew all Quebecers' passion for Canada and to forge a new synergy within the Canadian federal union.

Separate Sovereignty

Québec and Canada: Equal partners

Hon. Jacques Brassard, MNA, *in Quebec City*

The pro-separatist government in Quebec calls for its people to be recognized as a sovereign nation distinct from, but linked with, the rest of Canada.

In September 1994, the Parti Québécois came to power provincially in Québec with the mandate to proceed as soon as possible to a public consultation with a view to Québec's accession to sovereignty.

In the federal elections, held the year before, two-thirds of the federal Members of Parliament from Québec had been elected on the ticket of the Bloc Québécois, a party advocating, at the federal level, Québec's accession to sovereignty. In fact, these Members of Parliament then formed — and still do — the Official Opposition in the Canadian Parliament.

This combination of a majority of Parti Québécois Members in the Québec National Assembly and a majority of Québec's federal Members of Parliament from the Bloc Québécois gave the sovereignty proposal unprecedented legitimacy.

M. Brassard is the Minister of Canadian Intergovernmental Affairs in the Parti Québécois government of Québec. A teacher, he has been a Member of the National Assembly since 1976.

Hon. Jacques Brassard.

The new Québec government wasted no time before initiating the process that was to culminate in the second referendum on sovereignty. The first was held in 1980.

In the early months of 1995, Quebecers were invited to participate in the work of regional commissions on the future of Québec by proposing ideas for a declaration of sovereignty and discussing the main orientations of a sovereign Québec. More than 50,000 Quebecers of different origins accepted the invitation. A national commission subsequently summarized this work and made recommendations to the government of Québec.

Partnership

On 12 June 1995, the Prime Minister of Québec, Hon. Jacques Parizeau, signed an agreement with the Leader of the Official Opposition in Ottawa, Hon. Lucien Bouchard, (who succeeded Mr Parizeau in January 1996 at the head of the Québec government) and with M. Mario Dumont, the Leader of the Action démocratique du Québec, another political party represented in the Québec National Assembly. This tripartite agreement included a commitment to propose to Canada, before Québec's accession to sovereignty, a treaty of partnership similar in some respects to the European Union model, in order to ensure the free movement of people, goods, services and capital between the two states.

The Québec government vigorously supports the North American Free Trade Agreement and intends to participate by operation of law in this Agreement after Québec achieves sovereignty.

In September 1995, on the basis of the report of the National Commission and the tripartite agreement, the government tabled in the Québec National Assembly Bill 1, entitled an Act Respecting the Future of Québec. The Bill proposed that Québec become a sovereign country democratically and after a referendum supporting it. Under its terms, the National Assembly was authorized to proclaim Québec's sovereignty and to give effect to the declaration of sovereignty in the preamble of the Bill.

The Bill provided that the proclamation of sovereignty would be preceded by a formal offer of economic and political partnership with Canada. The Québec government was therefore bound to propose to the government of Canada the conclusion of a treaty of economic and political partnership on the basis of the agreement of 12 June, which was reproduced in the schedule to the Bill.

In addition, an orientation and supervision committee was established for the purpose of the negotiations relating to the partnership treaty, and, during the referendum campaign a few weeks later, M. Bouchard was named as Québec's negotiator.

Legislative plan

The first three provisions of the Bill clearly demonstrated the intentions of the Québec government:

1. The National Assembly is authorized, within the scope of this act, to proclaim the sovereignty of Québec.

   This proclamation must be preceded by a formal offer of economic and political partnership with Canada.

2. On the date fixed in the proclamation of the National Assembly, the declaration of sovereignty appearing in the preamble shall take effect and Québec shall become a sovereign country; it shall acquire the exclusive power to pass all its laws, levy all its taxes and conclude all its treaties.

3. The government is bound to propose to the government of Canada the conclusion of a treaty of economic and political partnership on the basis of the tripartite agreement of 12 June 1995 reproduced in the schedule.

   The treaty must be approved by the National Assembly before being ratified.

To ensure the continuity of institutions, laws, rights and freedoms, the Bill provided for the adoption of an interim constitution. It also provided for the creation of a constituent commission for the purpose of drawing up a new Québec constitution. The draft constitution would be tabled in the National Assembly, which had to approve its final text. The constitution would then also have to be submitted to a referendum before it could become, once it had been approved, the fundamental law of Québec.

Rights, borders and responsibilities

The new constitution of Québec was to state that Québec is a French-speaking country and to impose upon the government the obligation of protecting Québec culture and ensuring its development. It was to include a charter of human rights and freedoms and, insofar as the territorial integrity of Québec was respected, would provide guarantees regarding the rights of the English-speaking community and the aboriginal nations.

Section 10 of the Bill provided details concerning the territory of a sovereign Québec:

10. Québec shall retain its boundaries as they exist within the Canadian federation on the date on which Québec becomes a sovereign country. It shall exercise its jurisdiction over the land, air and water forming its territory and over the areas adjacent to its coast, in accordance with the rules of international law.

The Bill provided additional details concerning Québec citizenship, the currency that would have legal tender in Québec and the participation of Québec in international treaties, organizations and alliances. It ensured the continuity of the laws, of the payment of pensions and benefits to Québec citizens, and of licences and permits, contracts and the courts of justice.

The Bill also contained provisions concerning the conclusion of an agreement with the government of Canada on the equitable division of the assets and liabilities of the federal government.

Lastly, section 26 of the Bill set a maximum of one year for the negotiations with Canada on the partnership treaty, unless the period was extended by order of the National Assembly, and reserved Québec's right to proclaim sovereignty unilaterally if negotiations with Canada proved fruitless.

The referendum

The referendum on sovereignty was held on 30 October 1995. Quebecers were asked whether they authorized the National Assembly to proclaim sovereignty in accordance with the Bill and the tripartite agreement of 12 June.

Participation in the referendum was at a rate rarely achieved in a Western democracy (about 93 per cent), and the government's option garnered 49.4 per cent of the votes cast, while 50.6 per cent of the voters expressed their disagreement. The vote in favour of sovereignty was much higher this time than in 1980, when 40.4 per cent of Quebecers voted for that option.

As in 1980, the Prime Minister of Canada and several Members of his government participated actively in the referendum campaign and stressed the irreversibility of a result in favour of sovereignty. The Québec people exercised their right to decide their own future and intend to continue to do so freely.

Opinion polls since the referendum show an increase in support for sovereignty, which is now the option of choice for a majority of Quebecers. Under Québec law, no other referendum on sovereignty can be held before the next general elections, which must take place by the fall of 1999.

For the present (which one editorialist recently dubbed the "inter-referendum" period), the Québec government feels that, although Québec's citizens did not authorize it to take the path to sovereignty immediately, neither did they give it — at 49.9 per cent support for sovereignty — the mandate to take part in constitutional negotiations with the government of Canada in a process of renewal of the Canadian federation.

Representing the people

Since Québec is still a member of the federation and its citizens are still contributing, through their taxes, to the financing of federal programmes, the Québec government views its relations with the federal government from the vantage point of the promotion and defence of Québec's interests. In general, Québec intends to operate on a one-on-one basis with Canada and to conduct its intergovernmental affairs on a people-to-people basis.

In a recent speech in the National Assembly, the Prime Minister of Québec re-affirmed the right of the Québec people to freely decide their own future and the right of the National Assembly to proclaim Québec sovereignty unilaterally, if necessary, after the next referendum on sovereignty is held.

It is to be hoped that Québec will enter the new millennium with the heightened pride and dignity that accession to sovereignty will give it.

A Constitutional Solution

The evolution of Canadian federalism

Sen. the Hon. Gérald-A. Beaudoin, OC, QC, *in Ottawa*

A Canadian Senator from Québec traces Canada's constitutional history to support a call for a more creative approach to developing a less centralized federation.

The Canadian constitution of 1867 is one of the oldest in the world. It was the first federal constitution in the British Empire, and Canada was the first federation to combine a parliamentary regime with the system of responsible government.

The Constitution Act of 1867 outlines the distribution of legislative power: section 91 lists the federal powers; section 92 the provincial powers; section 93, a special article, allocates education to the provinces, and sections 94A and 95 deal with concurrent powers.

A Supreme Court, established in 1875, exercises since 1949 ultimate control over the constitu-

Sen. the Hon. Gérald-A. Beaudoin.

Sen. Beaudoin, a lawyer and law professor, has been a Conservative Senator representing a Québec division since 1988. He was a Joint Chairman of two special constitutional joint committees of the Parliament of Canada in 1991-92.

tionality of federal and provincial legislation. The court is composed of nine judges, three of whom are trained in the civil law system and six in the common law tradition.

In 1982, a Canadian Charter of Rights and Freedoms was enshrined in the constitution of Canada.

Section 52 of the Constitution Act, 1982, states that the constitution is the supreme law of Canada and that any law that is inconsistent with the provisions of the constitution is, to the extent of the inconsistency, of no force or effect.

The French fact

Only one province in Canada is in its majority French-speaking. No matter how far ahead we cast our vision, a similar situation is unlikely to occur in any other province, even if, since 1870 when Manitoba was created, more than one French-speaking leader has had such a dream. In New Brunswick 34 per cent of the population is French-speaking.

If we wish to keep Québec within the Canadian federation – a solution which, in our view,

The Chamber of the Canadian Senate, where Quebec has regional
status on a par with each of the country's three other designated regions.

NCC PHOTO

is by far the best for both
Québec and Canada – Canadian federalism will have to be
rebalanced.

A too pronounced decentralization would undermine the
central Parliament and produce
negative results. Moreover, a
number of provinces do not want
this. They argue that it would
deprive them of their financial
wherewithal. They are much too
dependent for their survival on

the financial assistance of the
federal authorities.

Québec, however, would
reject a federalism that is centralized.

Everything depends, then, on
finding an acceptable degree of
centralization or decentralization,
suited to contemporary needs.

Provinces with sparse populations and low revenues do not
request the additional powers
that some Québec governments

may desire occasionally. This is
the dilemma of Canadian federalism, its existential difficulty.

Meech Lake Accord

Québec did not give its assent
to the patriation of the constitution from Great Britain on 17
April 1982. However, in 1985,
Québec, which is legally bound
by the patriation, wanted to
"politically return" to and be rec-
onciled within the Canadian

19

family, subject to certain conditions. Hon. René Lévesque, the Québec Premier, took this path with a long list of his own terms in the spring of 1985, and in May 1986 Hon. Robert Bourassa, whose party had now come to power, set forth five minimum conditions.

In August 1986, in Edmonton, the federal government and the other provinces agreed to give priority to Québec's "re-integration".

On 30 April 1987, at Meech Lake, the eleven First Ministers (Canada's Prime Minister and the Premiers of the 10 provinces) reached agreement in principle on the five points. Québec heard from some experts in May in its commission on institutions.

On 3 June 1987, in the Langevin Block across the street from Parliament in Ottawa, after nearly 20 hours of deliberations, the eleven governments agreed on the legal wording of the "Meech Lake Accord", enriched by a few safeguard clauses and amendments.

It remained only for the Senate and the House of Commons, as well as the Legislative Assembly in each province, to adopt in both official languages the amending resolutions. Debates followed in the federal and provincial capitals. At a conference of the eleven First Ministers on 9 June 1990, the Meech Lake Accord came under very heavy fire. Unfortunately, the Accord lapsed through the failure of the Manitoba and Newfoundland Legislatures to ratify it by 22 June 1990.

Studying national options

In the wake of the failure of the Meech Lake Accord, the federal government created the Spicer Commission, with a mandate to listen to Canadians in general, and the Beaudoin-Edwards parliamentary committee, with a mandate to propose amendments to the procedure for amending the constitution of Canada.

The Beaudoin-Edwards Committee tabled its report on 20 June 1991 and proposed, *inter alia*: a new amending formula based on regional majorities (Atlantic Canada, Québec, Ontario and the Western provinces) to replace the formula of approval by seven provinces with half of the population and the unanimity requirement, a constitutional guarantee of the civil law component of the Supreme Court of Canada; participation of the aboriginal peoples and territories in future constitutional conferences; entrenchment in the constitution of a provision authorizing the interparliamentary delegation of legislative powers, and the enactment of a federal statute allowing the government of Canada to hold, at its discretion, a consultative referendum on a constitutional proposal.

The Committee on a Renewed Canada was established in September 1991 to examine proposals formulated by the Canadian government in its document *Shaping Canada's Future Together*. This committee (the Beaudoin-Dobbie Committee, as it came to be called) tabled its report on 28 February 1992 and proposed a number of major constitutional changes.

These included: entrenchment in the constitution of a "Canada clause"; recognition of Québec's distinct society and the vitality and development of the official-language minorities; a constitutional guarantee, within certain parameters, of the inherent right of the aboriginal peoples to self-government; a new elected and more equitable Senate with a six-month suspensive veto over most Bills; a new distribution of powers; the limitation of the federal spending power; the withdrawal of the federal government from the following areas of provincial jurisdiction: tourism, forests, mines, recreation, housing, municipal and urban affairs; the federal government should also withdraw from: energy, regional development, family policy, health, education and social services; a statement of economic union accompanied by a non-judiciable social charter; a provision on the Canadian common market; the enactment of federal legislation enabling the government of Canada to hold, at its discretion, a consultative referendum on a constitutional proposal, and the constitutional entrenchment of the civil law component of the Supreme Court of Canada.

Finally, the Beaudoin-Dobbie Committee proposed a series of constitutional amending formulae, all of which would give Québec a right of veto.

On 28 August 1992, the Prime Minister, the 10 Premiers, the two Leaders of the territories and the four leaders of the aboriginal peoples of Canada reached an agreement, called the Charlottetown Accord, largely inspired from the Beaudoin-Dobbie Report although it differed in some major aspects. For instance, the Charlottetown Accord proposed an equal Senate (six Senators per province) and a much broader right to self-government for the Aboriginal peoples.

The Charlottetown Accord, however, was not ratified by Canadians. Two referenda held on the same day, 26 October 1992, one in Québec the other one in the rest of Canada, were clear: 54 per cent to 46 per cent were against that Accord. It was a failure.

Changing moods

Exactly one year after the referendum on the Charlottetown Accord, the Liberal Party of Canada led by Rt Hon. Jean Chrétien took power in Ottawa with a majority government.

Less than a year later, the Parti Québécois defeated the government of the Québec Liberal Party and Hon. Jacques Parizeau became Premier of Québec. As soon as he took office he tabled a draft Bill on Québec's sovereignty which culminated in a referendum on 30 October 1995.

The result was very close: 50.6 per cent of Québec voters voted against sovereignty while 49.4 per cent voted for it. Premier

Parizeau resigned and was replaced by Hon. Lucien Bouchard, former Leader of the pro-sovereignty Bloc Québécois (the Official Opposition in the Parliament of Canada) and a former Minister in the national Conservative government which had tried to secure passage of the Meech Lake and Charlottetown Accords.

Although according to surveys a clear majority of Quebecers are willing to stay in Canada, the willingness of that majority depends on the Prime Minister to deliver constitutional amendments or offers.

The Parliament of Canada has adopted a resolution recognizing the distinct society concept for Québec and has passed a Bill to the effect that a constitutional amendment would need the consent of the five regions of Canada (Québec, Ontario, East, Prairies and British Columbia) before it can be proclaimed.

It is a first step in the right direction, but it is not enough.

Premier Bouchard has said that there will not be another referendum on independence before another provincial election. We have a few months, perhaps a year or two, to make adequate constitutional offers.

Here are my suggestions on the division of powers, on the distinct society concept and on the formula of amendment.

The division of powers

The division of legislative powers must respond to our needs. So, it must be tailored. It varies from one federation to another. Our division of powers has not been amended often since 1867; but it has considerably evolved as a result of court decisions — for the best, I believe.

We must have great respect for the division of powers: it is the hearth of federalism. We should respect the actual division of powers as interpreted by the courts, for example, in the field of social security and social programmes. That would mean a lot for Canada. There is no need to decentralize more in that field.

Adjustments, if any, should be of a financial nature.

We should not hesitate to recognize as provincial matters what we have called the six sisters: tourism, forestry, mines, housing, municipal affairs and recreation. We have been talking about that for some years. Now is the time to act: the federal authority must withdraw from those fields.

Concurrent powers are not numerous enough in our federation. There were two at the beginning (agriculture and immigration); another followed in 1951 (old age pension) and, finally, supplementary benefits in 1964. We may perhaps add some others, like culture, for example, with provincial paramountcy and telecommunications with federal paramountcy.

The federal spending power is a jurisprudential creation since 1937. We should recognize that power in the constitution; however we must have parameters, as was suggested in the Meech Lake Accord. We must constitutionalize the right for provinces to opt out of federal spending programmes, with compensation. The equalization payments from Ottawa to lower-income provinces have been constitutionalized; this is right.

Manpower training is a field of provincial priority. We must be ready to settle this problem.

The "watertight" division of powers is no longer strictly exact today. It was relatively possible in the nineteenth century to draw two lists of exclusive powers. It is not so at the end of this century. At our request, governments intervene more and more, but not always for the best. We must accept some crosschecks and ask the courts to create interpretative rules that would help refinine the division of powers.

We must not, in my opinion, introduce in Canada the theory of "subsidiarity" which is in vogue in the European Union. Competence must not always be based on the importance of the problem to be settled. We would otherwise centralize too much. I

would prefer, by far, a rebalancing.

We may *perhaps* decentralize three powers: personal bankruptcy, inland fisheries, and marriage and divorce.

The place of Québec in Canada

In my opinion, Quebecers will stay in the Canadian federation if they feel adequately recognized; if not, they will choose a nation-state. In my opinion, it is more than an identification problem; they want the constitution to spell out that they are different because of their language, culture and civil law. It is a fact. It is a question of recognition.

We in Canada remember the famous phrase of Lord Durham: "Two nations warring in the bosom of a single state". It was said in 1839. Trace back even further. In 1774, England itself restored French civil laws in Québec. Imagine for a moment: to restore French laws in a British colony! That is a recognition!

It is the reality that is important! If the words "distinct society" are taboo, replace them with others. We must be creative, imaginative.

There is more than one nation in Canada; there is more than one people in Canada. The Constitution Act, 1982, talks about the "aboriginal peoples". Canadian case law refers to "aboriginal nations". Francophones certainly form a "people". It is a reality firmly established by history over four centuries.

Some Quebecers are ready to leave the federation. We must motivate them to stay. For that, they must be recognized in the Canadian institutions. Federalism has been very much influenced by Québec. It should continue to be so.

Québec must also be recognized in the amending procedure. I do not see how we can bypass a right of veto for Québec in the constitution. It could be a regional veto; it could be the unanimity formula as was proposed in the Meech Lake Accord for ten topics.

The Supreme Court in the Ford

case has used the concept of "visage francais" to recognize that Québec may in an act of the Legislative Assembly give French a clear paramountcy. It is an interpretation that is close to the "distinct society" concept. It is an interpretation that does not give additional legislative powers.

The federal government has referred to the distinct society concept, the federal spending power and manpower training in its Speech from the Throne. Those elements were to be on the agenda of the First Ministers Conference that was called for 21 June in Ottawa.

At this time, the Minister of Justice of Canada has agreed to take part in a court action between lawyer Guy Bertrand and the government of Québec over the legality of the Parti Québécois government's measures to promote sovereignty for Québec, including the holding of separation referenda.

The constitutional debate in Canada includes a juridical dimension and a political dimension. Those two dimensions are parallel and will be discussed in the months ahead. The Canadian constitution does not mention the right to secession or the referendum. Two referenda on the question of secession have taken place in Québec, one in May 1980 and the second in October 1995.

One group puts the accent on the formula for constitutional amendment which for secession would require unanimity. The second group, that is the government of Québec led by Hon. Lucien Bouchard, rests its case on a referendum and principles of international law. This debate will continue for months.

I think that we should concentrate on constitutional offers. This is what we call Plan A. If the offers are meaningful, Québec, in my opinion, will stay in Canada. This is what Hon. Jean Charest, the national Conservative Leader, is recommending.

THE CASE FOR STRENGTHENING FEDERAL POWERS

Pourquoi décentraliser le pouvoir davantage au Canada ? Nous sommes déjà la fédération la plus décentralisée du monde. Le gouvernement fédéral est tout à fait dans ses droits lorsqu'il entend participer à la politique sociale, et les gouvernements provinciaux ne sont pas forcément « plus près du peuple » que lui. Enfin, on a exagéré le degré de double emploi et de chevauchement qui existe entre les deux paliers.

by Andrew Coyne

Of all the ills that might be said to afflict Canada, the one thing we are *not* suffering from is an overly centralized system of government. Far from devolving still more powers to the provinces, as Robert Young advocated in the March issue of *Policy Options*, I will argue that if anything the pendulum has swung too far in the direction of devolution already, and that if we were serious about reforming the federation, we should find there was more need to strengthen federal powers than provincial.

I do not propose to discuss this in the context of the much-supposed need to make "offers" to Quebec. The truth is we have used Quebec as a scapegoat for a more general inability to think clearly about the federation and, more particularly, about the uses of federal power. When Quebec nationalists demand that a long list of powers should be transferred to the province, they find an all too ready echo in other provincial capitals, especially when this can be dressed up in the name of saving Canada. But we can hardly save the country by destroying it, which I am afraid is what the devolution movement amounts to.

Let me lay before you three very simple propositions. First: *The only reason to have a federation is to have a federal government.* If all we wanted to do was inhabit this frozen shelf on the northern US border, we needn't call it a country. If all we wanted to do was get along with each other and be friends, we could live as 10 sovereign states, sign treaties, exchange ambassadors, maybe even form an alliance of sorts, and everything would be swell. But we would not be a federation.

What marks a federation out from other sorts of arrangements is the presence of a federal government, whose legitimacy, like that of the provincial governments, derives from a popular mandate, and whose power, in those responsibilities the people choose to assign to it, is not dependant on the wishes or desires of the provinces. It represents the Canadian nation, in its way, just as the provinces collectively do in theirs. It is not the residual of the provincial governments, with whatever powers are left over after they are through. Nor is it their emissary, nor their handmaiden, nor their bank machine, nor any of the other roles to which the premiers would like to consign it.

Second: *The only reason to have a federal government is to do federal things*: to exercise those powers that it would be impossible or unwise to entrust to the provinces. These are not mysterious. They are Federalism 101: to represent the nation abroad, as in defence or international trade; to govern in matters that cross provincial boundaries, such as the currency, transport and communications, or for which the federal fiscal power is required; to ensure that provinces, acting within their own jurisdictions, do not burden, impede or infringe upon other provinces; and, last, to protect the rights of local minorities from local majorities.

But we will not entrust it with those powers, we will not consent to be ruled by this government, unless we see ourselves as one nation, as a single self-governing people. This is the third proposition: *There is no federation without the nation*. Yet the palpable and occasionally explicit belief among much expert opinion is that there is no such thing as a Canadian nation, but only two, or three or hundreds, depending on which racial or ethnic groups they choose to recognize as "real" nations, to which the "artificial" Canadian nation must defer.

But one part of it is also the ongoing campaign to denude the federal government of any effective role in the country. Do not get me wrong. I have no desire that Canada should be a unitary state. I do not believe that all wisdom resides in Ottawa. I am not, needless to say, a fan of Big Government, and I do not think that the nation is defined by its federal Crown Corporations. But while it is not the federal government that makes the nation, it is equally true that unless there is a common sense of nationhood, we cannot hope to govern ourselves federally. Which explains the vicious circle in which we now find ourselves. Lacking legitimacy, the feds have failed to act where they should; and having failed to act, lack legitimacy all the more.

The clearest way to understand how nutty the situation has become is to compare our own situation to other countries. As a matter of fiscal record, we are already the world's most decentralized federation: from a postwar peak of 70 percent, the federal government now retains scarcely a third of all government revenues for its own purpose. Even in Switzerland, the central government's share is 40 percent.

We are the only federation in the world without a working internal common market, nor any means of enforcing it. In every other federation in the world, that is a recognized constitutional responsibility of the federal government. Only in Canada is the matter left to negotiation between provinces, as if between sovereign states, a process in which the federal role seems to fall somewhere between caterer and the Harvard Conflict Resolution Group.

We are the only federation in the world whose every province may borrow at will, on any amount, on any market, without regard to the consequences for the rest. Even Europe, which is not a federation, recognizes that this is nonsense, if they hope to maintain a common currency.

We are the only federation in the world without an effective second chamber repre-

senting population as it is divided into member states. In no other federation in the world has the First Ministers Conference, or its equivalent, become the sort of parallel government — unaccountable and unconstitutional — that it has become in Canada.

We are the only *country* in the democratic world whose Constitution allows governments to ignore fundamental human rights the same Constitution solemnly guarantees. Needless to say, we are also the only federation in the world that has adopted as its most solemn principle the notion that the whole thing may be dissolved at any time, on the vote of one province, at a time that suits the Premier of Quebec's family commitments.

So: I think we are at least entitled to ask: In what specific ways does Canada suffer from excessive centralization? How precisely are the provinces suffering under the federal yoke? The premiers like to complain a lot about national standards in social programs, as if they were being dictated to by some foreign power called Ottawa. But the fact is that there have always been enormous variations in the way in which social programs are delivered, even before the new Canada Health and Social Transfer. If the programs are in poor repair, it is hardly fair to blame the feds. Whatever design flaws they may have, they reflect the thinking when they were implemented — at every level of government.

Contrary to what the rhetoric would imply, the federal government does not directly regulate health, welfare or higher education, and can not under the Constitution. When it offers provinces federal funding in exchange for their compliance with national standards, it is simply setting the terms and conditions under which it will spend its own money, which under the Constitution it is entitled to spend on just about anything it likes. It is the provinces, then, who presume upon federal turf, not the other way around. The point is, it is a contract: if they do not want to live up to the standards, no one is forcing them to take the money. But they need the money; that is why they do so much bellyaching. You will notice that no one is telling the feds to stop sending the cheques. So it is not a matter of "put up or shut up." What the provinces want Ottawa to do is put up *and* shut up.

So whence this demand for devolution? I have heard several arguments, none of them persuasive. The first is simply to declare, in a tone meant to suggest resignation to the inevitable, that, well, "Ottawa is broke." *Ergo*, no more federal transfers for social programs.

Rubbish. The federal government is more than halfway to balancing its budget on the basis of reducing the cash portion of the transfer to $11 billion — not zero. Had it moved sooner, cut deeper, it need not have cut even that much out of federal-provincial transfers. And had it been serious in reforming the two largest single budget items — Old Age Security and Unemployment Insurance — health, higher education and social assistance might have been spared altogether. If it has chosen to cut the latter, and not the former, it is simply because the provinces were the path of least resistance — at least, compared to tackling the old folks.

A second argument for devolution is to claim, with mild astonishment that anyone could find it controversial, that "we're just resorting the division of powers to the original terms of the 1867 constitution." Nonsense. The federal role in funding social programs, as I mentioned, is entirely within the 1867 Constitution. More to the point, if we are serious about going back to the BNA Act, why don't we revive the power of disallowance, the power of reservation, the Peace, Order and Good Government clause, and a battery of other federal powers to over-ride provincial legislation.

I am not suggesting we should — well, maybe I am — but the point is that it is an utter perversion of the truth to claim that the Fathers of Confederation, meeting in the waning days of the American Civil War, intended the BNA Act to be a declaration of provincial rights.

Third, there is the more general argument that the provincial governments are "closer to the people," and that therefore power should wherever possible be in provincial hands. Piffle. What is closer about a provincial government than a federal? That might have been truer in the days when the major means of transportation was a snowshoe, but communications have come a little way since then. And while it might seem that a government answering to fewer citizens would be more accountable than a government that must take account of the needs of 30 million, the reverse is more often the case.

Coyne's Law on this is absolute: the closer the government, the less accountable it is. Think about it: most people could name their federal MP; at a stretch, they could give you their representative in the provincial legislature. But few know who their city councillor is, and even fewer would know the name of their school trustee. Accountability in a modern democracy is a matter of attention, not geography. We pay attention to federal politics because it is at the centre, the focus of hundreds of national journalists, the common subject of discussion, not to say disgust, for millions of Canadians

Fourth, devolution is urged in order to end the dreaded "overlap and duplication." This is a little like the old "waste, fraud and abuse," the favourite campaign target of politicians who have no intention of cutting spending. When you actually get into the books, you find that there is not as much of it as all that. Or if overlap and duplication is such a problem, why is it always presumed that it is the federal government that should withdraw?

We should not take is as a given, in any case, that "overlap" is always to be deplored. I do not think it is useful to look at jurisdictions as watertight compartments, exclusively federal or exclusively provincial. Rather, there are, or may be aspects of each that are appropriately federal, and aspects that are appropriately provincial. If, for example, the federal government were to assume the power to enforce the economic union, and therefore to strike down provincial regulations that impeded the free flow of goods, services, capital and labour, it would be entitled to intervene in any number of provincial jurisdictions — though only in this restricted capacity.

This is the limited-government case for strong federalism. I do not care for "cooperative federalism," so long as that is taken to mean the federal government cooperates while the provinces do whatever they damn well please. Getting in the provinces' face is a large part of what a federal government is *for* — to limit provincial powers, so far as the individual exercise of these threatens the national interest, or minority rights. In the same way, the provinces can act as a check on an overpowerful federal government. The federal-provincial relationship should properly be viewed not so much as a division of powers, but as a balance of powers.

I think this is especially important for conservatives to bear in mind. Many conservatives have taken up the devolution case with evangelic zeal, thinking that if only they can be rid of Clutter-on-the-Rideau, they will have one less level of government to worry about. It does not seem to have occurred to them that by devolving the powers of one government to 10, they may not divide government, but rather multiply it. Think about it: do we really want 10 CRTCs mucking up the nation's airwaves? That is the limited-government case against devolution in a nutshell: it is not that the federal government is losing powers, but that the provincial governments would be getting them. Rather than fighting over which level of government should exercise power, in other words, it may in some cases be that none should. To put it another way, if no government exercised power, maybe we would not be fighting so much over which one should.

Indeed, get to its roots, and you find the case for devolution is based on some fairly statist assumptions. If you want the government to be doing a lot, if it is to be charged with managing society and the economy in a detailed, hands-on way, then of course it can only hope to do that for a very small population, say the size of a village. Of mud huts. Governments in large, complex societies just do not have that much information. But if you prefer that government take a much less discretionary role, essentially limited to setting the rules of the game, letting markets work, and redistributing the results according to some very simple formula like rich to poor, then it is possible to extend the same government's jurisdiction over a much larger population base.

Let me give you an example. If you want the universities to be run by the government, to be directly funded, regulated and controlled by government, then yes, you might prefer that they should be run by the provincial government. But if you prefer that universities should be more autonomous, that they should have to compete more vigorously for students' custom, and if, therefore, you are drawn to a model that would send public funding not to the universities but to the students, who would then pass it on to the university of their choice — well, the feds can cut the cheques just as easily as the provinces.

And indeed, there would be every reason to prefer that the feds should do it, so as to allow students to take that funding with them anywhere they choose to go, across the country. That is real devolution: when students decide where the money should go, not provincial bureaucrats. You cannot get much closer to the people than that. If you are going to devolve power, in other words, why stop at the provinces? Why not cut out the middle man? The market for universities, after all, is national, or international, not provincial. Yet under present arrangements, the funding stops at the border. So long as out-of-province students remain a net source of additional costs, and not additional revenues, then we will have the absurdity of the province of Nova Scotia declaring "Goodness, our universities are too popular. We'll have to shut them down."

This takes us to the fifth, final and best argument for devolution — a model that is often called "competitive federalism." Or rather, it would be an argument for devolution, if we were living in a unitary state. For the case for competitive federalism is really the case for federalism — as opposed to the confederalism to which we are rapidly converging.

If we wish some powers to be exercised by a lower level of government, it is not because the smaller government will always do things better — which seems to be the implicit assumption behind the "subsidiarity" argument. That is not always true of firms, and there is no reason to think that it should always be true of governments. One could find as many reasons to think the federal government would do a better job — economies of scale, a larger talent pool to draw on, and so on — as the contrary.

The case for competitive federalism is not that the provinces are better at governing than the feds, but that some provinces are better at it than others. With many different governments operating in the same field, it is possible to compare their approaches, learn from their successes and failures, and borrow the best from each.

But just as there is a role for government in private markets — not as manager but as referee — so there is a role for the federal government to referee the competition between provinces, even in areas of provincial jurisdiction. As with private markets, it should not presume to interfere too far. Some advocates of national standards seem to think it is the business of the federal government to save the provinces from themselves, which betrays a shaky grasp, not only of federalism, but of democracy. If the people of a province, in their wisdom, elect a government with a different vision of social policy than that prevailing elsewhere, that is their privilege — until and unless this affects others outside its borders.

The bedrock federal role, it seems to me, is to ensure the portability of these programs, an extension of its constitutional responsibility to guarantee the mobility of citizens. We do not need the federal government to tell the provinces what colour to paint the hospital walls. We do need a federal government to tell the government of British Columbia, in the matter of residency requirements for social assistance, not to treat Canadian citizens as if they were foreigners.

More broadly, it should ensure that provincial programs do not work at cross-purposes with one another, each province shovelling its snow onto it's neighbour's driveway; for example, issuing welfare recipients one-way bus tickets to the next province. Broader still, national standards might be used to put a floor under provincial social programs, to ensure that certain basic minimums are maintained, so as to prevent a ruinous "race to the bottom." This might again be justified in the name of mobility: if a province were to scrap public health care, it would certainly make workers from other provinces think twice before taking a job there.

It is fine to say that the provinces could just agree to preserve these standards among themselves. But if the provinces are so keen on national standards as to make federal prodding unnecessary, then they cannot possibly object to it either: at worst, it would be irrelevant. What, in any event, is the point of standards the premiers set for themselves? The purpose of setting rules, presumably, is to force people to do things they might not do otherwise. Either the constraint binds, then, or it does not. If it does, how is it to be enforced? And if it does not, then we have a solemn and binding agreement among the premiers that each will do whatever he likes.

It is true that as federal transfers diminish, so does federal leverage. But rather than simply wash our hands of national standards altogether, I think it is time we looked at equipping the federal government with other means of enforcement. If it can no longer buy its way into provincial jurisdiction, what about the legislative route? I do not think you would need a constitutional amendment. It seems to me that so far as there are national dimensions to these programs, the federal govern-

ment would be well within its rights to invoke the Peace, Order and Good Government power in defence of the social union — just as it could probably use the existing trade and commerce power, if it so chose, to enforce the economic union. At any rate, it would be worth a Supreme Court reference. All that is really lacking is the will.

If none of the arguments for devolution hold water, if the evidence points in fact to the need for a stronger federal role, why, then, is devolution so much discussed, so widely agreed, so often urged? Simple: it is to mask the devolution of powers to Quebec; to make the paying of ransom to nationalist blackmailers less odious. But I said I would not discuss that.

Andrew Coyne is National Columnist with Southam News. This is adapted from a debate with Tom Courchene.

The Parliamentary System

For many years scholars and critics of Canada's government have suggested that modifications to the parliamentary system need to be made in order to have the system do what it is *supposed* to do: adequately represent the voices and views of the Canadian public. In recent years, criticism of the Canadian Parliament has increased in a number of different respects, including (a) who its members are, (b) how they are chosen, (c) how the Parliament is organized, and (d) how responsive the Parliament is to the public. Each of these questions is addressed in the readings here, which also examine fundamental changes in the Canadian parliamentary system as well as the results of the 1997 parliamentary election.

The first essay in this section asks about the general issues that representatives of the people feel are important in Canadian politics. Author David Docherty interviewed members of the 34th and 35th Parliaments and describes the types of issues that they feel are most important to their respective publics. After discussing the importance of these issues, Docherty suggests that members of Parliament could gain more public respect by devoting more time to communication with the public. At the very least this would add to the sense of "legitimacy" that the public would feel about the Parliament.

A discussion of "who" members of Parliament are must include sheer demographics, and the second article in this section discusses these characteristics. Daniel Girard of *The Toronto Star* shows that the new House of Commons elected in 1997 is dominated by male, middle-aged, university-educated members. Discussion of the occupations, gender groups, and age groups represented, as well as other characteristics of MPs, is also included in this essay.

But the data clearly show that women are significantly underrepresented in the House of Commons, and if the House is a democratic and representative body this should not be the case. Or should it? In an article titled "Women: Why the House Is Not a Home," Lynda Hurst asks why women have not been more successful in becoming a significant presence in the House of Commons. After describing the barriers in Canadian politics and society that women have already overcome, we are shown the role of parties and social institutions in not promoting women candidates for Parliament as vigorously as they could have. In fact, in the newest House of Commons women make up only 18 percent of the members, which very clearly is not representative of the proportion of women in the general population.

While women are generally underrepresented in the House of Commons, women from ethnic and racial minority groups are especially underrepresented. In an essay focusing upon *minority* women in the 35th Parliament, Jerome Black describes ethnic and racial representation in Parliament over the last 33 years, and tries to explain why minority representation has been so much less than an equitable proportion would suggest. Black shows that the barriers that work against women generally work even

more strongly against *minority* women. He concludes that the Canadian political system has a long way to go before it can be satisfied with its progress in this area.

Even if members of Parliament were to represent the Canadian public demographically better than they do today, that would not necessarily mean that they could actually represent their views in the Parliament. Colby Cosh shows us that, even though the House of Commons is supposed to be a democratic and representative body, in fact its methods of operation are not democratic at all. Cosh describes what he calls an "iron rule" of parliamentary government and explains that individual legislators have difficulty actually representing the views of their constituencies because of this as well as because of party discipline. The question is: how can parliamentary government coexist with effective representation of geographic districts? Cosh concludes that new technology and new access to information may play a significant role in the resolution of this problem.

But there are mechanical factors at work, too. The way that borders of electoral districts are drawn can have an effect upon who is elected to the House of Commons. An article by James Hrynyshyn describes an attempt by the Liberal Party to prevent a redrawing of electoral districts prior to the 1997 federal election—as required by electoral laws passed years earlier—so that they could keep the boundaries that had elected them to office. Members of Parliament elected to office in the previous election did not want to have to worry about new borders for their districts and possible increased opposition in their districts, and they wanted the 1997 election to be exempted from procedures agreed to earlier. In the end they were unable to prevent the process from moving forward, and election districts were redrawn according to law.

One issue that has been part of the debate over Parliament and parliamentary institutions since the creation of the Canadian federation has been the role of the appointed Senate in the Parliament. Senator Normand Grimard returns to that issue and describes the current balance of political parties in the Senate. After several years in which the leadership of the Senate was not of the same party as the leadership of the House, both Houses are again controlled by the Liberal Party. Is now an appropriate time to return to the issue of Senate reform? The issues of the debate are straightforward: when the (appointed) Senate agrees with the (elected) House it is an unnecessary and expensive institution; when it disagrees with the House and blocks House legislation it is an expensive institution that is undemocratic and threatening to popular sovereignty. What is to be done? Grimard suggests that now may be a good time to return to the question of whether the Senate is needed at all and how its structure and role might be recast to be more appropriate for contemporary politics.

The final essay in this section focuses upon Prime Minister Jean Chrétien. In this article, *Maclean's* correspondent Anthony Wilson-Smith examines the record and behavior of the prime minister in the period leading up to the 1997 federal election and tries to use a longer perspective to ask, ultimately, whether or not Chrétien is "up to the job."

Looking Ahead: Challenge Questions

What are the factors that most need to be changed to do a better job of representing women and minorities in the House of Commons?

Is an appointed upper house an appropriate political institution in a contemporary Canadian Parliament? Why or why not? If the Senate is to survive, should its method of selection be changed—to election or selection by provincial governments? Should its powers be limited? Explain your answer.

What should be the role of political parties in an elected parliament? Does the concept of legislative party discipline threaten democratic government in Canada? Could parliamentary government exist *without* organized and influential parties in Parliament?

What Kind of Representatives do Canadians Want?

by David C. Docherty

Observers of the House of Commons cannot help but notice that the mood and decorum in the House of Commons deteriorated almost immediately after the close NO vote in the Quebec referendum. As the aftermath of the referendum unfolds, and the federal government cedes more power to the provinces, the roles and responsibilities of members of parliament may come under closer scrutiny. This article is based on surveys and interviews with members of the 34th and 35th Parliaments undertaken by the author as part of a larger project on member's views of representation.

There are many reasons for the scepticism of Canadians toward our politicians. Party discipline keeps some members from voting as they otherwise might; pension plans seem too generous; there is a sense among the public that political parties listen to the public only during elections; they see a fascination with constitutional reform that has little to do with the day-to-day lives of most citizens; and we see a continual power struggle between levels of government over power and scarce resources.

Political scientists André Blais and Elizabeth Gidengil found that over 80% of Canadians believe that politicians have no intention of keeping the promises they made during election campaigns.[1] In the 1993 election 80% of Canadians felt that soon after arriving in Ottawa, MPs would lose touch with the people they were elected to serve.[2] The public sees members of parliament as following a classic trustee view of representation, where members are supposed to make decisions based not on what their constituents want, but what elected legislators think best for the riding and country as a whole. It is a view the public is not happy holding, as they wish their

legislators would be more immediately responsive to riding demands and opinions.

Canadians, it seems, do not think federal politicians are doing the job they were elected to do. It is clear that there is a gap between what the public wants and expects politicians to do, and how members of parliament themselves see their job. What Canadians think is the proper role of a federal representative differs substantially with the views held by legislators. For citizens and politicians, the first step in closing the gap is understanding where the break lies. Exactly what do Canadians want in a representative and what do representatives think Canadians want of them.

> *Of all of these problems, perhaps the most serious for individual politicians is the charge that they do not listen to the women and men who elected them.*

A December 1993 Gallup poll asked Canadians to rank the importance of five different responsibilities of federal legislators. A similar question was asked of MPs in the 34th Parliament (1988-1993) and non-incumbent candidates in the 1993 federal election. The responses of

David C. Docherty is an Assistant Professor of Political Science at Wilfrid Laurier University in Waterloo.

From *Canadian Parliamentary Review,* Spring 1996, pp. 8-11. © 1996 by the Committees and Parliamentary Associations Branch of the House of Commons in Ottawa. Reprinted by permission.

successful Liberal and Reform candidates (now rookie MPs in the 35th Parliament) are used in this analysis.[3]

The comparison among veteran office holders, new members of parliament and the general public is quite telling. It is clear that what Canadians want from their MPs is not what MPs think is important. Interestingly, rookie MPs reflect the views of citizens on questions of representation to a much greater degree than do veteran legislators. In this light, it does appear that MPs lose touch with the public they are elected to serve. Time spent in office make MPs forget the desires of those individuals who sent them to Ottawa.

this form of district service. But time spent in the nation's capital has seemingly drawn members away from this task. Veteran MPs rank this duty third.

According to members of parliament, however, their lack of interest in communicating government policy or protecting the riding does not indicate a lack of concern on their part with the plight of their constituents. Members of the 34th Parliament indicated that their most important duty was to help individuals who had problems with a government department. Interestingly this is the duty that Canadians ranked last. This is where the true gap lies. Canadians do not see the job of MP as

Ranked Importance of a MP's Duties

Responsibility	MPs, 34th Parliament 1988-93	Rookie MPs 35th Parliament[4]	Public
Protect interests of constituency	3	1	2
Helping people who have personal problems with government	1	3	5
Ensuring bureaucracy is administering government policy	5	5	3
Keep in touch with constituents about what government is doing	4	2	1
Debating and voting in Parliament	2	4	4

So where does the gap lie? What exactly do voters want and what are MPs happier doing. According to the public, a member of parliament should spend more effort on communicating government policy. For Canadians, the "keeping in touch" function was the most important job of an MP. As candidates, both new Liberal and Reform MPs ranked it second. Members of the previous parliament ranked it fourth of five. That the public ranks "keeping in touch" so high compared to veteran legislators, helps in part to explain why citizens feel that politicians do not listen to the public. Members of parliament do not see this as an integral part of their job description.

The public also thinks that an MP should exert more effort on riding wide matters. Close behind communicating, in the eyes of citizens, is acting as a riding advocate. Riding advocacy means ensuring that decisions made in Ottawa do not adversely affect the member's constituency. Canadians, therefore, seem to be suggesting that members of parliament have a duty to act as a collective representative. As candidates in 1993, Liberal and Reform members also placed a premium on

one of helping individuals, at least not compared to larger, riding wide functions. Given that members think this is their central task, it is little wonder Canadians think MPs do not listen or respond as they would like.

Recognizing where the deviation between public wishes and legislator's views on representation rests is much easier than identifying the cause of this discrepancy. From a legislator's perspective there are numerous possible reasons that they might view individual service as their primary responsibility. First, members see such work as an effective way of maintaining their reputations as problem solvers. People in the riding who encounter problems with government agencies or departments expect MPs to help resolve these difficulties.[5] As one member of the 34th Parliament stated, "Helping people will not get me re-elected. But not doing it will sure get me defeated" (Interview July 1993). This member recognized that local service has few direct electoral benefits but remains a requisite part of their job.

Members also take pleasure in the fact that they are often successful in helping people in their ridings. By

31

contrast, tackling larger public policy issues within an executive-centred parliamentary system is more frustrating. Members may be more likely to find victory in solving individual concerns than they are in attempting to make sweeping policy changes. As a result, there may be a greater attachment to working on problems that can be resolved. As one rural MP explained, "Not only is this important work, but it is good work. After a frustrating few weeks in Ottawa, it is nice to go to an event [in my district] and see someone who says 'Thanks for helping me with my pension' or whatever" (Interview October 1994). These types of reflections were common among most veteran legislators.

Further, helping people means avoiding partisan involvement, or perhaps even more importantly, conflict with ones own party. Given the primary role of party discipline within the Canadian legislative system, it is not surprising that many members emphasize activities with little or no partisan content. Acting as a local trouble shooter means avoiding conflict with your party, leader and government. One veteran member summed up this attitude nicely by comparing constituents to consumers. "We [MPs] love constituents who have troubles. It is black and white. A constituent is always right, and we just have to convince the bureaucracy that they are wrong" (Interview, September 1995).

All of this suggests that one-on-one service has two benefits for members. First, within their ridings it accentuates their ability to get things done, thereby increasing their local profile. Whether or not the electoral benefits are direct or even present is secondary. Members avoid this work at their own risk. Second, it provides an opportunity for members to demonstrate their effectiveness, despite their status in the House. Members can resolve problems locally without being in cabinet or holding any other position of authority. Additionally, such local work does not force members to take a position that might clash with party policy.

Yet the emphasis that members of parliament place on local service does not come automatically with their election. In fact, as the Table on the previous page suggests, an emphasis on individual service may well be a learned response.

Neither Liberal nor Reform candidates seemed terribly enthused about having to do individual case work if they won office, ranking it third of the five responsibilities. Again, this suggests that candidate views on questions of representation are closer to the public than experienced politicians. Yet even here the difference among groups are notable. Candidates do not emphasize one-on-one help like veteran politicians do, but neither do they shun this work, as the public would have them.

Further, once in office, many of these new rookie MPs, Liberal and Reform alike, have come to accept this as a more important part of their job. Interviews with some of these new lawmakers six and eighteen months after their 1993 election revealed that many were not prepared for the high demands that individual constituents placed on them. Although the interviews were selective and therefore not generalizable, they did uncover hints that the first couple of years of office transform the representational views of these newcomers.

> *Many rookie MPs, after being immersed in the work world of elective office, indicated that they spend far more time on this one-on-one service than they thought they would.*

One Reform member, who prior to his election expressed little desire for such work, explained his transformation just six months into the job. "My constituency office spends all their day on this, and I spend a good part of mine doing this. But if people are coming to us for help we have to provide it. It is part of my job" (Interview March 1994). Many other first time members, Liberal and Reform alike, indicated that demand alone made them realize the importance of this part of their job.

A Liberal rookie echoed such thoughts when she stated "my predecessor told me this was a busy constituency office, but I had no idea how busy until I was [elected]. It is perhaps the least glamorous part of my work, but once you realize that they [constituents] have no place else to turn to, and after you help them, you understand it is the most vital service we provide" (Interview October 1995). Many other rookies gave similar accounts of how they have come to appreciate the importance of one-on-one problem solving. The dilemma for politicians, rookies and veterans alike, is that not enough voters share these views. Despite the number of people turning to constituency offices for help, most voters do not see this as an important function.

It appears, therefore, that Canadians are less charitable toward citizens who need assistance working their way through government programs than are our elected representatives. And maybe this is proper. Elected representatives should be helping people. The problem is, that the longer an MP spends in Ottawa, the more they come to believe this part of their job is their most important responsibility and the more energies they devote to this function. At the same time, they are alienating themselves from those Canadians who do not need this type of assistance.

Members of parliament could go a long way to regaining public respect by devoting more of their time and efforts on the communication function. Canadians want to be kept informed of the goings on in Ottawa, and not just from the media. Members could start thinking of how to increase their presence in their ridings and improve on their ability to communicate with their constituents. But doing so will not be easy, nor will it leave others unaffected. The more emphasis they place in performing one task, the less time and energy they will have to maintain their present duties. That would be too bad.

Notes

1. Andre Blais and Elizabeth Gidengil. 1991. *Making Representative Democracy Work: the Views of Canadians.* Volume 17, Royal Commission on Electoral Reform and Party Financing, (Toronto:Dundurn Press).

2. Harold, Clarke, Jane Jenson, Larry Leduc and Jon H. Pammett. 1995. *Absent Mandate: Canadian Electoral Politics in an era of Restructuring.* 3rd Edition, (Toronto, Gage Press) p. 178.

3. The response rate for members of the 34th Parliament was just over forty percent for non-cabinet ministers. The response rate for candidates was lower (33%). However, a subset of he 1993 candidate survey respondents, those individuals who were successful in their bid for office, includes half of all rookie Liberal and Reform MPs in the 35th Parliament. It is this subset that is used in this examination. BQ MPs participated in the 34th Parliament survey but not in the candidate survey.

4. Although the responses presented in this column are calculated from rookie Liberal and Reform MPs, these individuals responded to the questions while candidates for office in 1993, and therefore reflects their views prior to their election.

5. See John Ferejohn and Brian Gaines. 1991. "The Personal Vote in Canada" in Herman Bakvis ed. *Representation, Integration and Political Parties in Canada.* Volume 13, Royal Commission on Electoral Reform and Party Financing.

Snapshot of the new Parliament

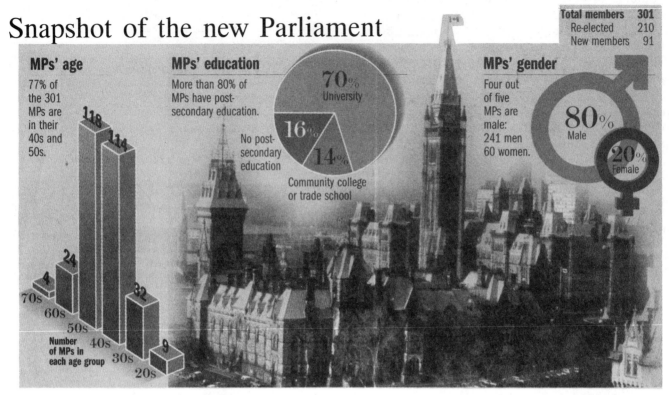

MPs' age
77% of the 301 MPs are in their 40s and 50s.

118
114

24
4
70s
60s
50s
32
Number of MPs in each age group
40s
30s
9
20s

MPs' education
More than 80% of MPs have post-secondary education.

70% University

No post-secondary education

16%

14%

Community college or trade school

MPs' gender
Four out of five MPs are male: 241 men 60 women.

80% Male

20% Female

Total members 301
Re-elected 210
New members 91

Educated, middle-aged males dominate Parliament

BY DANIEL GIRARD
QUEEN'S PARK BUREAU

If you're male, middle-aged and university-educated, listen up.

It would appear that your country wants you.

Of the 301 people elected to Canada's 36th Parliament last Monday, 80 per cent—241—are men, 77 per cent—232—are in their 40s or 50s and nearly 70 per cent—209—had some university education.

Voter turnout, at 67 per cent nationally, was well below the average 75 per cent in the previous dozen federal elections and part of that could be due to Canadians seeing no real need to make big changes.

While nearly 1,700 candidates were vying for a seat in the House of Commons, Canadians chose just 91 new faces. And some of those weren't really new, as more than a half-dozen had previously been MPs.

Sure, there was the usual complement of lawyers—nine—and small business owners—10—among those newly elected, as well as provincial and municipal politicians—15—who graduated to the bigger arena.

There are also seven teachers and five real estate agents.

But it's also clear you don't have to have university training or be a corporate big shot to be one of Canada's lawmakers.

Some 16 per cent of MPs—49—do not have any post-secondary education, while 14 per cent—43—attended community college or trade school.

There are seven tradespeople among the newly elected, as well as three company presidents and five social workers.

And among those making their way to Ottawa is a man who has a lot of experience working with those known to bury their heads in the sand.

One of the Reform MPs is Gerry Ritz of Battlefords-Lloyd-minister in Saskatchewan. He's an ostrich farmer.

What they did

Occupation of the 91 new members before they were elected:

Small business owner	10
Lawyer	9
Municipal politician	8
Teacher	7
Tradesperson	7
Provincial politician	7
Marketing/sales	6
Provincial government bureaucrat/aide	5
Public affairs/consulting	5
Social worker	5
Real estate agent	5
Company president	3
Trade unionist	2
Nurse	2
Doctor	2
Police officer	2
Farmer	2
Airline employee	1
Journalist	1
Pastor	1
National park employee	1

CATHERINE FARLEY/TORONTO STAR

Women: Why the House is not a home

BY LYNDA HURST

FEATURE WRITER

I F YOU'D asked equal rights activists 20 years ago when they thought women would finally break through into federal politics, they'd have told you the late '90s.

It was going to take two decades to shake political parties out of their reflex sexism and closed-shop lethargy; two decades to make women see they had to participate directly in government policymaking, not just plot and protest from the sidelines.

It was going to take that long before the pool of capable women was big enough and willing enough to take on an institution historically dominated by men—and how they think the other half should live.

Breaking down the barriers would be tough, but by the end of the '90s, women would be well on their way to filling half the seats in the House of Commons, or at least be past the critical mass point of 30 per cent. It was inevitable, they said; wait and see.

It's 20 years later.

No one can argue that the pool of competent, savvy women isn't now big enough. Women have flocked into business and the professions, into municipal government, media and academia; by extension, they're surely champing at the bit to get into federal politics.

The parties? They've long been on record as seeking (if not always obtain-ing) a higher female blood count, fielding record numbers in 1993.

So, the upcoming election is going to be the one, right?

Don't bet on it.

Female MPs comprise only 18 per cent of Parliament—precisely 53 women out of 295 men, 37 of them Liberals. That's an all-time high but it is also the product of the 1993 Liberal sweep in which, as more than one commentator has pointed out, the party could have run a goat and got it elected.

A tidal-wave election tells you nothing about how women are really faring politically, and it's why analysts are uncomfortable forecasting the numbers this time out. But then again, few are even talking about women running for office. For a once red-hot issue, it has grown curiously cold.

In part, that's because the economy still blankets the political agenda. But it's also because women now see that getting their own into office makes little difference, says a disenchanted Judy Rebick.

The former head of the National Action Committee on the Status of Women (NAC), now TV host, who ran and lost for the provincial New Democrats in 1987, says flatly that the political system neutralizes women.

"Those women in Parliament haven't raised the gender impact of government policies, and with rare exceptions over the years, the abortion law, say, women MPs never have," she says. "The partisan nature of politics mitigates against it. It homogenizes them."

Women in Parliament

Top six

Rank	Country	Seats	Women	%
1	Sweden	349	141	40.4
2	Norway	165	65	39.4
3	Finland	200	67	33.5
4	Denmark	179	59	33.0
5	Netherlands	150	47	31.3
6	New Zealand	120	35	29.2

Falling behind

Rank	Country	Seats	Women	%
21	Canada	295	53	18.0
41	U.S.	435	51	11.7
50	U.K.	651	62	9.5
72	France	577	37	6.4
83	Japan	500	23	4.6

SOURCE: Geneva-based Inter-Parliamentary Union

Political scientist Carolyn Andrew says ordinary women are enormously frustrated by the way social policies have been hammered in the past decade, first during Brian Mulroney's government, with its 40 female MPs, then with the current one and its 53.

"Having more women in the Commons hasn't changed anything," she says. Even pressure groups on the outside have backed off the fight for more women in office.

NAC, once the country's strongest advocate for political equality—calling at one point for constituencies to have two MPs, one male, one female—has turned its increasingly muted voice away from mainstream politics on to minority issues.

The Committee of '94, a high-powered, non-partisan women's group set up in the mid-80's to promote 50 per cent female representation by 1994, disbanded a couple of years ago, foundering with the arrival on the political map of far-right women politicians.

"Reform gave us pause," admits Wanda O'Hagan, the former chair. "Were we going to support all women running for office, or just some? What if they weren't pro-choice?"

The group ran out of steam before resolving the questions.

In the upcoming election, the parties have the same female candidate goals as last time, but now covering 301 ridings: 25 per cent for the Liberals, 20 to 25 per cent for the Tories, the now-usual 50 per cent for the NDP. None of them achieved it in 1993; only the Liberals sound remotely confident of making it this time.

Reform expects to field the same 10 per cent, but is adamantly opposed to target-setting. "We don't believe in cocooning or cubbyholing women or any other group," says spokesman Ron Wood. "We've got no youth wing, no women's wing, no nothing."

Women's participation is routinely the second or third item on the agenda at party meetings

Liberal campaign chair David Smith says he thinks the party will hit its goal of 75, "but I have to tell you, if we weren't pro-active, we wouldn't be where we are, not *remotely*."

Smith says women's participation is routinely the second or third item on the agenda at party meetings. "We always get asked, 'What are you doing about women?' "

But they're not lining up at the gate: "You'd think there would be more running by now . . . but they still have to be encouraged."

The baby-boom generation of women is well into its 40s, educated, confident, demanding of equality as no generation before. Not all of them would agree with Rebick that women are fated to be silenced or underused in Ottawa.

Single mother of four who became MP says success in politics is doable, if not easy

They know all about critical mass theory and how greater numbers do have major impact. Thirty per cent did it for the Scandinavian countries, most of which are now well over that count; Sweden has more than 40 per cent female representation.

Women are now increasingly influential inside party structures, shaping policies and platforms. So what happens when it comes to running for office?

"They're looking at politics and saying 'Who needs it?' " says Senator Marjorie LeBreton, former appointments adviser to Mulroney and aide to his three Tory predecessors.

That saddens her because, in her 35 years on the Hill, LeBreton knew many of the standard-bearers who took Ottawa on in more sexist times; Judy LaMarsh, Flora MacDonald, Ellen Fairclough. . . . "Women who really wanted to do something for the country."

They still exist, says Doris Anderson. And there's no big mystery why they're not swarming forward.

Cynicism about politics and government has affected both sexes, says the noted feminist and writer, "but with women, there is the added feeling that the system is skewed against them—and they're right."

Practically speaking, most women don't have the money or the monied connections to mount a nomination, let alone an election campaign, she says. That, and

having young children, has always been the main reason given for women's apparent exclusion from the process. But to many who've made the leap, they're starting to sound like excuses.

Have a young family and can't disappear to Ottawa during the week? So don't, says Bonnie Brown, Liberal MP for Oakville-Milton. Get involved in non-partisan local politics instead. She was a single mother of four who learned her political craft over 17 years on the school board and Oakville regional and town councils before running federally in 1993.

"Ottawa doesn't need young people of either sex, she says. "It needs people with some life experience under their belt."

And while it was tough raising the $55,000 for her first federal campaign, it was doable. Just find yourself a good fundraiser, Brown says, in her case a most efficient "bag lady."

"A male candidate would only have had to make 55 calls to get $1,000 cheques from each. My 'bag lady' had to get 1,000 donations of $50 and $75. You have to be determined. I was."

Since the mid-'80s, the three main parties have had funds to help women once they're the designated candidate, averaging $1,500 to $2,000 per woman. Reform, predictably, does not. ("Deb Grey said she'd resign if we ever set one up," laughs Wood.) But elections can cost many times that, depending on how many voters are in the riding, which determines the spending limit.

Only the provincial Tories have a Women In Nomination fund to help them over the crucial first hurdle; its federal counterpart and the other parties say helping one would-be candidate over another interferes with the selection process. Only the NDP has a spending limit, $5,000, on nomination races; they can cost up to $20,000 in the other parties.

Some financial help may now exist, but the parties' commitment to run women in winnable ridings is still lip service, says Anderson, the former high-profile editor of *Chatelaine* who was approached by all three in the '70s.

Indeed, 53 were elected in 1993, but 276 women ran.

One study of women in competitive ridings found that fully 50 per cent had experienced "at least one negative incident," such as changing the date of nomination meetings or stacking the vote with special interest groups. A sudden rush of freshly minted party members who were pro-life supporters caused a furor in the Liberal nomination race between two women and a man in Ottawa's Nepean-Carleton riding earlier this month.

Those tactics may not be specifically anti-female, "but they're dirty and underhanded," says Anderson, "and women don't like them."

It's why the NDP, the most vocal of parties in its promotion of women, is so opposed to airlifting them in, as the Liberals did in four ridings last month, bypassing the nomination process.

"You have to get the riding organizations to fix themselves," says NDP spokesman Hugh Blakeney. "You have to remove the barriers against women, not appoint around them."

But even if the playing field were levelled, the kind of women the parties say they're seeking is increasingly inclined to take a pass. Precisely because they've now entered fully into other professions, the best and brightest of them are as little attracted as high-calibre men to political life.

For a woman, as former PM Kim Campbell pointed out, life in Ottawa can be "unbearably lonely." And that's just the start of it, says Donna Dasko, vice-president of Environics Research.

"The job insecurity, the career interruption, the (uncompetitive $64,400) salary, the commuting back and forth—they're daunting for anyone, male or female. On top of that, public office doesn't have the authority and prestige it used to. A whole set of psychic rewards have gone."

Lawyer Libby Burnham, a long-time Tory activist and fundraiser who's crossed party lines to support female candidates (co-chairing New Democrat Barbara Hall's mayoralty campaign), agrees a key problem today for many professional women is the over-all financial insecurity of entering politics, not the cost per se of a campaign.

"If you decide to run, you can jeopardize your long-term career and financial position in life," she says. "It takes several years for the pension to kick in, and if you run and are defeated, where do you go to get re-established?"

Women may be turning off just as political strategists are turning on to them.

Unlike Anderson, political scientist Sylvia Bashevkin, whose 1992 book, *Toeing The Line*, chronicled the history of female MPs since Agnes Macphail became the first in 1921, says the parties probably *are* more sincere in the '90s about bringing women into the fold.

"They want caucuses that have depth and quality, and because of what women have to go through to get there, they know they're getting that with them"

But keeping women committed to a party is a problem. Baskevkin is blunt about what smart women are going to ask themselves: "Do I want to put all this energy and money into getting elected to end up a trained seal on the back benches?"

That was Catherine Swift's reaction before the last election when the Liberals approached her, even making noises about a cabinet post.

The high-powered president of the Canadian Federation of Independent Business wasn't tempted for a moment.

"I didn't need the grief," she says. "I have two kids, my life is busy and deranged enough as it is, and I happen to think the work I do is altruistic in itself."

When she told the party scouts, there was incredulity.

"They live in such a hothouse environment that they can't comprehend why you wouldn't want to run."

A New Dimension of Social Diversity

Minority Women in the 35th Parliament

by Jerome H. Black

The election of 53 women in the 1993 general election provided further opportunities for reflection on the significance of gender in elite-level politics. One important perspective, given added significance by the record level of women elected, carries on the tradition of assessing the impact of women in the House, particularly their possible influence in relation to policy matters that are of central concern to many women in Canadian society. Representation is another area for reflection and particularly the fact that women still remain considerably under-represented relative to their population incidence. This article explores an additional, and as yet largely unresearched, dimension associated with elected women, their ethnoracial diversity. Using systematic methods of categorization, it documents the number of minority women in the 35th Parliament. Their election in 1993 in significant and unprecedented numbers is an important justification for such a focus, as is the fact that without explicit attention to their double minority status, as both women and ethnoracial minorities, an understanding of their experiences as candidates and MPs is likely to be incomplete.

A variety of interesting queries suggest themselves as relevant points of departure in looking at minority women. For example, are the hurdles on route to Parliament higher or different for minority women than they are for women and minorities taken separately? Similarly, once inside Parliament, are they confronted with a particular set of constraints linked to their background? Does their approach to parliamentary politics reflect their special background? Is preference given, if at all, to preoccupations reflecting their distinctiveness as women, as minorities, or both?

Adding meaningfulness to the value of answering these and other questions about the implications of

double minority status is the fact that a notable number of women with minority group origins were indeed elected in 1993. Even the most casual inspection provides some sense that something new occurred that year. The unprecedented election of not one but two women of colour, Jean Augustine and Hedy Fry, immediately comes to mind. Other newly elected women as well, particularly Eleni Bakopanos, Maria Minna and Anna Terrana, can be fairly easily identified as having roots in their (Greek and Italian) ethnic communities. Nevertheless, the attention paid to the election of minority women MPs has been largely informal and anecdotal, so that the true dimensions of their presence remain to be documented. Certainly, there has yet to be any rigorous gauging of how the 35th Parliament compares with earlier ones in terms of social diversity.

Jerome H. Black is Associate Professor of political science at McGill University.

From *Canadian Parliamentary Review*, Spring 1997, pp. 17-22. © 1997 by the Committees and Parliamentary Associations Branch of the House of Commons in Ottawa. Reprinted by permission.

The Problem of Categorization

Because ethnoracial origin is a multidimensional phenomenon, and not always easily measured, determining the ancestral backgrounds of parliamentarians is not a simple matter. The impediments have been carefully set out in a recent paper which classified all 295 MPs elected in 1993 along origin lines,[1] but which did not address gender distinctions. A brief summary of the methodological issues dealt with in that essay can serve as an instructive prelude to the categorization results broken down by both origin and gender.

The classification effort in the existing paper on the 35th Parliament was purposefully narrow to emphasize the dimension of objective condition, rather than subjective sentiment. That is, the analysis was directed at determining categorical membership in ethnoracial groups and not at evaluating the nature and extent of felt or expressed attachment to the heritage group. In focusing on minority status as a background characteristic, it was understood that no assumption could be made about particular subjectively based patterns of identity. This would mean in the present context, for instance, that not all women classified as having a minority background necessarily regard their heritage as a significant factor in their personal careers; fewer yet would regard it as salient for their public lives. It was also understood that highlighting the objective dimension did not imply that the study of the subjective side of ethnicity and race is unimportant. Quite the contrary, differences in the kind and degree of expressed ethnoracial identity would, in fact, constitute critical factors for many analytical purposes, such as consideration of the antecedents in support of policies of concern to multicultural communities.

A categorization approach is no less valuable, however. In fact, it is a necessary starting point for incorporation of the subjective dimension, since expressed attachment can only be gauged relative to the category of potential attachment. Moreover, by itself, an objective approach is necessary for allowing judgements about the important issue of the incidence of minority individuals in elite positions relative to their general population numbers, typically framed in terms of the goal of proportionality. The motivating concerns are not only about the statistics and symbolism of representation but as well about the lack of the group's presence in the legislature. Related questions about the legitimacy of the institutions themselves and the distribution of opportunities for access into positions of power also motivate attention.

In other ways, the classification effort was expansionist in design, by allowing for the possibility of categorizing individuals according to more than one ancestral stream. Such a procedure harmonizes with the cumulating census record which has shown increasing numbers of Canadians taking advantage of opportunities to report origins that are multiple in character.

This work also stands out in contrast to the, albeit few, existing studies that have generated single-origin classification results for earlier cohorts of MPs.[2] The methodology employed for the 35th Parliament further distinguished itself by adopting a multiple measurement strategy in order to maximize reliability in the categorization effort.

The predicament is that while there is much to commend the use of two traditional methods of measurement, biographical research and last name analysis, each is limited by particular problems.

Biographical material could be relied upon, and even exclusively, if MPs clearly signalled, in the printed record, what their ancestral origins are. Unfortunately, explicit indications of ethnicity and race are only given infrequently. Consequential reliance on other biographical details such as country of birth can be helpful but, as indirect "markers," they can be misleading and must be used judiciously. One study, for example, wrongly classified Simon de Jong, of Dutch background, as a visible minority apparently because his birthplace was Indonesia.

For their part, etymological approaches which examine the last names of MPs are justified by the often discernible and close association between the nature of surnames and particular ethnocultural and/or areal origins. At the same time, there are both inherent difficulties and procedural practices that constrain the methodology as well. Obviously, when individuals change their family name or, as has happened more in the past, have had their names altered by dominant individuals and groups, surnames no longer serve as indices of ancestry. This decoupling works to underestimate the incidence of minority origins since the change is typically in the direction of the dominant group, with anglicization being especially prevalent. A similar directional bias stems from the practice, which is typical fare, of ignoring the maternal line of ancestry. This can lead to the misclassification of minority women who married across the minority-majority divide and

Table 1
Estimates of the Ethnoracial Origins of MPs in the 35th Parliament, and by Gender

	All MPs		Women MPs	
Ethnoracial Origins*	Percent	Number (A)	Number (B)	B/A
Majority (British and/or French)	65.4	193	33	.17
Majority-Minority	9.2	27	8	.30
Minority	24.1	71	11	.16
Aboriginal	1.4	4	1	.25
	100	295	53	

*Condensed results from Black and Lakhani, "Ethnoracial Diversity in the House of Commons."

assumed their husband's name. Similarly, there is the risk that the partial minority status of MPs, both male and female, who have mothers from minority communities will not be recorded. Other practices, however, may operate to exaggerate the number of minority individuals, including the tendency to rely heavily on British surname dictionaries. This likely occurs because minority origins are assumed if the surname cannot be located in dictionaries referencing British origins.

These concerns were handled through the adoption of a multiple measurement strategy, which entailed not only the employment of both biographical and surname analyses (to offset each other's weaknesses) but the use of survey methodology as an additional and distinctive approach. Each MP was sent a single-item questionnaire which replicated the 1991 census question on ethnic ancestry. Though based on self-report, the question clearly elicited origins as an objective condition and constituted the primary basis for categorization for those 49% who responded. The remaining cases were categorized relying on both multiple biographical information (country of birth, religion, community involvement) supplemented by a visual assessment to help in the determination of visible minority status, and as well a surname analysis carried out on the last names of the MPs and their mothers and fathers (and based on an unusually large number of surname dictionaries covering noncharter as well as charter groups).

In sum, the methodological approach adopted in the classification of ethnoracial origins reflected an eclecticism typically not evident in exercises of this nature. As a result, classification errors have been

greatly minimized; certainly, it is highly unlikely that the broader patterns identified are distorted images of reality. Nevertheless, since it is unrealistic to claim that no errors have been made, some modesty is called for, one indicator of which is frequent reference to the results as estimates.

Ethnoracial Origin and Gender in the 35th Parliament

Table 1 presents the distribution of origin classifications in the current Parliament resulting from the application of this methodology. Briefly, the overall pattern shows that 193 of the MPs elected in 1993 were estimated to have British and/or French origins, while 4 were classified as having aboriginal origins, in full (3) or in part (1). Seventy-one MPs were estimated as having minority origins, about 24% of all Members. Included in this category are 53 individuals with European background, 4 who have Jewish roots, 1 Chilean, and 13 with origins officially regarded (by Statistics Canada) as most likely associated with visible minority status. A further 27 MPs, about 9%, were deemed to have multiple origins which spanned the majority-minority categories (overwhelmingly consisting of British and other, nonFrench, European combinations). If the mixed category is factored into the overall tally, then the number of parliamentarians estimated as having at least "some" minority background reaches 98.

Of more immediacy here, the data corroborate the sense, informally gained, that women with minority backgrounds entered Parliament in 1993 in notable numbers. Altogether, eleven women were categorized as likely having origins exclusively associated with minority communities, that is, nine in addition to

Augustine and Fry (as members of visible minorities). Five of the nine women have origins concentrated in Southern European countries with the remaining four having collectively more diverse backgrounds (Croatian/Norwegian; Hungarian; Jewish; Polish). These women make up about 16% of the minority group as a whole and, except for one, are all Liberals.

A further eight women were estimated to have multiple origins rooted in both majority and minority communities. The fact that they comprise a relatively larger proportion of their particular category (about 30%) may hold some significance worthy of further reflection, but for present purposes it suffices to note that their inclusion bumps to 19 the total number of women with at least some minority aspect in their background. It is British ancestry that is the prevalent majority group component for these women. For five of them, it appears to be twinned with Croatian, Dutch, Ukrainian, German, or Polynesian ancestry. For two other women, British heritage is combined with two minority lines of ancestry, Icelandic/Norwegian and German/Finnish. Finally, for one of them, majority links are to both French and British communities and are combined with German and Italian origins. Here, too, most are Liberals.

It might be appropriate to acknowledge here that the ordinary expectation is for women in this combined majority-minority category to identify less strongly with the minority dimension of their background than women who have a minority-only heritage. Intuitively, a partial majority heritage may work to diminish self-assessment as a minority. That said, it can also be noted that some self-assessment does occur. During the course of interviews with some of these women, it became quite clear that they indeed attributed some relevance to that part of their background outside of the majority context. Inclusion of such women in the counting exercise is not entirely inappropriate.

Comparisons with Earlier Parliaments

It might be tempting to dismiss or underestimate the significance of the total numbers of minority women and what they mean for indicating added social diversity in the composition of the House. After all, the 19 minority women constitute only about 6% of all MPs. Moreover, the fact they make up about 19% of the entire (broader) minority category (i.e., 19 of 98) –virtually the same percentage of seats held by women as a whole – might be taken as evidence of a rather ordinary state of affairs. Moreover, some of the women in the 35th Parliament who were identified as having minority backgrounds were, of course, incumbents who were first elected in 1988 or even earlier.

Such reservations, are diminished when the makeup of previous Parliaments is brought into consideration. This is evident on the basis of an entirely new classification analysis which was undertaken for women elected to previous Parliaments and which provides the basis for longitudinal tracking.[3] See Table 2.

Before the 1980s, the presence of women in the federal legislature registered as little more than a minor blip. Even as their numbers increased noticeably over that decade, their share of the seats lagged far behind the proportion held by men. By 1988, the 39 women in the 34th Parliament still only made up about 13% of the House. With such a low threshold, it did not take much for a new record to be established in 1993.

The argument that the 1993 election was exceptional in producing an unprecedented number of minority

Table 2
Majority and Minority Women in Parliament, 1965-93

	1965	1968	1972	1974	1979	1980	1984	1988	1993
# Women MPs	4	1	5	9	10	14	27	39	53
% Women MPs	1.5	0.4	1.8	3.4	3.6	5.0	9.6	13.2	18.0
Among Women MPs									
% Minority	0	0	0	11.1	10.0	7.1	3.7	5.1	20.8
% Min. and Maj.-Min	0	0	20.0	22.2	20.0	14.2	3.7	7.7	35.9

women MPs is strongly corroborated by the data. Before that election, very few such women had been elected as parliamentarians. Over the entire 1965-88 period, there were apparently eleven instances in which minority women, including those with a mixed background, won seats–which is about 10% of all those held by women. Even these figures slightly overstate the case since two of the women had repeat victories. The first woman with roots exclusively outside of the two charter groups appeared to first enter the federal legislature only in 1974.

In doing so, Simma Holt (of Jewish background) became a colleague of Monique Bégin, who herself was first elected two years earlier, apparently the first women with a "hybrid" (French and Flemish) background. Over the next four elections little changed. By 1988, it was possible to count only two women MPs with minority origins and as many as three by including the mixed category. This translates into about 5% or 8%, respectively, of the 39 women elected to the 34th Parliament. Five years later, the corresponding percentages were noticeably higher; about 21% for the minority-only category, 36% for the two categories combined.

Differences across the last two elections can be even more dramatically portrayed by comparing percentage changes for the separate categories of women and minorities. For women as a whole, their expansion from 39 to 53 MPs is tantamount to an increase of about 26%. For minorities as a whole, the percentages appear to be much larger, perhaps as high as 46% if the mixed category is excluded, perhaps as high as 102% if it is included.[4] However, dwarfing these percentages by far is a figure of 550% representing the increase from 2 to 11 minority-only women MPs, or 633% reflecting the change more inclusively considered (from 3 to 19).

Conclusion

While it remains to be seen whether or not subsequent elections will confirm this pattern, it is clear that at this point the presence of minority women in the 35th Parliament constitutes a distinctive feature in the evolution of the legislature's composition. Understanding both this development and its implications ought to loom large as a study goal. Research on the former dimension will need to acknowledge that three of the minority women were among the nine or so women that Mr. Chrétien, using newly acquired powers of direct appointment, designated as the party's standard bearers, thus sparing them the necessity of fighting a nomination battle. Still, these designations cannot account for all of the growth in the number of minority women elected in 1993.

Also limiting the explanatory reach of the phenomenon of candidate appointments is the fact that most of the designated women were actually from majority communities (and who, except for Georgette Sheridan in Saskatchewan, were defeated in the election). Further, it is not unreasonable to suggest that Jean Augustine and Maria Minna, designated in Toronto constituencies, were swept into the House in part because of the exceptional Liberal wave and the split in opposition voting. At the time of their appointments, it was by no means a foregone conclusion that they would win. Only Eleni Bakopanos (in Quebec's Saint-Denis riding) had been selected for a riding that the Liberals had actually won in the previous election.

Since the appointment of women was, in some measure, justified by the acknowledgement that women continue to have a more difficult time winning nomination contests, these designations actually draw more attention to the broader questions of recruitment and access, including the specifics of the nomination process itself. Indeed, one might ask what these designations actually imply about the particular impediments that minority women face. Relatedly, what about those who contested (and won) their nominations? Did they have to overcome greater obstacles? That there is something of value to explore with these, and similar, questions is suggested by a preliminary consideration of responses gathered through interviews with MPs. Some minority women did, in fact, make explicit reference to the double burden they felt they carried and to the discrimination, often subtle, occasionally overt, they faced along both fronts. At times, the constraints imposed by a male world of politics and by an English-French one were viewed as operating in independent and perhaps additive fashion.

However, complaints were also voiced about the men within their very own communities who, it was believed, were reluctant to share power and therefore in their actions constituted additional and distinctive barriers. At the same time, this sentiment did not prevent these women from sympathizing with the problems that their male counterparts faced as minorities. They were especially quick to point out the hypocrisy of those majority politicians who accused minority individuals of mobilizing their ethnic communities to win nominations, when in the past the same mobilization had been undertaken on behalf of the majority politicians.

Such mobilization efforts by themselves do not differentiate between the political approaches adopted by minority men and women; many on both sides of the gender divide regard their community ties as a resource base which, quite naturally, should be brought to bear in the political arena. What may differentiate between the two groups, however, is the greater importance for minority women of organizational work and office-holding at the community level. Though more work is needed on this notion, there is at least a first-blush sense from the evidence that their access experiences were distinctive in the way they relied more on active community involvement and formal positions as stepping stones towards parliamentary office.

A variety of distinctive experiences and reactions within the parliamentary setting itself was also evident from the interview information. One minority female MP, for example, expressed how difficult it was to know if the slights she has experienced, such as witnessing credit being given to someone for the same idea she had initially expressed, were because of gender or origin. Concerns were also raised by many MPs, including males, that minority women were merely being used in a perfunctory way, as individuals who could provide double token value. On the other hand, a few minority women themselves complained that men, including their co-ethnics, discounted their promotions (as parliamentary secretaries, committee chairs, etc.), claiming they were the product not of hard work but of gender considerations.

Notes

1. Jerome H. Black and Aleem S. Lakhani, "Ethnoracial Diversity in the House of Commons: An Analysis of Numerical Representation in the 35th Parliament", *Canadian Ethnic Studies* (forthcoming).

2. A few, fairly early studies are cited in Black and Lakhani ("Ehnoracial Diversity"), as are two, more recent ones which merit specific mention here. One is R. Ogmundson and J. McLaughlin, "Trends in the Ethnic Origins of Canadian Elites: the Decline of the BRITS?," *Canadian Review of Sociology and Anthropology* 29 (1992), 227-41, which classified MPs in the years 1965, 1975, and 1985, but without any detailed specification beyond a broad single-origin "other" (nonBritish, nonFrench) category. More specific classifications of ethnicity and race were provided by Alain Pelletier, covering the entire period from 1965 to 1988. "Politics and Ethnicity: Representation of Ethnic and Visible-Minority Groups in the House of Commons," in Kathy Megyery ed. *Ethno-Cultural Groups and Visible Minorities in Canadian Politics: The Question of Access.* Volume 13, Royal Commission on Electoral Reform and Party Financing (Toronto: Dundurn Press), 1991. Some limitations in Pelletier's analysis are noted in Black and Lakhani ("Ethnoracial Diversity").

3. Of course, it was impractical and, in many cases, impossible to survey past parliamentarians, so the categorization was based on biographical and surname approaches alone. This variation in method, it should be noted, does not appear to compromise judgements about trends. First, the same elaborate versions of the two traditional approaches used for the 35th Parliament were also employed for the earlier Parliaments. Second, there were extra efforts made to gather biographical information from a wider range of sources, including magazine articles and the like. Thanks are owed to Chris Anderson for assistance with this phase of the data collection.

4. The comparison is based on Pelletier's estimate of 48 minority MPs for 1988 ("Politics and Ethnicity"). See Black and Lakhani ("Ethnoracial Diversity") for an argument that Pelletier has probably underestimated the incidence of minority MPs.

The elected dictatorship

Can Parliament be made an adequate instrument of democracy? Easily

The floor of the House of Commons is only a few yards wide, but when Toronto MP John Nunziata crossed it to talk to Jean Chretien on December 1, it must have seemed like one of the longest walks of his life. Mr. Nunziata was evicted summarily from the Liberal caucus in April after voting against the 1996-97 budget. By failing to abolish the Goods and Services Tax as they had promised in 1993, the Liberals, felt Mr. Nunziata, had betrayed their constituents. Despite support from voters, however, Mr. Nunziata has had trouble mapping out a political future. Jean Chretien has no hesitancy about not signing the nomination papers of democratically-selected candidates: before the last election, he summarily appointed Liberal candidates in five ridings, some of which had already held nomination contests. Mr. Nunziata could have run as an Commons independent, but that is something that only four people have done successfully

in the last quarter-century. So he swallowed his pride and crossed the floor—a symbolic defeat, some said, for government accountability to the citizenry.

The inner cabinet's iron rule over MPs makes it hard for them to stick up for their constituents in situations like his. As a result, our modern Parliament has become a rubber stamp: once seen as a sort of absurd and impotent national debating society, it has now become less than even that, as premature closure of debate becomes standard practice and the governance of the land is done by executive fiat. Right now, however, there are a couple of dim signs of positive change on the parliamentary horizon.

Perhaps no one has described the existing conditions better than John Nunziata himself. "The real power, the ability to influence, is concentrated in the office of the leader of each of the parties," Mr. Nunziata said in an August 9 speech in Toronto. "It is most pro-

nounced in the case of the government, where the power is in the Prime Minister's Office...Surprising as this may sound, in fact this country is run by half a dozen people, half of whom are unelected. This may not be something that Canadians realize, but it is something that they should be extremely concerned about. These unelected officials have a tremendous influence over public policy and the careers of individual MPs. They determine who is rewarded and who is punished."

Canadian federal governments are accountable to the populace once every five years, but in the interim, there is little that elected representatives can do to influence policy; once a decision is taken by the government, there can be no deviance. This becomes truer and truer with each passing decade.

"This is one of the legacies of Pierre Trudeau," explains David Somerville, president of the National Citizens Coalition. "He studied under Harold Laski at the London School of Economics, and one of Laski's famous observations is that parliamentary government is really incompatible with socialism. Parliament is unsuited to carrying out constant detailed intervention in people's lives, because of the time-consuming process of subjecting laws to debate and committee scrutiny. What Laski proposed, and Trudeau adopted, was the use of large amounts of 'enabling legislation': a bill is passed into law as a kind of skeleton, delegating powers of regulation to the Governor in Council [the cabinet], and the government can then change the law in whatever way it pleases without putting it before the MPs."

Hence, a quarter-century of "enabling legislation" of the sort that gave us metric in 1975, when cabinet altered a law allowing both Imperial and metric measurements so that it banned the older system outright. Today, it is one of the Liberals' favorite tools. The Draconian firearms regulations created under Allan Rock's controversial C-68 are all subject to unilateral change by cabinet. Another 1995 bill put forward by Sheila Copps created a cumbersome new regulatory regime for energy efficiency; green-minded administrations of the future can toughen up energy policing infinitely without the by-your-leave of our elected officials.

A particularly controversial current example is the new regulations created by David Dingwall's tobacco-advertising legislation. The government has hitherto had to push Tobacco Products Control Act changes through the slow-grinding mill of the Commons. But now, with the procedurally-accelerated passage of the bill, Mr. Dingwall will acquire the right to unilaterally make new law on tobacco advertising, packaging, and promotion. "A theatre group accepting tobacco company funding could not allow one of the characters to smoke on stage," pointed out *Globe and Mail* columnist Terence Corcaran on December 4. "Journalists could be muzzled . . . retailers and distributors can be raided and their products seized without warrant and based on arbitrary regulation."

As cabinet arrogates such rights to itself, what little is done inside Parliament is inceasingly circumscribed by procedural bullying. In 1956, the electorate was so outraged by the St. Laurent government's use of closure that it voted Tory the next year. In the Mulroney era, however, the closure vote and a similar tactic, the invocation of "time allocation," became commonplace, being used dozens of times and always inciting Liberal fury in the pro-

cess. "But bad as we thought the Mulroney government was, the Liberals have surely displaced them in the record books," says Reform deputy house leader John Williams. "They've cut off debate with time-allocation three times in the last *ten days*. And, in fact, it would have been *four* had we not agreed to help expedite the passage of [the tobacco law]."

New statistics released on December 6 show that the 35th Canadian Parliament has passed, in all, 123 bills. Twenty-eight of these—or nearly one-quarter—have been passed after the government used time-allocation motions and closure motions to shut down debate early. These now-routine gag motions would not, perhaps, be startling if they were used to push through minor bills without major national implications. But it has been used to help bake some of the government's hottest potatoes. After the 1995 Quebec referendum, for example, Jean Chretien used it to get his unity package passed after less than three days. It was used in March 1994 to suspend the redrawing of electoral boundaries, and in June of that year to ram through a quarter-billion-dollar Indian land claim in the Yukon. It figured in C-68, and now it seems almost an inevitable end to any slightly heated Commons debate. The bill banning the motor-fuel additive MMT got through that way at the end of November, as did the Judges' Act changes which conferred extra cash on Supreme Court Chief Justice Antonio Lamer.

Why are we stuck with such an autocratic system? "My simple explanation is that when there's so little that divides the parties, it's much more important for their members to stand together," says Richard Schultz, a McGill University political scientist. "It is different now with Reform on the scene, but with pre-1993 conditions, which may well return after the next election, the Liberals and Tories don't differ an awful lot. It's been leadership-driven—personality-driven. And as a result the prime minister has so much power over the backbenchers. Our MPs are essentially short-term amateurs, unlike politicians in Britain."

According to Mr. Schultz, the problem of too much executive power is not a new one in Canadian politics. A brief post-Confederation "Golden Age" saw the House of Commons bristle with "loose fish," MPs who withheld party affiliation to try to win more attractive offers from either side. But the secret ballot and simultaneous general elections, both introduced in 1875, undercut MPs' local power and made "loose" hold-outs

less valuable to majority governments. "Since then," says Mr. Schultz, "we have been a more top-down, executive-controlled parliamentary system than any other country that follows the Westminster model. We have a more rigid party discipline than anywhere else, and far less input from individual MPs and MPs collectively."

Nonetheless, says Mr. Schultz, throughout most of this century MPs have not been quite the eunuchs they are now. To him, and to many other political scientists, a turning point was 1965, when the Pearson government moved to deflect criticism over the "inefficient" nature of the annual debate over the government estimates. Before that, a part of each parliamentary year was given over to an all-party quizzing of cabinet ministers, in keeping with the 13th-century Magna Carta principle that the Crown should have no money until the grievances of the people were redressed. If the estimates were not approved by the end of the fiscal year—and the opposition, at that time, had the power of filibuster—a situation similar to the 1995 shutdown of the U.S. federal government could have followed.

But the public, in an era of greater faith in big government, found that process tedious and inexplicable. Pearson, in a move made permanent by Mr. Trudeau in 1968, devolved questioning of ministers onto the parliamentary committees, taking it out of the hands of the House proper. More important, a regulation was instituted whereby the estimates for the ministries would be deemed to have been approved on May 1 if they had not been accepted by the committees by then.

Thomas d'Aquino wonders whether that has not primed the explosion in spending we have seen since the 1960s. "Going back to the Magna Carta, one of the checks and balances we've had—in a system that doesn't have many—is Parliament's power over the purse," says the longtime president of the nonpartisan Business Council on National Issues. "That was the original *intent* of Parliament: to make sure that the king couldn't act without the consent of the bill-payers. This has left our parliamentarians with only Question Period as a vehicle for accountability. They can try to embarrass the government or ask questions about the way it's operating. But its ability to exercise significant influence over how money's going to be spent? That really does not exist."

The good news is that a return to pre-1965 conditions is not out of the question. A special five-person Commons subcommittee on the Business of Supply was created 18 months ago as part of a deal to get the Reformers to drop a filibuster in the Treasury Board com-

Rumblings within Reform

At times, the life of a Reform MP is rough. The party has pressured its caucus members to give up their pensions, to throw a blanket over their more politically incorrect opinions, and to coordinate their House of Commons questioning with their caucus comrades. Now some are fussing over that section of the Reform Party Blue Book which mandates that where their judgement and conscience conflict with "the consensus of the will of a majority of the constituents," the latter shall prevail. In 1993, Reform candidates for Parliament were required to sign a pledge that they would honour this stipulation and act as the vessels of their constituents' wills. But some of those who signed in 1993 do not think they should be made to do so again.

"I signed it last time around," says Edmonton MP Ian McClelland. "But I am of the opinion that we would greatly strengthen our party if we said that on moral-ethical issues, people are obliged to represent their own values, provided those were made known to the voters in advance. If people have not been able to make a judgement on me, and I hide my opinions, then

of course I should not be given the freedom to vote my conscience. But if I was upfront about my innermost values in the first place, and I was voted in anyway, I should have the right to represent those views. But my quest is to change our party position on that," Mr. McClelland hastily adds, "not to be a lone wolf. I've lived with it this long."

There could very well be "lone wolves" in the party slate at the next election, however. Some Reformers do not like the idea that they may be forced to vote against their consciences on sticky ethical issues such as gay rights, euthanasia, and abortion. So far, the party shows no sign of dropping the formal pledge requirement. But chief strategist Rick Anderson acknowledges the possibility that a constituency association could send a candidate through without making him do it. "The pledge is not a *sine qua non*—that's too strong," says Mr. Anderson. "But it is still considered to be one of the core principles of the party . . . The executive council has indicated that this

could be grounds for refusing to recommend the signing of a candidate's papers, and has recommended that it be grounds for local associations to nominate candidates."

Personally, I think we should rethink the policy," says Calgary Reform MP Stephen Harper, who bears the reputation of a social moderate amongst the crusty, traditionalist Reformers. "The goal of every MP in the party should be to have these issues put to public referenda, but in practice it is going to prove difficult to get all the MPs to vote the constituents' wishes, even if they sign the pledge." However, says Mr. Harper, "I send a cautionary note to those who feel they simply must vote their wishes over those of the voters. A lot of people are going to ask themselves: 'If an MP is not prepared to listen to me on moral issues, where there's not a lot of technical expertise required to make an informed judgment, when *are* they going to listen?' "

—*C.C.*

mittee. Its report, due in March, will end up being debated by committee of the whole Commons. According to Mr. Williams, it will call for a return to a single Commons-wide debate on the parliamentary estimates. "[Liberal chairman] Marlene Catterall and I are singing from the same page," says Mr. Williams. "I really it's going to happen."

If history really does repeat itself, however, the report's most likely fate is that of the 1985 McGrath Report, commissioned from an all-party team by Brian Mulroney. Jim McGrath called for more power to be devolved onto committees and for several other democratizing reforms that would give more power to MPs; his report, however, mouldered on the cabinet's shelves and is now forgotten. Nonetheless, MPs Catterall and Williams place great trust in their secret weapon: a raft of heavy-hitting committee witnesses from the Pearson era who say that the effects of the removal of debate on the estimates have been disastrous.

Indeed, the report calls for more than

just a rectification of the 1965 move. Even in committee, says Mr. Williams, "parliamentarians only get to vote on 30% of the federal spending. The other 70% is merely given to us for information purposes; it's statutory program spending, like for unemployment insurance, which was permanently approved when the initial legislation was passed." Thus, the spending in ongoing programs is never debated or voted on, and never has been. The Williams-Catterall committee hopes to change that, seeking to introduce periodic, full-blown evaluations of ongoing spending on a cyclical basis. "Once every, say, 10 years," says Mr. Williams, "we take these big programs, evaluate them from a public-policy point of view, and ask the minister for changes. We'll get the chance to formally investigate the way this 70% of the public money is spent."

The report could even include, as Mr. McGrath's did, recommendations for changes to Canada's uncommonly tough rules about when a government beaten in a division is

required to resign. Under the Canadian system, the ruling government has traditionally felt obliged to drop an election writ after any defeat on a major bill. In Britain this is not so, and as a result, back-benchers are free to respond to constituents and block unpopular legislation. The British system of party discipline, unlike ours, contains gradations of urgency, and even on the most urgent votes, MPs are relatively free to go against government, because the occasions mandating a governing party's resignation are very highly circumscribed. Margaret Thatcher often introduced important bills without making them tests of confidence, and her own back-bench beat her several times, the most famous example being over the controversial 1986 poll tax.

Could Canada have been spared the GST if it had laxer confidence rules? (It is worth noting that the Senate held the tax up for an entire summer by virtue of the fact that its parliamentary procedures have never been streamlined the way Pearson did the Commons.) John Nunziata thinks it might have been, and sees freer votes in the House as a means of restoring democratic accountability to Parliament. "Allowing free votes on *every* issue would show true leadership in this country—whether it is the leader of the government or of any of the opposition parties." Mr. Williams will not go that far, but he concedes that it "would allow parliamentarians to stop worrying about party lines and start representing the taxpayers."

There is another set of measures that may soon return from the parliamentary past—namely, the 1920s, when a number of progressive-minded provinces (including Alberta) allowed the citizenry to petition the government to hold binding referendums on important issues. This August, the Ontario government released a discussion paper on direct democracy. "We're looking at the possibility of government-initiated, opposition-initiated, and citizen-initiated referendums," said Premier Mike Harris at the time, noting that the "wisdom of the people" defeated the 1992 Charlottetown Accord. If there is such an experiment, and it works out, it could spread quickly: the Alberta government considered citizens' initiative this summer, and the rural back-benchers pressing for it were put off only with promises that the issue will eventually return to the table. Direct democracy might ultimately make its way to the halls of federal power, providing Canadians with the means to thwart any unsavory ambition of Mr. Nunziata's ruling half-dozen.

Citizens' initiative has long been a cherished policy plank of the Reform Party of Canada. Draft legislation has been in the works for almost two years, and the party finally unveiled its Citizen-Initiated Referendum Act on October 30, 1996, when it received first reading in the House of Commons. Introduced as Private Member's Bill C-343 by Reform direct-democracy critic Ted White, the bill would force the government to hold a referendum on any measure petitioned for by 3% of the voters in the prior federal election. Petitioners would present their motion to the Clerk of the House of Commons and then would have a year to gather the required signatures. The Clerk would reject any motion that did not contain a statement of its net cost to the federal treasury, and that statement would be printed right on the referendum ballot. To save money, referendums could be held concurrent with elections, and could eventually be conducted electronically.

"As far as I'm concerned, the current parliamentary system is completely incompatible with the Information Age," says Mr. White. "The old red herring from old-line parties was that MPs had to consider bills very carefully and were in a better position than the public to make judgments on them. But that's just horseradish. Today, most MPs don't even read the bills. They are told how to vote by the whip. Parliament has become a place for the enactment of a party agenda, and the wills of bureaucrats, rather than being there to enact the will of the people...If a government feels it has an agenda that is in the best interests of the people, more transparency and more participation would mean it had to spend more time convincing the people that 'this is what we should do.' Can that really be bad for Canada?"

—Colby Cosh

LINES IN THE POLITICAL SAND

"There has to be a good reason if the Senate is going to exercise powers it shouldn't have."

by JAMES HRYNYSHYN

W hat if the government of Canada tried to do away with one of the fundamental tenets of democracy? What if the media paid little or no attention to the story? Even worse, what if the only hope for a reprieve lay with a collection of party hacks and bagmen in the Senate?

Incredible? Yes. But true. Believe it or not, the Senate did come to the rescue of democracy, saving Canadians from a government prepared to see the current electoral map —based on 1981 census data — stay in place.

The story begins in February 1994, just a few months after the Liberals' election victory. The government benches were rife with rookies, many of whom senior party organizers had never expected to see in office. Chrétien was riding a wave of unprecedented popularity. He had yet to introduce any legislation of consequence, and his most remarkable accomplishment to date was cancelling contracts signed by the previous government: expensive military helicopters and the Pearson Airport deal.

But on February 15, Elections Canada unveiled the proposed changes to the federal ridings, as mandated by the Electoral Boundaries Readjustment Act. Ontario would get four new seats, B.C. two, and of the existing 295 seats, 264 would be redrawn — a typical readjustment by any standard. The changes would take effect on January 16, 1997. It was the third time the ridings had been redrawn since the act was passed 30 years earlier, and veteran MPs were blasé, regarding it as an unavoidable minor inconvenience.

But the rookies, particularly those from southern Ontario, were worried about the possibility of Reform Party candidates taking advantage of the creation of six new ridings. Of the 98 Ontario Liberals then sitting in the Commons, 93 would see their ridings redrawn. Apparently, as former Liberal MP turned independent Senator Marcel Prud'homme sarcastically remarked, they hadn't yet learned how to trade campaign managers across riding boundaries.

 From *The Canadian Forum*, May 1996, pp. 25-27. © 1996 by Canadian Forum, Ltd. Reprinted by permission.

Chrétien's response was to introduce Bill C-18 — an Act to Suspend the Electoral Boundaries Readjustment Act of 1964. In effect, the Liberals had decided electoral reform could wait until after the next election. It was greeted, literally, with cheers from the backbenchers assembled at a caucus meeting in Parliament Hill's Centre Block. So happy were they that other Grits, like Vancouver rookie Ted McWhinney, made no attempt to hide their surprise.

"There's a huge backlash from the new members," he observed. "They fought one election and they don't want to do it again on entirely new boundaries, or fight each other for nominations."

Another B.C. newcomer, Anna Terrana, had different thoughts; she was "troubled" by the implications of the bill. B.C. would gain two seats under the new riding order, after all, and she saw no reason to postpone those additional seats until after the next election.

While House Leader Herb Gray was insisting the bill was written to reform an out-of-date redistribution process, Toronto's John Nunziata, a marginalized Liberal and former member of the Rat Pack, was telling anyone who asked that it had nothing to do with improving redistribution and everything to do with mollifying frightened rookie MPs.

"People were looking at how they were affected personally," he told Norm Ovenden of the *Edmonton Journal*. "That's where the pressure came from. Their personal kingdoms were being eroded or in some cases obliterated."

The Liberals' frankness can be attributed in part to the weakness of the opposition on the issue. The Bloc Québécois was vowing not to run another federal campaign and cared nothing about future ridings. The Reform Party did object to the bill, but, in the absence of a curious press gallery and without the ability to do anything more than delay a vote, their protests were little more than bluster. C-18 passed through the House a month later, thanks to Chrétien's first (but not last) use of closure, which cut off debate.

The next step, however, confronted the Liberals with a more serious obstacle. In the Commons, the lack of public concern worked to the government's advantage, but in the Senate it proved a major drawback. The Conservatives were eager to undermine the Chrétien government, as long as it didn't mean antagonizing the public. Many were still smarting from the previous summer's public relations disaster, when they were forced to reverse a decision to increase their housing allowance by $6,000. Bill C-18, they concluded, was the perfect target: there were serious constitutional issues at stake, and the Senate could claim it was

defending the democratic principle of "one person, one vote". It was a chance to regain lost pride.

Led by the scholarly Gérald Beaudoin, who chaired the Senate's Legal and Constitutional Affairs Committee, Tory senators found a long list of experts and former electoral boundary commissioners to denounce postponing redistribution as an affront to democracy. They pointed out that Section 51 of the Constitution calls for a redistribution of federal ridings after each decennial census. The bill would kill two years of work by the existing commissions, turn the update clock back to zero and freeze it there for two years while Parliament came up with a new riding update law. Without the bill redistribution would take effect in 1997.

Because the process takes two-and-a-half years to complete, new ridings wouldn't be ready until late 1998 — after the next expected election. If C-18 passed, the next election would be fought using the old ridings based on population data gathered in 1981. Already, ridings such as York North in metropolitan Toronto are home to more than 250,000 people, while others have fewer than 30,000. The formula laid down in the Constitution calls for an average of about 100,000.

Beaudoin, known in Parliament as a "pit bull" on points of law, says the Senate had a "constitutional obligation" to fight the bill. "We were defending the principles of democracy."

The Tory majority in the Senate voted to amend the bill to ensure the $4 million worth of work by the existing commissions wasn't undone and reduced the suspension period to six months.

The reaction from the Chrétien government was predictable outrage about the unelected Senate "meddling" in MPs' affairs. But in the end, they compromised: the commissions would remain intact, with the freeze shortened to nine months, beginning after the release of the riding commissions' reports in the fall — sufficient to ensure that the ridings would not be scuttled. C-18 received the Senate's blessing on June 15. Equality of votes had been restored, and, for a while, it looked like the tawdry tale had come to an end.

But the Liberals had another card to play. A few weeks later, the Commons' Procedure and House Affairs Committee, led by Kingston Liberal Peter Milliken, opened hearings on the drafting of replacement riding update legislation. It was clear from the beginning that the committee's work was little more than a side-show to the true Liberal strategy.

The government charged Milliken with examining four possible "improvements" to the law: a cap on the number of seats in the House; the method of selecting the electoral commission members; the rules governing the drawing of boundaries; and the involvement of MPs in the process.

The first item was a non-starter, since the number of seats is governed by formulas laid down in the Constitution, and not even Chrétien was prepared to open that can of worms.

The second, commission membership, also turned out to be a bogus issue. Each province has a three-member panel, the chair of which is chosen by the chief justice of the province, while the other two commissioners are appointed by the Speaker of the Commons. No one had any complaints about the process, and all the Milliken committee could do was suggest that the positions be advertised, a meaningless gesture, since the tiny pool of experts from which membership is invariably drawn hardly needs to be alerted to the job openings.

The boundary-drawing rules also escaped serious revision. Only the fourth subject proved useful: MPs would no longer have their own set of hearings to complain about proposed riding boundaries, a provision universally derided as a vestige of the days of the gerrymander.

The only other significant elements to emerge from the committee were a recommendation that MPs have a veto over the Speaker's appointments, and the creation of a partial riding update after each off-year census (those held in years ending in a "6" in addition to the existing system, which follows censuses carried out in years ending in a "1"). Both these measures were attacked in the Senate on constitutional grounds.

Lack of content notwithstanding, the government turned the Milliken report into Bill C-69, which, like its predecessor, passed the Commons with barely a ripple. Most members of the Parliamentary Press Gallery continued to assume that the public was far less interested in the story than were their MPs.

Unfortunately for the Liberals, C-69 suffered the same fate in the Senate as C-18. Beaudoin and the constitutional experts denounced the bill. Their main criticism was that it included an immediate repeal of the existing riding update process, again setting the clock back to zero and guaranteeing that the next election would be fought using the old boundaries. The Conservatives were having none of it. They stalled the bill for months, narrowly outvoting Liberal senators more than once. It finally died in early February when Chrétien prorogued Parliament. Though any bill can be revived, House Leader Herb Gray hinted that, as C-69 was in the Senate, resurrecting it would be "complicated" — parliamentary code for "very unlikely".

Tory Senator Lowell Murray, government leader in the Senate for the Mulroney years and a 30-year backroom veteran on the Hill, says he was surprised by the Liberals' willingness to tamper with the democratic process. But it makes sense when you consider the composition of their caucus. Back in early February 1994, backbenchers were being asked to swallow a legislative agenda that many found less than palatable. There was recognition of homosexual rights, gun control and more cuts to unemployment insurance. Perhaps, says Murray, Chrétien decided to offer them their old ridings in exchange for their acquiescence on less popular matters.

In the Commons, the lack of public interest worked to the government's advantage, but in the Senate it proved a major drawback

Basically, says Nunziata, that's exactly what happened. Of course, Nunziata is quick to point out that the Tory senators would never have turned electoral boundaries into a crusade if they hadn't recently been stung by their party's worst election defeat in history.

Murray concedes that partisan politics did play a role, more with C-69 than with C-18. But the latter, he says, raised questions of principle that transcended party lines. Not everyone in the Senate wanted to risk the wrath of the public over something as arcane as riding redistribution. After all, says Murray, "there has to be a good reason if the Senate is going to exercise powers it shouldn't have."

The reason proved strong enough to convince the rest of the Tory senators over the last two years to devote their time and energy to blocking the two election reform bills. By the time the Liberals achieved a tenuous one-seat majority in the Upper House (through the suspicious resignation in late January of Tory Senator John Sylvain and his replacement by Liberal MP Shirley Maheu), Conservative strategists were preparing to pull out all the stops to prevent C-69 from passing.

Then the bill died. As far as Murray, Beaudoin and their colleagues were concerned, the Senate had done its part.

But the story may not be over. Rumours are circulating that Chrétien may call an election as soon as this fall, before the new ridings take effect in January 1997. If that happens, he will have won — and the Senate will have lost — the battle to save Canadian democracy.

James Hrynyshyn is a freelance journalist in Ottawa.

Is Senate Reform a Dead Issue?

by Senator Normand Grimard

The Conservatives formed a majority in the Senate before February 1, 1996. The resignation of Conservative Senator John Sylvain and his replacement by Liberal Shirley Maheu then reversed the proportions. At the time of writing, the political make-up of the Senate is as follows: 51 Liberals, 50 Conservatives and three independents, for a total of 104 senators. While a majority of one or even several votes in the Senate does not necessarily mean a nerve-wracking balancing act, the possibility of defeat is always there, especially in important votes on matters of principle. Party discipline can always break down. This article looks at some recent developments in the Senate and considers whether Senate reform should be put back on the political agenda.

The Senate seems to provoke a mean-spiritedness so obstinate, so close-minded, so doctrinaire, that it verges on caricature, and this is true even when the aim is its reform. Mordecai Richler, an author not often cited by French-speaking Quebeckers, wrote of the Meech Lake Accord that was reached in 1987 and rejected in 1990: "each Canadian province would now have a role in choosing its senators, which is to say it could reward its own superannuated bagmen and other political nonentities rather than those favoured by Ottawa."[1] I begin my remarks on this negative note as a contrast to four or five examples demonstrating just how well Canada's Upper House retains its valuable qualities in the contemporary context.

Over the past year, the Senate has "made the news" (according to people who do not make a practice of covering us) several times. The first was the vote on the Pearson Airport Bill, on June 18, 1996. This bill limited the right of private investors to claim damages as a result of the government's decision to cancel the deal they had made. Because Liberal Senator Herbert O. Sparrow voted

A lawyer, Normand Grimard was appointed to the Senate in 1990. He is author of L'indispensable Sénat : Défense d'une institution mal aimée, Éditions vent d'ouest, Hull.

From *Canadian Parliamentary Review*, Spring 1997, pp. 7-10. © 1997 by the Committees and Parliamentary Associations Branch of the House of Commons in Ottawa. Reprinted by permission.

with the Opposition, the outcome was 48 votes in favour, 48 against, undoing a victory the government majority had assumed to be a foregone conclusion.

A little later, on November 26, 1996, the support of four Liberal senators and two independents gave the Conservative Opposition enough of a majority (46-35) to block the constitutional amendment doing away with the denominational school system in Newfoundland. In constitutional matters, however, rejection by the Senate holds for only six months, as set out in section 47 of the *Constitution Act, 1982*, and the Commons can vote to reverse the Senate's decision. In this instance the Chrétien government requested and got such a vote in the House on December 4, 1996. The loophole provided by section 47 was also used by the Mulroney government in 1987 to revive the Meech Lake Accord, which had been blocked in the Senate by the Liberals one month earlier. As I wrote in 1995, "Although new in law, this provision is no longer a theoretical one."[2].

Was the shift away from denominational schools in Newfoundland a violation of freedom of religion? Governments (not only that of Newfoundland) and churches clashed on this point. It could be argued for a long time. Another reason for the vocal opposition to the measure was probably the fear that abolishing "term 17" in Newfoundland would weaken the rights of official-language minorities in other provinces (such as Quebec). Be that as it may, the Senate once again proved its independence, even though the resolution ultimately, and to no one's surprise, passed by a second vote in the Lower House.

Again in 1996, the Senate served as a lightning rod for both hostile and favourable opinion on the gun control legislation. And heaven knows the fax machines were humming! Bill C-68 passed as well in the end. To go back a little further, the Upper House defeated a bill in 1993 that sought to merge the Canada Council and other cultural funding bodies. In 1991, it blocked Bill C-41, which would have re-criminalized abortion after the Morgentaler decision disallowed the former *Criminal Code* provisions.

That date should be noted. The Mulroney government was still in power, and former Cabinet Minister Pat Carney and five other Conservative Senators voted against the government. Senator Maurice Riel, former Speaker of the Upper House, remarked during the sitting of December 3, 1996:

> The Senate decision on abortion, which was subjected to a free, non-partisan vote in the Senate, is a very good example of the moral and social responsibilities of senators, and hence of the importance of their duties.[3]

I have been a senator since 1990. I am sure I could look further into the past than that and find other breaths of fresh air that have been forgotten, or that have been studiously ignored because they came from the Upper House. But it is clear by now, I think, that not being elected gives senators the advantage of being able to vote more freely, according to their conscience.

Even if they were to be elected, we would have to hope that their ability to make unfettered judgements could be retained, although the electoral mandate would, in my opinion, make this less likely. Obviously I am dealing in a great many "what ifs".

The idea of an elected Senate is definitely a popular one. For example, the leader of the Progressive Conservative Party, Jean Charest, wrote to me towards the end of 1996:

> Senate reform is a very important matter. A number of proposals have been put forward, and I am sure that other people will be addressing the issue. Personally, I am still pondering which option to support, while bearing in mind that our Party's rank and file want to see the Senate modernized.

Mr. Charest is not alone in his attitude: probably a majority of ordinary Canadians, parliamentarians, political leaders, journalists and academics would support the idea of an elected Senate as a way of increasing its credibility. Their opinion is among the more reasoned and moderate. I respect the good faith of all these colleagues and other intelligent individuals.

However, I will continue to believe that a combined formula of election and appointment, half and half, as senators retire or resign their seats, would meet Canada's needs just as well, and perhaps even better.

Combining election and appointment would give us the best features of both systems. I would limit the term for all new senators to ten years. Ten years, not a day over! The number of senators would rise from 104 to 130 because of fairly substantial changes introduced to combat Western Canada's feeling of injustice. My proposals remain purely castles in the air for the moment – I am well aware of this, and it does not bother me.

A Disputatious History

George-Etienne Cartier, the emblematic Montrealer and French Canadian of his day, the friend of John A. Macdonald of Kingston, 290 kilometers to the west, was one of the Fathers of Confederation in 1867. In a biography of Cartier, Brian Young has this to say:

> For years he opposed the abolition of the upper house of the Canadian legislature, on the ground that it acted as a protector of property, and he objected to universal suffrage since in his opinion only the lazy or vicious failed to meet property qualifications.[4]

As a 19th century bourgeois and owner of considerable property, Cartier also opposed the elimination of the provincial upper houses. In Cartier's view, something was needed to keep in check what we can imagine him calling "the excess energy of the Members of the Lower House". Right or wrong in perceiving such a need, he saw an appointed Senate as the required check rein. He even wanted to set the property qualification for becoming a senator at $8,000[5]; as we know, it was finally set at $4,000.

At the dawn of the 21st century, few politicians would argue that the Senate should be the official guardian of private property. But the deluge of criticism began to make itself felt the moment the Senate was created in 1867, and it has not stopped since. There would be no point in denying it. Nor does complaining about it win the slightest sympathy, since some people's minds are so firmly made up, and not just in favour of reforming the Senate either. They want it done away with. The shelves holding studies on the Senate's future – whether public or private, initiated by government task forces or academics, dealing only with the Senate alone or integrated into constitutional revision as a whole – buckle under the weight. To those studies must be added thousands of newspaper articles. Even Senate committee reports as thorough and thought-provoking as *Of Life and Death*, by the Special Senate Committee on Euthanasia and Assisted Suicide, chaired by Senator Joan Neiman, are scarcely given more than lip-service attention.

For the past 35 years, bursts of constitutional enthusiasm have been entangling us in an endless debate over all the possible meanings of some twenty terms: special status, Confederation, cooperative federalism, profitable federalism, renewed federalism, cultural sovereignty, two nations, the principal homeland of French Canadians etc. Quebec independence, and its off-shoot, sovereignty association, are still more drastic ways of posing the problem of the relationship between francophones and anglophones.

> **But whether one likes it or not, Senate reform is also part of the process of learning to get along together.**

Senate reform will determine the scope of the provinces' influence in Ottawa. Will the Senate become the voice of the provinces? Or of the regions? The 1987 Meech Lake Accord would have involved the provinces in the appointment of senators. The Charlottetown Accord, repudiated by referendum in 1992, would for all practical purposes have meant the Triple-E Senate wanted by the West. But neither of these attempts succeeded.

Prime Minister Jean Chrétien now has an easy riposte in the House for the leader of the Reform Party. If Mr. Manning wanted a different kind of Senate, he should have supported one of the two Accords. In the meantime Mr. Chrétien continues to appoint senators in the traditional way. He even appears to have rejected the *pro-Meech*-style consultations with the provinces that former Conservative Prime Minister Brian Mulroney practised.

Moreover, new appointees have been somewhat older than Mr. Mulroney's. On February 1, 1997, the 19 senators appointed by Mr. Chrétien were between 50 and 73. Four[6] of them sworn in at the age of 70, will not even qualify for the parliamentary pension, automatic after six years of service, since senators must retire at 75. Other amendments have resulted from increases in the number of Senate seats due to the entry of new provinces and territories into the federation (a change that could reasonably be expected), from the limited constitutional veto given the Senate in 1982, and from the reform of parliamentary committees, which has been beneficial to the Senate as well as the Commons since 1970.

One question, however, remains: what should the Senate's role be in the legislative process? Can it block legislation? As an unelected body, how far can it go in opposing legislation? When must it give way? What should its attitude be to a piece of legislation it regards as badly constructed or unworthy of a place among Canada's statutes?

I doubt if there is "one" single position to adopt as our guide. Defining such a position should be done by all the parties in turn, taking public opinion into account. Senator Allan MacEachen, who steered the Liberal Opposition in the Senate through the impassioned debate on the GST in 1990, recognized this in his farewell speech of June 19, 1996:

> I believed when I came into the Senate as I do now, that the Senate has a legislative role and the authority to amend and to defeat; but, in doing so, it must make all those careful calculations that will ensure that it is not bringing opprobrium upon itself in so doing.[7]

I regard this cautious attitude as being all the more important where money bills are concerned, given the undisputed role of the elected House. Equally, each time the "less partisan" Upper House becomes more partisan, the result is conflict of the kind that Senator Guy Charbonneau saw at its worst in 1990 during the debate over the GST.

To sum up, the Senate is an unappreciated institution, and as I said in 1995:

> I am writing to describe these feelings but also with the hope that those who come after me will be able to rescue our Upper House from this labyrinth – I doubt that I will see it myself!

> Disparaging senators is a common practice. If they worked seven days a week and agreed to have their salaries cut in half they would still be regarded as parasites by a portion of the population, simply because they are not elected. This may seem harsh, but it is a conclusion based on remarks made to me, sometimes even – more woundingly still — by friends.[8]

And I am not the only one to have observed how widespread this negative opinion is. The question that troubles me, however, is this: what are we to think when the Minister of Intergovernmental Affairs, the Honourable Stéphane Dion, can say to a Calgary businessman, "We Quebeckers do not want to hear a word about the Senate"?[9] If the Minister currently responsible for the Constitution does not want to discuss the Senate because that would annoy his province, Quebec, who is going to modernize it?

Far from changing the Prime Minister's attitude, the quasi-defeat in the 1995 Quebec referendum seems hardly to have made a dent in Mr. Chrétien's aversion to talking about the Constitution. And in what may well be an election year, his aversion is unlikely to diminish.

Notes

1. Mordecai Richler, *Oh Canada! Oh Quebec!*, (Toronto: Penguin Books), 1992, pp.151-2.

2. Normand Grimard, *L'indispensable Sénat*, (Hull:, Vents d'Ouest), 1995, p.140.

3. Senate *Debates*, December 3, 1996, p.1253.

4. Brian Young, *George-Etienne Cartier, Montreal Bourgeois*, (Montreal: McGill-Queen's University Press), 1981, p.19.

5. Young, *op.cit.*, p.75.

6. One of them, the Honourable Jean-Louis Roux, appointed at the age of 71, was fated not to draw a pension as Lieutenant-Governor of Quebec either, cf. *Le Journal de Montréal*, November 6, 1996, p.2.

7. Senate *Debates*, June 19, 1996, p.747.

8. Grimard, *op. cit.*, pp.188-9.

9. *Macleans*, January 13, 1997, p. 20.

IS HE UP TO THE JOB?

BY ANTHONY WILSON-SMITH

ELECTION '97

For those who have ever wondered what a prime minister does for fun, here is an example. In early April, Jean Chrétien was in British Columbia for several events that included a lunchtime meeting with Liberal candidates in a McDonald's restaurant in Surrey. After lunch (Big Mac, large fries with no ketchup and cola for the Prime Minister), Chrétien decided to visit the restaurant staff behind the counter. He shook hands with several cooks and servers, then spotted a woman working at the drive-through window. "Would you mind?" he asked, stepping past her with a smile. The next three customers pulling up to the window were given, along with their orders, a smile, a proffered handshake and the announcement "Hi, I'm Jean Chrétien, the Prime Minister." The predictable result, one Chrétien aide recalls, was "utter astonishment. One woman looked as though she didn't know whether to giggle or faint."

Memories are made of such things—if any of those patrons could later find anyone who believed them. Other than that, there are several prospective lessons to be drawn from the latest escapade of Jean Chrétien, full-time prime minister and sometime prankster. One, for political friends and allies, is that as he approaches a June 2 election, the 63-year-old Chrétien has lost none of his zest for both his life and his job. "He just loves doing the unexpected," says Eddie Goldenberg, his senior adviser and alter ego of more than 25 years' standing. The other potential outcome, for Chrétien's optimistic oppo-

nents, is that he will soon need such practice for a new career if his decision to go to the polls only 43 months into his present mandate proves to be a bad one. "The Canadian people," says Reform Leader Preston Manning, "are just waiting for the opportunity to hold this government and this prime minister accountable."

If that is the case, they will soon have their wish—and no one will have more at stake than Chrétien, whose place in history will be determined, at least in part, by the result. But the man who would lead Canada into a new millennium remains, to many people, no more familiar than he was when he took power in 1993. Is the real Jean Chrétien the glad-handing flag-waver that Canadians have come to know and—outside Quebec at least—often

Even after 3½ years in office, the Prime Minister remains an unknown quantity

love during the past three decades? Can a man who was first elected 37 years before the end of the century have the vision and gumption to lead the country into another one? And after all this time in public office, in a period when politicians are reviled more than revered, why would he even want to?

As the Liberals begin the campaign, Chrétien is, in the words of Finance Minister Paul Martin, "far and away the party's biggest, most important asset." But some skeptics, even within the party, would argue that the title now belongs to Martin himself. Chrétien, after three years of revelling in the highest popularity ratings of any prime minister in the last half-century, has during the past six months often appeared to have lost his fabled political antennae, stumbling from malapropism to misstep to outright muck-up. From his handling of the Goods and Services Tax, and tussles with Quebec, to a series of recent, and lavish, pre-election promises that tarnished the party's carefully established image of frugality, the Prime Minister's recent behavior has raised the question: is he up to it? "There is," says a senior Ontario Liberal organizer, "a very real fear that our support could melt very quickly."

That feeling is most acute in Ontario, where Liberal fears of Conservative Leader Jean Charest—seen as a younger, more charismatic, similarly middle-of-the-road and equally devout federalist version of the Prime Minister—run the highest. In Toronto, despite the divided state of the present opposition, some Liberals now mutter dark predictions about a minority government, and claim that many voters perceive Chrétien as being out-of-touch and out of ideas. Among the concerns cited: the near-loss in the 1995 Quebec referendum, the government's seeming inability to decide on a strategy for national unity, Chrétien's increasing isolation in office, and his unwillingness to articulate a specific vision of where he wants to take the country.

Perhaps more than anything else, the latter point could be the party's Achilles heel. The last budget, says Martin, "marked the turning of a corner" from a preoccupation with deficit reduction to new priorities. But so far, Chrétien has not made clear what those priorities will be. They could range from tax cuts and continuing reduction in government spending to the creation of new programs such as day care or enhanced funds for health care. But at this point, concedes one Liberal adviser, "no one knows because we haven't told people properly. And perhaps we haven't told people because we don't really know."

Then there is Quebec. In this century, no prime minister from that province, before Chrétien, has failed to win a majority of seats on his home turf. This time, it is virtually certain that the Bloc Québécois, under new leader Gilles Duceppe, will repeat its success of 1993 and again win most of Quebec's 75 ridings. Chrétien faces a stiff re-election fight in St-Maurice from his bitter rival Yves Duhaime, a one-time acolyte who later became a Parti Québécois minister. If Chrétien loses, and even if the Liberals win the election, there will be enormous

pressure from both inside and outside the party for him to step down before another Quebec referendum. And if he wins, the question remains: can he handle the issue when it again arises—as it inevitably will?

Despite such concerns, the Liberals' ad campaign and overall strategy will revolve almost entirely around the Prime Minister. In doing so, they are again placing their destiny in the hands of a leader who, as described by close associates, is a bundle of contradictions. Jean Chrétien is portrayed as alternately complex, straightforward, playful, withdrawn, ruthless, forgiving, just-plain-folks, a culture maven, cautious, daring, progressive, firmly anchored in the past, a whiz at deciphering complex policy, easily bored and impatient with many issues, open to new ideas and arguments, and mulish in his stubbornness.

But there are several Chrétien qualities on which everyone agrees. "Jean," says Mitchell Sharp, his $1-a-year personal adviser and 85-year-old mentor "always knows exactly what he wants and can cut through any amount of double-talk to get to it." And, notes Penny Collenette, an old friend who is director of appointments in the Prime Minister's Office, "He is usually at his most comfortable when he is being underestimated." She adds: "Lots of people say they want to be like that, but not many really like others thinking they are less able than they are. In his case, he is so comfortable with himself that he accepts it, and uses it to his advantage."

The criticisms are, by now, familiar: he is said to be bored by detail, impatient to the point of being impetu-

POSTWAR POLLS

When Prime Minister Jean Chrétien issued the call for a June 2 election last weekend, he brought to an end Canada's shortest-lived majority government since the Second World War, elected to office just 43 months before. Since Confederation in 1867, in fact, only Sir Wilfrid Laurier in 1911, facing a Parliament and nation riven by the issue of free trade with the United States, went to the polls sooner, less than three year after winning a majority.

Majority Government Calling Election	Election Date	Months in Office Since Last Election
LIBERALS	June 27, 1949	48
LIBERALS	Aug. 10, 1953	49
LIBERALS	June 10, 1957	46
CONSERVATIVES	June 18, 1962	46
LIBERALS	Oct. 30, 1972	52
LIBERALS	May 22, 1979	58
LIBERALS	Sept. 4, 1984	55
CONSERVATIVES	Nov. 21, 1988	45
CONSERVATIVES	Oct. 25, 1993	59
LIBERALS	June 2, 1997	43

ous, out of touch with the national unity question, uninterested in anything more ambitious than cleaning his desk of paper by the end of every day. In fact, Chrétien's career in politics has been marked by a string of successfully overcome odds. He arrived in Ottawa as a unilingual francophone in 1963 and, within four years, had become the youngest person ever appointed to cabinet. In 1980, he served as Pierre Trudeau's lieutenant in the Quebec referendum battle, and was widely credited with reversing an early sovereigntist lead and co-ordinating the strategy that led to a 60-per-cent to 40-per-cent No victory.

In 1984, he made an unexpectedly close contest of what was supposed to be a runaway victory for John Turner during the Liberal leadership race. "That," says Goldenberg, "was when he showed the doubters he had real leadership qualities." And in 1993, Chrétien was widely derided as "yesterday's man"—before proving to be his party's strong asset in government.

As to the apparent contradictions in Chrétien's character, there is ample evidence to support the existence of all of those qualities. On a surface level, Chrétien spent much of his political career cultivating the bumpkin image of the "little guy from Shawinigan." In keeping with that role, he is a self-proclaimed pool shark, and takes pride in showing off the fact that he is in better physical shape than many contemporaries two decades younger. At the prime minister's retreat at Harrington Lake, one of the few places where he can find some measure of privacy, Chrétien delights in eluding the RCMP officers on security detail by racing at high speeds in his jet boat, the Red October. A mark of his lack of sophistication in another area is his ineptitude with almost any form of new technology, from videocassette recorders to computers. "The phone," says one friend drily, "is a real problem for him: all those buttons to deal with."

On another level, Chrétien has a healthy dislike of pomp and circumstance that many voters clearly identify with. "He is a person," says Eddie Goldenberg, "who is a lot more interested in the qualities of other people than in their social status." Stories of Chrétien's impatience and disdain for protocol are legion. In November, 1994, during a Team Canada trade mission to Asia, the Prime Minister decided to talk to New Brunswick Premier Frank McKenna about his plan to name New Brunswick native Roméo LeBlanc as the new Governor General. "He hauled me out of a reception and took me up to his suite," McKenna recalls, "saying he had to talk to me at once. When we got there, Mrs. Chrétien was in the living-room, sewing. So as not to bother her we went into the bedroom and sat down on the bed, where he laid the news on me."

Chrétien's difficulty with names is legendary, and he often resorts to word association games in order to identify people and places. When in Toronto, he and David Smith, the co-chairman of the Liberals' campaign team, often dined at an expensive French restaurant that closed last year. Chrétien could never remember the name, but always directed Smith to book a table at "the kidney place" (it was one of the few restaurants that featured his favorite meal, lamb kidneys, on the regular menu). He calls Fredericton MP Andy Scott "the disability guy"—because of the extensive work Scott has done in that area. In caucus meetings, he occasionally refers to longtime Newfoundland MP George Baker as boulanger—French for baker.

But there is nothing wrong with Chrétien's memory when his own livelihood is at stake. In the summer of 1993, he took his press secretary, Patrick Parisot, out for a boat ride on Lac des Piles, the Shawinigan-area lake where he owns his cottage. For more than an hour, Chrétien pointed at each of the dozens of cottages along the shore, identifying the owners by name, describing a bit of their family situation, and recounting exactly how each adult was known to vote federally and provincially.

In public, Chrétien seldom shows his anger—but most of those who have seen flashes of it say that is more than enough. "He is always very courteous in caucus," says Windsor MP Shaughnessy Cohen, "but it is always very clear to all of us that it would be a really terrible idea if we displeased him." It is not, associates say, so much what Chrétien says as the way he says it, biting off each syllable while a wintery chill emanates from his blue eyes.

Once, Peter Donolo, the Prime Minister's communications director, was summoned to see Chrétien after making a mistake that caused the leader some embarrassment in public. Donolo told the Prime Minister that he accepted "full responsibility," expecting the apology to close the matter. "Congratulations," hissed a sarcastic Chrétien, adding that such a gesture was of no use in getting him out of the mess. But for the most part, Chrétien's anger passes quickly. During a cabinet meeting, he launched into a blistering denunciation of one minister and, while in full rhetorical flight, got up from the table, poured a coffee and delivered it to the still-squirming minister.

Chrétien says that he has many acquaintances but few friends—and is quite blunt about his opinion that politics and friendship do not usually mix. Once, during a visit to Washington in 1993 while he was still opposition leader, Chrétien began discussing his views while having a coffee with Donolo, aide Jean Carle and a reporter. "You see these two guys here," Chrétien said, pointing at Carle and Donolo. "If you asked them, they would probably tell you they are my friends. But they are not. In politics, there is no room for friendship." His point was that a leader must sometimes make tough decisions that should not be affected by personal feelings, and the two were visibly taken aback. But Chrétien has often proven flexible about that rule—when it suits him. He appointed his close friend, LeBlanc, as Governor General; his longtime friend Robert Nixon, the former head of the Ontario provincial Liberal party, as head of the

Atomic Energy of Canada Ltd. Crown corporation; and his nephew, Raymond Chrétien, a career diplomat, as ambassador to Washington.

Like many politicians, Chrétien has a long and unforgiving memory when it comes to slights. Although there is no shortage of holdovers in government today from Chrétien's 1984 leadership campaign, few supporters of John Turner remain. Similarly, although Chrétien has treated Paul Martin with respect and decency after their often-bitter 1990 leadership race, Martin's supporters from that campaign have been all but shut out of key government positions and appointments.

Many of Chrétien's closest advisers are people he has known for at least a quarter of a century. They include Goldenberg, Sharp—for whom Chrétien served as parliamentary secretary in 1967—chief of staff Jean Pelletier, who attended high school with Chrétien, and the man usually acknowledged as his most important adviser after his wife, Aline: Montreal businessman John Rae. Others include Donolo, Collenette, Carle and policy adviser Chaviva Hosek.

That relatively small circle inspires powerful emotions among other Liberals that range from respect and reverence, to far ruder responses from some backbenchers. On one level, Chrétien goes to great pains to be accessible. Within the PMO, there is a rule that any backbencher asking to see Chrétien should be given a meeting within 48 hours—even if it means cancelling other appointments. At caucus meetings, cabinet ministers are instructed to speak as little as possible, and listen to the views of other MPs. Chrétien also keeps attendance lists of ministers at those meetings—and woe betide any minister absent without an explanation.

As well, with several exceptions, Chrétien has been very tolerant of MPs whose views clash with his own. One of those is Roger Galloway, a gruff Ontario MP from the Sarnia area whose private member's bill banning "negative-option" cable billing ran contrary to the wishes of cabinet—and was only blocked from becoming law at the last minute. That was only one of several occasions when Galloway has bluntly denounced his party's official position. But each time, he says, "The Prime Minister has gone out of his way after meetings to tell everyone that he understands my position and has lots of sympathy for it." And Cohen, another outspoken Ontario MP, praises what she calls "the Prime Minister's enthusiasm for straight talk at all times from all sides."

But in spite of Chrétien's devotion to caucus meetings—which he regularly describes as "the most important part of my week"—his major decisions usually are based on the advice of his inner circle. In a high-stress environment that usually leads to an equally high rate of turnover, the key people within Chrétien's PMO have remained in place for unusually long periods of time. They share several qualities: they are almost all from Central Canada; almost all are fluently bilingual and, with the exception of Hosek and Collenette, all are male.

All have more frequent access to the leader than most members of the caucus—and cabinet—and the advantage of being able to speak with Chrétien regularly in small, informal gatherings. As a result, says one adviser, "we can get things done quickly and easily. But we also live in a double bubble: we work tremendously long hours alongside the same people all the time, and our regular friends away from politics lose touch with us."

That can be both a boon and a bane—and Liberals, as well as many others, think the downside of that equation has become more evident in the past six months. "You've got a real bunker mentality in that office," says one Ontario Liberal MP from a rural riding. "If they didn't think of an idea, it doesn't exist. And if they did think of it, there can't possibly be anything wrong with it." Many Liberals concede that two issues have been particularly damaging for the party: the question of Quebec's constitutional future, and Chrétien's mishandling of the GST. On both, many Liberal backbenchers say their views were either ignored—or, even worse, suppressed.

On the issue of Quebec, there is ample evidence to support that belief. Prior to the October, 1995, referendum, Chrétien repeatedly told the caucus that the No side would easily win. But a prerequisite for that victory, he often said, was for MPs from outside Quebec to stay quiet on the issue, and leave the driving of the campaign to him. In the wake of the near-loss, many MPs, faced with a barrage of complaints from constituents, complained that they and other Canadians had been shut out—and the country nearly splintered as a result. But Chrétien, rather than acknowledge any errors, has suggested that it was only because of his efforts in the last week of the campaign that the No side averted defeat.

Chrétien's mishandling of his onetime promise to make the GST "disappear" marked a similar example of his unwillingness to admit error. As opposition leader, he was always wary of efforts by some party members to commit to abolishing the GST before a suitable alternative was found. Nonetheless, he was finally persuaded to make that promise after strong pressure from more left-wing members of the caucus. When the time finally came in early 1996 to acknowledge that the GST would not be abolished, Chrétien advisers say, he could not accept the idea that he was being asked to apologize for a promise that he had never wanted to make in the first place.

The result was an embarrassing series of public appearances in which he used tortuous logic to justify his belief that he had not broken a promise—and which culminated in a CBC town hall appearance last December in which he appeared alternately defensive and abusive towards questioners. Even his most loyal advisers cringe at the memory of the incident; one calls it "the closest thing we've had to an unmitigated disaster."

Others fear that its impact still lingers. And in spite of the Prime Minister's continued high popularity ratings, there are two examples of electoral disaster that have eerie parallels for Chrétien: one involving former U.S. president George Bush, the other the case of a Liberal prime minister from Quebec, Sir Wilfrid Laurier, 86 years ago. In Bush's case, he enjoyed some of the highest popularity ratings in polls in American history less than a year before the election—but went down to humiliating defeat. One reason, all too familiar to Chrétien, was Bush's inability to articulate a vision of where he wanted to take the country during a second term. Ultimately, many Americans came to regard him as a decent man but a flawed politician, one whose best days were behind him.

In Laurier's case, the potential parallels are even more disturbing. The June 2 election, only 43 months into the Liberals' mandate, will mark the earliest that a majority government in Canada has gone to the polls since Laurier did so in 1911. After less than three years in power, Laurier's government, torn by controversies over free trade with the United States and the Naval Services Act that severely damaged Liberal popularity in Quebec, was resoundingly defeated. In an opening speech in that campaign, Laurier said: "I am branded in Quebec as a traitor to the French and in Ontario as a traitor to the English. . . . [But] I am a Canadian. Canada has been the inspiration of my life." Parts of the same speech could easily have been given by Chrétien, who regards Laurier as his greatest political hero and inspiration. Despite the high regard historians now accord Laurier, when he died he was widely considered a failure. And that is one similarity that Jean Chrétien, heading into what is likely his final political campaign, cannot bear to even contemplate.

• *Do you think Prime Minister Jean Chrétien is up to facing the problems that will confront Canada after the next election? Post your views in the election section of the* Maclean's *Forum* (www.canoe.ca/macleans).

The Supreme Court and Its Role in Canadian Politics

The members of the Supreme Court come under increasingly close scrutiny both by those who nominate and appoint them and by the general public. This scrutiny now includes a close examination of their lifestyles and personalities as well as of their ideologies and decisions.

The role of Canada's Supreme Court is also still evolving. The first article in this section describes the current role of the Supreme Court of Canada and suggests that it has been put in a novel—and a bit uncomfortable—political role in recent years. In some cases members of Parliament are avoiding making decisions in controversial areas, and disputing parties are subsequently taking the questions to court; the problems end up before the Supreme Court of Canada, which is unable to avoid becom-

ing involved. Accordingly, the Supreme Court of Canada has had to make some very difficult decisions in recent years in areas that previously had been outside of the domain of the Court but which, because of the inaction of the "political" actors of the government, have become the responsibility of the Court.

Because the individuals who are on the Court are so important in shaping government policy, it becomes increasingly important to appoint Supreme Court justices in the most open and rational way possible. Jeffrey Simpson of *The Globe and Mail* argues that a "better way to make Supreme Court appointments" is needed, because despite the crucial role that the Supreme Court plays in the Canadian political system in legal issues, in deciding the nature and future of Canadian federalism, and in other areas, a secretive process for appointing candidates to the Court continues to be the primary vehicle for filling these critical positions. Simpson describes alternative methods of appointing justices and suggests that if the Court is going to continue to be so important to Canadian politics, then the legitimacy of the justices demands a better method of appointment.

This is even more clear when we look at how Court decisions are made. David Beatty of *The Globe and Mail* argues that the members of the Supreme Court of Canada are not governed by any overriding philosophy of government when they make their decisions but rather seem to be guided by their own *ad hoc* personal views. He suggests that this is not only undemocratic, since the justices are not elected, but that it does not lead to the development of any coherent philosophy of government for the rest of Canada to follow since it is not clear that any *theory* is behind the Court's decisions. He suggests that now may be a good time to discuss the appropriate role of the Court as a maker of law and policy rather than the popularly elected Parliament if that is the direction the Court is going to follow.

But often the problem is not just that we do not understand how justices are appointed and how they make

decisions, but that *they* are not the ones making key decisions. The next selection describes the key role of law clerks in the Canadian government and shows that these unelected, publicly invisible actors play a crucial role in what the courts do. Even though law clerks are not a formal part of the public policy-making process in Canada, this article suggests that they have far more influence over policy than most people would recognize. Clerks often are asked by judges to frame decisions for them, to provide alternative decisions, and to suggest arguments to make in judicial decisions. This, clearly, gives the nonelected and nonratified clerks a great deal of influence in the political process.

More than this, the courts generally are having a hard time just keeping up with demands made upon them. Tracey Tyler of *The Toronto Star* suggests that there is a significant backlog of cases in many judicial jurisdictions, resulting in violations of guidelines handed down by the Supreme Court of Canada dealing with how quickly judicial actions need to be resolved. Tyler describes how serious this situation is, how it came about, and what can be done to resolve the problem before it reaches crisis proportions.

Looking Ahead: Challenge Questions

What is the *political* role of the Supreme Court of Canada today? How would you compare the Court's *political* role with the *political* role of the Parliament of Canada?

How are members of the Supreme Court appointed? Is this appropriate given the role of the Court in the Canadian political system? What might some alternative methods of appointment be?

If we do not want law clerks having a significant influence on judicial decisions, what are our alternatives? What can be done to reduce the backlog of legal questions in the Canadian judicial system? Can this be done without giving law clerks a great deal of discretionary power?

Politicians defer to high court

Top judges are deciding issues legislators don't want to touch

BY DAVID VIENNEAU
OTTAWA BUREAU CHIEF

OTTAWA—Reform MP Jan Brown was recently approached by a reporter and asked to identify the judges on the Supreme Court of Canada. Rather than confess her ignorance, she feebly guessed, "Maude Barlow."

Wrong. Barlow would probably accept the promotion but she remains with the Council of Canadians, the anti-free trade lobby group. After this was pointed out, the Calgary MP stormed off in a huff.

Brown need not have. The reality is the vast majority of Canadians would probably be unable to name any of the seven men and two women who make up the highest court in the land.

Maybe it is time Canadians started to pay attention.

Increasingly, the high court is being asked to make tough decisions affecting the lives of law-abiding Canadians and the expenditure of millions of tax dollars. Often it's because politicians do not have the courage to do so themselves.

It's a conundrum that has not escaped the attention of Supreme Court Chief Justice Antonio Lamer. Using uncharacteristically blunt language, he recently told a Toronto audience that the judiciary did not seek to become arbiters of social policy.

"The truth is that many of the toughest issues we have had to deal with have been left to us by the democratic process," Lamer said.

"The legislature can duck them. We can't. Think about abortion, euthanasia, same-sex benefits to name a few."

For those who don't know, the members of the court are Lamer, 62, and Justices Gérard La Forest, 69, Claire L'Heureux-Dubé, 67, John Sopinka, 62, Charles Gonthier, 66, Peter Cory, 69,

> **'The truth is that many of the toughest issues we have had to deal with have been left to us by the democratic process. The legislature can duck them. We can't.**
>
> —SUPREME COURT
> CHIEF JUSTICE
> ANTONIO LAMER

Beverly McLachlin, 51, Frank Iacobucci, 58, and Jack Major, 64.

All are eligible to serve until age 75, although L'Heureux-Dubé, Cory and Gonthier could retire now and receive full pensions.

The role of the judiciary forever changed on April 17, 1982, when the Charter of Rights and Freedoms was proclaimed. Until then, the doctrine of parliamentary sovereignty was the fundamental principle of Canadian law. It meant laws and penalties imposed by

Parliament and the legislatures had to be obeyed by the courts.

The Charter, by entrenching into law guarantees such as freedom of expression—previously assured only by tradition—changed all that. It gave the courts the power to overrule decisions made by elected politicians.

When the Supreme Court began its 1994-95 sitting last September, it outraged Canadians by citing the Charter to rule a man could not be found guilty of rape if he was too drunk to know what he was doing. The federal government was forced to enact a law to correct the legal loophole.

When the session ended this month, the court again stunned the public by invoking Charter guarantees to throw out murder charges against two Ontario men because the crown took too long to bring the case to court.

In between, it handed down 113 judgments, including two historic equality rights appeals that captured the attention of a divided public and a nervous federal government, which worried about the billion-dollar cost of extending benefits to homosexuals and single and divorced mothers.

As it turned out, it need not have.

The court deferred to government, and in the process, broadly stated that maybe Canadians can not afford the guarantees the Charter of Rights and Freedoms entitles them to.

The court ruled 5-4 that impoverished, elderly homosexual couples are not entitled to the same federal social benefits as needy heterosexual couples. It then ruled 5-2 that custodial parents must continue to pay income tax on child support payments they receive from their former spouses.

"Government must be accorded some flexibility in extending social benefits," Mr. Justice John Sopinka wrote in the gay-rights ruling.

"It is not realistic to assume that there are unlimited funds to address the needs of all."

The decisions were greeted with a collective sigh of relief by the government. But groups representing minority groups angrily maintained the high court had passed up a golden opportunity to put some teeth in the equality rights provisions of the Charter. Instead, the majority judges endorsed traditional family values.

Section 15 of the Charter states everyone is entitled to equal protection under the law regardless of race, national or ethnic origin, color, religion, sex, age or mental or physical disability. However, under Section 1 of the Charter, these rights are subject to reasonable limits, such as cost.

Margot Young, a University of Victoria law professor, says the court missed a historic opportunity to extend social benefits to homosexuals and custodial parents. Instead, it opted for the safety of the traditional family unit: mother, father and children.

"It showed a real lack of courage under the guise of deference to the legislature," Young said in an interview.

Not everyone agrees. Joel Bakan, a University of British Columbia law professor, says when the court does extend rights, as it did when it ruled people 65 and over are eligible to collect unemployment insurance, it does not guarantee taxpayers will have to cough up more money.

When the court resumes sitting in the fall, it will be asked to hear appeals on the validity of Canada's child pornography law and on whether an otherwise stellar citizen, Robert Latimer, should have received a life sentence for murdering his severely disabled daughter.

Again, the court will be in the position of pleasing some and outraging others. So be it, says Lamer.

"Judges are not in the business of making decisions with the objective of pleasing as many people as possible," he says.

"Judges are in the business of deciding difficult questions according to law, whether it pleases or not."

Needed: a better way to make Supreme Court appointments

Jeffrey Simpson

OTTAWA

PRIME Minister Jean Chrétien will have not one but two appointments to make rather soon to the Supreme Court of Canada.

Mr. Justice Gérard La Forest of New Brunswick announced this week his intention to leave the court next month. Mr. Justice Peter Cory of Ontario, who turns 72 in October, will likely not be far behind.

Despite the prestige and intellectual challenge of serving on the Supreme Court, plenty of lawyers and judges would pass on an appointment. The hours are long. The isolation is considerable. The workload, especially in the Age of the Charter of Rights and Freedom, is heavy.

As the court has emerged into the public eye, courtesy of the Charter, its decisions have fired controversies not just on the pages of law-review journals but in newspapers and political platforms. Judges, being hu-

man, don't like their decisions attacked (including by newspaper columnists), a distaste made more acute by their inability—by convention—to respond.

There will be candidates, of course, and from these Mr. Chrétien will make his selection. The process will be secretive—consultations with the bar and discreet informal inquiries. Even campaigns for some prospective candidates will be waged quietly, such as those that sprang up for Toronto lawyer Mary Eberts and Ontario judge Rosalie Abella when prime minister Brian Mulroney had to make an appointment. (He selected Mr. Justice Frank Iacobucci.)

This furtiveness and secrecy, however, are no longer appropriate. The Charter has thrust the judiciary, and especially the Supreme Court, into public debates in ways completely foreign to the situation in pre-Charter days.

A majority on the court has used the Charter to expand considerably

the rights of the accused, to the consternation of some appellate and trial judges, of police forces, certain provincial attorneys-general and policy makers in the Justice Department.

The court has made landmark rulings on the ambit of aboriginal rights, with the most recent judgments disappointing those who sought an expansive interpretation of those rights. Rulings on the "equality rights" sections of the Charter have pushed it directly into areas of social policy and even tax policy.

Deference to legislatures, central to U.S. jurisprudence and legal commentary since U.S. Supreme Court chief justice John Marshall's rulings in the early 19th century, is now central to Charter debates and Supreme Court rulings in Canada.

The court, in other words, touches the daily lives of Canadians as never before. Yet the appointment process does not touch them at all. From the political ether emerges a name, and soon he or she dons the ermine robes and begins work.

If Mr. Chrétien was a reform-minded Prime Minister instead of an institutional conservative, he might consider changing the selection method to make it more publicly consultative while avoiding the occasional excesses of the U.S. Senate ratification process. (The U.S. proceedings can produce fierce political debate, as in the cases of Robert Bork and Clarence Thomas, but it often works quite well, as in those of David Souter, Ruth Bader Ginsberg and Stephen Breyer.)

In 1995, the eminent University of Toronto law professor Martin Friedland produced a long report for the Canadian Judicial Council that recommended a better way.

Prof. Friedland suggested creating a nine-member committee to recommend two or three nominees for the prime minister. The committee would be made up of two members from the province or provinces from which a nominee hailed, three lawyers chosen by such institutions as the Canadian Bar Association and four representatives from the federal government.

If the prime minister chose a name that was not on the short list, some sort of confirmation hearing about his selection should then be held. "This system," Prof. Friedland wrote, "would give the government the right to go outside the list, but would put considerable pressure on it not to do so . . ."

Other scholars and institutions have recommended new selection procedures, so Prof. Friedland's is by no means the only possibility, though it is a highly sensible one.

Given the court's importance now in Canadian society, and given the opportunities presented by two coming vacancies, it's time to try a new selection process. After being used for a couple of appointments, it could be fine-tuned.

Such a change presumes, of course, that Mr. Chrétien is interested in institutional reform. Nothing in his political track record suggests he is, for Supreme Court appointments or anything else.

Order in the Supreme Court! Ad-hockery is running wild

LAW / *Something is very wrong in the Supreme Court of Canada. Judges have come to believe they have the right to vary the rigour of their review depending on which right or freedom is at stake and what kind of law is before them.*

BY DAVID BEATTY
Toronto

LAST month's decision by the Supreme Court of Canada striking down the federal law prohibiting tobacco advertising was one of its most controversial. Commentators attacked it from all sides.

Globe columnist Andrew Coyne saw it as a threat to the liberty of Canadians because it did not take freedom of expression seriously enough. Osgoode Hall Law School professor Allan Hutchinson condemned it as elitist and anti-democratic because it made public regulation of private corporations more difficult. Columnist Jeffrey Simpson said the logic of allowing the court to make political decisions of this kind requires us to rethink the procedures we use to select judges, so we can learn something about their legal and political philosophies before they get on the bench.

Any time a decision of the court is attacked from both the left and the right, Canadians should take note. It should be a warning that something has gone very wrong in the third branch of our government.

It's time to re-examine the role we think judges should play in political controversies like these. The decision in the tobacco-advertising case should force us to be clearer about what we mean when we claim that ours is a system of government under the rule of law.

Even though the commentators criticized very different aspects of the case, implicitly they all condemned the judges for doing politics instead of law. For all of them, the decision was illegitimate because it was the legal and political philosophies of the judges that determined the outcome of the case, and not any rule or principle of constitutional law.

Everyone who reads the decisions of the Supreme Court on a regular basis knows the commentators are right. It is widely recognized among members of the legal profession that each of the judges has developed his or her own distinct legal and political philosophy about what the Charter of Rights and Freedoms means and what the role of the court should be. One can read numerous judgments like the ones in the tobacco-advertis-

ing case where the personalities of the judges shine through.

No one who is familiar with the court's judgments could have been surprised to see that Madam Justice Beverley McLachlin wrote for the majority. It was equally predictable that Mr. Justice Gerard La Forest would author the lead opinion for the four dissenting justices who voted to uphold the law.

In earlier cases, both of these justices had shown they have very different views of what the Charter means and what the court's role should be. Judge McLachlin, favoured to be the next Chief Justice of Canada, is unquestionably the champion of free expression, while Judge La Forest, the second most senior judge on the court, has built his philosophy of law on a principle of judicial restraint. The tobacco-advertising case marks one of the few times Judge La Forest hasn't been able to persuade his colleagues to defer to the politicians when issues of social and economic policy are at stake.

Of course, these are only two of many differences that make each judge's legal profile distinctive from all the others on the bench. In other cases, a different principle or idea and combination of judges might carry the day.

When the judges split the way they did in the tobacco-advertising case, it must be that at least one side based its decision on a theory or principle of law that doesn't fit with the Constitution.

===

Although the practice of judges relying on their own legal and political philosophies to decide whether a law is constitutional is well settled and accepted by all members of the court, it is, in the end, impossible to justify or defend.

First, it is grossly undemocratic. It makes a mockery of the idea that Canadians are a sovereign people, in control of their own destiny, when a policy—one regarded as a model in many parts of the world—can be struck down just because a bare majority of the judges have more sympathy for Judge McLachlin's belief in the priority of free speech than they do for Judge La Forest's call for judicial restraint.

Second, allowing judges to base their decision on their own under-

standing of what the Charter means and how rigorously its rules ought to be enforced makes it virtually inevitable that some—or even all—of the judges will make rulings that are themselves unconstitutional. In any case when the judges split the way they did in the tobacco-advertising case, it must be that at least one side based its decision on a theory or principle of law that doesn't fit with the Constitution.

The difference between Judges McLachlin and La Forest is a conceptual one, about what the Charter means and what principle governs the case. Both of their theories cannot be right.

Either judicial restraint was appropriate in this case, as Judge La Forest believed, or, for the reasons (about the importance of free expression) that Judge McLachlin gave, it was not. If law is to have any meaning, both theories cannot be true. The Charter does not speak with a forked tongue.

It is important to stress that this practice—of the judges basing their decisions on their own personal views about what the Charter means—has evolved gradually.

In the beginning, some of the most prominent members of the court (including Brian Dickson and Bertha Wilson) advocated a much more objective approach. In the first few years after the Charter was entrenched, these two judges envisaged a role for the court in which they and their colleagues would measure the constitutionality of every law they were asked to review against two basic tests of necessity and consistency.

Had the judges restricted their review of the tobacco-advertising law to ensuring that it satisfied the basic rules of the Charter, it is hard to imagine that it would have been invalidated.

The law seems virtually identical to the provisions of the Criminal Code which prohibit hate speech and which the court has already approved. If our lawmakers are entitled to restrict the latter because of the psychological harm it may cause, consistency requires that other potentially harmful modes of expression can be regulated in a similar way.

The debate about the job of the judge that occurred on the court in the early Charter cases did not last long. Today, members of the court believe they have the right to vary the rigour of their review depending on which right or freedom is at stake and what kind of law is before them.

As the tobacco-advertising case reminds us, the question of how judges should measure the constitutional validity of the laws and regulations they are asked to review remains unresolved. It will not go away. And we ignore it at our peril.

Canadians should see the tobacco decision as an appropriate occasion to renew the debate about whether the shape and substance of lawmaking in Canada should be controlled by the personal philosophies of nine judges rather than by the basic rules of (constitutional) law.

David Beatty teaches in the law faculty of the University of Toronto. His most recent book, Constitutional Law in Theory and Practice, was published by the University of Toronto Press in May.

Clerks labor to keep justice in balance

By David Vienneau
OTTAWA BUREAU CHIEF

OTTAWA

ONE OF CANADA'S top judges had a rather unorthodox method of deciding cases—he instructed his law clerk to write two opposing judgments, then picked the more convincing of the two.

The judge is never named, but the anecdote is used in a soon-to-be published paper to illustrate the growing influence law clerks have on the nine judges who sit on the Supreme Court of Canada.

These law school graduates not only help write the judgments, they also recommend which appeals the judges should hear and then prepare critically important documents for those they do.

There are 27 of them, three per judge. Yet, they anonymously toil away in obscurity, deliberately ordered to stay as far away from the public and the media as possible.

They are, in effect, members of a secret society.

Toronto lawyer Lorne Sossin, who clerked for Chief Justice Antonio Lamer in 1992-1993, has written a paper called *The Sounds of Silence: Law Clerks, Policy Making and the Supreme Court of Canada* that examines the relationship between judge and clerk.

"The fear seemed to always be that you'd have this kind of sensationalizing attempt to tell secrets or remove skeletons from whatever closet they had been hiding in," Sossin said in explaining why he broke with tradition.

"That fear seemed to have a chilling effect or a silencing effect on talking about the issues that weren't scandalous

by any stretch but that were relevant to anyone who is interested in how the place works."

The highly coveted position of clerk to a Supreme Court judge is offered to top law school graduates from across Canada. The one-year job pays $37,241 and in some provinces, including Ontario, it is a substitute for a year of articling that is required before a lawyer can be called to the bar.

Clerks help to write the rulings that often shock Canadians, something that's accepted in the U.S. Supreme Court

---

Sossin emphasizes that the conclusions in the paper are based on his own court experiences and on conversations with other former clerks, none of whom want to be identified. He also notes that each judge employs his or her clerks differently.

The 44-page paper, which is to be published in the *University of British Columbia Law Review,* does not delve into the personality quirks and failings of any judge nor does it reveal tales of infighting among them.

But it does state unequivocally that the clerks help write the rulings that

often shock Canadians, something that is accepted as the norm at the United States Supreme Court. American law clerks are often asked when they apply for a job how many Supreme Court rulings they authored.

After a case has been argued, some clerks are asked to do a draft of all or part of a decision, which the judge then uses as raw material to edit, revise and rework, Sossin writes. With other judges it is the reverse: They will give a skeletal first draft to the clerk, who is then expected to add the flesh of research.

Some lawyers grumble that the increased reliance on clerks may have contributed to a growing inclination by the court toward releasing lengthy rulings with multiple concurring and dissenting opinions. Others note that formerly turgid judicial writing has improved dramatically since the clerks first came on the scene in 1967.

Sossin says it would be a mistake to give too much credit to a clerk, because ultimately it is the judge who signs the decision who must take the criticism or the accolades.

"How much of a particular decision is actually written by a clerk, and how much by a justice, does not strike me as a very interesting issue, akin to speculating as to whether a minister actually penned a speech or had a staffer write it, or whether the idea for a policy initiative originated in the Prime Minister's Office as opposed to the mind of the Prime Minister," he writes.

"It was rare that a justice would disseminate a clerk-authored draft of a judgment (to other justices) without making significant input, though it was equally rare that the disseminated draft of an opinion would contain no input from a clerk."

Sossin says the approach of the "eccentric" judge who asked his clerk to prepare differing opinions illustrates how important clerks can be to the decision-making process.

"It gives judges a lot more flexibility on how they approach decision making than they would have if they were working on their own," he says. "It seems to me that is why clerking developed in the first place."

Clerks are also charged with drafting important legal documents for the justices before they decide whether to hear an appeal of a lower court ruling. They also make recommendations on whether to grant leave, although many of these are ignored. Once the court decides to hear an appeal, the clerks sift through mountains of legal documents from each of the parties and provide the judges with a synopsis of each.

"Justices now organize their decision-making workload on the basis of the presence of clerks—this affects how many judgements a justice may take on, how long a justice takes to produce a judgment and how much detail or original research is incorporated in the judgment," Sossin writes.

After an appeal has been argued, the clerks often take straw poll among themselves to decide what the outcome should be. Sossin says some are also not above trying to persuade a "swing" judge's clerk to support their judge's position.

The court began employing clerks in 1967, when five judges hired them. The following year all nine justices employed clerks. In 1983, each judge hired two clerks and in 1989 they added a third.

Some have moved on to greater prominence, including: Industry Minister John Manley, Madam Justice Louise Arbour of the Ontario Court of Appeal, prominent Toronto lawyer Neil Finkelstein, Katherine Swinton, a renowned University of Toronto constitutional expert, and David Matas, a Winnipeg human rights lawyer.

The third clerk was added in 1989 to help the court cope with the Charter of Rights and Freedoms. It radically changed a judge's job description by giving judges power to overrule political and social decisions made by elected politicians.

Instead of dealing strictly with legal issues, judges suddenly found themselves being asked to resolve major social questions, such as the constitutionality of a law banning abortion and whether to allow Sunday shopping.

Sossin says this may be where clerks have had the greatest impact on the court. They act as sounding boards for monastic-like judges, some of whom are old enough to be their grandparents, on some of the key social and political issues the court has dealt with.

"The generational gap clearly gives to the justices a wealth of experience and expertise, but the youth of the clerks, the fact they may bring more diverse perspectives to the court than do the judges, and the fact that they have recently progressed through law school may offer a countervailing balance in the determination of which cases deserve to come before the court," he writes.

"More broadly, law clerks ease the isolation which is part and parcel of the life of a justice at the Supreme Court."

In the early 1970s, women rarely were hired as clerks. But in recent years they commonly comprise a majority of the clerks. The most common characteristics of the clerks through the years? They were almost all white and hailed from affluent families.

Most graduate from one of seven law schools: McGill, Osgoode Hall, University of Toronto, University of Ottawa, Dalhousie University, and the Universities of Alberta and British Columbia.

The nine members of the court are Chief Justice Antonio Lamer, 63, Gérard La Forest, 70, Claire L'Heureux-Dubé, 68, John Sopinka, 63, Charles Gonthier, 67, Peter Cory, 70, Beverly McLachlin, 52, Frank Iacobucci, 59, and Jack Major, 65.

JUSTICE IN JEOPARDY
LAST OF THREE PARTS

Court backlog crisis looming again

BY TRACEY TYLER

LEGAL AFFAIRS REPORTER

NEWMARKET

ASKOV II. Or perhaps, Son of Askov.

Whatever you choose to call it, a second major trial backlog is rumbling across the province, and the epicentre of impending disaster is here.

Backlogs were the culprit in the 1990 "Askov crisis," which led to 50,000 criminal charges being tossed out because of delays in coming to trial.

Now a confidential document prepared by the attorney-general's ministry for Ontario's Management Board of Cabinet confirms what criminal lawyers have suspected for months: Newmarket

Critics of 'investment strategy' wonder who is doing the screening

is "the worst backlogged court in the province," the document says.

In practical terms, that means approximately two cases a week, mainly impaired driving charges, are being tossed out of court because of unreasonable delay, according to the document, a copy of which was obtained by The Star.

Or, as Toronto criminal lawyer Lisa Pomerant put it last week: "I had a case

today where the charge was 29½ months old."

Trials here are being set as long as a year away and, recently, a defence lawyer sat slumped in a chair in the corridor waiting for the start of a client's bail hearing that was supposed to have begun three days before.

Meanwhile, 38 of 61 court locations in Ontario are on "red alert" for having cases tossed out for taking longer than eight months to bring them to trial, the ministry documents say.

The irony, of course, is that the problem has developed despite the fact the attorney-general's ministry has spent $22.9 million since 1990 to make certain that court backlogs don't happen.

The impetus was the "Askov crisis," in which the Supreme Court of Canada ruled that a person had a right to be tried on criminal charges within six to eight months. As a result of the ruling, conspiracy to commit extortion charges against Elijah Askov were stayed. Tens of thousands of criminal charges that had been in the system more than six to eight months were subsequently thrown out of court.

Since then, the attorney-general's ministry has assigned crown attorneys to "screen," or review, charges before they come to court, promptly assemble evidence and disclose it to the defence, with whom they are to have a "pretrial conference" in the hopes of resolving legal issues—if not the case itself—before a trial.

The Ontario Crown Attorneys Association, which fears up to one-third of prosecutors will lose their jobs as a re-

sult of government cost-cutting, has warned the public that this method of scrutinizing cases—known as the "investment strategy"—will collapse if crown attorneys are laid off.

However, an examination of the investment strategy system, based on information contained in the confidential ministry document, as well as the observations of unhappy defence lawyers, reveal that it's had far from perfect results.

The percentage of cases going to trial has dropped—from 12 per cent to 9 per cent, which translates to 18,000 fewer actual cases. That's led to a subsequent saving in expenditures for legal aid and police witnesses.

However, the investment strategy was supposed to reduce the number of charges in the system, cut back on trial time and speed up the flow of cases from the time of arrest up to that point.

In absolute terms, the number of cases in the system has risen, many trials are taking longer, and many cases are moving more slowly than when the measures were put in place 18 months ago, ministry figures show.

For instance:

■ The charges pending trial have increased substantially. There were 165,000 in February, 1993, but 190,000 this past July.

■ Judges in the Ontario Court, provincial division, are sitting longer. For example, they spent 51,240 hours on trials and other matters in 1995 compared with 48,802 in 1992.

■ Twenty-nine per cent of all criminal charges are taking longer than eight months to hear, whereas the standard set

Court hours

Number of hours Ontario Court of Justice – General Division operates including motion, pretrial, civil and criminal court hours.

Hours, thousands

How long it takes

Average trial times (in minutes) by charge type in Ontario Court – Provincial Division.

Charge	Prior to Jan. '94	After Jan. '94
Theft and possession	163.5	68.1
Firearms off.	90.4	151.8
Homicide	228.4	1,495.8
Child victim off.	105.9	299.0
Property off.	123.4	191.8
Robbery	106.7	349.5

SOURCE: Ministry of the Attorney General
TORONTO STAR GRAPHIC

Arthur Martin, was appointed by then-attorney-general Howard Hampton in 1991 to examine pretrial procedures.

Its recommendations, in part, gave rise to the investment strategy. Fully implementing its recommendations provincewide would have taken $23 million. As it was, the province spent $12 million on hiring 60 prosecutors to do the pretrial work.

Hampton had spent another $11.9 million immediately following the Askov crisis to hire prosecutors, appoint more judges and build new courtrooms.

But defence lawyers say putting more money into the system won't eliminate other problems with the investment strategy, including:

■ Inconsistency. Charges are not being screened with the same rigor from one court district to another, says Bruce Durno, president of the Criminal Lawyers' Association. For instance, crowns in one area might be willing to reduce a charge of assault causing bodily harm to the lesser offence of assault, whereas crowns in another area might not budge, he said.

Brendan Crawley, a ministry spokesperson, says unequivocally that "there is no inconsistency" between regions.

However, several months ago, stories began circulating among members of Durno's association that retired police officers and secretaries in crown attorneys' offices were doing the screening of the charges. This has not been substantiated.

■ Non-screening. Despite assurances by the crown to the contrary, sexual and domestic assault charges are invariably sent to trial regardless of the strength of the evidence, Durno says.

■ Swelled bureaucracy. In a recent column in the Criminal Lawyers Newsletter, editor David Schermbrucker says the investment strategy system has given rise to a "fetish for bureaucracy."

One problem, Schermbrucker says, is that while pretrial conferences are supposed to be an opportunity to arrange a plea bargain, the bargaining power is often reduced by this point.

The reason? Crown attorneys who screen the charges after they are laid often state a plea bargaining position on a "charge screening form," and the crown at the pretrial conference is reluctant to deviate from it, he says.

by the Askov case is that no jurisdiction should have more than 15 per cent of cases taking this long.

What happened? The ministry, in its confidential report, says the investment strategy system is not inherently flawed. Virtually all lawyers applaud the principle. In fact, an Askov II, as the ministry refers to it, would have occurred long ago had the new measures not been in place.

The ministry says part of the problem stems from significant changes to the law on disclosure, which has lengthened court proceedings while defence lawyers argue about whether the crown has ful-

filled its requirement to provide all relevant evidence.

The ever-expanding jurisprudence surrounding the Charter of Rights has also increased court time, says the ministry, which also blames "the most generously funded legal aid plan in the country" for giving "aggressive and well-trained" defence lawyers the resources to argue the law.

But perhaps most significant is the government's refusal to provide sufficient funding for the system.

The Martin Committee, a group of crown attorneys and defence lawyers headed by retired Court of Appeal judge

Quebec

The tempo and temper of Quebec nationalism has fluctuated over many years with the ebb and flow of public opinion, specific policy issues, political personalities, miscalculations in electoral strategies and fortunes, the rise and fall of "Meech Lake," and, most recently, the extremely narrow defeat of a question regarding negotiation toward sovereignty in a referendum in Quebec in 1995. In this section six articles discuss current debate over the nature of contemporary Quebec and its place in a Canadian union.

The Quebec population continues to be of (at least) two minds in this regard, with a significant proportion committed to remaining within a Canadian federal union and a significant proportion committed to an independent and sovereign Quebec. A third significant block of Quebec voters is apparently open to short-term forces of campaigns and to the precise wording and context within which the election takes place. To a very large extent, it is still not entirely clear how important the actual wording of the precise question will be when the *next* referendum comes about, as many of Quebec's political leaders promise will be the case soon.

The first article in this section focuses upon economic federalism and inquires about the relationship between fiscal federalism and Quebec separatism. Kenneth G. Stewart asks how federal domestic economic policy affects the movement to sovereignty in Quebec and suggests that there is a strong relationship between these two factors. He contends that decentralization of responsibilities has encouraged provinces to be more active than they otherwise might be; in Quebec's particular case it has encouraged a network of cross-subsidies that have contributed to the erosion of Ottawa's influence in Quebec.

The question of the precise *type* of federalism that exists in Canada is the subject of the second article, which focuses on the general topic of "renewed federalism." M. Jean-Marc Fournier searches for an answer to the question of Quebec's role in a Canadian federal system and suggests that a new model of Canadian federalism must specifically address the subject of provincial diversity as well as the provinces' need for greater authority. Not all provinces are alike, and they cannot all be treated in the same manner. If the federal government respects this diversity, a future together is indeed possible—one that could include Quebec.

But other factors in the provinces are visible and very sensitive policy areas also in Quebec. Language is primary among these. The third article in this section discusses the politics of language and the *kinds* of bilingualism that are possible, for it turns out that "bilingualism" can mean more than one thing. One alternative is to replace the current policy of national bilingualism—where theoretically all parts of the country are actively bilingual—with a policy of "territorial bilingualism," in which single languages are dominant in different areas of the country, rather than two languages being officially equal everywhere in the country. That is, Quebec might be essentially unilingually French while other areas of Canada might be essentially unilingually English, although either language would be legally acceptable in the entire country. Ray Conlogue suggests that this is what is in fact happening in Canada today and that the government should try to approach this policy outcome in a rational and planned manner.

The next series of three essays reflects a very visible and widely discussed exchange of letters between the federal minister of intergovernmental affairs, Stéphane Dion, and the deputy premier of Quebec, Bernard Landry. In the first essay Dion takes issue with several statements of Quebec premier Lucien Bouchard regarding Quebec's ability to secede from Canada and suggests that Bouchard is being inconsistent in his arguments. Dion argues that Quebec must determine what its position is on some key issues in international law and then stick with them, rather than supporting positions only when they work in Quebec's interest and renouncing them at other times.

Landry replies promptly to Dion that Ottawa's position threatening to block the will of a majority of Quebeckers was antidemocratic. He suggests that a bare majority of Quebeckers have the power to act as they see fit and that bare majorities have been adequate in other constitutional situations. He concludes that Ottawa was using a form of blackmail in its relations with Quebec.

Dion responds that Quebec is unclear in its positions and that if Quebec has the power to pull out of Canada then identifiable units of Quebec could pull out of an independent Quebec. If Quebec leaves Canada it might not leave in exactly the same form and dimensions that it occupies today. He concludes that Quebec does not have a legal basis for unilaterally seceding from the rest of Canada.

Looking Ahead: Challenge Questions

What is the likelihood that Quebec will decide to separate from the rest of Canada? If it does make such a decision, what will the new Quebec look like?

Which argument(s) about Quebec's right to secede unilaterally from the rest of Canada is/are most compelling? If Quebec secedes from Canada, should portions of Quebec have the right to secede from Quebec and remain with Canada?

What is the relationship between independence and economic policymaking? What would the effect of sovereignty be on Quebec's economy? Is it reasonable for Quebec to seek political independence with continued economic union with the rest of Canada?

FISCAL FEDERALISM AND QUEBEC SEPARATISM

Le « fédéralisme fiscal » a créé un vaste réseau d'inter-financement au Canada, ce qui a engendré des rapports de dépendance qui suscitent un sentiment de frustration aussi bien chez les « donateurs » que chez les récipiendaires. Selon l'auteur, cette dynamique a attisé le séparatisme au Québec. Il réclame l'instauration d'un nouveau régime de relations financières fondé sur le principe suivant lequel ceux qui jouissent des bienfaits procurés par les programmes publics devraient en défrayer les coûts.

by Kenneth G. Stewart

To the English Canadian mind Quebec is an enigma, the reasons for Quebec's dissatisfaction with the country a bewildering puzzle. Has any country in the world been as accomodating to a linguistic minority as Canada? Is it not the case that existing constitutional and legislative arrangements provide the province with virtually complete autonomy in the areas of language and culture, and with great independence in many other areas as well, including immigration? Should it be necessary to effectively bribe the province to remain within confederation, the bribes taking the form of federal largesse in a multiplicity of programs ranging from dairy quotas to equalization payments? In their longstanding rejection of any option involving outright separation of the province, do not Quebeckers themselves recognize the historical symbiotic unity of the nation and the essential role that Quebec plays in creating a uniquely Canadian culture? How does one reconcile this with

 From *Policy Options*, June 1997, pp. 30-33. © 1997 by the Institute for Research on Public Policy. Reprinted by permission.

widespread support for political leaders committed to separation, to a point that includes the election of openly separatist governments in 1976, 1981 and 1994, the election to 53 of 75 federal seats members advocating separation in some form, and a 49.6 percent vote in the last referendum in favour of pursuing a separatist agenda?

The thesis of this essay is that the emergence of separatism in the last three decades is related to Canada's system of fiscal federalism. Because this system is so complex that it is not understood by the vast majority of Canadians, it is useful to begin by reviewing its essential features and history. Prior to 1957 the fiscal responsibilities of Canada and the provinces were divided along lines such that, to a very large extent, those who were taxed were in turn the beneficiaries of that taxation. In 1957 the government of Louis St. Laurent introduced a system of equalization payments from well-off provinces to poorer provinces having the laudable objective of equalizing the public services available to all Canadians. This was followed, in the 1960s and early 1970s, with the establishment and expansion of a variety of cost-shared and other social programs. These fall into essentially two categories: federal transfers to individuals, and transfers from the federal government to the provincial governments. The most important examples of the former are unemployment insurance and pensions; the latter consist primarily of transfers associated with the financing of health, education and welfare.

These programs were created in a historically unique spirit of generosity and social progress of which Canadians have rightly been proud. At the same time they have had two noteworthy consequences which were not anticipated. The first is that the financing of these programs has given rise to one the highest debt levels in the industrialized west, second only to Italy among the G-7 countries, and a comparatively high tax burden. Indeed, a recent study by C. Good, in the *Fraser Forum*, that takes explicit account of intergenerational transfers found that "...the Canadian government sector is overspending at a vastly greater rate than its US counterpart," "...current government fiscal policy is not sustainable," and "... in order to provide for long-term government solvency, Canadians must face substantial and permanent declines in government expenditure, permanent increases in taxation and permanent declines in transfers."

The second noteworthy consequence is that this system of fiscal federalism has led to vast cross-subsidies between individuals and regions that have served to undermine the economic and political foundations of the country in a way that is only now coming to be fully appreciated.

The erosion of the economic foundations of the country, particularly in the areas of government expenditure and finance, is now well documented. As just one example, surely the single most misguided program is Unemployment Insurance (UI), now Employment Insurance (EI), which generates cross-subsidies not only between individuals and regions but also across industries. By subsidizing seasonal industries at the expense of nonseasonal ones, workers have been attracted to low-skill seasonal employment. In addition to resulting in a self-propagating expansion of UI/EI payments, there has been an artificial inducement for excessive numbers of workers to enter low-skill industries which cannot, ultimately, support them. When the natural resource base upon which the industry depends is exhausted, as has happened in the east coast fishery and may be close to occurring in the west, large numbers of low-skill workers are left to demand compensation. By this process the coastal communities of Atlantic Canada, have been reduced in a generation from proud self reliance to embittering and pitiable dependence on handouts from the rest of the country.

The many problems with UI/EI specifically, and Canada's patchwork quilt of income security programs generally, have been well known for many years. The 1986 report of the Newfoundland *Royal Commission on Employment and Unemployment* noted that "[t]he income security system as a whole, in Canada and in Newfoundland as a province of Canada, was never designed rationally to serve a set of well-defined goals..." and further found that the UI system "...undermines the intrinsic value of work..., undermines good working habits and discipline..., undermines the importance of education ..., is a disincentive to work..., undermines personal and community initiatives..., discourages self employment and small-scale enterprise..., encourages political patronage..., distorts the efforts of local development groups...," and "... has become a bureaucratic nightmare."

These are the reasons the 1986 report of the federal *Commission of Inquiry on Unemployment Insurance* concluded that "... a fundamental transformation of the design of the program and of the structure of the organization was essential." Yet a decade later the essentials of the system remain much as originally conceived. Instead of being willing to use the experience of the past 30 years to recognize the weaknesses in Canada's social programs and revise them accordingly, there is a tendency to view the original 1960s conception of these programs as a sacred trust to be defended at all costs.

Less well understood is the erosion of the nation's political foundations that has taken place during this time as a result of Canada's system of cross-subsidies. Direct transfers of funds from the federal to the provincial governments are associated primarily with three program categories: "Established Programs

Table 1:
Net Federal-Provincial Transfers, Fiscal Year 1991/92

Province	Total ($ millions)	Per Capita ($)
Newfoundland	881	1,536
Prince Edward Island	189	1,446
Nova Scotia	698	775
New Brunswick	907	1,249
Quebec	2,984	436
Ontario	− 5,015	− 506
Manitoba	762	697
Saskatchewan	388	390
Alberta	− 809	− 321
British Columbia	− 986	− 306

Source: T. Courchene, *Social Canada in the Millenium* (Toronto: C.D. Howe Institute, 1994), Table 17.

Financing" of health care and post-secondary education; the Canada Assistance Plan for the financing of welfare; and the equalization payments referred to earlier. Professor Thomas Courchene of Queen's University has computed the net transfers arising from these programs; his figures are reproduced in the Table. They indicate that, as intended, these payments have the effect of transferring income from the "have" provinces of Ontario, Alberta and British Columbia, to the remaining seven provinces. In per capita terms by far the greatest beneficiaries are the four Atlantic provinces; however their populations are small — in total no more than one third that of either Quebec or Ontario. In contrast, although its net per capita transfers are relatively modest, due to its population, by far the single greatest beneficiary of Canada's system of fiscal federalism is Quebec.

In regions that are beneficiaries of the system two effects are notable. The first is a natural tendency to resent the system. Dependency breeds contempt for those upon whom one is dependent. Sometimes this resentment takes the form of denial that one is a net receiver of transfers; at other times it takes the form of claiming that the subsidies are entitlements having some objective historical basis. The other side is the resentment of the system by those who pay the bills, a resentment that has developed rapidly in recent years as the inequities and perverse incentives of the system become more apparent.

Paradoxically, the second notable effect on the receiving provinces is to attempt, where possible, to negotiate an expansion of the system and an increase in the payment flows. The

Atlantic provinces, Manitoba and Saskatchewan, because their populations are relatively small, are limited in their ability to do this. There is only one province that both benefits from the system and has a large enough population to give it the political clout to negotiate in earnest for an increase in the benefits it receives: that province is Quebec.

Negotiation, of course, can take a variety of forms, and often it is in one's interest to negotiate in a way that does not reveal ultimate objectives. In addition to negotiating within a given set of rules, one may seek to change the rules so as to improve one's negotiating power. In doing this, it is unwise to motivate the proposed rule changes in these terms; instead it is preferable to cite other pretexts, such as historical, cultural or linguistic grievances, real or invented. At times good negotiation may take the form of engaging in brinkmanship and aggressive rhetoric which cites injustices of the past, of which there are always some to be found.

It is important that these observations not obscure the objectives of the current Quebec leadership, which undeniably seeks separation. Why would such a leadership be elected to power by a populace that, for the most part, does not share that goal? For the same reason that I might elect firebrand Marxists to the executive of my union local even if I believe that Marxism is nonsense; I may simply believe that they will be the best negotiators.

Canada's system of equalization and transfer payments, and federal sponsorship of other social programs such as unemployment insurance, was originally conceived in part as a unifying influence. Instead, by creating vast cross-subsidization between regions which decouples the benefits of expenditure from the costs of taxation, it has had exactly the opposite effect of balkanizing east and west and serving as a propellant to separatism. Just as unemployment insurance and welfare sometimes have an economic effect on individuals contrary to that which was originally intended, so too has fiscal federalism had unanticipated political consequences.

The parallel I have drawn between these political and economic effects extends in another disturbing direction. In the same way that Canada seems stuck in a '60s time warp in trying to deal with the economic consequences of fiscal federalism, a similar myopia seems to pervade its political consequences. Instead of seeing the system as an incentive which incites Quebec to ever higher levels of political brinkmanship, modifications to the constitutional rules governing its negotiation that favour the province are proposed as a solution. The history of the past three decades shows just what to expect of all attempts to buy off Quebec in this way: in any system of cross-subsidies the political action will always come to revolve around the nature and magnitude of the subsidies, and regardless of what specifics are negotiated there will always be demands for increased subsidies.

This is why there must be no constitutionally recognized special status for Quebec. A "distinct society" clause would likely become a basis for further demands that will include the perpetuation and expansion of the existing system of fiscal federalism. A constitutional veto will, for all time and regardless of the relative size of Quebec's population, make it possible for less than one quarter of the country's population to extract concessions from the rest in return for permitting any constitutional change whatsoever.

Instead the solution to Canada's political and economic problems requires a funda-mental rethinking of fiscal federalism in a way that resurrects the principle that, at least at the margin, those who benefit from public programs should also bear their cost. This will not, of course, end separatism among some elements of Quebec society: that will always be present in some form. But it would reduce the incentive of the Quebec populace to elect leaders who are then in a position to advance their own separatist agenda. Such a rethinking will be met by strident, even violent, opposition from the powerful vested interests, regional and otherwise, that the present system has created. But Canadians must ask themselves what kind of country it will ultimately be easier for Quebec to leave: a financially sound Canada, or a dissipated one?

Kenneth G. Stewart is Assistant Professor of Economics, University of Victoria.

Interprovincial Role
Quebec: Looking for change

M. Jean-Marc Fournier, MNA, *in Quebec City*

Quebec's provincial pro-federalist party advocates constitutional reform to create greater national unity by respecting provincial diversity and authority, says the party's constitutional spokesman.

During last October's referendum, Canada came within a hair's breadth of breakup. Many observers now believe Canada has a last chance to embark on long-awaited reforms. If this opportunity is lost, the separatist movement will not disappear — it may even gain momentum.

Besides this motive for change, many Canadians want to renew federalism simply to strengthen their country. Quebec federalists are looking for these Canadians to lead their fellow citizens away from confrontation with Quebec and towards reform.

Competing interests, common concerns

Leadership in change is therefore urgently needed. But what change? Each stakeholder group has its own agenda. Quebecers want constitutional recognition of their identity and a guarantee that no constitutional amendment will ever again, as in 1982, be adopted against the will of their National Assembly.

The federal government wants a stronger economic union. Western Canadians seek better representation in central decision-making institutions. Aboriginal peoples want recognition and self-government.

Beyond this diversity, there is

M. Jean-Marc Fournier.

M. Fournier, a Liberal, is the opposition critic for Canadian Intergovernmental Affairs and has been a Member of the Quebec National Assembly since 1994. He is a lawyer.

one issue which is widely supported in all regions of the country: rebalancing of federal-provincial spending and legislative responsibilities.

The spending issue did not crop up overnight. From the Second World War onwards, the federal government gradually intruded into various spheres deemed by the constitution to be of provincial jurisdiction. It did so thanks to its general power to tax, which it used beyond the requirements of its own responsibilities.

Aided by post-war prosperity, and responding to popular demand, the central government went about building a set of social programmes now heralded by some as Canada's hallmark *vis-à-vis* the United States. Most of those programmes have a redistributive effect, not only between rich and poor Canadians, but also between prosperous and disadvantaged regions. This redistribution permits all provinces to offer their population roughly equivalent services.

However, with this federal spending in areas of provincial jurisdiction came an undesirable evolution of Canadian federalism as well. With federal money came federal priorities and federal control.

In the absence of an effective interprovincial standard-setting mechanism, Parliament adopted rules making its contributions to jointly financed programmes in areas of provincial jurisdiction conditional upon provincial respect of federal standards set unilaterally.

Moving beyond its jurisdiction

Such measures to make the nation uniform run contrary to the spirit of federalism, a system of government designed to permit diverse regional and national communities to participate fully and freely in a large political union.

In theory, each order of government in a federal state should be sovereign in its own jurisdiction. But unilateral federal norms in areas of provincial jurisdiction have in practice subordinated the provinces to the central government.

The federal government also initiated other self-delivered,

Reprinted with permission from *The Parliamentarian*, July 1996, pp. 229-231. © 1996 by The Parliamentarian.

fully funded programmes in areas of provincial jurisdiction, often without the consent of those provinces which had the means to deliver them themselves. These initiatives led to duplication, waste of money and, in Quebec at least, to a costly popularity contest between federal and provincial bureaucracies.

Although subsidiarity is the organizing principle of federations, Ottawa started spending in policy areas that the provinces are able to manage.

This unfortunate evolution blurred the constitutional division of powers. For example, although health care is constitutionally a provincial responsibility, many Canadians outside Quebec now believe the federal government to be its guardian. Lines of accountability have become unclear; each level of government can now blame a problem on decisions taken by the other.

Unity in harmony

Yet, all these inconveniences do not remove the need for a common standard-setter. If we believe in the free movement of labour, capital, goods and services throughout our economic union, then we must accept a certain amount of harmonization of standards between provinces, or at least mutual recognition of distinct standards.

For example, if we believe in the free movement of labour, then it is in citizens' interests that provinces agree on a minimum level of health insurance coverage.

If we want savings to flow freely to investment opportunities across the land, then the provinces must either harmonize their respective financial regulations or recognize each other's.

If we want our firms to achieve economies of scale before venturing into international markets, then we must continue to liberalize access to markets within Canada.

Traditional nationalist thought in Quebec has resisted the very idea of common standards in areas of provincial jurisdiction — a misguided position to my mind. By analogy, the European Union example has shown us that common standards are not bad *per se* as long as provincial governments freely consent to let themselves be bound by a decision-making process in which they participate. What should be resisted are unilaterally-set federal norms.

This position is gathering momentum. The report to the Ministerial Council on Social Policy, a task force set up last year by provincial governments (all except Quebec's separatist government which boycotted the group) to examine social policy reform, states that the use of federal spending power in areas of sole provincial or joint federal-provincial responsibility should not allow the federal government to unilaterally dictate programme design.

Ottawa has shown some willingness to change. For example, Federal Finance Minister Hon. Paul Martin's 1995 budget increased provincial autonomy by rolling previously separate transfers to provinces for post-secondary education, health and welfare into a single block transfer which provinces can allocate according to their own priorities.

Yet these initiatives, however encouraging, still fall short of what most provinces and think-tanks expect in terms of reform. Clearly, if we are to rebalance Canadian federalism, the provinces must offer Canadians a credible alternative to the federal government as the common standard-setter.

Interprovincial initiative

During their upcoming conference in August, the provincial Premiers will discuss ways to strengthen interprovincial decision-making. Quebec federalists hope they will make headway on this issue.

Some analysts and many federal officials doubt the provinces could ever devise an effective decision-making process — for good reason. Until recently, inter-provincial conferences have achieved little. There were to be no losers, so no votes were taken. The agenda, therefore, had to avoid controversy.

Undoubtedly, if the provinces wish to manage their own affairs they will have to address the difficult issues even when consensus seems out of reach. Since Quebecers and other Canadians alike want a more transparent government, I suggest deliberations between provincial representatives be made public. All parties would thus bear the pressure of public opinion.

The crucial issue of decision-making must also be addressed. One could imagine many rules for interprovincial decision-making. But whatever the chosen formula, it will have to meet two objectives: first, it will have to reconcile the 10 provinces' equality in rights with their inequality in demographic and economic weight, and secondly, it will have to prevent a coalition of only large or of only small provinces from driving the decision-making process.

Interprovincial decision-making should take place in areas of exclusive provincial jurisdiction which bear upon Canada's economic and social union. It would speed up negotiations flowing from the 1994 Internal Trade Agreement. It would stimulate current interprovincial co-operation in areas such as recognition of diplomas and professional standards. It would replace current unilaterally-set federal standards in areas such as health and welfare. Unilateral federal spending initiatives in areas of provincial jurisdiction would also be subject to provincial consent.

No new institution need be created. The provincial Premiers' conference need only be transformed. Provincial delegations to the conference would continue to emanate from the executive branch of government.

These proposals only pertain to areas of exclusive provincial jurisdiction. Canada also needs a mechanism to deal with federal-provincial interdependence in areas where both levels of government have a role to play. Environmental protection, immigration and transportation are obvious examples.

These broad policy areas include matters of both local and country-wide impact. Hence they cannot be attributed in whole to either level of government. We must divide them into smaller policy areas which could then become the exclusive

public scrutiny. Canada already has a First Ministers' Conference which deals with federal-provincial issues. Some Canadian authors have suggested this conference be transformed into a more efficient tool of federalism.

Time to act

If the provinces and the federal government make progress on

taken before the next Quebec general election, probably even before the upcoming federal election.

Such an agenda for rebalancing and recognition is not unreasonable. Alberta Premier Hon. Ralph Klein has pledged to chair the provincial Premiers' conference like no one before. Several Premiers have expressed their willingness to recognize Quebec.

Now is the time to initiate

The historic Chamber of the Quebec National Assembly.   LOUISE LEBLANC PHOTO

responsibility of one level of government.

As suggested by numerous academics, business leaders and provincial Premiers, subsidiarity should become the operating principle of this exercise.

The ongoing task of reviewing policy areas and allocating responsibility to governments must be accomplished within a transparent institution open to

rebalancing Canadian federalism, they will be responding in part to the call for change Quebecers expressed through the result of the referendum. The other part of their response will come when they recognize the existence of a national community within Quebec.

The time-frame for such responses is not open-ended. Actions must undoubtedly be

change, change that will make provincial and federal governments co-operate, respect each other and seek to empower citizens. Change that will show Quebecers they were right to reject separation, and prove to all Canadians that their federation can indeed adapt.

Change that will give Quebecers and Canadians new confidence in their common future.

UNITY SOLUTIONS

Arrêt! You are entering a French-speaking area

A Vancouver economist suggests that we replace our current bilingualism with a system where language is based on territory, as it is in Belgium and Switzerland.

BY RAY CONLOGUE
Quebec Bureau
Montreal

QUEBEC'S close brush with secession has prompted a good deal of soul-searching in think tanks and in the halls of power about renewing the Canadian federation.

Language is a prominent issue. In spite of modest progress in the past 30 years, francophones have little faith in current policies. A 1995 survey by André Blais at the University of Montreal, for example, showed that a majority of Quebec's francophones believe their language would be more secure in an independent Quebec.

For this reason, the C.D. Howe Institute recently published a proposal by Simon Fraser University economist John Richards on a new approach to language policy. He advocates replacing our current bilingualism, where language rights attach to the individual citizen, with territorially based language rights modelled on those used in such countries as Belgium and Switzerland.

Lying behind these models are two opposed ideas of how to protect a minority language in a modern democracy. Canada's policy, as articulated in the 1969 Official Languages Act, is called "personality bilingualism." It calls for services in both official languages throughout the country. English speakers are also encouraged to become bilingual, so that speakers of the minority language feel they are accepted as equals.

Advocates of "territorial bilingualism" argue that it is idealistic and even naive to think that majority language speakers can be persuaded to view minority speakers as equals. They point out that John Stuart Mill, the father of liberalism, said that minority languages were especially unwelcome in democracies because they impede communication among citizens.

The answer, say the "territorial" people, is to separate the two languages geographically, as most countries already do. Canada is alone in building a language policy mainly on the "personality" principle.

Professor Richards contends that a switch to a territorial model would be relatively simple because most French speakers in Canada are concentrated in one province. He believes a constitutional amendment giving Quebec broad power over the public use of language would largely do the job. By arresting possible future inroads by the English language, such an amendment would assuage the concerns of "Joe Lunchbucket in Trois Rivières [who] votes for the *Oui*," he said in a recent interview.

"I'm a pragmatist. I don't think we need major monkeying about with our institutions. We just have to look at where we've got it wrong." In his view, language—rather than vague notions like "distinct society"—is the key.

A problem is that English Canadians have largely accepted the American-style model of individual rights enshrined in the 1982 Charter of Rights and Freedoms. French Canadians, on the other hand, bristle at the notion that language is an individual rather than a collective concern—and Prof. Richards agrees: "Language can't be left to individual choice because the spillover effects of one person's language choice affect the value of other people's language."

He argues that a minimum population of about four million people is required to produce a full range of "language goods" (the cultural products, from books to television, necessary to a modern society). In our current system, which he castigates as a form of "linguistic free trade," majority and minority speakers compete freely throughout the country—and the minority language loses. Once it drops below a critical mass, it may collapse altogether.

> Francophones outside Quebec are now being assimilated at the head-spinning rate of between 40 per cent (in Manitoba) and 74 per cent (in British Columbia) with each generation.

Quebec's response has been a series of "collectivist" laws, of which the most controversial is Bill 101, the Charter of the French language. Passed in 1977, it established French as the obligatory language in the Quebec workplace and obliged most immigrants to educate their children in French. It was one of the irritants that led to the passing of the Canadian Charter of Rights and Freedoms five years later. Prof. Richards likens the subsequent conflict between these two charters to a "chronic disease" in the Canadian political system.

In its pure form, territorial bilingualism solves the problem by creating a zone where the majority language has no status whatever. In Switzerland, for example, a citizen who moves from Zurich (in the German zone) to Lausanne (in the French zone) is obliged to function in French. His children must go immediately to a French school. He shouldn't expect to find anything,

not even a train schedule, printed in two languages.

Prof. Richards is not advocating this hardline model for Canada. But he feels that the core idea of a guaranteed zone for the minority language is essential, and he observes that "the Quebec government has *de facto* insisted that this principle apply to Canada" since the early 1970s.

Although it is not widely remembered today, the members of the Royal Commission on Bilingualism and Biculturalism (the Bi-Bi Commission) debated the merits of these approaches in the mid- 1960s. Territorial bilingualism made more sense, but it left "local minorities" (in Canada's case, the English in Quebec and the French outside it) without legal protection. Unwilling to face this awkward consequence, the commissioners chose the personality principle.

Why does Prof. Richards believe it has failed? "I start with my personal experience," he explains from his home in Vancouver. "My wife is *pure laine* French and our daughter attends a French school. But it is almost impossible to get her to speak the language." His daughter reflects what he feels is a prevailing attitude that French makes little sense in British Columbia. "You shouldn't try to introduce more political unity than people really want."

In his view, the rough-and-tumble political deals of Canadian history, from the Quebec Act of 1774 through to the British North America Act of 1867, recognized this reality in a common-sense way. A territorial division of language rights would make sense in this tradition.

But the 1982 Charter upset the apple cart by suggesting that freedom of language could be a fundamental human right. This was a radical extension of what is usually thought of as human rights, but a lot of English Canadians bought into it. Now, for the first time, an anglophone in Vancouver could feel *personally* affronted if the language "rights" of an anglophone in Montreal were infringed upon. "Michael Walker of

the Fraser Institute bluntly says he sees 101 as an affront to individual rights," notes Prof. Richards with some dismay. The Supreme Court reinforced this impression by attacking the bill in 1988 and striking down some of its restrictions on the English language.

Francophones, even federal Minister of Intergovernmental Affairs Stéphane Dion, will never accept such attacks. Mr. Dion has called Bill 101 "a great Canadian law" because it frees francophones from feeling "constantly obliged to justify their survival in North America."

Specialists like University of Toronto political scientist David Cameron increasingly feel that it was a mistake in the charter to marry "language and culture issues to the language of human rights." But not all agree with Prof. Richards' solution.

Alan Cairns, a charter defender who teaches constitutional law at the University of Saskatchewan, says the charter is more flexible than Prof. Richards thinks. It's true the Supreme Court used it to attack Bill 101, but much of Bill 101 survived and is now reluctantly accepted by Quebec's anglophones.

Kenneth McCrae of Carleton University worked with the Bi-Bi Commission and has studied territorial bilingualism in Switzerland, Belgium and Finland. He feels that Prof. Richards is "trying to put an end to the endless litigation"— which ranges from the Bill 101 case to challenges of unilingual parking tickets—"but I'm not sure his plan is very realistic." Prof. McCrae agrees that Canada should use the territorial principle, but adds that it is not a cure-all. "These things don't get settled ultimately. You manage conflict, and it's always changing."

WHILE the debate continues, Canada seems to be heading for territorial bilingualism whether we like it or not. Francophones outside Quebec are now being assimilated at the head-spinning rate of between 40 per cent (in Manitoba) and 74 per cent (in British Columbia) with each generation. In Quebec, anglophones have declined from 13 per cent of Quebec's population in 1961 to less than 9.5 per cent today, and migration of English speakers from elsewhere in Canada has virtually stopped.

This leads demographers like Charles Castonguay at the University of Ottawa to argue that "personality" bilingualism can no longer be defended honestly. "Sheila Copps recently appeared before a House of Commons committee and claimed that the assimilation of francophones outside of Quebec has been halted," says Prof. Castonguay. "The gap between reality and the fiction described by the Heritage Minister is becoming larger."

Territorial bilingualism may describe reality better, but it also deprives majority-language speakers who happen to live in the minority zone (read: English Quebeckers) of legal protection. It may increase the pressure on them to assimilate or leave. But, says Prof. Richards, "there is no escape from making explicit choices about winners and losers in linguistically contested regions." In Quebec, French has the "better moral claim."

Not surprisingly, prominent Quebec anglophones take a dim view of this. Jack Jedwab, Quebec director of the Canadian Jewish Congress who has recently written a book called *English in Montreal*, agrees that Quebec's anglophones are "experiencing a loss of vitality" while francophones outside Quebec are in a state of crisis. But instead of writing off both groups, he feels that the present policy of bilingualism should be more vigorously enforced.

Prof. Richards answers that his plan allows for anglo-Quebeckers to retain their current status if they agree not to expand their presence. This also disturbs Mr. Jedwab, who says he has "trouble with the idea of French having a better moral claim."

He points to "excesses" of Bill 101, such as forcing anglophones who move to Quebec from other provinces to educate their children in French (struck down by the courts), as proof that anglophones can't be abandoned to negotiate along with the Quebec government.

However, Dermod Travis, a 36-year-old Vancouverite who moved to Quebec five years ago and has organized a group called Forum Quebec to mediate between French and English, feels that "you could devolve language and cultural power to Quebec with the proviso that it be subject to Quebec's own charter of rights" even though Quebec's charter is not a Constitution. He feels that younger anglophones, comfortable in French, have a greater trust in the good intentions of francophones.

McGill University chancellor Gretta Chambers is distressed at the idea of entrenching territorial bilingualism in the Constitution. But she agrees that Quebec must assume authority over language. "Anglos here must stop saying [as a negotiating tactic] that they are part of Canada and Canada is going to save them," she says.

In her view, Bill 101 is legitimate in its attempt to sustain the French population by compelling immigrants to become francophones. "Anglophones are starting to accept that their population cannot grow in Quebec. But they want to save their institutions and have a communal life."

Prof. Richards argues that there would be a better chance of that happening if the rest of Canada would get off Quebec's back. He admits that under his system the English in Quebec "would become more clearly a minority group. But I believe a majority of [francophone] Québecois are as tolerant as the rest of the country."

The fact that Prof. Richards sees even a modest future for English and French minority communities means that he is quite a distance from hardline territorial bilingualism. But Prof. McCrae, the Canadian authority on the subject, feels that this is wise. "We need a made-in-Canada solution, a multiple solution. I'm less optimistic than I was 20 years ago about uniform solutions for whole countries."

Prof McCrae feels the Richards plan would have the symbolic merit of completing the unfinished work of the Bi and Bi Commission, which dissolved in acrimony after writing only six of its 10 proposals. "The other four parts would have addressed the question of the two majorities," he recalls.

Prof. Richards calls this inability to find a solution for the two majorities a case of Canadian "moral failure." By "retreating into liberal discussions about free choice," we have avoided difficult "moral arguments about language policy." But he believes that there is fresh support for change—particularly in the West.

"More and more people have a view of the federation that isn't incompatible with that of moderate Quebec nationalists. On cultural matters, there's more acceptance of the rationale of what I'm saying among government officials in Edmonton than in Ottawa."

Ray Conlogue is The Globe's Quebec Arts Correspondent and the author of Impossible Nation: The Longing For Homeland in Quebec and Canada *(Mercury Press).*

Stéphane Dion: 'These grave questions cannot be avoided'

VERBATIM / *Canada's Intergovernmental Affairs Minister takes issue with Quebec Premier Lucien Bouchard for both denying the relevance of law and invoking it when it suits him.*

Before the annual premiers conference last week, Quebec Premier Lucien Bouchard sent an open letter to New Brunswick Premier Frank McKenna, strongly criticizing him for having sent a letter of support to a group of Quebec municipalities that wish to remain part of Canada if Quebec secedes. (Mr. McKenna later said he was supporting not partition, but the group's call for Canadian unity.) "Your intervention in this file constitutes not only an unprecedented inference by a provincial premier in Quebec affairs," Mr. Bouchard wrote, "but comes in support of a fundamentally antidemocratic position that international law and the history of peoples have rejected many times."

Yesterday Stéphane Dion, federal Minister of Intergovernmental Affairs, wrote an open letter to Mr. Bouchard. Here is the text, based on a translation from French by Mr. Dion's office:

BY STÉPHANE DION

Ottawa

DEAR Premier:
The open letter you recently sent to the Premier of New Brunswick, Mr. Frank McKenna, was brought to my attention, and I read it with interest. I will consider it as a contribution to public debate about the procedure by which Quebec might eventually become an independent state, an issue of great importance to Quebeckers and other Canadians.

Your argument is based on three rules that you claim are universally accepted: that a unilateral declaration of independence is supported by international law; that a majority of "50 per cent plus one" is a sufficient threshold for secession; and that international law rejects any changes to the borders of the entity attempting to secede. We are convinced that such assertions are contradicted by international law and state practice.

Let me start with the question of a unilateral declaration of independence. The Government of Canada has always maintained that if Quebeckers expressed very clearly a desire to secede from Canada, then their will would be respected. As you know, this position is highly unusual in the international community. Most countries do not allow constituent parts to secede under any circumstances. For example, the constitution of the French Fifth Republic, that of General [Charles] de Gaulle, provides that *"La France est une Republique indivisible"* [France is an indivisible republic], while the U.S. Supreme Court has found that our neighbour forms an "indestructible union."

The Government of Canada has never contested the right of the Government of Quebec to consult Quebeckers on their future, but it has affirmed that the provincial government cannot have a monopoly on the establishment of a fair process that might lead to secession. There is no democratic country in the world where the government of a province or other constituent entity has been allowed to determine these procedures unilaterally.

Neither you nor I nor anyone else can predict that the borders of an independent Quebec would be those now guaranteed by the Canadian Constitution.

===

The vast majority of international law experts, including the five experts consulted by the [1991 provincial] Bélanger-Campeau commission [on the future of Quebec], believe that the right to declare secession unilaterally does not belong to constituent entities of a democratic country such as Canada. If you believe otherwise, I invite your government to ask the Supreme Court of Canada for the opportunity to submit your arguments on these questions as part of the present reference.

TURNING to the "50 per cent plus one" rule, it should be noted that it is customary in a democracy to require a consensus for serious, virtually irreversible changes that deeply affect not only our own lives but also those of future generations. Secession, the act of choosing between one's fellow citizens, is one of the most consequence-laden choices a society can ever make.

It is no accident that all instances of secession effected through referendums have been supported by a clear consensus. It would be too dangerous to attempt such an operation in an atmosphere of division, on the basis of a narrow, "soft" majority, as it is commonly called, which could evaporate in the face of difficulties.

If I had enough space, I would cite a series of examples from other countries in which a referendum verdict that was too uncertain was not acted on, for decisions much less important than the breakup of a country. But let us confine ourselves to your secession project.

In the white paper that led up to Quebec's Referendum Act, it is noted that, because of the consultative—and not decisive— nature of referendums, "it would be pointless to include in the law special provisions requiring a certain majority vote or rate of participation." When the bill was tabled on April 5, 1978, its sponsor, Mr. Robert Burns, spoke of the "moral weight" of a referendum won on the basis of "a clearly and broadly expressed popular will."

You yourself acknowledged on June 15, 1994, that an attempt at sovereignty with a slim majority would adversely affect "the political cohesion of Quebec." And on Sept. 12, 1992, in the case of a simple constitutional referendum (on the Charlottetown accord), Mr. Bernard Landry [then vice-president of the Parti Québécois, now Deputy Premier] linked the legitimacy of a Yes vote to obtaining a substantial majority in Quebec.

As for the question of territorial integrity, there is neither a paragraph nor a line in international law that protects Quebec's territory but not Canada's. International experience demonstrates that the borders of the entity seeking independence can be called into question, sometimes for reasons based on democracy. For example, you are no doubt aware that France insisted on partitioning the island of Mayotte from the Comoros at the time the latter gained independence because the residents of Mayotte unequivocally expressed their desire to maintain their link with France.

Even the most prominent secessionists do not agree that Quebec's borders would be guaranteed if secession were being negotiated. When he was a professor of international law, Mr. Daniel Turp [now a Bloc Québécois MP] stated his belief that, in the event of Quebec separation, Quebec's aboriginal peoples would have the right to remain in Canada if they so chose. During the recent federal election campaign, Mr. Gilles Duceppe [leader of the Bloc Québécois] also pointed to the special geographic position of Quebec territory occupied by aboriginal peoples and suggested the issue might be referred to an international tribunal.

Neither you nor I nor anyone else can predict that the borders of an independent Quebec would be those now guaranteed by the Canadian Constitution.

THESE are crucial questions which, so that they can be better debated on their substance, require your government to choose between two contradictory positions. In effect, you are saying simultaneously (1) that the procedure leading up to secession is a purely political matter, in which case the established law demonstrates you are right and those who contest the procedure you intend to follow are wrong.

If you hold the first assertion, you must alert our fellow citizens that you are prepared to plunge them into a situation of anarchy, outside the legal framework, which is not done in a democracy. If, on the contrary, you hold the second assertion, you must produce the rules of law that support your position and agree that our reference to the Supreme Court is a constructive and necessary exercise of clarification, whether or not its outcome is in your favour. One thing is certain: You cannot continue to deny the relevance of law while invoking it when it suits you.

The Government of Canada is convinced that Quebeckers will never choose to renounce the deep-rooted solidarity that unites them with other Canadians within this great federation, which we must always strive to improve. Our being together gives us one of the best qualities of life in the world. We acknowledge, however, that the spirit and practice of democracy must be respected in all circumstances, even the very unlikely and sad prospect of Canada's partition.

Reconciling secession with democracy is such a difficult undertaking that no well-established democracy has yet attempted to do so. These grave questions cannot be avoided if you persist in your project of secession. Our fellow citizens expect their elected representatives to debate these issues in a calm and level-headed manner. This debate on the procedures that would apply concerns us as Quebeckers first and foremost, because an attempt at secession in an atmosphere of confusion would profoundly divide our society, but it also concerns Canadians as a whole, all of whom would be affected by the breakup of their country.

Bernard Landry: Ottawa's line is anti-democratic

JUST WHAT WAS WRITTEN / *The Deputy Premier of Quebec replies to the federal Intergovernmental Affairs Minister.*

The text of a letter sent on Tuesday by Quebec Deputy Premier Bernard Landry to federal Intergovernmental Affairs Minister Stéphane Dion, whose own open letter to Premier Lucien Bouchard was printed here on Tuesday. Mr. Landry's letter has been translated from French by Patrick Van de Wille, researcher in The Globe and Mail's Montreal bureau:

BY BERNARD LANDRY
Quebec

Mr. Minister:
The open letter that you released to the media yesterday confirms, unfortunately, the anti-democratic slide that your government has taken over the past few months with regard to the question of Quebec's future.

You reiterate the very grave statements made by your Prime Minister, who would refuse to recognize a 50-per-cent-plus-one democratic decision that Quebeckers would make in favour of sovereignty. It is absolutely incredible that a democrat, whoever it may be, could defend such a position.

To justify yourself, you invoke the impact that a sovereignty decision would have on future generations. However, Quebec entered Canada without a referendum and with a parliamentary majority of only a few votes, and Newfoundland joined the federation with a result of only 52 per cent. These decisions had impacts for future generations. Do you propose to declare null and void the entry of these two provinces into the federation? Obviously not. According to you, does a simple majority suffice to enter Canada but not to leave it? That would be absurd.

It is the Quebec people in its entirety that took the decision to stay in Canada in 1980 and 1995; it is the Quebec people in its entirety that will become sovereign if it so decides in a majority.

We must look elsewhere for the truth. Now that you fear a sovereigntist majority in the next referendum, you are turning your backs on democratic principles and you want to alter the rules of the game. Your refusal to indicate the level that would satisfy you (66 per cent? 99 per cent?) shows the incoherence of your position.

Your approach is similar with regard to the territorial integrity of Quebec. On this subject, Quebec's political parties are unanimous in condemning militant partitionists. Democracy and justice are the stakes in this debate. The partitionists claim that certain No voters have more rights than Yes voters. Sovereigntist voters, in 1980 and 1995, accepted with good grace the majority decision. According to partitionists, certain No voters could ignore the majority, refuse the verdict and change the rules of the game.

According to you, Quebeckers should trade in their right to vote and renounce their freedom of choice in exchange for a promise of constitutional change—which never took place in the nine years that Quebec was run by Liberals who were clamouring for it.

That is a terrible injustice, [discriminating] between Quebec voters. You never speak out against this injustice. Is it because you think that the cities and regions that voted Yes in 1980 and 1995 also have the right to leave Canada's territory? Surely not.

It would be easy enough for your government to declare clearly, in a single, short sentence, that in the case of Quebec's sovereignty Canada would oppose any efforts to dismember the Quebec state. In fact, studies commissioned by your Privy Council, and reported in the media in 1995, point out that Canada

would have no legal argument to bring into question the territorial integrity of a sovereign Quebec. In the same way, these past few years, the Canadian government has recognized, in their territorial integrity, a good number of former provinces having left federated states—as it did for Slovakia, whose population was never consulted in a referendum. Canada did not then have the scruples that you now invoke. Do you think Quebeckers have fewer rights than citizens of Eastern Europe?

You have made the decision to lend your moral and political approval to militant partitionists by maintaining in this matter a creative fuzziness that serves them and does not honour you. All Quebeckers have been able to see, these past few days, how militant partitionists use intimidation, crowd pressure and procedural interruptions, all of which have nothing to do with municipal democracy or democracy plain and simple. That federalist municipal representatives are the victims of such tactics doesn't seem to move you, a fact they will duly note. As for us, we will join all democrats who denounce partitionists, both in substance and in principle.

The anti-democratic slide of which you are one of the architects does not limit itself to these arguments. For 15 years now, Quebec has had to endure a constitution that was imposed upon it, without referendum and against the clearly expressed wishes of both major parties in the National Assembly. The spite that your government showed to Quebec's election law during the last referendum, the cavalier fashion in which the National Assembly's request to designate its own Lieutenant-Governor was received, and the designation—against Quebec's wishes—of an *amicus curiae* [friend of the court] in a purely political appeal to the Supreme Court are just so many instances where you scoff at Quebec democracy, its government and its institutions.

Last Friday, you added another element to this list. In an interview,

you stated that English Canada must promise Quebeckers to recognize their uniqueness in the Constitution, but only on condition that they elect the Quebec Liberal Party in the next election. That is an odious example of blackmail. According to you, Quebeckers should trade in their right to vote and renounce their freedom of choice in exchange for a promise of constitutional change—which in fact never took place in the nine years that Quebec was run by Liberals who were clamouring for it. The sucker's deal that you are offering Quebeckers shows, it seems to me, the extent to which democratic principles are threatened in your lair.

You justify your arguments through your fear that Quebec would unilaterally declare independence. You and your colleagues brandish this hypothesis like a threat. However, it is publicly known that in 1981, when he was seeking to make Canada completely independent from the United Kingdom, the Prime Minister [Pierre Trudeau] reserved the right to resort to a unilateral declaration of independence in the event of a disagreement with London. His first choice, however, was to reach a friendly agreement with the British government. Am I to understand that you now maintain that in the event of a disagreement with London you would have opposed a formal declaration of independence by Canada?

Obviously not. Your objections only hold for Quebec. They don't apply to Canada, or to Newfoundland, or to other countries.

However, the Quebec approach is similar to that which was envisioned at the time by the Canadian government, with the major difference that it would be founded on a democratic decision by the Quebec people. Allow me to quote the speech given in May of last year in the National Assembly by the Quebec Premier:

"By proposing a formal offer of partnership and a period of one year to negotiate the necessary arrangements, we clearly affirm that our first choice is a negotiated resolution to the matters of interest to us: common economic territory; a sharing of responsibilities as far as debt and assets are concerned; a common organization for managing our partnership.

"If Canada and the provinces want to use this period to settle their internal legal problems and adopt the appropriate resolutions, the government of Quebec will not oppose this. We have always maintained that it is in the interest of both Canada and Quebec that this transition to sovereignty take place with calm, mutual respect, and reciprocal good will.

"We must add, however, that if Canada rejects our outstretched hand, if Canada wants to impose vetoes on us, holds us within the federation against our will, then we will leave it by declaring sovereignty."

QUEBEC sovereigntists, long before the federal government, have reflected on and made proposals for the transfer period that would occur between the sovereignty vote and the accession to sovereignty. Long before you, we proposed an orderly process based on negotiation and conflict resolution. Long before you, we declared that all these matters would be resolved with calm voices, without recourse to force, as Mr. Bouchard clearly repeated during his Centaur Theatre speech.

Dozens of nations have achieved their sovereignty since the Second World War. Among them, not one had the democratic tradition that Quebec can take great pride in. Not one, then, was as well prepared to achieve that transition and assume its sovereignty. It is about time that your government acknowledged this and abandoned its anti-democratic temptation. It is about time that your government declared itself ready to accept the democratic will of Quebeckers if it should be in favour of sovereignty, and to engage then—in our mutual interest—in negotiations, the success of which would render useless any recourse to unilateral action on either part.

Stéphane Dion: 'I am entitled to insist on a process that is clear'

JUST WHAT WAS WRITTEN/ *The federal Intergovernmental Affairs Minister takes issue with the response by Bernard Landry, Quebec's Deputy Premier, to Mr. Dion's first letter.*

The text of an open letter sent this week to Quebec Deputy Premier Bernard Landry by Stéphane Dion, federal Minister of Intergovernmental Affairs. Mr. Dion's first letter appeared here on Aug. 12, and Mr. Landry's response on Aug. 14. (Those on the Internet can read the earlier exchange—or comment on the unity debate—by visiting The Globe and Mail's National Issues Forum at http://forum.theglobeandmail.com/forum/nif on the World Wide Web.)

DEAR Deputy Premier:
The citizens who have elected us are entitled to have us discuss the procedures of secession frankly and thoroughly. I was therefore delighted that you wrote on behalf of your government in response to my own letter of Aug. 11. I hope that this beginning of a dialogue between us marks the end of your government's regrettable attitude of seeking to discredit your critics so as to avoid a debate of substance.

Now that both our letters have been the subject of widespread media coverage, and many of our fellow citizens have had time to familiarize themselves with their contents, permit me to go a little further.

For my part, I am not accusing you of being a poor democrat. I am simply reproaching you for not adequately considering your arguments.

Above all, I note that you have not responded to my three objections regarding the process you plan to follow to make Quebec an independent state. I shall review those three objections in the order in which you raised them in your letter: majority rule, the question of territory and the consequences of a unilateral declaration of independence.

First, I noted that in all cases of secession where a referendum has been held, it has always been to confirm the existence of a clear consensus. You have not denied that fact. Rather, you have maintained that a simple majority in a referendum in Quebec would be sufficient to declare independence, citing the processes that resulted in the creation of the Canadian federation and in Newfoundland's entry into Confederation. You conclude that it would be absurd if it were more difficult to leave Canada than to enter it. It is in no way absurd.

Human societies consistently ensure that more care is exercised in dissolving than in creating an association. Democracies do this at all levels of social life. For example, the laws are drafted in such a way that it is easier to get married than to get divorced, and to create corporations in law than to dissolve them. The United States Congress is considering passing legislation that would offer statehood to Puerto Rico on the basis of a referendum result of "50 per cent plus one," on the condition that it clearly be a definitive, irreversible entry into a federal union that proclaims itself to be "indestructible."

Democracies set more stringent requirements for separation than for union because the risks of injustice are much greater in the case of separation. In effect, a just way needs to be found to break the ties of solidarity and allegiance forged over time, while dividing up the assets that have been jointly acquired. It is better to ensure that populations truly wish to break up before embarking on such a step.

Today, all of Canada belongs to Quebeckers and to other Canadians. Quebeckers are entitled to the assurance that they will not lose Canada unless they have very clearly renounced it. Our government would be acting irresponsibly if they tried to negotiate a breakup without solid confirmation that this is truly what Quebeckers want.

SECOND, I pointed out the absence of any legal basis on which Quebec's borders would be inviolable while Canada's borders would not be. There again, you did not contradict me.

Instead, you are asking that any possibility of modifying Quebec's borders in the event of negotiations on secession be excluded *a priori*. The Government of Canada is against partitioning Canadian territory, and is thus against partitioning Quebec territory. It may be, however, that in the difficult circumstances of negotiating secession, an agreement on modifying borders would become the least unfavourable solution. Our fellow citizens must be aware that such things can happen.

Third, I noted the absence of any legal principle, international or otherwise, that would create a right to a unilateral declaration of independence in a democratic country such as Canada. According to almost all the experts consulted, there is no legal foundation of this type. It would appear that you have not been able to find one either. We have referred this precise question to the Supreme Court because it is important to have the opinion of the highest court in the country. We believe that the position we are defending before the court is in accordance not only with international law, but also with international practice.

You point out that Canada and the international community have recognized the emergence of many new states since the Second World War. You ask why the Government of Canada does not state that it is prepared in the same way to recognize a unilateral declaration of independence contemplated by your government in the event of a breakdown in negotiations whose framework you had established alone.

The answer is that no government in Canada can commit itself to recognizing a secession in advance, in the abstract, without knowing its concrete conditions. This position seems to us to be the only reasonable one and is in accordance with normal international practice, under which no constituent entity of a state

should be recognized as independent against the will of that state. Since 1945, no state created by secession has been admitted to the United Nations without the approval of the government of the predecessor state.

WITHOUT the support of the Canadian government, a declaration of independence by your government would not be recognized by the international community. Other countries would regard your attempted secession as a Canadian

---

Imagine the chaos that would ensue if your government unilaterally told Quebeckers that they must ignore the courts, the Constitution, the federal government and the international community, and henceforth recognize only your authority, your laws and your taxes.

---

matter to be dealt with in accordance with our democratic and legal traditions. You well understand that Mr. [former Quebec premier Jacques] Parizeau's "great game" of diplomacy last time would not have changed this.

The international community's dislike of unilateral declarations of independence is not legal quibbling. It is a condition of the system of legal and orderly government without

which our societies could not function. Imagine the chaos that would ensue if your government unilaterally told Quebeckers that they must ignore the courts, the Constitution, the federal government and the international community, and henceforth recognize only your authority, your laws, your regulations and your taxes. Your unilateral declaration of independence would divide Quebec society in an utterly irresponsible manner. It would be a complete departure from the democratic traditions of our society. It is very dangerous in a democracy for a government to place itself above the law but nevertheless require the obedience of its citizens.

We must avoid such a situation at all costs. You desire the independence of Quebec. I want to preserve the unity of Canada. I am convinced, however, that we are both concerned that our disagreement be resolved in a peaceful and orderly manner, respecting human rights.

Mr. Deputy Premier, you think that being a Canadian prevents you from fully being a Quebecker. I think that being both a Quebecker and a Canadian is one of the most fortunate things that life has given me. You want to choose between Quebec and Canada and to force me to choose, although I have no wish to do so. At the very least, I am entitled to insist on a process that is clear, legal and fair not only to me, but also to the seven million human beings who are both Quebeckers and Canadians, and to the other 22 million human beings who enjoy the good fortunes of having Quebec as part of their country.

If we are all to agree on such a procedure, we must discuss it calmly and in a levelheaded manner, as our fellow citizens wish us to do.

Yours sincerely, Stéphane Dion.

The Provinces in the Canadian Federation

Canada's federal structure is one of its most significant political characteristics. The fact that Canada's population is spread out like a 300-mile-wide ribbon across the continent—over 90 percent of Canada's population lives within 300 miles of its southern border—puts a strain on Canadian political unity. When this is combined with Canada's federal distribution of power, a structure that gives provincial governments relatively more political power in relation to Ottawa than American states have in relation to Washington, D.C., it makes Canadian federalism a much more *decentralized* political structure than that which is found in other federalisms.

This means that it is more difficult for the federal government to plan policy than it is in other federal political systems. The federal government in Ottawa not only has to be concerned about the nature of the policy that it wants to enact, but it must also be prepared to negotiate with the provincial governments for the *authority* to enact that policy. In fact, the governments of Canada—the federal government and the 10 provincial governments—will on occasion spend as much time in discussion of the question of *which* level of government has authority to make policy than it does on *what* the policy should be.

In this section six selections discuss the vast differences among Canada's provinces and the relationship between the provinces and Ottawa in making policy decisions. The first article, "Not 'Distinct Society' but 'Distinctive Societies,'" examines the differences between the words "distinct" and "distinctive." Alastair Taylor suggests that in Quebec's quest for recognition as a "distinct society" it might be more appropriate for Quebec to seek recognition as having a "distinctive society," which would apply to the other provinces as well.

Edward Greenspon, correspondent for *The Globe and Mail (Toronto)*, presents two essays that relate to the federal-provincial relationship. In "Provinces Muscling in on Federal Territory," he shows that one of the greatest sources of tension between Ottawa and the provinces has to do with which level of government shapes public policy. Many of Quebec's recent political demands are not significantly different from those of other Canadian provinces, and Greenspon contends that if this were recognized by other provinces it might reduce tension between Quebec and the rest of Canada.

In his second essay, "Ottawa Plays Tough Guy with Provinces," Greenspon suggests that the federal government in Ottawa is not going to give in to the demands of Quebec and the other Canadian provincial governments. The proper strategy for Ottawa, he advises, is to be active and visible and to get its case out before the public.

In Alberta the primary topic of discussion is financial expansion. While it is true that Alberta made a number of cuts in its social programs, public opinion has recently begun to convince the government of Ralph Klein that the time has come to rethink this policy. With the improved financial health of the province, the government has changed its policy and is restoring health care programs at a remarkable rate.

One of the key issues in politics in Saskatchewan has nothing to do with Quebec at all, and little to do with relations with Ottawa, but rather focuses upon more negative issues. In "The Stolen Revolution," reporter Shafer Parker Jr. examines the legacy of the government of Grant Devine and the Progressive Conservative Party there. Parker suggests that the Devine government not only left a huge debt but also left a record of criminal activity, witnessed by numerous criminal indictments of its leaders.

A final essay on provincial government examines the Atlantic provinces. Wayne Hunt shows us that the threat of Quebec separation has served as a catalyst for the creation of a "maritime union" among the Atlantic provinces. This kind of political alliance would strengthen those provinces, especially if Quebec were to leave Canada, "cutting off" the Atlantic provinces from the rest of the nation.

Looking Ahead: Challenge Questions

What is the significance of who has control over a given policy area—the federal government in Ottawa or the provincial governments has control over a given policy area? Take health or education policy as an example and discuss how policies might develop if Ottawa were in complete control and if the provincial governments were in complete control.

How different are the concerns of the province of Quebec from the concerns of other Canadian provinces? How

UNIT 5

much do they overlap with the concerns of the other provincial governments?

How does Canadian federalism make coordinated policy making more difficult for the federal government in Ottawa? What role should the provincial governments play in providing more social services? How active should the federal government be in ensuring that all Canadians have similar standards of living?

While the federal government cannot prevent all regional disparities, what should be the role of the federal government in helping provinces to deal with social problems?

NOT "DISTINCT SOCIETY" BUT "DISTINCTIVE SOCIETIES"

Le concept de « société distincte » ne passera jamais. Il repose sur une logique de rupture et cette même logique pourrait mener au déman-tèlement du Québec. L'auteur propose plutôt la notion de « société distinctive », qui favorise l'intégration tout en reconnaissant la diversité.

by Alastair M. Taylor

Canada is at a constitutional impasse, marked by the term "distinct society." And as a consequence it raises crucial questions. How logical — or inexorable — is Quebec's claim to be recognized as "distinct" in its society and culture? How can we get beyond this stumbling block?

Focussing on the lexical meaning of the root verb *distinguere*, we can differentiate between "distinct" and "distinctive." The *Oxford English Dictionary* defines "distinct" as: not identical, unlike, different in kind or quality, separate. In turn "distinctive" is defined by the *OED* as distinguishing, a characteristic feature or quality, and by *Webster's* as marking a difference. Both adjectives convey the concept of unique or "one of a kind."

Because the defining character of "distinct society" emphasizes "different" and "separate," the relationship between a "distinct" and any other society takes the preposition "from." With this emphasis upon uniqueness and separateness, the word describes the position of Quebec separatists since in "distinct society" inheres the inexorable logic of secession and the consequent creation of an independent nation-state.

But where does "different in kind or quality" stop — and with it the invocation by others of the logicality of secession and unilateral declarations of independence? Surely the First Peoples in Canada have an even greater claim to be called "unique" and "distinct." Quebec's francophones share with anglophones a common Indo-European language ancestry; a common Christian ancestry; and a common racial/ethnic ancestry. The First Peoples share none of these ancestries — but they can claim a territorial ancestry which indeed is unique: they were here first. And since they have an unanswerable claim to having created "distinct" societies, they have in logic the strongest claim in the northern half of this continent to choose as their right to secede from the Canadian federation.

Meanwhile, on the basis of linguistic and cultural criteria, the anglophones and allophones have as valid a claim to be regarded as "distinct" and "separate" within the present boundaries of Quebec itself. True, Quebec's civil code is distinct and unique within Canada as a whole, but can not anglophones claim that common law should be regarded as no less distinct and unique — and hence should be applied, if not within a separate Quebec state, then by the anglophones in a jurisdiction of their own?

Here we come to a critical problem that inheres in the application of any "distinct society" thesis: the logic of infinite regression. It baffled the inventiveness of statesmen and cartographers when drawing up the Peace of Versailles, where Woodrow Wilson discovered to his chagrin that with the breakup of defeated empires there was seemingly no end of claims by ethnic and cultural minorities to be granted national status with internationally recognized boundaries. Both the Canadian Federation and an independent Quebec are subject to the same process of cultural and territorial fragmentation. How can it be stopped? The superordinate polity could prevent a subordinate entity from exercising this logic, but this woud violate the right of self-determination. The other method is to forgo the fragmenting process at the outset.

Syntactical consequences of "Distinctive Society"

Here the key definitional concepts are "distinguishing" characteristics, features and qualities, which as a result "mark a differ-

From *Policy Options*, May 1997, pp. 47-50. © 1997 by the Institute for Research on Public Policy. Reprinted by permission.

ence." The relationship demarcating "distinctive" societies takes the preposition "among" — that is, among societies of which each is distinguished by qualities that make it for one reason or another "one of a kind" or "unique." But not "separate."

The basic characteristic of "distinctive" can be illustrated by familial relationships. A family is interconnected (genetically and socially) to form a recognizable unit, and its relationships are marked by interactions "among" all its members. In this way, a given family has its own collective identity and status. At the same time, each member is unique (as attested by its one-of-a-kind birth certificate), while his or her individual physical, emotional, intellectual and behavioural traits combine to categorize that individual as "distinctive."

Distinctiveness recognizes and applauds "diversity within unity" at whatever societal level it occurs.

Distinctiveness recognizes and applauds "diversity within unity" at whatever societal level it occurs. And by its inclusion of uniqueness coupled with distinguishing cultural and linguistic attributes, it avoids the pitfall of infinite regression and the bifurcating road that leads to cultural and territorial fragmentation.

Some political consequences for the Canadian Federation.

Canada has always recognized the existence — and primacy — of more than one language, legal system and cultural genesis. "Distinctiveness" was enshrined in the BNA Act, such as in Parliament's use of two official languages, even as French-Canadian rights had been sustained in the Quebec Act of 1774. The concept of two founding peoples was in turn strengthened in recent years by creating machinery to foster and advance bilingualism and biculturalism.

But this bi- and bi- approach could represent at most a halfway step in the evolution of Canadian society. The concept of two founding peoples was historically fallacious since it failed to recognize the presence as a founding people of this country's first inhabitants. Today, the Canadian social fabric is more "distinctive" and polyglot than ever, as attested by current immigration trends and numbers, which have altered the original dualistic ethnic pattern to the point where presently a majority of the City of Vancouver's residents have English as a second language.

Confederation also sanctioned socio-political distinctiveness based upon demographic actualities. It recognized all the provinces, large and small, as equal in their juridical status, while granting PEI the right to send four MPs to Ottawa, thereby compensating for its inferior demographic stature. Given the distinctiveness permeating their constitutional principles, why should Canadians want to single out one of the 10 provinces to have the unique juridical right to be regarded as "distinct" with all the implications which that term syntactically possesses? This would mean that while all provinces are juridically equal and culturally distinctive, Quebec is more equal and distinctive than the others.

Distinct society is a retrogressive step toward cultural and educational homogenization, mandated by a separatist ethic and governing party whose nationalism is based not on civic but ethnic criteria. "Distinct" is tied into that form of logic set forth in Aristotelian two-valued orientations, expressed as "either/or." This dualistic logic was employed in the formalization of the nation-state system, resulting in a geopolitical patchwork quilt with each patch boundaried off from the others — and which gave governments a free hand in handling domestic affairs. But in today's world, either/or is becoming all too simplistic and counter-productive: in the case of separatists this mind-set excludes viable alternatives to their *idée fixe*. Those alternatives are found in a multi-relational logic, expressed as "both-and."

Already we can see the poverty and inadequacy of the either/or options in which Quebec's separatists have trapped themselves. Its chief urban centre, Montreal, cannot be homogenized or unilingualized, and attempts to dismember its cosmopolitan linkages and force all residents into the procrustean bed of separatist conformity has already caused anglophones and allophones to consider having to invoke in turn the logic of infinite regression. Demographic projections can now set the time frame when Montreal Island emulates the City of Vancouver by having a population for whose majority the speech of the superordinate polity will have become a second language. Driven by the same linguistic motivation as Quebec's francophiles, why should the Island's linguistic majority then not demand a new distinct state within a distinct state? On the Island itself, should not the dynamics of ethnicity logically call as well for a sociopolitical boundary along the axis of St. Laurent Boulevard? Absurd? But already the geopolitical situation is absurd. There is a spectre haunting Quebec, the spectre of the fragmentation that derives from this logic of infinite regression. Because the Cree possess a First Peoples distinctness that needs pay allegiance to no other society, they have the strongest of reasons to demand the right of self-determination — yet if they secede from Quebec, the latter will be both territorially and economically crippled, perhaps irrevocably.

Concluding observations

"Distinct society" may accommodate the beliefs and aspirations of some of the separatists in Quebec, but it cannot accommodate those of the federalists either within Quebec or elsewhere in the Canadian Federation. Conversely, "distinctive" cannot be expected to accommodate diehard separatists who will insist on achieving their aspirations on unilateral terms. Nevertheless, it could satisfy the aspirations of Québecois who are asking for assurances that their cultural and linguistic "uniqueness" is both recognized and safeguarded. If we must have a constitutional provision, but one that is acceptable throughout Canada, then let us enshrine the recognition of cultural and linguistic distinctiveness for all provinces and territories.

Is it possible for "distinct" to transform into "distinctive"? The American experience — although the most traumatic in its history — provides an affirmative answer. Slavery was the dominant ideological element that thrust Americans into a civil war where, ironically, the most venerated of Presidents today rejected the secessionists' claim to self-determination in order to preserve the Union. And today a South which prides itself on its historical and cultural distinctiveness may well be the most patriotic American region. Transcending narrow logic, Southerners celebrate national holidays by proudly waving together the Stars and Stripes and Stars and Bars. Canadians have needed no bloody encounters in order to celebrate the dual distinctiveness of the Maple Leaf and the Fleur-de-lys.

In any case, our concepts of nationhood are undergoing a sea change. The nation-state system was based upon territorial separatism and absolute values, summed up in the overarching concept of "sovereignty." But in today's world, that concept is being rapidly transformed, thanks to the accelerating removal or overriding of national boundaries in the movement of goods, peoples, technologies and ideas. Where in the past "independence" was the key expression of a society's status, today's realities are replacing it with "interdependence." If we correlate "independence" with "distinct," an analogous correlation holds true between "interdependence" and "distinctive" — in which entities share similarities of political structure and process while retaining their individual and distinctive culture patterns.

In this overall evolution toward global interdependence, Canada is well positioned to play a distinctive role in the family of nations. A federal society which has never espoused the melting pot ethos, it stands now, with very few other viable national polities, as a model of multiculturalism and pluralism. Within the emerging global paradigm of interconnectedness and reciprocal activities, Canada has no wish to separate itself from this new reality, yet it continues to be as distinctive in the family of nations as the maple leaf within the planet's family of floral genera.

Distinct society is a retrogressive step, mandated by a separatist ethic whose nationalism is based not on civic but ethnic criteria.

As our final observation, we would argue that the concept of "distinct society" and its logical potential consequences should be rejected for two reasons. In stressing uniqueness in terms of separateness, it goes against this century's evolutionary drive toward multiculturalism and interdependence. To adopt this stance could have the effect of isolating Quebec as an ethnic entity, and possible future ethnic nation-state, from full participation in a world *sans frontières*, or even being accepted as an equal partner — no more and no less — "among" the other regions of the Canadian Federation. But Quebec's loss must be shared as well by the rest of Canada. To constitutionalize "distinct society" and hence enshrine the distinctness of one of its entities "from" all the others, must inevitably accord *de facto* recognition to the logic of infinite regression, and thereby provide a juridical precedent for disaffected elements elsewhere to call for the further fragmentation of the

Canadian Federation. This is because "distinct society" is a two-edged sword: it cuts at the bonds of political unity at every level, and can be employed whenever the forces of ethnic-cultural division and separateness become dominant.

For these same reasons, we should be prepared to adopt the concept of "distinctive society," which recognizes and applauds diversity among all the Federation's entities — whether in Newfoundland, Quebec, British Columbia, or the Inuit and Dene communities north of the 60th parallel. Although initial steps have already been taken to constitutionalize "distinct society," it is not too late to propose amending the term to "distinctive society" — and to have the term apply to all of Canada's "distinctive societies." Westerners and Canadians in other regions will almost certainly oppose "distinct society," but I believe a majority would applaud the more inclusive concept that all regions and cultures are equally "distinctive." And in so doing, we can again make use of the root verb *distinguere* to pay tribute to the peoples of Quebec — be they francophone, anglophone, allophone or Cree — as not only *distinctifs* but *distingués*.

Alastair Taylor is Professor Emeritus, Political Science and Geography, Queen's University, Kingston.

Books Available/Livres disponibles

The following books are available for review. Please contact *Policy Options* to receive a copy

Les livres di-dessous sont disponibles à nos bureaux. Si vous voulez contribuer une critique de livre, communiquez avec *Options politiques*.

Senator Al Graham, *The Seeds of Freedom: Personal Reflections on the Dawning of Democracy*, The Canadian Peacekeeping Press, 1996

Liesbet Hooghe ed.,, *Cohesion Policy and European Integration: Building Multi-Level Governance* Oxford University Press, 1996

G. Bruce Doern and Stephen Wilks, eds., *Comparative Competition Policy* Oxford University Press, 1996

Caroline Andrew and Sanda Rodgers eds., *Women and the Canadian State* McGill-Queen's University Press, 1997

Wallace Clement ed., *Understanding Canada: Building on the New Canadian Political Economy* McGill-Queen's University Press, 1997

Provinces muscling in on federal territory

Premiers seek greater control over social policy, financing

BY EDWARD GREENSPON

Parliamentary Bureau

ST. ANDREWS, N.B.—The provincial premiers emerged from their annual conference here this week intent on further pushing back the frontiers of provincial leadership in key areas of national policy making.

The premiers want to take even greater control over social policy and, for the first time, assume a leadership role in shaping the financial arrangements at the heart of federal-provincial relations.

The premiers opened up a new front by asking their finance ministers to meet, without Ottawa, and recommended a plan for handling fundamental issues such as equalization, federal transfers and taxing authority.

It is highly unusual for provincial finance ministers to meet as a group without the federal government, particularly when dealing with issues that go to the core of the federal system. The order from the premiers marks a further extension of provincial assertiveness.

But the premiers view their move as flowing naturally from the larger role they have assumed in social policy since financial arrangements

such as the Canada Health and Social Transfer and the equalization program helped bankroll the system.

The premiers' final communiqué indicates their finance ministers are to consider a radical agenda. The document talks about the way in which the system of federal transfers to the provinces reduces accountability, suggesting that they will examine the possibility, among others, of demanding that Ottawa hand over some of its taxing authority.

The wealthier provinces, upset at the way in which Ottawa shortchanges them in national programs, secured language that says governments must "ensure that individuals are treated as fairly as possible no matter where they reside in Canada." Provinces like Ontario have been calling for some time for equal, per capita funding of social programs, except for equalization.

Although they are a long way from decisions, the obvious trade-off of per capita grants would be to enrich the equalization program. The provinces privately discussed at this meeting different approaches to equalization that would effectively increase Ottawa's payments to the seven have-not provinces by, in the

least-generous formulation, nearly $1-billion a year.

But agreement between the three wealthy provinces—Alberta, Ontario and British Columbia—and the rest will be hard won, even before they sit down with Ottawa. As Saskatchewan's Roy Romanow admitted yesterday, "The devil is in the details."

But their very willingness to begin going down that road without Ottawa once again underscores the extent to which provincial premiers have cut the federal apron strings. They no longer just make demands on Ottawa, but are increasingly carrying the ball as to how the federation should evolve.

Meanwhile, the premiers continue to press forward on devolution in the social area, even after gaining control last year over job training, social housing and other areas of responsibility.

They used their meeting to call on Ottawa to put its youth- employment programs on the table as well. The federal government, fearful of becoming irrelevant to Canadians, had expressly kept youth programs out of the mix when it agreed in 1996 to hand job training to the provinces.

The premiers also issued a warning against any slippage on the harmonization of environmental standards, another part of the so-called rebalancing agenda. And they castigated Ottawa for its "recent unilateral and intrusive legislative initiatives" on endangered species and the proposed Canadian Environmental Protection Act. These measures must not be reintroduced without prior consultation with the provinces, the premiers stated.

All of these measures—and much more—add up to what the premiers are dubbing the 80-per-cent solution, a phrase widely borrowed from Mr. Romanow. By this, the premiers mean that 80 per cent of the solution to national-unity problems lies in demonstrating to Quebeckers practical, non-constitutional ways that the federation can function more to their liking.

Moreover, Ontario Premier Mike Harris maintained that the other 20 per cent—progress on the constitutional file—is linked directly to the first 80 per cent. The launching of a constitutional process, which the premiers will consider at a meeting within the next two months, depends on winning Ottawa's co-operation on the rebalancing agenda, he said, and on demonstrating success in these areas to Canadians, especially in Western Canada.

Although Quebec Premier Lucien Bouchard refused to sign an Ontario paper on social-policy arrangements, which is to serve as the basis for negotiations on such matters as national standards, enforcement and use of the federal spending power, other premiers are convinced he came close to giving it a try. Many continue to be convinced that an accommodation, in the form of further decentralization, is not impossible.

In his public comments, though, Mr. Bouchard took a decidedly harder line than the other premiers. "I think that you are caving in to the federal government when you accept to transfer responsibilities which have been ours, the provinces', for the last 130 years. I don't understand that."

Opposition Leader Preston Manning said the premiers conference left him optimistic about the chances of both unifying the country and rebalancing federal and provincial powers.

With a report from Karen Unland in St-Jean-sur-Richelieu

Ottawa plays tough guy with provinces

Federal government no longer walking on eggshells when dealing with provincial ambitions

BY EDWARD GREENSPON

Parliamentary Bureau Chief

OTTAWA—Stéphane Dion's summertime letter-writing campaign is part and parcel of a new postelection assertiveness on the part of the Chrétien government in its relations with the provinces.

The Intergovernmental Affairs Minister's correspondence with Quebec Premier Lucien Bouchard and Deputy Premier Bernard Landry underlines a determination in Ottawa to take the initiative in matters involving Quebec and a willingness, even an eagerness, to do so in a provocative manner, federal government officials say.

"We are less reluctant to be in their face," a senior Liberal strategist commented.

Nor is this emerging pattern confined to Quebec. When the premiers, at their meeting in St. Andrews, N.B., this month, proposed that Ottawa hand over to them the money it spends on youth-employment programs, Prime Minister Jean Chrétien was quick and sharp in rebuking them.

This same attitude was also much in evidence in Ottawa's handling of the dispute over the Nanoose Bay weapons range with B.C. Premier Glen Clark, including its attempt to discredit him by leaking information of a private meeting.

And in an episode that attracted little attention outside Quebec, Human Resources Minister Pierre Pettigrew, one of the Chrétien cabinet's major accommodators, refused to accede to Quebec's financial demands in agreeing to hand over control of parental and maternity benefits to the provincial government. The Parti Québécois government broke off talks this month.

The truly noteworthy aspect of the failed negotiation, federal officials contend, was the manner in which Ottawa played its hand, including getting out its side of the story with off-the- record briefings with Quebec journalists by Mr. Pettigrew's staff. More often in these matters, the province has always taken the lead in putting its spin on events.

"Typically, we're not very good at getting out ahead. This was a departure," said an official involved with the dossier. He conceded that the resulting media coverage was "not as favourable as we might have wanted," but that it was an improvement over past experience and a portent of things to come.

All this is in sharp contrast to the highly conciliatory, we-aim- to-please posture struck by the federal government in the period between the Quebec referendum in October of 1995 and the federal election this year that returned Mr. Chrétien with a second majority government.

Even before the referendum turned sour, the federal Liberals were planning to reach out to the provinces in its aftermath. In a letter of Sept. 27, 1995, to then-environment minister Sheila Copps, Mr. Chrétien called for a period of "national reconciliation which will follow the referendum" and urged her to settle outstanding disputes with provincial colleagues.

This quest to demonstrate—to Quebeckers above all—that the federal system could accommodate change had a crescendo in a preelection blitz of deal making.

Ottawa handed over job-training and housing programs (along with billions in cash), increased immigration-settlement funds to provinces such as British Columbia, Alberta and Ontario, loosened federal control over the salmon fishery on the West Coast and even agreed to build a bridge to the Vancouver airport as a sweetener for Mr. Clark.

But the Liberals now look back on these deals, especially in British Columbia, and wonder what political credit it gained them. Their dreams of a major breakthrough in the province were dashed. In Quebec, they made moderate gains, but there was little evidence that the high-profile devolution of job-training powers made a contribution. "There was no payoff," a Liberal strategist said.

As well, federal ministers have judged that their harder-edged Plan B approach to unity is finding favour in most parts of the country and, with the deficit almost licked, they aren't feeling as much on the defensive about a robust federal role.

Mr. Chrétien, a politician from the weather-vane school, was only committed to decentralization for pragmatic reasons.

Senior Liberals emphasize that they aren't seeking fights with the provinces. Mr. Chrétien has welcomed the decision by the premiers to meet on national unity, and Ottawa is hoping for a joint initiative on youth employment, in line with the agreement last year on a new national child benefit.

Perhaps the most striking thing about the new assertiveness is Ottawa's aggressive tone. Mr. Dion's letters have been very much in the face of his Parti Québécois adversaries. In his letter this week to Mr. Landry, he wrote: "I am not accusing you of being a poor democrat. I am simply reproaching you for not adequately considering your arguments."

Federal officials say they are no longer interested in walking on eggshells in Quebec and that they have come to believe that raising the rhetoric helps them get their case into the media.

As a case in point, they cite an otherwise unspectacular speech Mr. Pettigrew delivered last February to a partisan crowd of young Liberals in Quebec. At one point, arguing that Ottawa's contribution to Quebec cultural industries had far outstripped that of the Quebec government for many years, he let slip with a curse word, saying Quebec had not put *un maudit cent* (a bloody cent) into culture.

The comment generated headlines in Quebec, mostly because of the fact that Mr. Pettigrew swore. The federal government was pleased by any coverage that even remotely challenged the assumption that Quebec is the sole protector of language and culture.

"That made a deep impression on us," one of the federal strategists reflected last week. "We led the news for two days in a row. If it had been a normal bland comment, that wouldn't have happened."

The top Liberals around Mr. Chrétien concluded there is value in expressing positions bluntly and provocatively. And so Mr. Dion, who comes naturally to that style, has been let loose.

Alberta reopens the big spending tap

In the end there was a real long-term cut of about 15% in healthcare,
but demand is rising on all sides to undo the whole Ralph Revolution

In November 1995, laundry workers protesting outsourcing started a wild-cat strike against the Calgary Regional Health Authority. When Ralph Klein intervened personally in the negotiations, and later had then-health minister Shirley McClellan cancel $93 million in budget cuts, the press was thunderstruck and in some quarters the end of the Klein Revolution was proclaimed. Mr. Klein had done what he had promised never to do: "blink" in the face of interest-group pressure. But today, blinking is no longer a news story: the Klein government is restoring healthcare spending so fast that it has developed a full-fledged case of political Tourette's syndrome.

Yet the government's attempts to soothe public anxiety about healthcare have served only to keep it at the top of the political agenda. The Angus Reid Group released its latest Alberta survey on December 13, and while Tory numbers remain strong—they led the Liberals 65% to 22% and have an overall approval rating of 71%—people are still nervous about the health system. Eight hundred Albertans were asked by Angus Reid in November to name the two most important issues facing the province and 53% mentioned healthcare. It was cited more than twice as often as any other subject.

Every month of the year has seen health-care splashed across Alberta headlines. After the laundry workers' strike, things were relatively quiet until February, when it was revealed that the Capital Health Authority had exhausted its emergency cash reserve and could not put off service cuts which it had been delaying for two years. Other health authorities had taken the "front-loading" approach, cutting quickly to get debt servicing costs down right away, but the CHA inherited a $37-million deficit from its predecessor hospital boards in 1995. Doctors, nurses, and other front-line workers in Edmonton began to besiege the government openly with demands for spending. Meanwhile, Calgary's authority proceeded with controversial plans to close two city hospitals while rural authorities wrung their hands over an ongoing physician shortage.

The regional health authorities (RHAs) were created in 1994 to handle just such budget challenges. As Premier Klein infamously confessed on December 5 on Dave Rutherford's radio show, neither he nor any of his advisers ever had a "clear" province-wide "vision" of what the health system would look like when the budget-trimming was through. It was the RHAs that were supposed to innovate, remodel their regions, and create efficiencies. But in 1996 they turned into just another cash-demanding interest group—and politically the most dangerous of all for the Conservative government.

"Decentralization was supposed to take the government off the hook," says David Taras, a University of Calgary political scientist. "But people know who they've elected—not RHAs, which are political appointees—and they know who's responsible. Ralph is the symbol, in this province, of what goes right and what goes wrong, and he's a symbol of what's happened to the healthcare system, for good or bad. There was no way for him to download the responsibility to the RHAs, which don't have any real public visibility; eight of 10 Albertans probably don't even know what they are." Result: a painful retreat from health budget plans that made the PCs look like Napoleon leading the Grande Armee out of Russia.

At one time, the government had hopes of relieving pressure on the system by allowing private clinics to bill the government for medical services and the patients for "facility fees." Jane Fulton was appointed deputy minister to implement that program, which could have reduced waiting lists by taking non-urgent procedures out of hospitals and half-way out of medicare. But the Liberal government in Ottawa insisted on a strict construction (indeed, stricter than has been traditional) of the Canada Health Act's bans on extra-billing. To dodge ongoing federal fines, which eventually topped $3 million, the province nationalized the private eye and abortion clinics in late May and dismissed Ms. Fulton.

Despite this defeat, the premier at first stood firm on funding levels. "Of course those people who are involved in the system would like to see more money put into it," he said in mid-April. "With respect to health, what the public wants generally are assurances that the healthcare system is going to be there

 From *Alberta Report*, December 30, 1996, pp. 9-11. © 1996 by United Western Communications, Ltd. Reprinted by permission.

for them when they need it. But they don't want to see a lot of money poured into the system." Following this principle, the government tried to placate the Capital Health Authority without increasing the health budget, lending it $7 million of the $21 million its board had asked for. The condition of this loan was that Dr. Lyle Oberg, head of the provincial standing policy committee on health, would investigate the CHA's finances and come up with ways to help save the $21 million.

But there followed what came to be called the Leak of the Week campaign. Doctors, enraged with the premier's intransigence, started directing media attention to patients injured or ill-treated by "the system." Ralph Klein was to blame for clinical outrages as diverse as, in two high-profile cases, a fatally misdiagnosed appendicitis and diarrhea-stained sheets. The Oberg review committee was struck on May 1 and the Leaks of the Week began almost immediately. By June 24 the government was in full retreat, committing $235 million in new money to the 1996–97 and 1997–98 RHA budgets, writing off the $7-million loan to the CHA, and extending another $7-million loan which would also be written off. And when the Oberg report came out on July 3, proposing further austerities and efficiencies, the likelihood that it would be completely ignored was already widely presumed.

Premier Klein spent August cooking up a campaign to win the public back on healthcare, and now it has become the singular obsession of his government. The Liberals have said that they intend to make the spring election a referendum on the government's handling of the portfolio. In response, the Conservatives have been trying to craft common care guidelines for RHAs. Meanwhile, concerns from constituents were so loud that the government announced 1997–98 budget details a full three months early, on November 26. Under the new terms, health spending will grow 3.4% next year, and another 3.7% in each of the two years after.

By 2000, the painful Klein health cuts will basically have been cancelled out, at least in nominal dollars. That is still an extraordinary achievement, given that the real value of those dollars, compared to the number of people being treated, will have declined considerably over that time—certainly no less than

LARRY STEVENS

What Albertans Care About

"In your opinion, what is the most important issue facing Alberta today? And what is the second most important issue?"
—November 1996

Healthcare/Hospitals	53%
Education/Schools	27%
Jobs/Unemployment	25%
The deficit/Spending	22%
The economy in general	14%
Government cutbacks/ Spending cuts	7%
Bad leaders/Government	4%
Crime	3%

Source: Angus Reid Group

15%. But it is still bound to be disappointing to fiscal hawks, if only because the cries for more cash are as loud as ever. Significantly, the Angus Reid poll placing health at the top of the public agenda was taken immediately after the November 26 restored-spending announcement, not before.

According to Larry Bryan, a Calgary physician and former CEO of Foothills Hospital, the reason the public forced the government to turn so soggy was that it failed to publicize the goals and nature of health reform. "That's what they've done the worst of all on," he says. "They've left the public in the dark and there's a lot of conflicting information." The Leak of the Week publicity, amplified by the Liberals (as when Grant Mitchell read out his "roll of the dead" on the first day of the Legislative Assembly's fall session) overshadowed achievements that physicians applauded and had helped plan.

"A lot of progress has been made in reorganizing hospital care," says Dr. Bryan. In Calgary, he notes by example, two hospitals have been closed, inciting some outrage, but this has enabled new service centres to be put in under-served areas of the city; downtown now has a storefront care centre so that its indigents do not have to go across the river to the General, and there is money for a new hospital on the growing south side. Other services, such as kidney dialysis and eye surgery, have been moved

out of overcrowded hospitals and into community storefronts.

"Moreover, heart surgery and trauma services have been consolidated in both Edmonton and Calgary," says Dr. Bryan. "This was widely decried as a cost-cutting move, but the papers never reported that that's not why it was done." Clinical studies have proven that the more volume that heart and trauma centres handle, the higher their patient survival rates. "No money was taken out of those programs—it was a purely medical decision, based strongly on the literature. But people don't know that."

If all goes well, they will never need to know it, either. The RHAs and the doctors seem, for the moment, relatively content with the new RHA funding levels. But the November reinvestment announcement may herald new strife in a different quarter. While RHA funding rises until 2000, physicians' gross billings for the province have been capped at $737 million a year until then. Doctors are already in a squeeze and have exceeded the cap for 1996; they will have to refund the excess, just as last year they pocketed the $11 million they came in under the $759 million cap.

Richard Plain, a University of Alberta health economist, thinks that the Klein government intends to punish the Alberta Medical Association for its "antics"—namely, throwing political monkey wrenches into the reform process while certain of its own behaviours went unchecked. "While hospitals were being closed left, right and centre, physicians carried on business as usual; it was only in 1995 that we finally had a small decline in the growth of physicians in Alberta," says Prof. Plain. "Since last December, the physicians have been actively participating in their 'crisis-a-day' media manipulation. Klein may be recognizing that he only got part-way through his reformation, and that to continue it, physicians are going to play a key role."

This role, thinks Prof. Plain, will be forced on doctors by the fact that their billings are capped at $737 million a year between now and 2000. Inflation, increasing overhead, and an aging and growing population are all going to make that cap tighter and tighter if nothing is done by the doctors themselves to change the way they practise and bill. "We're going to hear nothing but screams and squalling about the quality of healthcare—the doctors' litanies will be there as long as they aren't getting more cash in their pockets," predicts Prof. Plain. "But they've got to take a serious look at the management of the system because they're the major driver in healthcare—the RHAs are really just their workshops. The RHAs reduced their beds by 40% while the total number of doctors in the province increased. Now Halvar [Jonson, the health minister] is capping them long and hard."

Prof. Plain thinks that is appropriate, but he warns that the oversupply of doctors is not system-wide; some specialities are under-staffed and so are many rural areas of the province. "The AMA elects its president and its board by majority vote," he says, "and what's in the interests of the majority of doctors may not be in the interests of Albertans. That's a concern, but at least the government is getting around to a health-reform issue that it couldn't tackle in the first round of its mandate."

"Reform," however, is not the primary word in the government's vocabulary nowadays: the emphasis now is on "reinvestment." The ultimate legacy of the 1996 health unrest may be a series of 1997 moves to forestall a ripple of revolts against cuts that have occured in other departments.

The Alberta Liberals are certainly counting on such a ripple to pulse through social services, education, community services and others. "I believe healthcare is going to become symbolic of the incompetence of this government," says Grit health critic Howard Sapers. "People are going to start hearing about disasters in other departments, and it's going to change their view of whether this government can be trusted to steer this ship."

In the past few months, the government has ploughed more money into the Edmonton welfare system, cancelled the privatization of employment-standards enforcement, and jacked up capital funding for education and benefits for seniors. With oil royalty windfalls bestowing billion-dollar surpluses on the province, nothing else seems politically possible but to make government bigger once again.

Indeed, no less a libertarian than Treasurer Jim Dinning intimates now that guaranteed safe growth in government spending was the very reason for the cuts. "We were in a financial mess, but we took serious action to turn that round," he says. "As a result, we've built a stronger financial foundation, thereby securing those valuable social programs for the future; they're no longer subject to the whims of our fiscal yo-yo."

"The change process within the government bureaucracy, that's going to continue," says the treasurer by way of summary. "But if you're asking me 'Are these departments facing more cuts later on?' the answer is no. The cuts are over in health and education. But that doesn't mean you can't look for greater efficiencies and better ways to improve the quality of healthcare and education; that search will never end."

—*Colby Cosh*

THE WEST

The stolen revolution

How the corruption and incompetence of the Devine government impoverished Saskatchewan and discredited its provincial conservatives, perhaps forever

Authors Stephen Clarkson and Christina McCall opened their critically-acclaimed 1990 book *Trudeau and Our Times* with the memorable observation: "He haunts us still." In Saskatchewan, among conservatives at least, the same might be said of the scandal-ridden administration of former Progressive Conservative premier Grant Devine. Not only did the Devine re- gime accumulate the largest debt in the history of the province, but as a series of fraud charges and trials over the last two years involving nearly a third of the former government's second-term caucus has shown, the Devine team was more than incompetent, it was crooked.

Two weeks ago, former Saskatchewan Tory MLA Michael Hopfner be- came the sixth member of the Conservative government that ruled the province from 1982 to 1991 to be convicted of fraud. Three other former MLAs have been tried and acquitted while three more await trial. Yet another, Jack Wolfe, committed suicide last year before he could face the court. Former PC caucus communications director John Scraba has also been con-

A sadder but wiser party

Unfortunately the horses have already bolted but current Tory leader Bill Boyd certainly appreciated the importance of securing barn doors. Saddled with the un- enviable job of rebuilding the conservative party in the midst of an ongoing scandal, the plain-spoken farmer from Eston has learned from the mistakes of former Saskatchewan Conservative premier Grant Devine. Mr. Boyd says that he has put in place the mechanisms necessary to pro- hibit another fraud scheme like the one that sank his predecessors.

"We've adopted an unlimited zero-tolerance position to- ward all law-breaking," he reports. "If an MLA is charged with a crime, he is immediately relieved from his position. And if he is convicted, we remove him from the party." For proof of his inflexibility on this point, Mr. Boyd points to convicted fraudster Gerald Muirhead, the MLA whom he expelled from the party soon after he became leader in November 1994.

"We've tightened up our caucus accounting procedure," he reports. All cheques now require a triple signing author- ity. At the end of every month all accounts are reviewed by all sitting MLAs, including Mr. Boyd. An annual audit by an independent auditor of all accounts, designed to make sure "that every expense is invoiced, receipted, and paid for," completes the picture. When asked if an annual audit was not part of past procedure, Mr. Boyd admits it was not. But today the Conservative chief says he "intends to make our accounting procedures more exacting than those of any other party."

Mr. Boyd is anxious to separate himself and his party from any trace of the "old Tory" willingness to use the letter of the law to flout its spirit. When Saskatchewan Tory Eric Berntson, now a senator, appeared to be using parliamen- tary privilege to avoid testifying in former MLA Michael Hopfner's fraud trial, the Conservative leader sent him a pointed letter which he released to the media. "I find it most unacceptable that you would choose to abuse an out- dated parliamentary privilege in this manner," Mr. Boyd wrote. "Those who are called to testify should do so without hesitation. Your reluctance to appear at this trial is dam- aging the integrity of both our federal Parliament and our provincial Legislature." At the same time, he wrote Prime Minister Jean Chretien and asked him to revoke parlia- mentary privilege "as quickly as possible, so that MPs and senators are required . . . to appear in court just like any other Canadian citizen."

After former caucus chairman Lorne McLaren was con- victed of diverting $125,000 from the Conservative caucus to the Progressive Conservative Party, Mr. Boyd agreed to pay that amount back to the government. Later he was accused of "dithering" because some time passed before the money was repaid. But Mr. Boyd explains that the delay was a result of the new accounting procedures he had es- tablished. "The $125,000 was paid within days after we were invoiced by the speaker," he says. "That was our past problem, paying for things without proper accounting pro- cedures." And to those who complain that he paid the money from the secret Regina PC Metro Council Fund, Mr. Boyd retorts that there is no difference between that pud- dle of discreetly-donated cash and the Tommy Douglas House Inc. fund maintained by the New Democrats. Mr. Boyd says he hates what happened to his party because it betrayed conservative philosophy. "True conservatism means carefully conserving taxpayers money," he says. "People should view the Devine administration, not as a failure of conservatism, but as a failure of individuals who belonged to our party." He is, says Mr. Boyd, "intensely frustrated and disappointed" with what went on. "The bot- tom line," he concludes, "is that no one should be above the law."

—*S.P.*

Government by winks and nudges

Tory apologists put the Saskatchwan Tory fraud scandal down to neophyte MLAs who were innocently sucked into wrong-doing by too much opportunity combined with excessive political naivete. Former finance minister-turned Ontario businessman Lorne Hepworth—one of the many former Conservative politicians who has left the province—suggests that the multiple frauds might have occurred "because there weren't enough lawyers in the Devine cabinet to keep them on the straight and narrow."

The suggestion that a government needs lawyers to explain the difference between right and wrong to its MLAs is a novel one. That job generally falls to party leaders. But premier Grant Devine and former deputy premier Eric Berntson have maintained resolutely that they had no idea a large group within their caucus, some of whom were cabinet ministers, were stealing taxpayers' money. Testimony at Hopfner's trial alleged that Mr. Devine funnelled $45,000 from PC caucus funds to former caucus chairman and convicted fraudster Lorne McLaren and knew that nearly half a million stolen dollars had been squirrelled away in a Martensville bank. The court also heard allegations that Mr. Berntson, who is now a senator in Ottawa, was involved in the illegal diversion of $125,000 in caucus funds to the PC Party. However, no evidence was put forward directly inculpating Messrs. Devine and Berntson in the fraud.

Hopfner was found guilty of defrauding the public of $57,348 through false expense claims, although he was acquitted of two other charges and vows to appeal his conviction. He was a piker compared to McLaren, who pleaded guilty to defrauding the public of $837,000, stealing $114,200 from the Conservative caucus and diverting $125,000 in public money from the caucus to the PC Party of Saskatchewan. The remaining four convicts—ex-cabinet ministers all—defrauded taxpayers of smaller sums. They are Joan Duncan ($12,405), Harold Martens ($5,850), Ray Meiklejohn ($4,500) and Grant Hodgins ($3,645).

Those acquitted include Bill Neudorf, John Britton and Lorne Kopelchuk. Still to be tried are Harry Baker, Sherwin Petersen, and John Gerich. Another former Tory MLA, Gerald Muirhead, was convicted of a communications allowance fraud not related to the larger scheme. He used a false invoice to purchase a saddle and accessories.

The main caucus fraud scheme was complex. Caucus employee and convicted fraud participant John Scraba was the administrator, although he denies inventing it. The heart of the plan involved diverting a quarter of each MLA's government communications allowance to a central fund. The fund would ostensibly allow the caucus access to more expensive forms of advertising—particularly radio and television—that they couldn't afford as individuals. Scraba has testified that at one time or another all 38 sitting Tory MLAs between 1986 and 1991 contributed to the fund.

To access the money, Conservative MLAs signed expense claims that were submitted to the Legislature along with an invoice from one of four numbered companies that Scraba has established. The invoices, usually for radio advertising, newsletters, and other communications services, were then approved by the Legislature's financial services office, and cheques were issued to the companies. Many of the invoices Scraba submitted, however, were for services never performed, or for MLA expenses that were either illegitimate or non-existent. At Hopfner's trial, RCMP Sergeant John Leitch told the court that just $229,000 was spent on advertising while $517,335 went to the Conservative caucus back account. That money eventually funded

victed of fraud. RCMP Inspector Sid Bloxon predicts that more charges will be laid. David Smith, a professor of political studies at the University of Saskatchewan, says the trials are exposing one of the worst cases of government corruption in Canadian history. Prof. Smith describes the Tory malfeasance as "different in kind, not just degree" from anything the country has ever seen.

How so many corrupt and spendthrift politicians could form a government—twice—remains an open question. Mr. Devine's crew first came to power in 1982 with 57 seats, the largest majority any party has ever won in the province, in part because they offered voters a clear alternative to the NDP's socialist principles that had for so long dominated Saskatchewan governments. Instead of increasing government intrusion in people's lives, the Tories promised less. And instead of looking to government to provide a basis for the province's economy, the PCs would, through tax incentives and elimination of red tape, encourage business and economic growth. Mr.

Devine said his government would end the gasoline tax, phase out the 5% provincial sales tax, and reduce the provincial income tax by 10%. In short, he would open the province for business.

In part, the Devine Tories accomplished what they set out to do. Their privatization program included Sask-Oil and SaskPotash. Now known as Wascana Energy Inc., and Potash Corporation of Saskatchewan (PCS), both companies are wildly successful. Indeed, Saskatoon-based PCS is on its way to becoming the biggest fertilizer company in the world. It was also the Devine government that put the uranium producer Cameco on the road toward privatization, a process almost completed today and one that has put hundreds of millions of dollars back into government coffers. "Even the oil upgraders are making money today," Mr. Devine notes. "It's ironic that every time the Romanow government goes to New York to borrow money they point to the success of industries we put on the map."

Despite Mr. Devine's conservative ideals, however, insiders report that he

was fundamentally unwilling to grapple with the details and stresses of daily government administration. And in that lay the seeds of his downfall. Anxious to curry favour with an electorate conditioned to big, generous government, from the beginning Mr. Devine promised voters more than the province's income could sustain. Even his first campaign was marked by new giveaways. Because interest rates were soaring at 20%, be promised to buy down mortgages and keep them at 13.75%. And government spending on healthcare and education increased throughout his time in office. "In the early '80s the deficits were relatively small, only two or three million dollars per year," explains Lorne Hepworth, Mr. Devine's last finance minister, "and everybody thought they would go away when the economy got better."

But they did not go away, they just got bigger. Frightened before the 1986 election by their low standing in the polls, the Devine government pulled out all the stops with grants and low interest loan programs for farmers, home-owners and businesses. By the party activities or found its way into the pockets of individual MLAs.

Hopfner's unique defense strategy—the former hotel owner acted as his own lawyer—led to revelations not heard before in public. Called as a witness, McLaren was first to link Mr. Devine to possible fraudulent manipulation of cash. He told reporters outside the courtroom that when he was dropped from the cabinet in 1985 he asked Mr. Devine to help him financially. Several months later he was surprised to receive a personal cheque for $45,000 from former Rosthern MLA Ralph Katzman.

McLarens' explanation came after Mr. Katzman had revealed in court that on December 6, 1985, he transferred $455,000 from a Conservative caucus bank account in Regina to the Martensville bank near Saskatoon where he did his personal banking. Mr. Katzman, who has not been charged with fraud, testified that he doled out thousands of dollars to McLaren and two other MLAs.

Excitement ran particularly high in October when Hopfner subpoenaed Mr. Devine and Mr. Berntson to testify as part of his defence. Speculation was widespread that one of them might have to admit, either to masterminding the fraud, or at least to being privy to illegal goings-on.

Mr. Berntson fuelled the speculative fire when he claimed parliamentary immunity and appeared to be attempting to avoid the subpoena. But after a series of scathing newspaper editorials, along with a sternly worded public letter from current Saskatchewan Tory leader Bill Boyd, the senator finally agreed to appear.

In the end, however, the courtroom appearances of the two men were anti-climactic. Mr. Devine denied any involvement in the wrong-doing that has touched so many members of his government. He explained that his knowledge of caucus finances was limited and that he was too busy to supervise such matters. Off the stand, Mr. Devine said in an interview that the caucus manages itself and blamed some of the problems on poor accounting. "We had 50 members," he said. "Mistakes multiplied."

Still, Mr. Devine did not escape the Hopfner trial entirely unscathed. Taking the stand a month later, former MLA Myles Morin, who was PC caucus chairman when the money went to Martensville, testified that Mr. Devine had approved the transfer and that he would not have signed the cheque Mr. Katzman used without the premier's approval. "I made a phone call to the premier's office," he testified, "I asked him if he knew that Ralph had made this request of Joan [to put money in a Martensville account] and if that's what he wanted to have done. He told me 'yes'." Mr. Morin said he had no idea how much Mr. Katzman transferred Martensville because the cheque was blank when he signed it. Nor did he discuss amounts with Mr. Devine.

Mr. Devine continues to deny all knowledge of criminal behaviour. He refuses to address specifics, referring instead to a printed statement he put out immediately after Mr. Morin's allegations. "Recent public statements in the media implying my involvement and knowledge of illegal activity are misleading and false," he wrote. "I wish to state categorically and unequivocally that in my entire political career, I have never been involved in, approved, or condoned, or even been aware of any illegal activity or wrongdoing."

As for Mr. Berntson, he told the court that while it was "fair to say I know something of $125,000" that was transferred to the PC Party, he knew nothing of the specifics. Mr. Berntson said he had approved a transfer of funds to the party in payment for research the party had done on caucus' behalf and that he told his underlings it was all right to pay the party "if they could discover it was appropriate to do so."

—S.P.

---

time another election had to be called in 1991, the accumulated deficit had reached $4 billion. And when the NDP succeeded in forcing the government to back down from its planned privatization of SaskEnergy in 1989, the writing was on the wall for the Devine administration. Even party loyalists have written that a malaise set in that afflicted his leadership from then on.

In *Battleground: The Socialist Assault on Grant Devine's Canadian Dream,* Saskatchewan Tory loyalist Don Baron wrote that the failure to explain the benefits of privatization "was a reflection of Devine's greatest weakness, an ongoing one which had been apparent to many insiders for years. Devine has little aptitude in choosing his chief advisers and the members of his office team."

Mr. Baron quoted former *Saskatoon StarPhoenix* columnist Paul Jackson as saying that "Devine's credible initiatives on economic diversification, northern development and privatization were being drowned by incompetent political advisers on one hand and inept communications aides on the other." One gets the idea, Mr. Jackson said, "that half the Tory communications staffers haven't yet mastered the basic art of sharpening a pencil and those who have are now back in remedial English classes learning how to spell their own names." Little did Messrs. Baron and Jackson realize that the communications office wasn't merely incompetent. It was also corrupt.

Perhaps more than any other player, Dick Collver, who was Mr. Devine's predecessor as party leader, was responsible for the party's rise from the dead. When Mr. Collver came on board, the provincial Tories were only getting about 2% support in the polls. In 1975, he and six other Tories got themselves elected to the legislature, the first Tory MLAs since the 1930s. Then in 1978, the Conservatives jumped to 17 MLAs, and the Liberals, long considered the NDP's natural opposition, were wiped out. Mr. Collver resigned his leadership post after that election, paving the way for the Devine sweep four years later.

Speaking in retirement from Phoenix, Arizona, Mr. Collver says he got into Conservative politics because "if you believed in free enterprise and the power of the West there was nowhere else to go." He says that Saskatchewan had suffered under a socialist government "most of the time I was alive" and he was determined to make a change. However, he says now that in his attempt to do a make-over on a moribund party he sometimes allowed himself to be driven by expediency. "I started bringing in anybody I thought could get elected," he explains. "Unfortunately, quite a few of the people facing these silly fraud charges are people I recruited." Today, Mr. Collver laments that "Eric Berntson, Grant Devine and Lorne McLaren were all people that I convinced to join the party."

And some of those early candidates, Mr. Collver recalls, were not ready for public life. "I remember Ralph [former Tory MLA Katzman] came to the Legislature the first time wearing great big rubber boots," he recounts. "And that was the kind of image I was very anxious to avoid." But when he told Mr. Katzman to lose the boots, "he just took them off and walked around the legislature in his socks the rest of the day." There were many others of similar rusticity, he recalls. They were popular in their ridings, but "loose cannons" in the Legislature.

Mr. Collver is reluctant to characterize Mr. Berntson, except to say that "Berntson was the real leader of the party" after Mr. Collver stepped down. Instead, Mr. Collver retreats into circumlocutions. "I'd rather not describe Berntson," he says. Then, "I'm sure you're sensing my reticence. I don't [want] to comment because I understand he's being investigated. I've already told you I'm ashamed of how the party behaved, and if he [Berntson] was the real leader, then I'm doubly ashamed."

For Mr. Collver, the real shame in the demise of the Tories lies in the province's lost opportunities. "Their election was a golden opportunity to permanently change the province," he argues. "Now it's gone forever." He observes that "once the Conservatives got into power, they started worrying about themselves" and thus lost sight of their reason for being there. "Instead of governing in the best interests of the people, they sought only to get re-elected." And that is sad, he says, "because Saskatchewan could have been another North Dakota," a geographically and demographically similar state where, in the last four years a pro-business Republican administration has presided over the creation of 30,000 new jobs and an unemployment rate of 2.5%.

But instead of demonstrating the advantages of free enterprise to a formerly socialist province, the uncertain leadership style that many insiders report afflicted Mr. Devine's internal administration from the beginning eventually became apparent to all. "Devine backed away from a fight at several crucial moments," says Howard Leeson, a University of Regina political scientist and confidant of NDP Premier Roy Romanow. "That made him appear to be neither fish nor fowl to the voting public."

Mr. Leeson makes Mr. Collver's case that the Devine administration, in failing to keep its own house clean, has set back the conservative movement. "Liberal Premier Ross Thatcher started talking about North Dakota in the 1960s," he says. "But ever since the '50s it's been obvious that Saskatchewan can't attract developing businesses. We're always going to be a hinterland."

—Shafer Parker, Jr.

RENEWING THE CASE FOR MAR- ITIME UNION

La menace de la séparation du Québec devrait servir de catalyseur à la formation d'une « Union maritime ». Les provinces maritimes pourraient aussi s'inspirer de l'Union européenne pour créer dans cette région un secteur public plus petit et plus efficace, mieux apte à jouer le rôle que l'État doit jouer dans une société moderne et dans un environnement économique mondialisé.

by Wayne Hunt

"Will Canada Unravel?" The title was all too familiar for those with a vested interest in the subject. But what granted the article which followed a wider hearing was its place of publication: in the September/October 1996 edition of *Foreign Affairs*, an influential academic journal favoured by policy makers of various persuasions. Briefly put, the author argued that the US must make preparations not just for Quebec separation but for a continued balkanization of the territories ranged along its northern border. The survival of Atlantic Canada was left as an open question.

Predictions of this nature excite controversy and gain temporary media attention from outside of Canada. But in the present instance a positive purpose can also be served. The attention can act as a spur to strategic thinking inside our own country. This thinking must turn around the deeply entrenched view that eastern Canada is overly as well as overtly dependant upon government. In other words regional patronage is not just done, it is seen to be done. This perception can become a self-fulfilling prophecy which steers entrepreneurial talent to growth centres elsewhere. In the past year, 1996, there was a marked discrepancy in employment growth. Quebec and eastern Canada posted job losses, while Ontario and the western provinces posted gains. However these aggregates do not in themselves tell the real story of how various communities and various sectors have adapted to the global economy.

Quebec will constantly barter for a better settlement for itself both within Canada and within the larger North American context. That is unlikely to change. Crises of national unity are the most predictable of patterns within Canadian politics. Sovereignty remains the ultimate goal of the present Quebec government. What has changed is the international context within which sovereignty is pursued. The individual economic sovereignty of nation-states has been dramatically altered by one massive geopolitical development: the ending of the Cold War. Lucien Bouchard's participation in the last Team Canada trade effort emphasized the fact that sovereignty must be pooled in the pursuit of larger trade objectives. Trade delegations, by their very nature, require a fluid coalition of participants. Negotiations with Quebec and with the various minority communities within Quebec — not least of whom are the first peoples — have highlighted the need for structural reform on a broad basis.

Atlantic Canada must seize the initiative here. The step toward full Maritime Union would go considerable distance toward destroying the myth that Atlantic Canada's is a dependency culture, dependent in the first instance upon non-renewable natural resources and, in the second, upon an all-too-renewable governmental largesse. Sustainable development has moved into the information age. At the same time reliance upon the government has decreased. Statistics supplied by the Atlantic Province's Economic Council have documented this transition. A recent report points out that the federal government's presence has decreased faster in Atlantic Canada than in other regions. Federal subsidies and capital support to businesses came to 12.7 percent of GNP in 1980 as opposed to 2.1 percent in 1994.

The bigger background has to do with the operation of the global economy. No nation

From *Policy Options*, April 1997, pp. 39-41. © 1997 by the Institute for Research on Public Policy. Reprinted by permission.

rests as an island, entire unto itself. Seismic shifts in capital markets and advances in information technology have ordered world politics. Institutions which have evolved over a long period of time have been obliged to come to terms with these changes. Consider the case of Great Britain. Basic constitutional change is likely to come by way of Tony Blair's "New Labour" government. This government has made structural reform of governmental institutions a priority. Tactical considerations have slowed the intended pace of reform with regard to the House of Lords but Canadians could take instruction from his example. Blair has studiously avoided the "c" word in order to avoid the rote-responses and old-line thinking that comes with terms like the "constitution." Instead he champions the cause of what he calls the project of democratic renewal," a project which he and others in his personal circle of advisors have tried to make as comprehensive as possible.

Eastern Canada's Atlanticist orientation and historic ties to the British parliamentary system make it receptive and open to changes that are taking place in Europe. Experience with the evolution of the EU has shown that a "two-track" approach is the most workable. Political reform starts with Maritime Union. To be successful this must proceed on a clearly defined, step-by-step basis. The end result must be less government and less regulation. But it must also be tempered by the humane recognition that smaller government has to mean not just smarter but kinder government. The public sector has a creative role to play as a shaping force in community life. This role cannot be confined to the establishment of a business climate; it must encourage a spirit of innovation and an independence of mind in all community endeavors. The proponents of Maritime Union must also be prepared to make strategic alliances with other reform-minded groups.

The most commonsensical way to proceed would be to have each of the four Atlantic legislatures take on a single responsibility for areas that all four handle on their own at present. Community-based debates about who would handle what would have to be resolved by a referendum. The first topic of discussion should be the field of education. At the conclusion of this exercise the overall authority for education would rest with one legislature but much of the debate about curriculum could — and should — remain at the local level. Education is a prerequisite for success in the global economy. In recognition of this

Bill Clinton has made education the priority for his second term in the US Presidency. Changes that are taking place south of our borders will impact immediately and directly upon us. A knowledge-based economy demands flexibility and creativity. In that economy education must be seen as a life-long process in which people must make career changes and retool themselves at pivotal points throughout their working lives. They must reinvent what they do in order to market themselves in new ways. And as it is for individuals, so too it is for governments. Atlantic Canada has reached a pivotal point. It must make a new departure without engaging the energies of those who have an interest in intergovernmental affairs. This is a particularly important objective to work toward at the outset of the discussion because it must be recognized that "specialists" have a professional interest in the *status quo*.

This, however, is only the beginning. The vexing problem of where to locate the capital has constantly plagued this debate. Again, it is useful to look at the experience of other countries for insights as well as guidance in this matter. Following the European example we could have a rotating premiership which would work in conjunction with a rotating capital. The Presidency of the European Council of Ministers offers a working model of this concept. Europe can also offer instruction on the second track, economic reform. Progress toward a European-style single market which allows for the free movement of goods and services has to be consolidated in Atlantic Canada as much as in the rest of the country. A European-inspired "variable geometry" which anticipates the core integration of one or two centres while others integrate at a different rate or move in a different direction would be appropriate here. Already we have "smart cities" which are developing a sophisticated computer network. They are forming "knowledge corridors" which extend into the economies of the US eastern seaboard, thus re-establishing lines of trade which reached their high point in what will soon be the previous century but one, the nineteenth century. Moncton and Halifax are two of the most noteworthy examples of cities that have re-engineered themselves in this manner and re-cast their thinking in this direction. As the Atlantic Province's Economic Council report noted, this region's exports reached the $10 billion dollar mark in 1995. In the report's own words, "Tough markets at home have driven Atlantic Canadian firms to look outward for new opportunities."

Structural change may come from another direction as well. The Royal Commission on Aboriginal Peoples has lobbied for a massive institutional transformation. In the short term this will not take place. After the federal election is over however, native issues will receive more attention and as the pace of reform increases from both the top down and the bottom up, self-government will become a living reality for a greater number of aboriginal communities. The wholesale transformation envisioned by the framers of the report clashes with the predisposition of those who are presently in authority in Ottawa, but this will change. So will the one-sided emphasis on deficit reduction and the management of downsizing. The next political cycle will be about vision and far reaching change. The implications of aboriginal self-government will have to be systematically thought out in association with the proposals for Maritime Union. Both movements share a commitment to the bettering of people's lives at the community level. Shared as well is a commitment to the tearing down of barriers and the establishment of a dialogue which centres on honest, open debate. Both movements have used information technology to move beyond the limitations of a resource-dependent economy; both currently share a strategic interest in the maintenance of a strong federal government. Finally, both accentuate the fact that at present there is a serious imbalance between political institutions and the wider matrix of forces that work upon these institutions.

Much of the disenchantment with politics as currently practised arises from the failure of those in positions of public authority to think beyond partisan, short-term categories. This is bound to affect the long-term potential for economic growth. The so-called "Singapore school" has mounted a critique of North American capitalism from this perspective, effectively arguing that a lack of political discipline will inevitably carry over into a lack of economic discipline. Atlantic Canadians have the discipline to move beyond the present state of affairs and to recognize that change must come about not through a change in government but through a change in the way we govern ourselves. Maritime Union is a means to an end rather than an end in itself. It is a way for citizens to gain control over the forces that control their lives. In the managerial parlance that dominates public policy, it is a way to be pro-active rather than reactive. Or in a more time-honoured phrase, it is to master

our own destiny. To passively sit back and watch the country unravel is untenable. But what about the other opinion? Will the amalgamation and integration of Atlantic Canada be a movement toward "a more perfect union?" The answer has to come in the affirmative: in both senses of the phrase. Yes, it will perfect the workability of the public sector by adding to economies of scale and yes, it will involve integration into a larger American market. That, however, is not the point. That market is global as much as it is American. We are being globalized in the sense that we are taking our place in a world that has moved beyond nation-states and an ethnocentric sense of national identity. Organizations that represent human rights groups, labour, environmental or business interest have moved from a fixed national address into the fluid transnationalism of the computer era. At the start of this decade Robert Reich published an article in the *Harvard Business Review*. Its title made its point — "Who is US?" — and numerous commentaries both before and after its publication have confirmed the premise that a national and a corporate identity are no longer synonymous.

Canada's constituent parts are not about to be swallowed by an American monolith. This is a fear which grew out of another age. The assumptions of the past have been turned upside down by a combination of geopolitical and technological change. It is America's own sense of unity that is coming apart — even as it is being recast in a radically different form. To be part of the Boston metropole is to be part of one of the most economically, intellectually and culturally vibrant parts of the world. Atlantic Canada will take its place here with a spirit of confidence, assured that it can compete at the highest levels. Pierre Trudeau affixed Marcus Aurelius' slogan "citizen of the world" to his door when he studied at Harvard. Later he castigated Quebec separatists for appealing to people's fears rather than to their better instincts, for wanting to look inward rather than outward, for what he famously derided as the "wigwam complex." He went on to show by his own singular example that francophones could take their own place at the pinnacles of power.

The case for Maritime Union has to move forward in the same spirit.

Wayne A. Hunt is a Visiting Scholar at Harvard University's Kennedy School of Government and a faculty member of Mount Allison University in Sackville, New Brunswick.

Political Parties
and Elections

The most recent federal general election in Canada returned a Liberal majority government, but just barely. Postelection analysis suggests that among the main issues in the campaign were the past record of the Liberal Party under Prime Minister Jean Chrétien as well as the relations between Quebec and the rest of Canada. At the time that the election campaign began, the Progressive Conservative Party was beginning to recover under the leadership of Jean Charest from its electoral debacle under the leadership of Prime Minister Kim Campbell following the departure of Prime Minister Brian Mulroney. The Reform Party of Preston Manning was continuing to grow in popularity. The Bloc Québécois, under Gilles Duceppe, did not perform nearly as well as in the past. The New Democrats did better than predicted. Thus an examination of the results of the federal election may have left the Liberals with an absolute majority, but the House of Commons had a more mixed character than at any time in recent memory.

In this section seven articles discuss the dynamics of elections in Canada and consider the impact of the electoral system on the results of elections, a theme that was widespread both before and after the election. The first two articles describe how electoral systems affect the results of elections. The first of these looks at the 1997 election in Alberta. This election, using a single-member-district system, created an overwhelming legislative majority where a bare popular majority existed, something that critics have pointed out has happened in federal elections on several occasions in recent years. The article concludes that a system in which 49 percent of the voters received 24 percent of the seats in the legislature is not very democratic. The second article, an editorial in *The Globe and Mail (Toronto)*, supports the conclusion that Canada's electoral system creates majorities where they do not exist and hides minorities.

In the next article, "Elections Bring Polls and the Question: Can the Numbers Lie?" author Karen Unland shows that polls can in fact *influence* public opinion before an election in addition to measuring what that public opinion is. This article describes some of Canada's major public opinion organizations, explains how they operate, and describes how the "remarkably accurate" Canadian polls can go wrong.

The campaign for the June 1997 federal election is the subject of the next article, in which four authors describe in detail the positions of the political parties at the beginning of the campaign, show what happened during the campaign, and identify those events that most clearly affected the outcome of the race. They show how the Liberals managed to win despite a number of hurdles that needed to be overcome. Subsequently Anthony Wilson-Smith, in "Distinct Societies," examines the implications of the election's outcome for federal unity and claims that the election did nothing to pull the nation together. In fact, while the Liberals do have some representation in all provinces—a situation that is much better than some of their previous electoral victories under the leadership of Pierre Trudeau—the election outcomes do not reflect that a national healing process has taken place.

The final two articles offer some *post hoc* interpretation of the election results. "Sovereignty's Stumbling Bloc" suggests that the 1997 federal election campaign revealed serious divisions in the sovereignty movement in Quebec and discusses what the Bloc Québécois is going to need to do to regain its momentum. The last article, by *Maclean's* author Mary Janigan, evaluates the Liberal Party's performance in the campaign, suggesting that it was not paying attention to numerous political cues when it was designing its campaign strategy in 1997, especially in the final days of the campaign. In hindsight the Liberals had plenty of warning of the "slippage" of their support, and they did not act in time to prevent significant losses.

Looking Ahead: Challenge Questions

How can an electoral system affect the results of an election? What would the membership of the House of Commons look like today if Canada had a different kind of electoral system?

How important are polls in a federal election? How can they influence the results of an election? What kind of factors can cause a poll to find incorrect results?

How did Canada's federal political parties behave in the 1997 election? What challenges were faced by the Liberal Party? How did it deal with these challenges? Did the Liberal Party or the opposition parties do a better job in the campaign?

UNIT 6

Suppose your vote counted

DEMOCRACY (1)/ *The results in Alberta this week distorted voters' choices. The province is not alone in needing a new system.*

BY DAVID ELTON and PETER McCORMICK

THE Alberta election is over, and Ralph Klein has rolled to a massive win, decimating the opposition and increasing his majority in the legislature from the comfortable to the overwhelming. Given the high level of support that opinion polls showed throughout the campaign, this is hardly unexpected. If anything, it is a surprise that the Conservatives wound up with "only" 51 per cent of the popular vote and "only" 76 per cent of the seats; for a while, it seemed their support would top 70 per cent, which might have given them every seat in the legislature.

But notice the curious arithmetic built into this description. For the winning party, 51 per cent of the vote equals 76 per cent of the seats, while 70 per cent of the vote might have equalled 100 per cent of the seats. The flip side is that for the other parties, 49 per cent of the popular vote means only 24 per cent of the seats, while 35 per cent would quite possibly have given them nothing at all.

For those who naively thought that elections were about the accurate reflection of the popular will and the political voices of voters, this "new math" is rather startling. But they can comfort themselves with the thought that things could have been even worse; in British Columbia last year, the party that won the election received fewer votes than the party that lost. "Majority rule" indeed.

The culprit in the piece is the single-member riding. This process divides provinces into electoral divisions with more or less equal numbers of voters, each division electing one representative. The system is used across Canada—but almost nowhere else in the world except the United States and Britain.

Does this make any difference, except to the overdeveloped sensitivities of political scientists? It has certainly made a difference to Liberal voters in B.C. (and there were a lot of them), left to wonder why they are being governed by the province's second most popular party. And it will certainly make a difference to Albertans during the next four years, with an opposition so small that it will be hard-pressed to provide the critical review that holds a government accountable between elections.

But these provincial examples pale to insignificance compared with the way the electoral system has let us down at the federal level, and may well let us down again. In the House of Commons the Progressive Conservative Party was annihilated, reduced to an embarrassing two members—but in fact the Conservatives received more votes (16 per cent) than the Bloc Québécois (13.5 per cent), and almost as many as the Reform Party (18.7 per cent). Thanks to our electoral system, the Official Opposition in the national Parliament is not the second most popular party in the country in the most recent election, or even the third, but the fourth.

The next federal election may do little more than reverse the relative position in the popular vote of Reform and the Conservatives, while leaving the Bloc firmly in fourth place but still the Official Opposition. Meanwhile, the Liberals stand poised to repeat their landslide win of 1993, which was accomplished with barely 40 per cent of the popular vote.

Yet that is considerably less than the vote share in Alberta that has created such a pathetically small opposition. Sometimes 40 per cent of the popular vote means a solid election win; sometimes it means crushing humiliation and near annihilation. What a curious way to translate the votes of citizens into representatives in the legislature in the elections that are the core of what we mean by democracy. Isn't there a better way?

AS it turns out, there is. Most democratic countries use some form of proportional representation (PR), which means that a party with 40 per cent of the votes gets 40 per cent of the seats. In a province such as Alberta, PR could be easily implemented. Instead of 83 single-member ridings, imagine seven multi-member ridings: Northern Alberta, Central Alberta, Southern Alberta and then two ridings in each of Edmonton and Calgary, using the major river that conveniently divides each city. These seven ridings would each have about 12 members—most of whom would have been Conservatives based on this week's results, but with a solid number of Liberals, a scattering of New Democrats and even a Socred or two.

Debates in the legislature between elections would resemble the campaign that is waged just before elections: a diversity of voices represented proportionately to their popular support, and contributing to the democratic debate that sets public policy. And those tens of thousands of voters from Central Alberta and Southern Alberta and Calgary who voted for an opposition party would have someone from their own part of the province, rather than some MLA from Edmonton, to voice their concerns.

The first consequence of a genuine proportional-representation system would be that most of the majority governments in Canada would become minority governments—and that, say the opponents of PR, would be a calamity beyond description.

But this is a curious argument. The most important function of an electoral system, these people seem to be saying, is to protect majority governments from the voting preferences of the very people they claim to represent. And we as voters suddenly demonstrate a truly bizarre paralysis of imagination. Between elections, we complain about our system as four years of an "elected dictatorship" when the prime minister can do whatever he pleases so long as his party holds together. But during elections we tremble in fear of a minority government, which would mean that our votes had failed to elect a strong new dictator with enough seats in Parliament to ignore us until the next election.

The price of this lack of imagination is an electoral system that gave 49 per cent of Albertans only 24 per cent of the seats, that put the second most popular party in power in B.C., and that gives the country's fourth most popular party the primary responsibility for criticizing the national government and proposing alternatives.

Surely we can do better.

David Elton is president of the Canada West Foundation in Calgary. Peter McCormick is professor of political science at the University of Lethbridge.

Counting the votes so all votes count

A STRANGE democracy, this. On June 2, the Liberal Party of Canada translated 38 per cent of the popular vote into a majority in the House of Commons. The Bloc Québécois, capturing 11 per cent of the vote, was awarded 15 per cent of the seats. The Progressive Conservative Party, with nearly twice as many supporters, received less than half as many seats.

In the Canadian parliamentary system, votes are tallied riding by riding, and a single seat is assigned in a winner-take-all, first-past-the-post count. The system tends to produce majority governments, a result that has its virtues because majorities mean certainty and stability. But that stability is bought at a price: a devaluing of many votes, an exclusion of many voices, perhaps even a warped view of the country.

So, for example, while Alberta is painted Reform Party green on the electoral map, 45 per cent of Albertans cast their vote for a party other than Reform. Thanks to first past the post, those 45 per cent were rewarded with exactly 2 seats. Reform, with 55 per cent of the vote, gets 24 seats. Because of first past the post,

the mistaken impression is left that Reform is not just the strongest party in Alberta, but the only party. Who speaks for the 45 per cent of Albertans who didn't vote Reform?

Or look at Nova Scotia, where the Liberals were wiped clean off the map. Wiped off the map, yet nearly one in three Nova Scotians voted Liberal. In Ontario, which gave the Liberals their majority by awarding them 101 out of 103 seats, the Liberal share of the popular vote was below 50 per cent. More Ontarians voted against the Liberals than voted for them. You will not, mind you, see that result represented in Parliament. Reform and the Tories each won the support of nearly 20 per cent of Ontarians, support that translated into exactly one seat.

There is another way of, as it were, putting political behinds into parliamentary chairs. Proportional representation, assigning voices in the legislature based on shares of the popular vote, is used in many countries. Some say it fosters quarreling minorities, instability, even chaos. Just look at Italy or Israel, say the detractors. Defenders can point to

more successful examples: long-time practitioners such as Germany, and recent converts Japan and New Zealand.

The chart below gives you a sense of what Parliament would look like if the votes Canadians cast on June 2 had been counted using one of four possible proportional representation systems. First off, there's pure PR: three-hundred and one seats in the House of Commons, with one-third of one per cent of the national vote equalling one seat. Count the votes up that way and the Liberals fall from 155 to 116 seats, and lose their majority. The Tories nearly triple their seats, the NDP's numbers rise, Reform remains stable and the Bloc's seat count falls. Notice also that three small parties doomed to perpetual exile under first past the post—the Greens, Christian Heritage and Natural Law—also get a voice.

The Israeli system is essentially pure PR, but with a proviso that only parties clearing a hurdle or more than 1.5 per cent of the vote are awarded seats. (The Germans employ a somewhat more complex system with a higher hurdle of 5 per

What if Canada had proportional representation?
Four alternatives to the current system.

	1997 ELECTION, PERCENTAGE OF POPULAR VOTE	FIRST PAST THE POST	PURE PROPORTIONAL REPRESENTATION	ISRAELI SYSTEM	JAPANESE 2-VOTE SYSTEM	THE GLOBE "ADD 60" PROPOSAL
Liberal	38.36	155	116	117	139	178
Reform	19.34	60	59	59	60	72
BQ	10.73	44	33	33	38	51
NDP	11.04	21	33	34	28	28
PC	18.88	20	57	58	35	31
Green	0.42	0	1	0	0	0
Natural Law	0.29	0	1	0	0	0
Christian Heritage	0.23	0	1	0	0	0
Independent (John Nunziata)	0.13	1	0	0	1	1
TOTAL		301	301	301	301	361

Pure proportional representation: seats allocated as a percentage of the national popular vote.

Israeli system: a modified version of pure proportional representation, in which parties must clear a hurdle of 1.5% of the votes cast to be entitled to a seat.

Japanese 2-vote system: 60% of MPs elected in traditional ridings by first past the post; 40% elected according to province-by-province proportional representation.

The Globe's "add 60" proposal: Add 60 seats to the current Parliament, to be allocated among the parties according to proportional representation.

cent.) The smallest parties lose out because of the hurdle, but then again, the existence of PR might boost their support. For example, almost nobody in Quebec—2 per cent of voters in 1997—votes NDP, because it's a wasted vote. But what if an NDP vote in Quebec could translate into an NDP seat? What if the sum of Green votes could add up to a Green seat? PR changes the nature and in some cases the need for strategic voting.

Then there's the Japanese system: Citizens have two votes, with 60 per cent of the members of the legislature elected riding-by-riding according to first past the post, and 40 per cent elected according to province-by-province PR. This system retains the virtues of local representation that are lost in pure PR, because there would still be a member elected solely by the people of Pierrefonds-Dollard or Esquimalt-Juan de Fuca. But at the same time, two out of every five seats in the Commons would represent all of a province's voters.

Finally, there is a proposal this newspaper floated some months ago: Retain the current 301 ridings, but add to the Commons another 60 members elected by all Canadians according to proportional representation. The idea isn't carved in stone, but it has its virtues. It retains local representation and only slightly dilutes the first-past-the-post tendency toward majorities. At the same time, it allows for more votes to count and more voices to be heard. The regions get 301 seats, but 60 seats are reserved for Canadians voting not as Calgarians or as Albertans, but as Canadians.

Of course, even under the "add 60" proposal, the Liberals lose their majority. Then again, maybe a minority government is all 38 per cent of the vote deserves.

Elections bring polls and the question: Can the numbers lie?

*They are 'remarkably' accurate in Canada, one pollster says,
but there are three ways they can go wrong.*

BY KAREN UNLAND

Quebec Bureau
Montreal

IF you listen closely, you can hear it: the sound of fingers approaching telephone keypads, interviewers clearing their throats, calculators preparing to crunch numbers.

It is the sound of the great Canadian polling machine revving up for the next federal election.

Although Prime Minister Jean Chrétien has yet to make it official, Ottawa's soothsayers have read all the signs and are predicting a June 2 election. So it won't be long before a steady stream of numbers begins to dominate front pages and news broadcasts as pollsters set about telling politicians and the media what you think.

Political strategists and journalists will take these numbers seriously. They may be fond of quoting John Diefenbaker's declaration that polls are for dogs, but they would not spend thousands of dollars on each one if they did not consider the information useful.

But how seriously should voters take the polls that are about to bombard them? After all, they had John Major's Conservatives trailing badly in the 1992 British election, and he wound up with a majority government.

"Generally, the polls in this country have been remarkably accurate," said Michael Adams, president of Environics Research Group in Toronto. "Fortunately, we haven't faced the same embarrassment that British pollsters had in the last election."

This is not to say that Canadians are immune to bad polls. Maybe numbers don't lie, but pollsters can make mistakes, said Linda Dyer, president of Baseline Market Research in Fredericton.

"When polls are wrong, there's something wrong with the way the poll was done," she said.

There are at least three ways that a poll can go wrong: sampling errors, mistakes in question design and interpretation problems.

Sampling is the heart of the science of polling. The idea, based on probability theory, is that you can determine the opinions of a large group by surveying the opinions of a smaller, randomly selected sample and be accurate within certain parameters.

To advise you of the poll's accuracy, reports will include a cryptic statement following the sample size: "The poll has a margin of error of 3.1, 19 times out of 20," for example. This is the pollsters' way of saying that if you surveyed all eligible voters, you could expect the results to be 3.1 percentage points higher or lower than the poll results, 95 per cent of the time.

If the sample is too small, the margin of error will increase to the point that the survey is meaningless.

Few national polls in this election season will have inadequate samples and high margins of error. Even regionally, most national polls do all right.

But when it comes to interpreting national results at the provincial level, watch out. Most national polls will not have surveyed enough people in any one province, especially in the smaller ones, to determine public opinion with reasonable accuracy.

"We would not want to speak with much confidence about what people in Prince Edward Island think, because you may only have talked to 40 people in Prince Edward Island," Mr. Adams said.

FOR an indication of how people in the smaller provinces plan to vote, look to regional polls that have a healthy sample size rather than to the national surveys.

Another key to avoiding sampling error is ensuring that the sample is as random as possible.

"Sampling theory requires pure random samples," said Conrad Winn, chief executive of COMPAS in Ottawa. However, he added, "I don't know of any poll that uses pure random samples" because many people are unwilling or unable to respond when pollsters call.

Mr. Adams said telephone surveys are becoming harder to rely on to get a random sample, too. The sample can be skewed because some people are less likely to be home or are more likely to screen their calls.

A good poll will have a proper callback design to try to catch some of those people, said Gary Edwards, research director for Gallup Canada in Toronto. That's why overnight polls aren't quite as reliable as the ones that take a week to do, he said.

That brings us to the second major pitfall of polling: how the survey is designed.

Here we get into the art of polling, and the art is more fraught with danger than the science is, said Prof. Winn, who also teaches political science at Carleton University.

"Most error is not sampling error," he said. "Most error is design error."

The way a question is phrased affects how people respond.

For example, Jean-Marc Léger of Groupe Léger & Léger in Montreal said he doesn't include the names of leaders in questions gauging party support in Quebec "because too many people hate Jean Chrétien . . . and too many people like Jean Charest."

It is also important to list the parties in a question about party preference, said Claude Gauthier, research director for CROP, another Montreal-based polling company. Without that, "some people who are not very familiar with the parties will say, 'Well, I don't know the names of the parties,' " leading to a low rate of response or a high rate of undecideds.

Then there is the honesty question. While Mr. Adams feels that "only very few people would actually be perverse enough to lie to a pollster," Prof. Winn said it is quite common for people to fib to make a good impression.

This is especially common for questions about the issues people think are important; the respondent may not want to acknowledge being in favour of tax cuts, for example, for fear of sounding greedy to the stranger on the phone.

Alternatively, people may be honest at the time of the survey and later change their minds. That's why a careful interpretation of the poll results is crucial.

Pollsters insist polls are not predictions but indications of public opinion at the time of the survey. If a party commits a major gaffe between the time a poll is conducted and its results are reported, all bets are off.

"In politics, a day can be a century," Mr. Edwards said. "Whenever you look at a poll result, realize that it's a snapshot."

MR. Gauthier noted a poll done during the 1993 federal campaign in Saint-Maurice, Mr. Chrétien's riding. "It was quite obvious that if people voted the way they would like to vote, Mr. Chrétien would not be elected."

But the numbers don't necessarily tell the whole story. The poll prompted Liberals to fire up their engines and remind voters of the prestige of having the Prime Minister for an MP.

After winning the riding, Mr. Chrétien brandished the poll results that had had him losing—much as Harry Truman waved the "Dewey Wins!" headline after his surprise U.S. presidential victory.

"So we have to be very humble in our profession," Mr. Gauthier said.

If polls have this many pitfalls, maybe we shouldn't pay much attention to them at all. But pollsters maintain that their work still offers a reliable picture of public opinion, especially if we note the trends rather than any single poll.

It also can be argued that polls make election coverage less susceptible to manipulation. Before the news media sponsored their own polls, political parties selectively used to release the results of their own surveys, with no way to check sample size, question design and interpretation.

Without polls, Carleton journalism professor Alan Frizzell said, election coverage is limited to reporters' impressions based on a few interviews and personal observations. Voters benefit from both traditional reporting and polling, he said.

"Polls are an extension of normal reporting: They just ask more people and choose their sample in a more scientific way. In that way they're useful," he said.

But what if polls go beyond providing information and start to influence the vote? The jury is still out on whether polls can have a bandwagon effect or in some other way cause voters to change their minds. Just in case that is possible, it is illegal to publish poll results 72 hours before an election for fear that an inaccurate poll at that time would go unrefuted, thus misleading voters and possibly affecting the way they cast their ballots.

Pollsters and analysts tend to believe that voters don't pay as much attention to polls as journalists and politicians think they do, and so are unlikely to be swayed.

"Do [polls] have an influence? No, they don't," Prof. Frizzell said. "Could they have an influence? . . . What one might argue is that polling data may be more important in this election than in most elections, and the reason for this is the strategic vote."

That's when voters weigh their options based on information from polls and vote for the person most likely to defeat what they consider to be an undesirable candidate.

VOTERS

The fickle finger of folk

*By the end of the campaign, the Liberals had lost ground, Reform
had made gains and the other parties ended up where they were when
the campaign began. What happened in between? Were there distinct phases
to the campaign? And did any particular events have an impact?*

BY ANDRÉ BLAIS, ELISABETH GIDENGIL, RICHARD NADEAU AND NEIL NEVITTE

Special to The Globe and Mail
Toronto and Montreal

VOTERS took candidates on a rollercoaster ride during the 36-day federal-election campaign. A surge by the Conservatives parallelled a Liberal slump, followed by a Liberal recovery coupled with a surge by Reform. How did this happen and what explains the shifts?

For the past five months, we four professors of political science—one at the University of Toronto, two at the *Université de Montréal* and one at McGill University—have teamed up to study the 1997 Canadian election. Funded by the Social Sciences and Humanities Research Council of Canada, what came to be known as the Canadian Election Study sought to detect and understand how and why voters change their minds during campaigns. (This was the third one in a project that began with the 1988 election; a British Election Study adopted the Canadian methodology in the recent election.)

Political parties spend millions of dollars trying to get elected, and more than 12 million Canadians went to the polls this time out. The critical issue: How do people make decisions that ultimately affect all of our lives? Why do citizens accept some political messages and reject others?

This is the only Canadian survey that undertook daily tracking throughout the entire campaign. Each day a random sample of about 110 people across the country were interviewed. The interviews were 35 minutes long, during which respondents were asked 120 questions: How they related to political parties, what media they'd been exposed to, their attitudes to social programs and such issues as Quebec, the distribution of wealth, women, aboriginals, taxes, unemployment, the deficit, the trustworthiness of politicians—the whole shooting match.

Such surveys are the best way to get a fix on how voter preferences change. Even though our daily sample wasn't all that large, we reduced error by looking at "moving averages"—adding together the results of successive days. Analyzing what goes on behind these moving averages is a complicated business, and it is far too early (and risky) to draw firm conclusions. Still, the preliminary indications are that there was significant movement in how Canadians intended to vote.

By the end of the campaign, the Liberals had lost ground, Reform had made gains and the other parties ended up where they were when the campaign began. What happened in between? Were there distinct phases to the campaign? And did any particular events have an impact?

One graph shows how voter allegiance shifted during the campaign. Nothing much happened as the parties played their opening gambits, except for a little slippage in Liberal support. Then came the televised debates, clearly won by Conservative Leader Jean Charest. His party was rewarded with impressive gains in support, distancing it from Reform, transforming the campaign in Quebec into a three-way race and almost reducing the Liberal lead to single digits. But this surge in support was short-lived. The Conservatives' 10-point lead over Reform vanished and the Liberals recovered some of the ground they had lost at the height of the Charest Effect.

Was the erosion of the Conservative party's gains the result of Reform's hard-hitting television advertisement depicting Quebeckers

Charest, Prime Minister Jean Chrétien, along with Bloc Québécois leaders Gilles Duceppe and Lucien Bouchard, as threats to Canadian unity?

The ad attracted wide media coverage and was grist for much moral outrage. But did it have any impact on voters? Our results suggest not. As the graph shows, much of the Reform gain at the Conservatives' expense took place before the ad was aired. It may have cemented that support, but it could also have forestalled further gains. Support for Reform hovered just below 20 per cent for the rest of the campaign, level-pegged with the Conservatives. The bottom line is this: The campaign may have been shorter than other election campaigns, but it was still too long for Jean Charest.

The Bloc is down—but not out

As in 1993, the main determinant of how Quebeckers voted was opinion on sovereignty. The challenge for the Bloc Québécois was to convince sovereignists to continue to support the party. On this score, it was partly successful: Three-quarters of sovereignists said they would be voting for the Bloc. Leadership seems to have been a key factor in inducing defections: Former sovereignist voters who were switching to the Conservatives gave Mr. Charest a much higher approval rating on average (67 on a 100-point scale) than Mr. Duceppe (38).

The Bloc may be down but it's hardly out. True, it lost nearly one-quarter of its 1993 support, but that's only half the story.

It retains a majority of seats in Quebec, and the potential for a sovereignist party in Ottawa remains impressive. In our survey, 44 per cent of Quebeckers favour sovereignty (47 per cent are opposed and 9 per cent are undecided) and 64 per cent believe that the Bloc is the party that best defends the interests of Quebec.

So the big question is: Will the sovereignist voters who supported Mr. Charest return to the Bloc fold in a campaign conducted by a leader more charismatic than Mr. Duceppe?

There is little comfort for Quebec federalists on two counts: the emergence of Reform as the Official Opposition and the fact that support for granting Quebec distinct-society status is very limp in the rest of Canada (34 per cent).

Voters adrift

How loyal are voters? Not very. People's attachment to political parties has been weakening in recent years and voters are increasingly tempted too scan the horizon for alternatives. These trends make for a lot of volatility but they're not unique to Canada.

Party strategists know only too well that crafting a winning appeal is a juggling act. They have to attract new voters while keeping their long-time supporters in the fold. When it comes to retaining core support: Reform was clearly the most successful. Over the course of the campaign, only 17 per cent of 1993 Reform voters said they intended to defect to another party. Defection rates for the New Democratic Party and the Conservatives were twice as high.

Where did the "defectors" plan to go? More 1993 Liberals went to the Conservatives than anywhere else. Tory defectors divided evenly; half went to the Liberals and half said they'd go to Reform. Most Bloc defectors went to the Conservatives, and where Reform did lose support it too went to the PCs.

There are regional wrinkles, of course. In Ontario, more than one in five of those voting Reform in 1993 switched to the Tories. The tables were turned in the West, with more than one in four 1993 Tories going over to Reform, along with one in five Liberals. And in Atlantic Canada, almost two-fifths of 1993 Liberal voters switched to the Conservatives or the NDP. Most in-

triguing, perhaps, is the distribution of the "new" vote—those who didn't vote in 1993. Nearly half of all the new voters said they'd vote Liberal on June 2.

Pushing the wrong buttons?

Opposition parties may simply have targeted the wrong issues. Mr. Charest campaigned on tax cuts and Preston Manning on national unity, but neither issue was voters' top priority. Tax cuts ranked last out of seven issues in terms of importance to voters; national unity ranked only sixth. Barely 30 per cent of voters were able to tell us which party (the Conservatives) was promising to cut personal income tax by 10 per cent. And despite the parties' best efforts, neither of the issues moved. They

Sometimes perceptions run headlong into the facts. Three out of five Canadians think that crime has gone up 'over the last few years.' According to statistics, crime has actually gone down. Nearly two of five say unemployment has gone up since the Liberals came to power in 1993. It may feel that way, but the fact is that the unemployment rate actually went down.

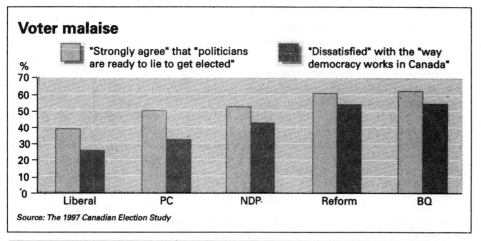

Voter malaise

☐ "Strongly agree" that "politicians are ready to lie to get elected"   ■ "Dissatisfied" with the "way democracy works in Canada"

Source: The 1997 Canadian Election Study

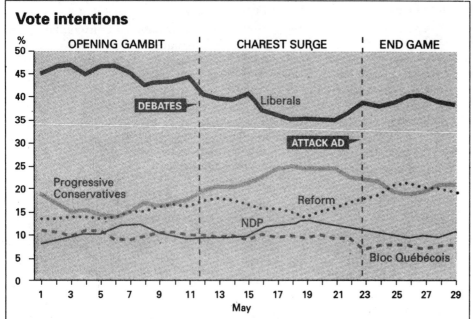

Vote intentions

OPENING GAMBIT   CHAREST SURGE   END GAME

DEBATES

Liberals

ATTACK AD

Progressive Conservatives

Reform

NDP

Bloc Québécois

May

Note: Respondents were asked 'Which party do you think you will vote for?' and given the choice of Conservatives, Liberals, New Democrats, Reform (outside Quebec), Bloc Québécois or another party.' The follow-up question for those who didn't know (the 'leaners') was, 'Which party are you leaning towards now?' Those who said they were certain they would not vote were excluded from the data.

Source: The 1997 Canadian Election Study

simply did not become more important to voters during the course of the campaign. Most striking, perhaps, is that national unity was never a top priority for voters even after Reform's attack ad was televised.

Jobs and keeping election promises mattered most, and voters gave the Liberals a failing grade on both. Two out of three said the Liberals had not done a very good job of creating jobs or keeping promises. To be sure, the party looked better on national unity but this wasn't a high priority anywhere. In a way, the more intriguing question is: Why didn't the Liberals fare worse? The

short answer is that voters had even less confidence in the other parties. When asked which party would be the best at handling these issues, the Liberals came out on top.

This was even true for the NDP on the issue that most preoccupied voters. The party was certainly in tune with the great majority of voters on unemployment. The problem was that voters didn't see it as the "best party" for creating jobs. It simply lacked visibility on the issue. For instance, only one voter in 10 could identify the NDP as the one promising to cut unemployment in half by the year 2001. The party's success in

the Atlantic provinces— where job creation dominated the voters' agenda—suggests that the jobs issue and visibility would have been a potentially heady mix.

A general malaise

There is no telling when cranky voters will seize upon an election as a chance to vent frustration. Certainly, the Liberals had some reason to worry. The Prime Minister's explanation for the early election call was not convincing. Cynics might construe the early call as raw political opportunism. The GST and "broken promises" theme also stalked the Liberals.

Like many other surveys, our research indicates that Canadians are irritated with the political class. Half the people interviewed strongly agree with the notion that "politicians are ready to lie to get elected." Politician bashing is widespread and fashionable. Perhaps that's why Canadian voters stayed away from the polls in droves—one third of them elected not to exercise their franchise.

Accentuating the negative may be popular, but there is evidence of a deeper political malaise. Four out of every five Canadians believe that members of Parliament soon "lose touch" with the people. One-third think that political parties "hardly ever" keep their election promises. And two out of five are not satisfied with "the way democracy works in Canada."

Troubling stuff. Also troubling is that these views have a partisan/regional spin, as the Voter Malaise chart shows. Not surprisingly, Ontarians, and hence Liberals, turn out to be the least dissatisfied. Reform and the Bloc provide homes for the deeply discontented.

Perceptions and reality

The unhappiness seems contagious and it colours everything. Perceptions matter not least during election campaigns. But sometimes perceptions run headlong into "the facts." For instance, three out of five Canadians think that crime has gone up "over the last few years." According to nearly all official statistics, crime has actually gone down. Nearly two of five say unemployment has gone up since the Liberals came to power in 1993. It may feel that way, but the fact is that the unemployment rate actually went down, and the number of unemployed did not change.

So why are perceptions so negative? It could be that people are simply in a funk. Or politicians may have done a poor job of advertising their accomplishments. All is not lost, though.

There are signs that Canadians have not given up completely on politicians or governments. Seventy per cent of Canadians believe that governments can do something to solve the unemployment problem. And almost 60 per cent think the government should be involved in job creation. That's something.

So why did the Liberals win?

Despite the discontent and despite the fact that 30 per cent of voters say their financial situation has worsened over the past year, everyone knew the Liberals would win. How did they manage this?

One possibility is that the party succeeded in staking out the middle ground. When asked about the tough choice between cutting taxes and improving social programs, 58 per cent of voters basically wanted to keep things on the course charted by the Liberals: Canadians are not willing to pay higher taxes to improve social programs but neither are they adamant about having tax reductions either.

Another possibility is that the Liberals succeeded in convincing enough voters of their argument that economic recovery required sacrifices, and that better times are just around the corner. One in three Canadians expect the economy to improve over the next 12 months—and fewer than one in 10 expect a decline. This guarded optimism must have loomed large in the Liberals' re-election. Voters were disenchanted, but they were also hopeful enough to give the Liberal government a second try.

The preliminary indications are that campaigns matter a lot. In 36 days, the Liberals almost lost their majority and Reform succeeded in wresting the Official Opposition status from the Bloc.

Our job now is to unpack the evidence and sift through an array of possible explanations, and pin down precisely what factors produced the intriguing shifts in voter preferences.

The 1997 Canadian Election Study team consists of André Blais of Université de Montréal, Elisabeth Gidengil of McGill University, Richard Nadeau of Université de Montréal and Neil Nevitte of the University of Toronto. The study is funded by the Social Sciences and Humanities Research Council of Canada. The fieldwork for the survey was conducted by the Institute for Social Research at York University. Research assistance was provided by Christophyer Kam and Martin Turcotte at the Université de Montréal. Interviewing started the day the election was called and continued until the last day of the campaign. A total of 3,922 eligible voters were interviewed. The average daily sample size was 110 respondents and the response rate was 60 per cent. The margin of error for the seven-day moving averages is 4 per cent.

Distinct Societies

The election leaves the nation splintered as never before

BY ANTHONY WILSON-SMITH

On the last day of what may have been Jean Chrétien's final election campaign, the Prime Minister went back to the place where his life and his political career both began. As he did in the 1993 election, Chrétien returned to Quebec's St-Maurice riding, where he was born in 1934, and where he first won election in 1963. Dressed in a dark suit and tie, he cast his ballot early at Ecole Ste-Marie on 33rd Street in the tiny village of Ste-Flore-de-Grand-Mère. Later, he retreated to his cottage at Lac des Piles to watch the results with his family. As in 1993, Chrétien appeared buoyant and said he was "confident." But again, there was cause for worry. In the last election, the Liberals appeared headed for a majority government—but feared that Chrétien might lose his own seat. This time, the reverse was true: Chrétien seemed likely to win his seat, but his advisers feared that the Liberals might not meet their goal of a second majority government. "It was not," sighed a dismayed adviser on election day, "supposed to be like this."

In the end, it was close on both counts. Chrétien won his riding—but after a surprisingly tough race. Nationally, the Liberals awaited a last-minute reprieve and got one—but only after a nail-biting election night. Shortly after the polls closed in Atlantic Canada, it looked as though their worst fears were about to be realized. In those four provinces, where the party won 31 of 32 seats last time out, the Liberals were reduced to 11 seats—and lost two cabinet ministers in the process. The losses continued across much of the country as Canadians voted in an election that has left the nation splintered as never before—even as it faces the likelihood of another Quebec referendum. A wild card in the inevitable unity battle to come will be Reform party Leader Preston Manning, whose tough stance against Quebec demands for a form of special constitutional status won strong support in the West—and equally strong antipathy in Quebec. His new status as official Opposition leader will further highlight tensions between Canada's regions.

For all the problems that lie ahead, Chrétien did succeed in his goal of becoming the first Liberal leader since Louis Saint-Laurent in the 1950s to win back-to-back majority governments. Even Chrétien's longtime leader, Pierre Trudeau, was never able to achieve that. But given the Liberals' close brush with minority status, Chrétien was reduced to putting the best face on a hollow victory. "I promise to do my best, and lead a government of integrity," he said in his victory speech. "This evening, the Canadian people have renewed their confidence in our team and in our program. I accept this honor." At the end of the night, the results in the next 301-seat House of Commons were Liberals, 155 seats; Reform, 60; Bloc Québécois, 44; New Democrats, 21: Progressive Conservatives, 20 Independents, 1.

On a superficial level, the new Liberal government will look and sound the same as its predecessor. But for the first time in Canada's history, the House of Commons will have five official parties—all with more than the 12 seats needed for formal recognition. That is more than just a mathematical curiosity: it reflects the political realities of a fractured country. Once again, the Liberals won seats in all of Canada's regions. But roughly two-thirds of their support comes from Ontario, where they won 101 seats, a fact that is certain to stir resentment about the province's inordinate influence over the rest of the country. And an unexpected savior for the party was Quebec, where the total of 26 seats was more than even the most optimistic Liberals expected.

Reform, which dominated the final two weeks of the campaign with its tough talk about the potential consequences of Quebec separation, swept past the Bloc Québécois to gain Opposition status. Manning, in a generally gracious speech, nonetheless called the result "a warning to the Liberal party." And, he said, Reform's rise was proof that "the old political landscape is changing." Still, Manning's delight at that achievement was muted by the fact that, again, his party failed to make

From *Maclean's* magazine, June 9, 1997, pp. 16-20. © 1997 by Maclean Hunter, Ltd. Reprinted by permission.

inroads in Central and Eastern Canada: almost all of his members will come from Alberta and British Columbia. In 1993, the party won one seat in Ontario; this time, it was shut out completely.

At Reform's election night headquarters in downtown Calgary, there was an air of expectation as results started rolling in. While a musician played softly on a grand piano in the lobby of the Metropolitan Centre, Reformers clinked glasses as they prepared to celebrate an expected breakthrough in Ontario. Buoyed by early reports that the Liberals were being battered in Atlantic Canada, the crowd of about 500 fell silent as Ontario returns showed Liberal support holding. Reform strategist Ron Wood could not hide his disappointment with Canada's most populous province, but also admitted he was not surprised. "You've got people in Ontario who have voted Liberal all their lives, including my aunt who's 97," said Wood. "They'd have to be struck by lightning to vote anything else."

The lack of an Ontario breakthrough, said University of Alberta political scientist Larry Pratt, suggested that Reform is destined to remain a western-based movement, similar to the Social Credit party of the 1950s and early 1960s. "Reform might have done better in Ontario had it moderated its attacks on Quebec," said Pratt. "But it also has to preserve its Alberta base, and that's the problem it faces."

Among the other three party leaders, the happiest is likely to be Alexa McDonough, who led the NDP to an unprecedented breakthrough in the Atlantic provinces—where it won eight seats. On election night, a casual observer at Halifax's historic Lord Nelson Hotel might have thought that it was the New Democratic Party, not the deeply wounded Liberals, who were about to form the next government. Bounding to the stage in the hotel's main ballroom as a standing-room-only crowd of supporters cheered and clapped deliriously, McDonough declared: "Tonight is about making history. And the next four years will be about making a difference."

Her own race in the riding of Halifax was supposed to be a tightly fought three-way contest between McDonough, Liberal incumbent Mary Clancy and popular provincial Tory Terry Donahoe. But McDonough won easily—and her party exceeded its wildest expectations, winning seven other seats in Nova Scotia and New Brunswick.

Another leader who revived a party from the near-dead—with only two seats in the last Parliament—was the Tories' Jean Charest. Now, the Conservatives have a solid base in Eastern Canada, and Charest's personal popularity in Quebec gives the party hopes for future inroads in that province—and makes him a key

player in a future referendum. But the party faces some formidable difficulties. Its brightest hope after Charest—retired Maj.-Gen. Lewis MacKenzie—was defeated in his first bid for elected office in the Ontario riding of Parry Sound/Muskoka. And the Tories have virtually ceased to exist west of Manitoba, failing to win any seats in their onetime strongholds of British Columbia and Alberta. In fact, despite the upbeat tone that Charest adopted in his election night speech, some Tories privately fear that he may not wish to stay on and face the disconcerting prospect of spending another four years rebuilding the party.

The Tories' most serious problems concern fund-raising—and some party strategists suggest that their showing could mean financial ruin. Insiders told *Maclean's* that the Conservatives were already about $2 million to $3 million dollars in debt when the election was called. But that debt was balanced, and secured, by a trust fund that would have comfortably settled it. Enthused by their prospects, and buoyed by Charest's favorable ratings from focus groups, the party decided to spend the full $11 million that Elections Canada allowed. Throughout the late winter and spring, in response to pleas from party bagmen, funds poured into Tory coffers.

As well, there were numerous pledges of hefty corporate and individual support. Insiders say that Tory fundraisers were getting almost as much money as the governing Liberals. But there was a catch: in many cases, the cheques were only *promised*. Delivery would come after the election. Insiders now fear that those cheques will never materialize. "It doesn't really matter what we want to do after the election," confessed one senior Tory. "We may have no choice. We may have to fold up our tent because we are bankrupt."

Meanwhile, for Bloc Leader Gilles Duceppe, the outlook is also bleak. Although the party rallied in the late stages of the campaign, he faced strong personal criticism—while the BQ campaign highlighted deep divisions in the sovereigntist movement. And the BQ lost the advantages that come with being the official Opposition—including extra funding and the right to ask the most questions during daily Question Period. That status was a major irritant to Canadians outside Quebec; in

CLOSE CALLS BY THE POLLSTERS

A comparison of the campaign's last four national opinion polls with the popular vote on election day:

	Angus Reid (May 24-27)	Strategic Counsel (May 25-27)	Gallup (May 25-28)	Environics (May 25-28)	ACTUAL
LIBERAL	36%	41%	41%	39%	38%
PC	24	19	22	20	19
Reform	19	18	16	19	19
NDP	11	11	11	11	11
Bloc	9	10	9	9	11

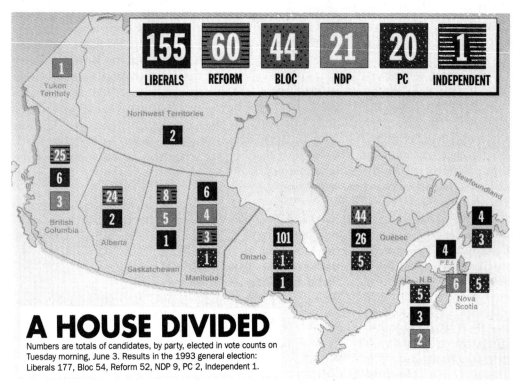

A HOUSE DIVIDED

Numbers are totals of candidates, by party, elected in vote counts on Tuesday morning, June 3. Results in the 1993 general election: Liberals 177, Bloc 54, Reform 52, NDP 9, PC 2, Independent 1.

For the most part, the impact of a revitalized opposition will not be felt until this fall, when the new Parliament convenes. But changes will become evident well before that. The first is the formation of Chrétien's cabinet, which will—by both necessity and desire—be quite different. Some familiar figures are nearly certain to be back in their previous portfolios, such as Finance Minister Paul Martin, Deputy Prime Minister Sheila Copps, and Foreign Affairs Minister Lloyd Axworthy. But in the previous cabinet, Chrétien's two strongest representatives from the four Atlantic provinces were Defence Minister Doug Young from New Brunswick, and Health Minister David Dingwall from Nova Scotia: both were unexpectedly defeated.

turn, when Bloc supporters saw Reform surpass their seat total on television at their Montreal election-night headquarters, they erupted into a furious chorus of boos.

Chrétien will likely move quickly to form his new cabinet—perhaps, some sources suggested, as early as

WHAT COMES NEXT?

The Liberals have had a bad fright. They have escaped with a very slight majority—but the voters are not content. Although it is clear that the Liberals must now pay new attention to their policies, their problem lies in *what* to do. They are caught in a dilemma: both wings of their party are angry with them. In the West, they lost many of their fiscally prudent, small-c conservative voters because their message was abysmally mixed. They were deficit fighters—but they announced plans for $6.5 billion in new spending before balancing the budget. They were national unity defenders—but they appeared to have no plan for Quebec. On the other side of the country, many of their seats slipped away because Atlantic Canadians were fed up with cuts to Employment Insurance and social programs—and exasperated by the introduction of the Harmonized Sales Tax. To add to the Liberals' woes, the new official Opposition, the Reform party, will scrutinize every announcement with renewed zealotry.

In such circumstances, the Liberals will likely be divided over just about everything. Many will want to spell out tough conditions for Quebec separation—while others will call for tactful silence. Many will opt to placate their more traditional base in Atlantic Canada with new spending, eroding their progress against the deficit—while others will hotly oppose those measures. For starters, the government will probably revive most of the 48 bills that died on the order paper when Prime Minister Jean Chrétien called the election. They include amendments to the Canada Labour Code to impose a partial ban on the hiring of replacement workers during strikes; constitutional changes allowing the replacement of Quebec's re-

ligious public schools with schools organized along linguistic lines; and an act to protect endangered species.

The Liberals will also attempt to keep most of their specific election promises (many were deliberately vague). They will cancel their own planned cuts of $5.4 billion over four years to the Canada Health and Social Transfer. They will allot $240 million for grants to students with dependants, $163 million for AIDS research, $28 million for breast cancer and $136 million to expand industrial research. But some promises may be swept under the carpet, such as $10 million for new works of art to celebrate the millennium—because they would simply act as red flags to Reform.

More important, voters should probably expect more spending announcements, especially for programs that benefit Atlantic Canada. The Liberals may grant a one-year extension beyond May, 1998, to The Atlantic Groundfish Strategy (TAGS), which provides generous benefits to unemployed fishermen. They will likely open discussions with the provinces to ensure that medicare eventually covers home care and perhaps pharmacare. They may increase the Child Tax Benefit, which is already slated to rise by $600 million to $6 billion in July, 1998. And they may channel more funds into infrastructure programs, apprenticeship programs, and research and development. In future, many Liberal MPs may simply want to throw money at job creation, ensuring that Ottawa no longer exceeds its deficit targets—and perhaps undermining the nation's financial health for the sake of their own electoral prospects.

MARY JANIGAN

this week. One reason is that the new government will have its work cut out for it. There is the looming likelihood of another Quebec election this fall—and if the Parti Québécois is re-elected, another referendum on sovereignty not long after that. At the same time, the debate over how to deal with Quebec, as well as several other key issues, has taken on a new edge with Reform's rise to official Opposition status. With the BQ in that position, much of the debate in the House of Commons was devoted to Quebec's alleged ill-treatment within Canada. And on other issues, such as health care and social programs, the Bloc usually adopted a left-of-centre stance.

Now, the tone in all of those areas is about to change dramatically. As the second-largest party in the new Parliament, Reform is about to ensure that Canadians hear much more about their wish for tougher stances on law-and-order issues, the need for further, deep reductions in government spending, and such radical proposals as privatization of the Canada Pension Plan. But the biggest change will be in the approach to Quebec. Reform revived its previously moribund campaign in the West when Manning began challenging Chrétien and Charest over their supposedly "soft" approach to Quebec sovereignty. Similarly, a controversial Reform television ad lumped the two leaders in with Duceppe and Quebec Premier Lucien Bouchard, and asked whether it was not time to have a prime minister from another province.

That tough approach is certain to be carried over into Parliament—and it will leave more than sovereigntists squirming. One likely example: polls show that a majority of Quebecers believe their province pays out more in tax dollars than it receives in return in services. If Chrétien tries to refute that claim by showing that Quebecers benefit from Confederation—as many studies suggest—Manning, in turn, is likely to seize on that as further proof that Quebec profits at the expense of other provinces.

That is one of the reasons why Liberal strategists were divided as to who they most wanted to see form the official Opposition. Shortly before election day, two senior Chrétien advisers discussed their opinions in an interview with *Maclean's*. One favored Reform because, that adviser said, "the Tories just hate them—and that makes a merger of the right-wing parties that much more unlikely in the near future." But the other adviser favored the Tories, citing fears that Manning will provoke many undecided Quebecers into supporting the Yes side in a future sovereignty referendum. "Every time he opened his mouth," said the adviser, "the Bloc jumped [in the polls] another couple of points."

But in the aftermath of a sharply divisive campaign, and with their own dramatically reduced majority, the Liberals may have little time to worry about the problems caused by other parties: they have enough of their own. For one, their razor-thin majority means they will have to enforce rigid discipline on their caucus to ensure that all MPs regularly attend votes.

VICTORS AND VANQUISHED

Once again, Canadians refused to hand out the darts and laurels quite as predicted. When the votes were counted, two prominent cabinet ministers lost their seats, while one party leader defied the pundits by winning her riding—and entry to the House of Commons—by a wide margin.

LOSERS:

David Dingwall A federal MP since 1980 and the Liberals' patronage godfather in Atlantic Canada, the minister of health lost Bras d'Or to NDP candidate Michelle Dockrill, a health-care worker.

Doug Young Voters in Acadie/Bathurst, a riding in northern New Brunswick, were clearly fed up with government cuts—and took out their anger on the combative defence minister. The NDP's Yvon Godin, a union activist who led protests against cuts to employment insurance, won by more than 2,600 ballots.

Dominic LeBlanc The son of Gov. Gen. Roméo LeBlanc lost to New Democrat Angela Vautour in the New Brunswick riding of Beauséjour/Petitcodiac.

Lewis MacKenzie Running for the Tories, the former celebrity peacekeeper was edged out by incumbent Liberal Andy Mitchell in the Ontario riding of Parry Sound/Muskoka.

Jan Brown A former moderate Reformer, Brown ran as Tory against Preston Manning in his home riding of Calgary Southwest but finished a poor third behind Liberal Paul Drager.

WINNERS:

Jean Chrétien The Prime Minister may be one of only seven Canadian leaders to win back-to-back majorities, but he barely scraped to victory in his own riding of St-Maurice. The Bloc's Yves Duhaime, a longtime political foe, trailed Chrétien by less than 1,000 votes.

Alexa McDonough The NDP leader ran away with the race in the riding of Halifax, scoring a first-time win for her party and blasting past Liberal incumbent Mary Clancy.

John Nunziata Kicked out of the Liberal caucus for demanding that the party keep its promise to scrap the GST, the Toronto MP retained the Toronto riding of York South/Weston as an Independent. Liberal Judy Sgro, appointed as a candidate by the Prime Minister, trailed Nunziata by about 4,000 votes.

Anne McLellan The Liberals' natural resources minister faced a tough challenge from Reform candidate Dean Kurpjuweit in Edmonton West, but squeaked through to retain her seat.

Gurmant Grewal Well-known local Reformer Gurmant Grewal won the new riding of Surrey Central, which has the largest concentration of Sikh voters in the country. In a contest against two other Sikh candidates running for the Liberals and the NDP, Grewal emphasized Reform's opposition to distinct society status for Quebec—evidence, he said, that his party stands for equality among Canadians.

Already, there are signs of strain within the party. The disappointing campaign, and the similarly dismaying result, seem likely to revive old divisions and provoke new ones. The most heated of those will be between supporters of Chrétien and Martin: although the two men's relations are generally cordial and respectful, the same is not true of their followers. Martin's supporters resented that, despite his high level of popularity, he was given a low-profile campaign role until the final weeks—when it became clear that all of the party's resources were needed. They also blamed John Rae, the longtime Chrétien friend, Montreal businessman and campaign cochairman, for a strategy they privately considered ineffectual, out of touch with voters' concerns and too Quebec-oriented.

On the other side, as the Liberals sank in the polls during the last 10 days of the campaign, confidantes of Chrétien began to mutter that Martin was responsible for the early election call. They said that he urged them to go to the polls because he had easily bested his deficit targets—and because interest rates might rise in the fall, slowing economic growth.

The other key factor in the equation is Quebec. Even as Chrétien takes credit for the No side's narrow win in 1995, and relishes the prospect of another scrap with sovereigntists, many other Liberals are much less enthusiastic about the prospect. They would vastly prefer the bilingual Martin, who regularly scores well in popularity polls in the province. As well: Chrétien's lacklustre performance in the campaign aroused fears that, at age 63 and 34 years after he was first elected, he has simply lost his fire for competition.

But of all the criticisms of Chrétien, that is the most unfounded: his competitive spirit in the final days seemed to burn as bright as ever. In fact, even as he was accepting congratulations on election night, Chrétien noted that "the Canadian people have given us a mandate for four years, and I intend to fulfill it." That message may have been aimed just as much at members of his own party as at those Canadians outside it. So often written off as "yesterday's man," Chrétien once again demonstrated that he continues, instead, to think more about where he will take the country tomorrow. His biggest challenge, in a deeply divided Canada, may be in ensuring that his party members are just as enthusiastic about that prospect.

With BRIAN BERGMAN in Halifax, BRENDA BRANSWELL in Sherbrooke, MARY JANIGAN in Toronto, DALE EISLER in Calgary and CHRIS WOOD in Vancouver

Sovereignty's Stumbling Bloc

On the face of it, it was the kind of campaign that federalists know too well: filled with mixed messages, missteps and public bickering over who should lead and what direction to take. In recent years, those who stand for a united Canada—in Quebec and across the rest of the country—have spent much of their time arguing with each other over the future form of the nation. But now, it was the sovereigntist side that appeared to be circling the wagons—and shooting inward. And the Bloc Québécois's 10 seat drop to 44 seats reflects the problems of a movement that is, at least temporarily, in disarray. "It is more clear than ever tonight that [constitutional] reconciliation between Canada and Quebec is impossible, and that sovereignty is inevitable," said Bloc Québécois Leader Gilles Duceppe, attempting to put the best face possible on his party's results.

Despite Duceppe's upbeat talk, the decline in the Bloc vote reflects Quebecers' disenchantment with the party since it shocked the nation by becoming the official Opposition in 1993. Even sovereigntists complained that, after Lucien Bouchard's departure in late 1995, the BQ lost its clear sense of direction. The party also fell short of the key target of 42-per-cent support that Bloc organizers privately set for themselves. That figure would have allowed the BQ to claim that it won the backing of at least half of francophone Quebec voters. "Below that," said Christian Bourque, the Montreal-based vice-president of the Angus Reid polling group, "you face a real crisis of direction in the party."

Among the questions already being raised: how long will the humorless, uncharismatic Duceppe stay on as leader? (In all probability, not very long.) How much of the movement away from the BQ was intended as a slap at Bouchard, and especially the stiff spending cuts his

The BQ lost more than its sense of direction

Parti Québécois government has imposed? (Quite a lot.) And how serious is the schism between those sovereigntists who favor a separate nation with few links to Canada—such as former premier Jacques Parizeau—and others, such as Bouchard, who want an economic and political "partnership"? (Very serious.)

Before the campaign began, strategists on all sides considered it likely that the BQ could come close to their 1993 total of 54 seats. But the final total might have been even lower had the federalist vote not split between the Liberals and Progressive Conservatives to the BQ's occasional advantage. The final showing will do little to ensure the political future of Duceppe, a onetime Marxist-Leninist whose caucus was split, often uneasily, between social democrats and small-c conservatives. Bouchard, who made his preference for Duceppe clear during the BQ's leadership race earlier this year, campaigned hard on his behalf, and stressed the importance of a strong BQ showing. Now, he must also share part of the blame.

On the other hand, sovereigntists can thank Parizeau for the fact that the BQ's final showing was not worse. The former PQ leader—no friend of Bouchard—turned a well-timed book tour into a one-man campaign for the Bloc. He attracted the largest and most enthusiastic crowds, and his presence doubtless resulted in thousands of BQ votes from disenchanted hardline sovereigntists who might otherwise have stayed home—or spoiled their ballots. If Duceppe steps down soon, it is not inconceivable that Parizeau—who toyed with the idea of running for the BQ leadership last year—might take a stab at replacing him.

In any event, the campaign both exposed and exacerbated divisions in the sovereigntist movement. The animosity between Parizeau and Bouchard is barely disguised; it springs, as much as anything, from deep ideological differences. "To say they are alike because they are sovereigntists," says one Quebec adviser to Jean Chrétien, "is like saying that the Prime Minister and Preston Manning are alike because they are both federalists." While Bouchard's ideal vision of a sovereign Quebec would include strong political and economic links to the rest of Canada, Parizeau's new nation would share the Canadian dollar—but little else. The campaign made clear that the two also disagree on the means of achieving that goal: Bouchard thinks Quebec should balance its books first, while Parizeau thinks that a sovereign Quebec would have an easier time balancing its budget because it would have all necessary monetary tools, such as tax policy, at its disposal—so government cuts should wait. "The trouble is," says one PQ backbencher, "both men make perfectly compelling arguments."

All of that should ease, but not dissipate, the worries of federalists. This fall, the Supreme Court of Canada is expected to rule on the federal government's challenge to Quebec's right to unilateral secession. If the judgment is in Ottawa's favor, as is considered likely, it would provide Bouchard with an ideal opportunity to call an election—one that polls suggest he should win easily. Moreover, the renewed strength of the Reform party comes as a comfort to many sovereigntists. "The reality," says pollster Bourque, "is that only about 25 per cent of English-Canadians support Reform." But the question, he adds, "is whether Quebecers will realize that—or presume them to be the authentic voice of the rest of the country." Already, the composition of the new House of Commons makes it clear that federalists and sovereigntists will once again be sparring vigorously—against each other, but also among themselves.

ANTHONY WILSON-SMITH

Unheeded Warnings

How the Liberals squandered their lead

BY MARY JANIGAN

A mere 10 days before last Monday's showdown, the Liberal high command was dangerously complacent, almost cocky. The election was viewed as a cakewalk to another term. Sure, there had been some slippage in British Columbia, Saskatchewan and Manitoba—but no one was overly concerned. Then, the bottom fell out of the campaign. Overnight, on Friday, May 23, the Liberals plummeted to the low 30s among decided voters in their own polls, sliding from potential majority to minority status. That drop, largely due to the party's declining fortunes in Atlantic Canada and the West, transformed the election into a nail-biting, hair-pulling cliff-hanger. And even though the Liberals squeaked through with a slim majority, the results left the party battered and bruised. "It was supposed to be a walk in the garden," said one rueful Liberal adviser. "That was wrong."

That may be the understatement of this intriguing campaign. Throughout the first 3½ weeks of the election, the Liberals were on automatic pilot because their support, although gradually slipping, was still comfortably high. But after that fateful Friday, Prime Minister Jean Chrétien and his rattled party found themselves in a new ball game. In desperation, they flung everything into a final 10-day pitch for support. They blanketed Vancouver and Edmonton with ads that denounced the Reform party's commitment to health care—in a bid to attract female voters who put higher emphasis on social programs. In Eastern and Central Canada, they concentrated their fire on Conservative Leader Jean Charest—because, to their horror, more voters, in every region, now believed he would make a better prime minister than Chrétien. In Atlantic Canada, they considered—but did not run—an unusual "contrition" ad that apologized for not providing full explanations of their economic plans. Instead, they ran ads vowing that spending cuts were over.

And they deployed the secret weapon they had been reserving, in case of emergency, from the start of the campaign: they invoked the memory of former prime minister Brian Mulroney. Day after day, cabinet ministers such as Deputy Prime Minister Sheila Copps, Liberal premiers such as Newfoundland's Brian Tobin, and Chrétien himself pointedly reminded voters that Charest had been a member of the highly unpopular Mulroney cabinet. "We had to blow up the bridge to Charest's credibility," says a senior Liberal. "It was our last card."

Through interviews with senior advisers from all parties, most of whom asked to remain anonymous, *Maclean's* has pieced together the campaign saga. It is a tale that will likely ensure that future governments think twice before they call an early election.

⋯

In retrospect, the Liberals were forewarned. Insiders say that, starting last December, party pollster Michael Marzolini, chairman of POLLARA, peppered the campaign strategy committee with closed-door presentations that recited the perils of an early election call. The Liberals had romped to victory in the Oct. 25, 1993, election—and, technically, did not have to go to the polls before the fall of 1998. The POLLARA warnings were stark. Go early, especially without a major issue, and the voters could rebel, asking why politicians were knocking on their doors when they had not produced the promised jobs. Wait, at least until the fall—and the voters might accept the argument that, even though there was more work to do on the economy, parliamentary tradition required an election. Campaign co-ordinator John Rae, campaign director Gordon Ashworth and Chrétien's principal secretary, Eddie Goldenberg, brushed aside those warnings. The economy was thriving; the government was well ahead of its deficit targets; interest rates might rise in the fall, slowing growth; the Liberals would secure their mandate before the Quebec election and referendum battles; and they were comfortably ahead in the polls. The momentum became unstoppable.

To the Liberals' dismay, their April 27 campaign kick-off became the first controversial event of the election. Chrétien seemed flat and unemotional as he read in a monotone from notes. He even stumbled over his explanation for the early call. Most of the nation appeared indifferent—but Manitobans, fighting rising floodwaters, were furious. Overnight, their opinion of Chrétien as a leader nosedived. And although the Liberals saturated the province with ads featuring their Manitoba team over the ensuing weeks, they never managed to recover.

It was an unimpressive start to two weeks of even more unimpressive Liberal campaigning. Strategists agree that the Liberals could not clearly define their so-called ballot question: what they wanted voters to ask themselves when they entered the polling booth. The Prime Minister was supposed to position himself as a prudent manager who needed a new mandate to proceed with job creation and the protection of social programs—in the face of Tory and Reform demands for a tax cut. But Chrétien muddied that message within days of the election call when he announced $6.5 billion in new spending. Insiders argued that he should never mention the deficit—because it meant little to Canadians' daily lives—unless he made the link between a balanced budget and job creation. But he rarely established that crucial connection.

As Chrétien proceeded placidly, almost half-heartedly, through his paces, Reform party Leader Preston Manning saw his chance. Last fall, to firm up his base in the West, Manning repeatedly visited party strongholds across the Prairies and in B.C. regions such as the Fraser Valley and the Okanagan. In January, he told his 49 MPs that they would have to take responsibility for keeping those seats, while his campaign would focus on winning another 50 targeted ridings: 20 in Western Canada, 25 in Ontario and a handful in the Atlantic provinces.

It was an astute move. Day after day, Manning moved across the country, pounding his Liberal and Tory opponents—and stressing how his platform differed from theirs. He secured copies of the Liberals' Red Book of policies before its release. "That allowed us to frame what their platform was about: 'Goodbye Red Book, Hello Chequebook,'" says Reform campaign director Rick Anderson. "It put them on the defensive." Reform support began to move up in British Columbia and Saskatchewan.

More important, Manning managed to overshadow his opponents. Between the Manitoba floods and the Bre-X Minerals Ltd. gold-mining scandal, there was little room for five parties on the news. In particular, coverage of Charest was often reduced to snippets of the leader announcing a policy tidbit from his platform. Eventually, Tory strategists realized that Charest himself should be front and centre, not his policies. They switched his daily events from factories or other sites meant to serve as backdrops to his policy announcements, to enthusiastic encounters with supporters. "We put our own campaign on ice," concedes a strategist. "We wanted voters to think about leadership for the future." That move also shifted attention away from the Tories' platform, which flung about numbers with reckless disregard for the basic laws

of addition—but which continued to hobble Charest throughout the campaign.

The only real movement prior to the May 12 and 13 televised leaders' debates occurred in Quebec, where Bloc Québécois Leader Gilles Duceppe began the campaign by stumbling from gaffe to gaffe. On April 29, at a cheese factory in Sorel, he sported a plastic hair net. Then, he made a near-fatal error: he fired a bus driver after he got lost en route to a campaign stop. Strategists now agree that *this* was the deed that was too much for Quebec voters: the bus driver was a real person, with family to support and bills to pay. Duceppe's standing plummeted.

⚜

The second stage of the campaign began when former Quebec premier Jacques Parizeau wandered—not so innocently—into the fray. In an excerpt from his new book (officially published on May 8), Parizeau hinted that he would have issued a unilateral declaration of independence if Quebecers had voted Yes in the October, 1995, referendum. Although the former premier subsequently backed away from this interpretation, the emotional issue of national unity was suddenly on the campaign table. And when the future of Canada was re-emphasized during the leaders' debates, it changed the election course.

Commentators in both English and French Canada agreed that Charest had performed the best. But with the exception of Quebec, where the Tories shot upward and the Bloc sunk to dismal lows, the fallout from the debates was slow to register. In the rest of Canada, the only immediate effect was a slight decline in Liberal and NDP popularity—and a slight rise in Tory and Reform support. Still, the renewed interest in Charest, especially in the wake of the second French-language leaders' debate on May 18, was enough to prod Reform strategists into highly controversial action. To maintain momentum, Manning began to point out that his two main opponents were Quebecers—and that Canadians from the rest of Canada deserved a voice in the unity debate. At the same time, within three days of that second debate, Reform filmed an explosive ad on national unity that lumped Charest and Chrétien together with Duceppe and separatist Quebec Premier Lucien Bouchard. It debuted on May 21.

Meanwhile, the NDP was lowering its sights from its targeted 50 seats. The party entered the campaign with nine MPs and a defiantly left-wing platform that combined $12 billion in annual tax increases with about $20 billion in new spending. Because leader Alexa McDonough cheerfully confessed that the NDP had no hope of forming the government, those proposals were largely ignored—while support for the New Democrats rose during the first two weeks of the campaign. But the party's frank admission eventually prompted many voters to assume that a vote for the NDP was a wasted vote.

As support slipped, strategists threw their formidable grassroots organization behind 26 high-profile candidates. That plan largely worked: Canadians who wanted to register a protest vote gravitated towards those candidates because they felt comfortable with them.

·☙·

On Saturday, May 24, as they peered at their polls, the Liberals rolled into the final phase of the campaign: the fight for their life. In the West, Reform's national unity message had rallied support behind a homegrown party that would assert a regional voice. In Atlantic Canada, with Charest poised to scoop up as many as 26 of the region's 32 seats—the Liberals had won 31 in 1993—the voters had finally put their lingering dislike of Mulroney behind them, partly because of their loathing of the Liberals' new blended sales tax. (In fact, the Liberals had to scrap an ad that featured their cabinet team because focus groups zeroed in on Copps's presence, which, in turn, reminded them of her broken promise to scrap the GST.)

In Quebec, the Tories, saddled with poor organization and many weak candidates, were waning. Boosted by Chrétien's assertion that he would not recognize a "50-per-cent-plus-one" result in a sovereignty referendum, the Bloc was regaining strength outside of the Montreal area—dashing Liberal hopes for major gains. In Ontario, opposition parties were pecking away at Liberal support: Reform in central rural ridings, Tories in suburban Toronto, and New Democrats in downtown Toronto and the north.

Panicked, senior Liberals honed their strategy. As their health-care ads saturated Edmonton and Vancouver, they ensured that party workers would take female voters to the polls on election day. They let Reform hurt itself in Ontario: that controversial ad lumping Chrétien and Charest with the separatists destroyed their critical margin of support within central Ontario, costing them most of the handful of seats that they had the potential to win.

Instead, the Liberals focused their attention on Charest's credibility. Party polling showed that the issue of leadership was a high priority for eight out of 10 potential Tory and Liberal voters: burned by past promises, they would not look at a platform unless they trusted a leader to implement it. In the last week of the campaign, provincial premiers attacked Charest's plans to transfer tax points to the provinces to pay for health and education, arguing that he would penalize poorer regions. When Charest countered that his critics were "liars," and when he was drawn into an ill-advised description of his relationship with Mulroney, the Liberals pounced in a coordinated attack.

Panicking Liberals attacked Charest's credibility

Strategists were divided, however, about what issue Chrétien should emphasize in the final days. Senator Michael Kirby urged that the emphasis be on health care. Rae insisted that national unity, especially Chrétien's strong stand against the recognition of 50-per-cent-plus-one results in a referendum, would carry the day. Marzolini repeatedly stressed jobs. In the end, the party stuck to its economic message: stay the course with a Liberal majority—and the jobs will come. The Liberals inched back upward, often a percentage point at a time, in their internal polls. In the end, enough of the Liberal vote survived for a slim majority. But the party has been chastened. And it is a sure bet that they will never, ever take their support for granted again.

FRANCE TAKES A LEFT

Nothing illustrates the road travelled by Canadian voters in the 1990s as clearly as the contrasting result in the French election last week. In Canada, only Alexa McDonough's New Democrats waved an economic goody bag, promising two million new jobs underwritten by about $20 billion in good old-fashioned government spending. In France, where unemployment is nearly 13 per cent, the opposition Socialists campaigned for the June 1 parliamentary election on an even more generous economic platform. The difference was that the Socialists won.

At times, the rhetoric in France sounded like Canada in the 1960s. The state was still the solution to economic woes, the Socialists argued. Privatizations would end. And the government would create 350,000 new public sector jobs, with 350,000 more jobs to come by slicing four hours from the 39-hour work week—without anyone having to take a cut in pay.

Despite the impracticality of those proposals in a nation fighting a ballooning debt, voters bought in. Rejecting President Jacques Chirac's attempts to modernize the economy, they tossed the centre-right parliamentary coalition out on its austerity plans and gave the keys to the treasury back to the Socialists and their Communist party allies. In Canada, the Liberals founded their reelection bid on their success in reducing the budget deficit. By the end of the French campaign, the desperate government was apologizing for even having tried. French voters looked at Canadian-style sacrifice—and chose nostalgia.

BRUCE WALLACE in London

The Politics of Culture

It has been said that no sooner did Canada move out from under British political, economic, and cultural domination, than it quickly fell under equally friendly but possessive U.S. influence. The politics of culture in Canada has traditionally involved a strong sensitivity to what—if anything—the government of Canada could (or should) do to protect and help develop a strictly *Canadian* culture, identifiably distinct from that of either the United States or the United Kingdom. Much debate has been devoted over the last 100 years to questions related to this problem: Should the government be involved in the "culture business"? How should it act, if it is going to act? What are the political and international political consequences of the government becoming involved in this area?

In this section eight essays consider how the unique political future of Canada has developed in recent years how Canadian cultural industries will affect Canada's future. The major issues in this discussion involve primarily two questions: what should be Canada's position in relation to the United States? Specifically, can Canada remain distinct from, yet friendly with, its large neighbor to the south? The second question relates to Ottawa's relations with Quebec: What should be the *cultural* relations between these two *political* adversaries?

The first article in this section focuses on Canada's bilingualism policy. In "Canada Talks the Talk," Murray Campbell of *The Globe and Mail (Toronto)* examines the government's bilingualism policy 30 years after it was introduced. The article presents a brief analysis of the effectiveness of the policy, describing how much French-English bilingualism has grown in Quebec and the rest of Canada. The cost of this program to the government is significant, but Campbell suggests that overall the policy is reasonably effective.

An article taking a different position is put forward by Ron Eade of *The Ottawa Citizen*. In "Open to Interpretation," Eade suggests that the policy of bilingualism is overwhelmingly expensive and only marginally effective. While the program has had some achievements, in the long run the French community outside of Quebec is being assimilated into an English-speaking environment that really is not bilingual at all. He suggests that the bilingualism policy should be abandoned.

The next selection focuses on the Canadian Radio-television and Telecommunications Commission, the CRTC. Laura Eggertson attacks a decision of the CRTC to not "delist" American channels to make room on cable systems for Canadian offerings. This had been a policy of the CRTC, but it was abandoned when the United States criticized Canada for doing this, and it led to a trade dispute with the United States when it was begun in 1994. The new Canadian policy has led to much concern in Canada about the vulnerability of the Canadian cultural industry to its larger American competition. This article demonstrates how and why the Canadian industry is vulnerable to the Americans.

A related article focuses on the Canadian Broadcasting Commission. In "The Juneau Report and the Gordian Knot of the CBC," Michael Valpy of *The Globe and Mail (Toronto)* examines how to sustain and expand a Canadian identity in the television industry. He shows that the CBC has received a good deal of public and governmental attention in recent years, and this article offers several suggestions on how to "fix" the CBC so that it can be competitive for years to come.

Another article on Canadian broadcasting policy suggests that the CBC may not be the answer to Canada's televison/cultural vulnerability. Ian Austen of *The Canadian Forum* suggests in "Culture between Commercials" that private television broadcasters may provide the most effective vehicle for maintaining a Canadian identity on television. Given the government's limited support for the CBC, private broadcasters may be the best alternative for promoting Canadian culture in this medium.

A very well-crafted and comprehensive article by Susan Riley examines several common myths about Canadian mass culture and its competitiveness in today's North American marketplace. Many nations are concerned about protecting their cultural industries, and Canada needs to act effectively if it wants its culture to remain identifiable and viable in the future.

Doug Saunders of *The Globe and Mail (Toronto)* discusses the issue of "Exporting Canadian Culture." He argues that there is a need for Canada's cultural industries to worry about their export potential in order to be financially competitive. The discussion focuses upon Canadian content in a global perspective. The irony is that while Canada's cultural industries are exporting very well, they are having increasing problems finding funding at home.

Finally, in an article returning to the topic of Canadian-American relations in the culture industry, Drew Fagan examines a recent ruling by a World Trade Organization panel that Canadian magazine practices violated international trade rules. This brief selection examines the Canadian government's cultural support programs that led to this finding.

Looking Ahead: Challenge Questions

Is the challenge to Canada's cultural independence primarily internal, from the United States, or global? Discuss your answer.

Is strengthening public broadcasting the most important means of protecting cultural sovereignty? Why, or why not?

What is the situation with respect to the official status of French and English in Canada? Is the governmental policy of bilingualism working? Can it be improved upon? How?

BILINGUALISM

Canada talks the talk

Three decades after the passage of the Official Languages Act it's time to ask: Has bilingualism been worth it? Have all those breakfast-food packages in English and French, the French-immersion courses and French classes for a cranky bureaucracy bound the country together more closely? Or is English Canada whistling in the wind?

BY MURRAY CAMPBELL
The Globe and Mail
Ottawa

THIRTY years after official bilingualism became a fact of Canadian life it is perhaps time to issue a report card on just how it is doing. What has been the point of the language laws, the bilingual signs, the school programs, even the bilingual corn flakes packages?

If we grade it on the basis of whether a once-cranky English Canada has learned to speak French, it qualifies as a success beyond most expectations: About 4.4 million people—more than 16 per cent of the population—can speak both English and French. The delivery of federal services from coast to coast in two languages is a reality. Hundreds of thousands of students have learned French in immersion programs. In Ottawa, the men and women who were in on the ground floor of official bilingualism wear Order of Canada buttons and pronounce themselves well pleased with their effort.

"It is, in my view, one of the most extraordinarily successful social revolutions ever brought about peacefully in a democratic country anywhere," says Max Yalden, a Torontonian who learned French as an adult and served for five years as the Official Languages Commissioner.

But if, as many anglos believe, the 1969 Official Languages Act was freighted with a higher design—the use of language to bind together two nations into one country—the marks on the report card get much lower, particularly in the West. "Canadian politics has been dominated by a language policy that provides no more than a chimera of the justice it promised nor of the unity it was supposed to guarantee," says Scott Reid, the bilingual author of a 1993 study, *Lament for a Nation*, that is highly critical of bilingualism.

Neither the supporters or opponents of Canada's language policies are likely to prevail anytime soon, but thanks to piles of government data and exhaustive academic analysis, the major linguistic trends in Canada can be identified. John Richards, a bilingual Simon Fraser University professor and former NDP politician, summarized them in a recent paper for the C.D. Howe Institute:

• French-English bilingualism has increased in both Quebec and the other nine provinces, from 13 per cent nationally in 1971 to 16 per cent in 1991. In Quebec, the rate rose to 35 per cent from 28 and in the rest of Canada to 10 per cent from 7.

• Outside Quebec, French is in decline with the exception of regions adjacent to Quebec, such as eastern Ontario and northern New Brunswick. Expressed in terms of mother tongue, francophones represented 4.8 per cent of the population of the nine English-speaking provinces in the last census, compared with 6 per cent in 1971. If home language is used, francophones are just 3.2 per cent of the population now and the vast majority are concentrated in New Brunswick and Ontario.

• The proportion of those who learn French as infants and still use it at home as adults is nearly 100 per cent in Quebec and 90 per cent in New Brunswick. But in the rest of Canada the retention rate is just 65 per cent, compared with 70 per cent two decades ago. Take away New Brunswick and Ontario and the rate falls to 40 per cent, compared with 51 per cent 20 years ago.

• Within Quebec, French has retained its status as the overwhelmingly dominant language. The proportion of anglophones has declined since 1971 after remaining stable for the previous 20 years, mostly in reaction to laws guaranteeing the primacy of French within the province.

The scope of the Official Languages Act was modest. It dealt with the public service and the provision of services in two languages. It said nothing about obliging Canadians to become bilingual or about securing Quebec's place in Confederation.

But there's no doubt the spirit of the times transformed Ottawa's initiative into something bolder, and for many people, particularly anglophones, the quest for linguistic equity was framed by the question of national unity.

And there's no doubt that it has transformed Canada in the past 30 years—a fact viewed with considerable satisfaction in Ottawa, no doubt because it has been most affected by the zeal of the B&B era.

Today, more than 63,000 public-service positions—about 31 per cent of the work force—are designated bilingual and meetings conducted in two languages are commonplace. Francophones now make up about 28 per cent of the public service.

This remarkable achievement reflects the toil of thousands of people over a great deal of time (it takes about 1,000 hours—at a current budgeted rate of $27 an hour—to make someone bilingual).

Many came grumpily and many left with atrocious accents in their adopted language, but the inarguable fact is that about 100,000 public employees have taken up a second language and that a public service that was once unrelentingly English-speaking is now irreversibly bilingual. "I believe that on the scale we've done it, Canada is unique in the world," says Judith Moses, executive director of the Public Service Commission's training-programs branch. "I'm told by world experts that this is an unparalleled experiment."

This education of the public service is mirrored by the phenomenal growth of French-immersion school programs in English Canada. In 1976, there were fewer than 18,000 students in French immersion; today there are more than 310,000—about 7 per cent of the English-speaking school system. Quebec does not offer an English-immersion program but English as a second language is compulsory from Grade 4 to the end of high school.

The experience of how much French these immersion children retain as they become adults is so far not encouraging. Birgit Harley of OISE concluded, after reviewing all the research, that the pattern of French use is generally rather limited for most immersion graduates and that, consequently, skills decline although perhaps not irretrievably.

So how much has it all cost? Can we do a cost-benefit study of bilingualism? Despite its successes, the larger criticism that current Official Languages Commissioner Victor Goldbloom has to deal with is whether the whole enormous bilingualism machinery is worth the cost.

He estimates the overall cost to the government last year—including two-language service delivery and federal transfers to the provinces for education—at $549-million (out of federal program expenditures of about $109-billion). The spending is about $105-million less than it was in 1992 because of cuts to in transfer payments and reductions in support for minority-language activities.

Critics, noting the interwoven costs of everything from public-service language training to the labelling requirement on packaged goods, say the cost is much, much more.

Scott Reid's "preliminary stab" in 1993 was an annual cost to the Canadian economy of $5-billion—of which $2.7-billion represented direct federal expenditures, $300-million was provincial spending resulting from federal initiatives and $2-billion arising from private-sector compliance with federal language regulations. He suggests that more than $50-billion has been added to the federal debt in the past two decades because of "the official-languages monster."

Dr. Goldbloom, relying on Treasury Board figures, dismisses Mr. Reid's figures. A recent report he commissioned, for example, found the average cost of compliance with bilingual laws and regulations was about $100-million a year—not the $2-billion that Mr. Reid suggested.

Whatever the price tag, bilingualism's defenders, as often as not, will shrug and say this is the cost of being a country. The real issue, they say, is what would be the cost of *not* having some sort of language regimen. "I think the language thing has always been fundamental to this country," says Mr. Yalden, who was language commissioner from 1977 to 1984. "You either come to terms with that or it tears the country apart."

Supporters of the federal official-languages policy believe it has been key in keeping Quebec in Confederation. Trouble is, it might also be contributing to Quebec's uneasiness.

Somehow, Canada has ended up with a system that also allows Quebec to operate under a more protectionist philosophy. While anglophones, for the most part, feel enriched by a culture in which two languages flourish, Quebec is suspicious of the federal power over language matters that makes this possible. Québécois accept both languages—their 35-per-cent rate of bilingualism is the highest in the country—but they resist the idea of official bilingualism inside the province for fear that French would be swamped.

Thus, the federal government and Quebec remain devoted to different language-policy visions. Ottawa pursues the notion of equality of French and English across Canada but tolerates the French-only unilingualism in Quebec.

Quebec's language charter, passed 1978, declares French to be the province's official language and is antithetical to the linguistic duality of the Official Languages Act. Polls show it is very popular among Québécois.

Dr. Goldbloom says Quebec's sense of collective destiny continues to clash with the rest of Canada's strong attachment to individual freedoms: "So unfortunately, even if we're bilingual and can communicate with one another we're ... not speaking the same language when we talk about individual and collective interests."

The result is that while anglophones in the rest of Canada accept official bilingualism, they detect a whiff of hypocrisy in Quebec's stance—manifest in its restrictive sign legislation—and increasingly endorse the so-called "tough-love" approach to constitutional negotiation. If this approach fails and Quebec does leave Confederation, the prospects would not be good that the elaborate official-languages structure would remain in the nine anglophone provinces.

Can anything be done? Does anything need to be done?

The Reform Party argues that the Official Languages Act should be scrapped and bilingual services continue only in areas with high concentrations of minority-language speakers.

Prof. Richards at Simon Fraser University argues that Quebec ought to be given explicit jurisdiction over language (subject to the maintenance of bilingualism within federal institutions) to calm the "perfectly reasonable" fears of Québécois about the survival of the French language.

Dr. Goldbloom makes the case for staying the course. He admits English Canada's good will has been tested in recent years by the discourse over Quebec. He argues that political leaders worry about these matters much more than the average person but accepts, nonetheless, that there is continuing tension about language matters all across Canada and pressure for radical changes.

"I think that we are doing reasonably well—not well enough, but reasonably well in responding to the historic existence of two languages in this country," he says.

Open to Interpretation

Are government language policies an extravagance or a necessity?

BY RON EADE

SPECIAL TO THE STAR

OTTAWA

TWENTY-SIX years ago, parliamentarians took up the Herculean call for national unity by ensuring institutional bilingualism for English and French across the land.

At least, that was the plan. Today, $11 billion later, nagging and emotionally charged questions persist about the policy's cost and impact.

While deficit-obsessed lawmakers cut provincial transfers and pick away at unemployment insurance, critics consider official language policy a $620 million-a-year extravagance that has fomented division, not unity, among Canadians.

The federal language policy has chalked up some tangible achievements

And they argue that if basic social programs are under scrutiny, official bilingualism should be, too.

Reform MP Bob Ringma is the latest to call for a review. The Bloc Québécois supports that call, but the other parties are not eager to debate it, particularly in

300,000 anglophone children across Canada are enrolled in French immersion, compared to 38,000 in 1977

the months leading to a sovereignty referendum in Quebec.

The root of eternal human division—personal attitude—determines how people view the policy.

There's no doubt Canada has come a long way since 1927, when the word *postes* first appeared on postage stamps, or since 1962, when the government finally made cheques bilingual.

The Charter of Rights in 1982 expanded the basis for linguistic legal challenges; a new Official Languages Act six years later extended the reach and primacy of the earlier version.

The federal policy has chalked up some tangible achievements. Among them:

■ About 29 per cent of 211,500 federal positions are designated bilingual, compared to 19 per cent in 1974.

■ More than 300,000 anglophone children across Canada are enrolled in French immersion, compared to fewer than 38,000 students in 1977.

■ Access to at least some bilingual federal service is available to 96 per cent

of Quebec anglophones, and 92 per cent of francophones outside Quebec.

■ Almost 4.5 million Canadians (16 per cent) are English-French bilingual, up from 2.2 million (12 per cent) in 1961.

"This much progress in such a relatively short space of time in itself must be counted as a considerable success," former official languages commissioner D'Iberville Fortier said in his 1991 annual report.

"It provides abundant proof of our ability as a nation to meet challenges head-on and to adapt in order to survive and grow together as a country."

Yet, through the years, public opinion has remained contradictory.

An Angus Reid-Southam News poll as recent as April, 1994, showed 64 per cent of Canadians gave linguistic duality strong or moderate support—about the same percentage as in 1990. Pressed further, however, 41 per cent agreed bilingualism is expensive, inefficient and should be scrapped.

Gauging the policy's real cost is difficult.

Treasury Board figures put the actual cost of federal language programs for 1993–94 at $584.8 million. That's expected to swell to $620.5 million in 1994–95, roughly equal to spending at the Canadian Space Agency, double the budget of Statistics Canada, and six times the annual operating tab for the National Capital Commission.

According to the languages commissioner, spending in 1993–94 included:

■ $242 million in transfer payments for provincial and territorial language programs.

■ $91 million for the translation bureau at the public works department.

■ $52.9 million for bilingualism bonuses paid to 62,200 public servants. The program was originally conceived three decades ago as compensation for secretaries only; it has since been repeatedly condemned by language commissioners as an unnecessary drain on federal coffers. (The Treasury Board estimates a payout of $81.1 million in 1994–95, reflecting a retroactive cost award for RCMP employees.)

■ $68.6 million for language training by employees of the Public Service Commission, federal departments, crown corporations and armed forces. (It takes 1,860 hours of training to reach a "superior" level of bilingual skills.

The official cost of bilingualism consumes just half of 1 per cent of the federal budget

In 1989, the languages commissioner reported 38,232 public servants had taken courses during the first 20 years of language training. However, 61 per cent of graduates had either left the public service or held unilingual positions for which their new language skills weren't needed.)

In total, these and other expenses add up to $10.7 billion since the Official Languages Act came into effect in 1969.

In some cases, the languages law created its own industries. Translation and interpretation since 1969 has cost $1.7 billion, while language training has cost $1.1 billion.

Ample as the price tag appears, the official cost of bilingualism consumes just half of 1 per cent of the federal budget, according to official languages commissioner Victor Goldbloom.

The Treasury Board figures have served to fuel suspicion and debate. Even a cursory examination reveals them to be a low-ball estimate that excludes numerous hidden expenses.

These include the cost of compliance by individuals, corporations and provinces with federal bilingualism rules, including English and French assembly instructions for children's toys; bilingual packaging; and minority-language school boards.

Other costs not factored in are paid time off for public servants who take language training; workers hired to replace those on language courses, and translation costs that can be buried in departmental budgets.

In one celebrated case in 1991, the national defence department awarded a $21.9 million contract to translate and print 100,000-page manuals for 12 new frigates. The costs were absorbed in the over-all budget for the ships, so didn't appear in official Treasury Board bilingualism estimates.

Reform researcher Scott Reid estimated the true annual cost to the Canadian economy at about $4 billion in *Lament for a Notion: The Life And Death Of Canada's Bilingual Dream*, published in 1993.

He included federal expenditures of $1.7 billion; provincial spending of $300 million incurred as a result of federal initiatives, and more than $2 billion in private-sector costs to comply with such dictates as federal bilingual packaging regulations. Other, less thoughtful assessments have put the number even higher.

"The truth is, no one knows the cost," says Ringma, Reform's official languages critic. "The accounting practices used for these programs have taken more twists and turns than contestants in a Chubby Checker dance-a-thon."

Conservative leader Robert Stanfield was under no illusion that official languages would be cheap when he supported the law 26 years ago: "What we are talking about will involve costs in any event. Confederation has always involved extra cost."

But, like many Canadians, Ringma questions whether the cost needs to be as high as it is.

He suggests state-supported French radio and television is a waste in British Columbia, where less than half of one per cent of the population speaks French at home.

"We're not saying 'Chop off all spending.' But we are saying there's a helluva lot of waste here."

Ringma has asked for a review of Canada's official bilingualism policy and the House of Commons will debate his motion again in October.

Only the Bloc supports Reform's call, but for its own reasons.

MP Suzanne Tremblay told the Commons the official languages law should be toughened.

"There is every indication that the francophone community outside Quebec is being assimilated, is losing ground where education is concerned, is getting poorer and generally does not have access to the federal services to which it is entitled in its own language."

CRTC abandons cultural red flag

Won't delist U.S. channels to make way for Canadian rivals

BY LAURA EGGERTSON

Parliamentary Bureau

OTTAWA—The federal broadcasting regulator has quietly changed a long-standing Canada-first policy that has been a persistent red flag to the United States.

The Canadian Radio-television and Telecommunications Commission has advised companies seeking licences for new specialty television channels that the commission will no longer delist U.S. channels to make room for competing Canadian ventures.

The CRTC invoked the old policy just once, in 1994, and triggered an acrimonious trade dispute by kicking Nashville-based Country Music Television off the air in favour of newly licenced New Country Network, a Canadian country music channel.

Even though the CRTC only acted on the old policy once, Washington fought it vigorously, charging that the policy set an important precedent of government expropriation without adequate compensation. That's the same principle the United States contends Cuba is abusing by allowing Toronto-based Sherritt International Corp. to reinvest in a nickel mine that Freeport-McMoRan Inc. of New Orleans was never compensated for when it was expropriated after the Communist revolution.

Even Canadian trade consultants often referred to the CRTC's decision to take CMT off the air as a "stupid" decision that needlessly enraged the United States and was a clear violation of the principle of national treatment—treating foreign corporations the same as domestic firms.

CRTC commissioners felt the old policy was justified in the past, when the CRTC was trying to develop Canadian services.

However, it doesn't reflect the new reality of the global marketplace, said Wayne Charman, the commission's director-general of broadcast, distribution and technology.

"We've reached a point now where things are pretty competitive. We've got a lot of services out there and we recognize the reality that it is difficult to take away services once they're there," Mr. Charman said yesterday in an interview.

The policy change was buried in another decision on Tuesday that announced the licencing of several new specialty channels, but was celebrated nevertheless south of the border.

"It's welcome news and it potentially avoids some future problems," said former U.S. trade negotiator Bill Merkin, now a trade consultant in Washington.

At the of the CMT dispute, tempers flared in Washington as U.S. trade representative Mickey Kantor accused Canada of "unjust expropriation," since CMT had already been on the air in Canada for 10 years.

CMT was at the time controlled by Gaylord Entertainment Co. of Oklahoma City and Group W Satellite Communications, a unit of New York-based Westinghouse Broadcasting Co. The companies had complained to Mr. Kantor, who launched an investigation and deemed the Canadian policy protectionist and in violation of national treatment standards.

In retaliation, CMT stopped playing videos of Canadian country stars on its U.S. network. As Washington threatened further action—either a challenge under the North American free-trade agreement or retaliation against Canadian cultural interests in the United States—the companies brokered a last-minute deal.

Gaylord and Group W took a 20-percent interest from Rawlco Communications Inc. of Calgary, owner of the New Country Network, which was then relaunched as Country Music Television (Canada) in September, 1996.

The agreement prevented the trade battle from escalating, but Washington stressed at the time that the CRTC policy itself was still an irritant that demanded attention and could be reopened at any time.

"The [U.S.] administration left the door open for future action were that policy ever to force another U.S. station off the air or to preclude the addition of a new U.S. service," Mr. Merkin said.

That door had recently been opened a crack. Representatives for CNBC, the U.S.-based 24-hour Consumer News and Business Channel, met with U.S. trade officials to signal they were having problems getting approval from the CRTC for a 24-hour broadcast in Canada, Mr. Merkin said.

CNBC did not ask for another investigation along the lines of the one involving Country Music Television. The meeting did, however, alert U.S. Trade Representative Charlene Barshefsky to potential trouble.

But the CNBC issue was also resolved in Tuesday's decision. The CRTC removed any restrictions from CNBC broadcasting, meaning it can operate on a 24-hour basis as it does in the United States.

CRTC commissioners did not know about any threat of U.S. action with regard to CNBC when they made that decision, Mr. Charman said.

A spokesman for CNBC said the organization was pleased by the CRTC's move and would not discuss what action it had contemplated if broadcasting restrictions had not been removed.

"I don't think that's an issue," said George Jamison, vice-president for media relations at the network's headquarters in New Jersey.

The Globe and Mail, which holds a licence for the all-business Report on Business Television, had opposed CNBC's request to be able to expand its programming to a 24-hour format in Canada, on grounds that CNBC would be competition for ROB TV.

The CRTC decisions remove a potential roadblock in the cultural area, which is destined to heat up this fall. Ottawa is expected to introduce new policies to defend the domestic magazine industry from U.S. competition after losing the tools it had employed to keep split-run magazines like Sports Illustrated out of the country, thanks to a World Trade Organization decision.

Those policies will be scrutinized by the Americans, both in the U.S. magazine industry and in government, for possible loopholes and a way in to the Canadian market.

THE WTO magazine decision and the new CRTC policy reflect changes in technology, which enabled Sports Illustrated publisher Time Warner Inc. of New York to use satellite printing to dodge the Canadian tariff code against split-run imports, and make cable channels difficult to restrict.

"Times are a-changin' and you can't just put up an Iron Curtain at the border and keep these U.S. services out," Mr. Merkin said.

"I think what the CRTC is doing is more a reality check for everybody, that technology is moving at such speed that whoever the Canadian service is, they have to be prepared to compete head-on with the U.S."

The Juneau report and the Gordian knot of the CBC

BROADCASTING/ *If we don't have the CBC, we don't have a country.*
So how do we fund the national public broadcaster?

Michael Valpy

LET'S all have a dream. Let's dream that, with yesterday's report of the Juneau task force on broadcasting and film, we now know how to fix the CBC. This will be like sorting out Northern Ireland and solving Bosnia. Big job, damnably difficult, needs prayers, not impossible to do.

The Juneau committee—former CBC president Pierre Juneau, TVOntario president Peter Herrndorf, Simon Fraser University communications professor Catherine Murray—gives us a workable, eloquent, convincing framework. But it's not everything. It falls short.

We'll have to fiddle with it, flesh it out in some places, point it in a different direction in other places. Fundamentally, however, we can accept that they have got it right and we can put our heads together to figure out how to achieve what they recommend.

WHAT do we do first? We end the arguments over whether we should have a CBC. If we don't have the CBC, we don't have a country.

Only the CBC bridges the country's two official language groups.

When you look at the box that accompanies this column, you'll see that private TV broadcasters in English-speaking Canada are basically foreign broadcasters. And much of what little so-called Canadian content they carry is U.S.-imitation programming designed for sale to the American market.

Without Canadian programming and film, without the broadcasting of Canadian stories, Canadian citizens will not be able to understand one another, will not be able to develop a national and community consciousness, will not be able to shape Canadian solutions to social and political problems, will not be able to transmit their values to their children.

We cannot be tourists in our own culture, not understanding how it works, not knowing the mechanics of its institutions, unable to speak its political language, not comprehending its authoritative mythologies.

Most of the stories we tell ourselves on Canadian television are foreign.

We have to have the CBC; we have to have it as a public broad-

caster. Owned by the people. It has to do a much better job.

WHAT do we do second? We recreate a CBC that is truly more *us*.

CBC-Radio does what we want public broadcasting to do. Television is what has to be fixed.

The Juneau committee gives us a vision of CBC-Television that has more distinctly Canadian drama, more children's programming, more good Canadian documentaries. As the committee says, it's not the choice of subject matter for programming that determines what is Canadian, it's the approach. It's the authenticity of cultural voice.

We can move toward the vision, the committee says, if we get commercials off television. Commercials drive programming; they tip the balance on English television to too much sports and too many American soaps (and, hence, so little children's programming in the afternoons).

I will set aside for today the circumstances for CBC's French-language television. Obviously Radio Canada is less in danger of being drowned by foreign programs. Let's focus on English-speaking Canada: Drama accounts for 41 per cent of all viewing in the anglophone market; Canadian drama attracts only about 10 per cent of that 41 per cent. Why? Because only about 14 per cent of all drama available on English television is Canadian.

We can move toward the vision, the committee says, if the CBC is provided with stable funding, and sufficient funding, to offer distinctive Canadian programming.

English-language Canadian television (including the CBC) provides 145 hours of original drama a year (and that figure is no doubt exaggerated, given the amount of U.S.-imitative drama). British television, in contrast, provides 1,300 hours.

For argument's sake, let's say British television serves a market three times larger than English-Canadian television. Three times 145 hours is 435 (virtually one-third of 1,300), an increase of 290 hours. The cost of producing drama in the United States is approximately $1-million an hour. In Canada, let's use half a million dollars an hour: $145-million to produce that extra 290 hours.

The Juneau committee says programming improvements—all programming improvements—for the CBC would require only $35-million in 1997–98, $70-million each year for the next three years and $100-million a year after that. The committee does not say how it arrives at those numbers.

It does not provide much insight into the market dynamics of television drama production. We don't get an idea, reading the report, of whether the CBC will have enough money to do what the committee says it should do, or whether it will be able to buy what the committee says it should buy.

But yes, let's get the commercials off. They do distort programming. They are the reason that prime-time sports accounts for 37 per cent of CBC viewing—an absurd amount, up from 20 per cent in 1985–86. (Sports brings in advertising and its production costs are low; French-

language CBC has done the same thing with variety programming.) Commercials result in programming that the advertisers want; they get in the way of our voices being heard; the market cannot dictate what a nation says to itself. They also take money, about $200-million a year, away from the private broadcasters.

WHAT do we do third? We come up with a better way to finance the CBC.

Making it more distinctly Canadian is the way to start. The Juneau committee poses the question: Why should Canadians want to put out a billion-plus dollars a year for something that looks like any commercial network? The revenue from commercials has to be replaced.

All over the world, wherever public broadcasters are financed by governments, their allocations are being cut and program quality is declining. The CBC will have $350-million in cuts imposed on it over three years. The corporation says the third-year cut, of $123-million, will severely affect programming and force the CBC, for example, to sell more commercials around the nightly national news hour.

(The Juneau committee, by the way, has accepted the full $350-million in cuts, even though Mr. Juneau

said before his committee began work that it would not be bound by the government's budgetary targets. Politically, it decided not [to] take the government on. It did recommend that the CBC be allowed to make up the third-year $123-million through annual 2-per-cent budgetary savings over five years.)

Financing by parliamentary allocation is no longer a good idea. For the future, the Juneau committee offers three financing options. All involve a dedicated fee or tax.

The most innovative—and the one that the CBC's telecommunications partners prefer (for obvious reasons, as explained below)—is a fee collected through the income-tax system. It would be almost invisible. It would be as universal as you could get, catching the one-third of television-watchers who receive the CBC via rabbit ears. It would be progressive; the rich would pay more than the poor. But the Juneau committee says, uh uh, the Finance Department would find it a difficult precedent.

The committee's second option is a communications distribution tax of 7.5 or 8.5 per cent; the higher amount would embrace the CBC's annual capital allocation as well as its operating allocation. The tax would be imposed on cable-TV and direct-to-home satellite services, long-distance telephone calls and other

Who's airing what

Percentage of viewing time devoted to Canadian and foreign programs 7 p.m. to 11 p.m.

ENGLISH

Station category	1984–85		1992–93	
	Canadian	**Foreign**	**Canadian**	**Foreign**
CBC	62.0	38.0	81.7	18.3
CTV	20.8	79.2	17.3	82.7
Global	7.9	92.1	17.4	82.6
Independent	16.4	83.6	17.9	82.1

FRENCH

SRC (Radio Canada)	72.1	27.9	90.9	9.1
TVA	46.2	53.8	66.3	33.7
TQS	54.8	45.2	47.6	52.4

Source: CBC Research (AC Nielsen). For TQS, the first year data shown are for 1986–87

transactions on the information highway.

This would increase the average monthly cable charge of $24 by between $1.80 and $2 (less, actually, because the committee recommends an end to the monthly charge of 65 cents in anglophone markets, and $1 in francophone markets, for CBC Newsworld and its French-language counterpart *Réseau de l'information*).

The committee says the tax would be sufficient to totally fund the CBC, giving it about $1.2-billion to $1.3-billion a year. It would be stacked on the existing 7-per-cent goods and services tax that applies to most telecommunications services.

The third option is the same as the second, except that the communications distribution tax would replace the GST on telecommunications services.

T HE committee has subtly recommended the second option.

It won't fly.

It will be seen as a tax grab. It will be labelled a user-pay fee, even though it is broadly based. It will almost certainly get cable subscribers upset, in a manner reminiscent of the furor last year when the cable companies tried to add new channels via "negative-option marketing."

It will lead to questions about why the government is imposing a tax on long-distance telephone-service providers (although the Juneau committee has research that says long-distance charges have dropped dramatically in the past few years and a tax on long-distance calls will not dampen demand).

The third option is so much more palatable, so much easier to swallow, so much less visible. Just replace the GST on telecommunications services.

What do we do most of all? We don't let the financing issue paralyze us. We don't do nothing. We accept the truth, that the CBC is necessary. We fix it.

CULTURE
BETWEEN
commercials

Private broadcasters can be a force for Canadian culture — if the Liberals act

by IAN AUSTEN

Who's the real Izzy Asper? Is he the media mogul whose Global Television Network was effectively heralded as a force for Canadian culture in a late February press release from federal broadcast regulator Keith Spicer? "We are pleased that the licensee has exceeded the minimum expenditure of over $30 million a year on Canadian programming," the CRTC chairman noted while announcing a seven-year renewal of Global's licence.

Or is he the man whose broadcasting vision was portrayed on a cover of *Maclean's* that appeared just a few days before Spicer's announcement? "Izzy's dream," as the magazine called it, was depicted by a series of television sets showing Global's programming highlights. Four displayed top-rated, U.S. network imports; the fifth featured Izzy's face.

While the magazine illustrator didn't include Global's new Canadian series, *Traders*, he was nevertheless much closer to the mark about Asper's record as a cultural force than Spicer's upbeat praise. Unfortunately, Asper — who wants to make Global the third national English TV network — has plenty of company. Despite years of effort and study, stacks of regulations and millions of government dollars, English Canada's commercial broadcasters remain largely distributors of the best Hollywood can offer. In short, we've been had, and amazingly, given

the current focus on the CBC's sins, hardly anyone seems to be noticing.

Take, for example, most media coverage of the CBC, National Film Board and Telefilm Canada mandate review committee's report. Predictably, reporters were fixated on the panel's suggestion that a modest tax on things such as cable bills should pay the CBC's freight. Almost entirely ignored was the section on Telefilm, the semi-invisible federal agency that's the biggest investor in most entertainment programming on private TV, including the much-hyped *Traders*. While the committee revealed lots of problems with CBC English TV, it was even harsher in its criticism of the private networks. "If the limited amount of Canadian programming (and particularly drama) on our television screens — and the disproportionate amount of time that Canadians devote to watching American programs — is not seen as a cultural crisis, it is only because English-speaking Canadians have grown too accustomed to this situation. It is not now, and never has been, a case of Canadian programs being provided and rejected by domestic audiences."

As the report suggests, the dismal state of private TV is hardly a recent development. Still, it's hard to imagine a more crucial time to start looking at private TV's invisible cultural crisis. As the CBC's resources continue to be squeezed, it becomes more important than ever to press

the point that private broadcasters aren't doing us a favour by producing Canadian programming — it's the price of some very valuable considerations from the government. Over the coming months, opportunities to address the issue will surface, including eight CRTC commissioners' spots, among them the chairman's, becoming vacant; an internal review by the Heritage and Industry departments of the CRTC's role and operations; Asper's station licence applications to create his national network; and growing calls for regulatory change prompted by the so-called information highway, calls that have been dominated by industry demands for less regulation and lower Canadian content requirements.

If you only read private broadcasters' annual reports and their CRTC submissions rather than watching their programming or even glancing at the TV listings, you might think they actually *are* major forces for Canadian culture. It's rare that a private broadcaster doesn't appear before the CRTC without an introductory videotape that includes some aerial views of the Rockies, Canada geese in slow-motion flight and perhaps a quaint Innu woman for good measure. When private operators actually produce a Canadian show, their publicity departments do their best to ensure that everyone knows about it —Asper posed with the stars of *Traders* for publicity photos and even did a walk-on part in one episode.

From *The Canadian Forum*, May 1996, pp. 14-19. © 1996 by Canadian Forum, Ltd. Reprinted by permission.

But nothing turns private broadcasters into greater patriots than the emergence of anything they perceive as a threat to their profit margins — whether it's tax changes, increased regulation, the advent of cable in the '60s or, more recently, direct-to-home satellites. Any decline in their financial performance, they warn in usually apocalyptic terms, will doom Canadian production, if not the very fabric of Canada itself. New forms of electronic communications are emerging as the latest enemy. Last year's Canadian Association of Broadcasters' convention lamely attempted to lay claim to that territory with its theme "Private Broadcasting: Canada's Voice on the Innovation Highway".

On the whole, waving the Canadian flag while filling the airwaves with American shows has paid off handsomely. Asper alone is estimated to be personally worth $600 million, much of it generated by his company CanWest Global Communications Corp. In the first six months of its current fiscal year, CanWest's Global—which broadcasts in Ontario, but does not include the company's Saskatchewan and Atlantic Canada operations—saw its profits rise 36 per cent to $66 million on revenue of $171 million. Most of that came from broadcasting popular U.S. sitcoms such as *Seinfeld* and *Friends*.

Asper's performance is not an isolated example. Last year, Vancouver-based WIC Western International Communications Ltd., owner of eight stations, a pay-TV network and half of the Family Channel, made $82.7 million. (The major English private network, CTV, has an extremely spotty financial record. However, its customers are for the most part its owners, including WIC, and their balance sheets are uniformly bright in large part because of the mostly American programming CTV provides.)

Despite all the extreme hype about a possible 500-channel universe and the current rush for more cable specialty channels, an over-the-air broadcast licence remains a re-

markably valuable piece of paper. Though only Belgium has more of its population connected to cable than Canada, when Canadians turn on the tube they overwhelmingly select conventional, over-the-air stations. The audience gap with the cable channels is startling. Government-owned (at least for now) TVOntario is that province's smallest over-the-air network in terms of overall audience. Nevertheless, most of the time, more Ontarians are watching TVO than all the English specialty channels combined.

Licences aren't the only gifts given to private broadcasters. Few steps have been as influential in shaping private broadcasters' programming strategies and balance sheets as the CRTC's introduction of so-called signal substitution. Under the scheme, major cable companies must replace U.S. stations' signals with local Canadian channels' programming if both are airing identical shows. The identical programs are, of course, overwhelmingly American. Under signal substitution, Canadian stations grab 100 per cent of the local audience for their commercials. Its unintended effect is less desirable. Signal substitution creates a powerful economic incentive for private broadcasters to flood key viewing hours with American imports that are sure to be popular with both audiences and advertisers: (The CBC also benefits from the rule when it airs U.S. shows, although the public network has vowed to eliminate its primetime U.S. programming by this fall.)

Substitution has been a constant trade irritant with successive U.S. administrations. In theory, it should be worth the price of that aggravation. Private broadcasters were supposed to take a chunk of extra ad revenue the scheme generated and use it to develop Canadian programming. A CRTC background paper boasts that, thanks to signal substitution, "millions of dollars are returned to the Canadian broadcasting system". Perhaps to the system but not necessarily Canadian programming, as former CBC president Tony

Manera points out. "This is a case where a public policy has been created to favour the interests of private broadcasters without adding any real benefit for consumers," says Manera, now a consultant after quitting the CBC in 1995 over cuts to its funding. "If the private broadcaster wasn't running those American shows, the consumer would still have access to them. But they'd just have to watch American commercials instead of Canadian commercials. So, big deal.

"I think the private broadcasters owe some return to the Canadian system."

Most private broadcasters have the good sense to always honour the minimum CRTC Canadian content requirements. There are some exceptions, but generally private TV stations must make sure that 60 per cent of their programming measured over an entire year is Canadian, including at least half the shows between 6 p.m. and midnight. Quantity isn't the problem; it's how the commercial operators reach the quota.

Asper's Global is a good example. The actual decision that renewed its licence reveals how the network became an overachiever: "The Commission notes...that Global's overexpenditures during the current licence term were made entirely on news programming and not on entertainment programming." Though Global and most private broadcasters have improved their performance, Canadian content on private stations remains overwhelmingly news and sports. Both attract ads and are relatively cheap to produce. But news shows that are heavily laden with U.S. network reports from abroad and Blue Jays baseball aren't really the stuff of national identity building. As well, neither sports nor news is what most viewers watch most of the time. Of the top 10 shows in the Toronto-Hamilton market early this year, none was a news program; one sports broadcast, CBC's *Hockey Night in Canada*, made ninth place. Most were imported American entertainment series that appeared on Global and CTV.

TVO chairman and mandate review committee member Peter Herrndorf gives private broadcasters some points for trying — at least a little. "Private broadcasters have done significantly better in the last 10 years. They do a lot more drama than anyone might have thought possible in the early 1980s." Not enough though.

"Having said all of that, compared to Australia, compared to Britain, compared to the U.S., compared to France; the commercial broadcasters here do quite modest amounts of indigenous programming. They still are locked to a considerable degree into that economic logic that's prevailed in Canadian broadcasting from the 1930s on."

The statistics back that up. There isn't any overall tracking of private sector performance by the CRTC, but it accepts a CBC study that found only 8.2 per cent of shows aired between 7 and 11 p.m. on Global in 1993 were Canadian drama or variety productions. The comparable figure for CTV is 7.9 per cent, while the CBC reached almost 17 per cent.

Indeed, the CBC research department's dismal findings may actually overstate the private networks' performance. Under the CRTC's and Telefilm's point systems for evaluating productions, some pretty strange things can qualify as Canadian content, especially co-productions. (The systems give up to 10 points for using Canadian talent such as actors, directors and cinematographers. A complex series of treaties, however, skews everything in the case of international co-productions.) CTV's "Canadian" offerings have included *A Family of Cops*, starring Charles Bronson as Milwaukee's police chief. Programs filmed in Canada primarily designed for sale in the U.S. market that meet the bare minimum Canadian content levels are known in the trade as six-pointers. They've also

become the greatest growth area in production, thanks in large part to the low value of the Canadian dollar. Turning parts of Toronto or Vancouver into Manhattan or Montana for a day certainly provides employment and revenue for independent producers, some actors and technicians. An occasional appearance by the odd Hollywood star is a nice diversion for passers-by, assuming they're not trapped in a film-related traffic jam. What most six-pointers do for Canadian culture, however, is at best unclear. Nevertheless, the push for more continues. The federal government's industry-dominated Information Highway Advisory Council, which reported last fall, was among the latest to join the cause. For cultural industries, it said, "[t]he objective must be a self-sustaining environment." Acknowledging that might not be completely possible, the report claims there's one way to reach most of the goal: "Government policies could do more to encourage the production of exportable content. As markets multiply and diversify, Canadian cultural products must stand out and appeal to consumers. They must strive to achieve maximum quality and marketability and not simply take up obligatory shelf space."

It's not hard to see from a pure business standpoint why private Canadian TV broadcasters have become essentially pipelines for U.S. shows. It costs about $700,000 to $1 million to produce a single hour of real Canadian entertainment programming — an eight- or more pointer. While there are a variety of funds and agencies to help finance the show, its chances for commercial success are dicey. Canadian programs receive only a fraction of the free publicity that falls on even the lamest U.S. shows. Three seasons passed before the CBC's *This Hour Has 22 Minutes* made two Canadian mass market magazine covers. "If it was an American show, it would have had 30 American covers by now and it would have had eight Canadian ones," says Herrndorf. By contrast,

the formula for success with simulcasting U.S. shows is dead simple. You buy a big American hit for about $90,000 a one-hour episode. Selling commercials is easy. Many advertisers prefer to drop their money on a simulcast of a U.S.-made sure thing such as *America's Funniest Home Videos* rather than an unknown Canadian product. Those ads should pull in about $150,000, leaving a gross margin of $160,000. With numbers like that, why would you do anything else?

Despite the economic woes of the Ottawa Valley, the annual fall fair in Renfrew, Ontario, continues to prosper. Last year, mixed in with the tractor exhibits, Super Peeler pitchmen and back-bacon-on-a-bun booths, there were two outfits pushing direct-to-home satellite TV systems.

The continuing obsession of Canadian broadcast policy makers with distribution systems rather than programming has guaranteed a lot of attention for satellite TV over the past two and a half years. But despite all the hype and concern, satellite TV remains a tiny niche product used mostly by people in rural areas with either poor or non-existent cable service. In Renfrew's armoury, the fairground's biggest hall, the Women's Institute was dishing out apple pie and TV dealer Ben Sauvé had perched a pizza-sized RCA DTH satellite dish on top of a massive Hitachi set. On the screen was one of the 175 channels — none Canadian — beaming into Canada's so-called grey market from Los Angeles-based Hughes DirecTV. The system's clear picture and crisp, CD-like sound certainly attracted attention. After they admired the screen, however, visitors consistently complained to Suavé about one major shortcoming: "Many people have been approaching us about it. But they're not interested right now because they want Canadian content. I'd say nine out of 10 want Canadian content."

Many of those nine, it seems, define Canadian content as NHL hockey on the Toronto-based specialty channel TSN. But sports isn't the only draw. Just before the fair opened, Linda and Brett Hodgins had dropped about $2,400 for a conventional, three-metre dish for their home east of Renfrew. Instantly they went from receiving two English channels—Ottawa's CBC and CTV outlets—to over 130. The range is bewildering and includes RTP Portugal, BBC World Service News, internal U.S. network and Canadian network news feeds. As her son watched *Barney* zapping down from God-knows-where, Linda said she was already longing for some of the local shows on CJOH, the Ottawa CTV station controlled by the Eaton family.

It's one of the great myths of Canadian broadcasting — one that serves private stations well and one that caught the fancy of the Information Highway Advisory Council — that no one watches Canadian shows. "When Canadian programming is available, people will watch it. But it has to be available," says Manera. The CBC's peak viewing time analysis, like other studies, shows that the audience levels for Canadian content roughly match the amount available. In 1993, 25 per cent of programming on all English stations between 7 and 11 p.m. was Canadian. It captured 24 per cent of the audience.

Boosting the number of Canadian shows is a problem that has plagued Canadian television from the beginning. Thirty-one years ago, the Fowler Committee looked at private broadcasting and produced findings that were echoed this year by the mandate review committee: "Their program schedules are unbalanced; they do not provide sufficiently wide variety, and do little to further the development of the Canadian consciousness." The establishment of Canadian content quotas in 1970, the creation of the broadcast fund at Telefilm 13 years later, the establishment of the cable industry's Canadian Program Production

Fund three years ago and a variety of tax measures were all hailed at their introductions as major steps to reversing the trend.

Most recently, an expanded range of cable specialty channels has been billed as Canadian broadcasting's salvation. Without exception, all the applicants for new channels have claimed that their services will be part of a new beginning for Canadian broadcasting. So far, there's not much evidence of that. "I am a sceptic about the specialty channels," says Herrndorf. "It's a nice thing to have. I happen to be a baseball fan, so I take full advantage of TSN. I like some of the things Bravo! does. But in many ways it's kind of a luxury. Given the economics of the specialty services, it is almost guaranteed that the level of complex original production they do will be minimal."

Sure enough, despite the specialty channels' bold promises to the CRTC, their production records have largely been disappointing. There are some exceptions, including YTV, Discovery and Bravo! to a certain extent. Most of the time, however, reruns and whatever's available at overseas program-buying shows are what specialty channels offer viewers. Reruns aren't necessarily a bad thing if they're Canadian programs. A second or third run is often what's needed to turn a profit. But reruns certainly don't add to the pool of Canadian programming. Programming that does get commissioned by specialty channels tends, on the whole, to be low end, what Herrndorf calls "pocket television". To a great extent, the whole specialty system has become a drain, drawing away ad dollars from over-the-air channels while making a minimal contribution to production.

The CRTC's answer to all this: a call for applications for even more specialty channel licences. Hearings begin this month, and the contenders, if anything, look less promising than the current bunch. They include The Horse Network: "All Horses, All The Time."

42. Culture between Commercials

Despite the less-than-inspiring history of the Canadian content crusade, there are a couple of approaches that still haven't been seriously explored. Neither particularly costs government money, which should be good news for the deficit-obsessed federal Liberals. Both, however, demand strong political will from Heritage Minister Sheila Copps and Industry Minister John Manley.

Politicians generally aren't keen to take a hard stand with private broadcasters. Most broadcast licence holders have strong political ties. Asper, for example, is a former provincial Liberal leader. On top of that, the industry has been adept at creating phony crises whenever it appears its cozy relationship is in jeopardy. Don't be surprised, for example, if you soon hear private broadcasters talking about their need for higher profits and less regulation because of the corporate takeovers sweeping American broadcasting and telecommunications following the near total deregulation of that market in January.

The most important issue for Copps has to be the CRTC and its eight empty chairs. Her closed-door review of the commission indicates that the government isn't happy with the state of the CRTC. Where that's headed is something of a mystery. Manley has talked ominously about making the agency better fit the Liberal Party's values—whatever they may be—and mused about the limited need for regulation in the future. Copps, on the other hand, continues to defend both the need for a CRTC and the importance of broadcasting as a tool for Canadian cultural objectives.

The dismal record of private TV isn't entirely the commission's fault, although the CRTC is obviously part of the problem. Much of the problem lies with the commissioners. That doesn't mean they're dupes of private broadcasters or a gang of fools. For the most part, commissioners are well meaning and work hard for their generous pay. The CRTC's caseload is exploding but hasn't been matched by a corresponding increase in resources. Hearings are seemingly endless, and it's a rare week when at least one commissioner doesn't nod off during some droning presentation.

Offsetting the commissioners' good intentions is their traditional background. With rare exceptions, they tend to be former broadcast or communications managers, journalists or politically connected lawyers, engineers or academics. Certainly those skills can be useful. But others with equally large stakes in broadcasting and communications — artists, consumer advocates, film directors, novelists, actors, musicians — have been conspicuously absent. "I don't know if I'd go so far as to say the CRTC doesn't work very well, but it really needs balance," says Sandy

W ith rare exceptions, CRTC commissioners tend to be former broadcast or communications managers, journalists or politically connected lawyers...

Crawley, president of the broadcast performers' union ACTRA. "The commissioners don't really take our needs into consideration the same way that they do the money people, who can afford to have lawyers, bring them big briefs, take them out to lunch all the time and constantly lobby to get their people appointed to the commission." (Crawley has applied for an appointment but isn't optimistic about his chances.)

This pattern of past appointments has created commissions that try to squeeze the objectives of the broadcasting act, such as Canadian content,

around the broadcast industry's corporate needs and desires. For most of the commissioners, the corporate world is where their ultimate sympathies lie. It won't be easy shifting that. One or two daring appointments, even in the chairman's job, aren't likely to be enough if recent U.S. experience is any indication. Spicer's equivalent there, FCC chairman Reed Hundt, is a former anti-trust lawyer who came to the job just over two years ago with hopes of improving children's programming and maintaining telecommunications access for the poor. Since then he's spent much of his time arguing unsuccessfully with most of his other commissioners over such limited measures as requiring the world's biggest broadcasters to show three hours of educational kids' shows a week. Last fall, *The New York Times* said Hundt is "looking more and more like the head of a dysfunctional family."

A balanced CRTC could be tougher on programming requirements. Other bodies internationally certainly aren't afraid to push the issue. CanWest was the top bidder, in cash terms at least, for the right to operate a new fifth national network in Britain. But the U.K.'s Independent Television Commission went for a much lower bid after it found fault with CanWest's programming plans, especially its high level of reruns.

But to really effect change in Canada, Copps and whoever succeeds Spicer must take a hard public stand and push private broadcasters to do more real Canadian drama. They should require real programming plans and budgets and make it clear to private broadcasters that keeping a licence will require a dramatic change in attitude. Obviously, it won't be easy. Even small steps by the commission in the past have provoked major propaganda assaults from private broadcasting. But if they now have the courage, Asper's national network quest certainly provides an opening for such a brave move. Australia shows such a step can be effective. While Australia

isn't next door to the U.S., its private networks have long been key sales targets of American program producers. The result was a domestic broadcasting system with programming that would be familiar to most Canadian viewers. Following government pressure, however, the three Australian networks — including one controlled by CanWest — all agreed to produce at least 100 hours of original, prime-time drama a year. In turn, they've been allowed to boost the amount of American programming they show in other programming areas and time slots. (The CRTC has a small measure along these lines, allowing a 150 per cent time credit for some Canadian dramas.) "I've heard very few complaints from the Australian private sector about that," says Herrndorf. "They seem to have come to the conclusion that both for identity reasons, prestige reasons and ultimately for profit this was a good deal for them."

W ill Copps take such a step? Historically, she's never been shy about speaking her mind, and the need for renewing the Canadian identity has never been greater. But the degree of the Cabinet's commitment to cultural issues is unclear. Much of the confidence instilled in Canadian cultural advocates by Copps's Cabinet appointment and the Cabinet's subsequent rejection of Borders Bookstores' plans for the Canadian market by Investment Canada faded in March when the budget further fuelled the CBC's funding crisis. Copps's main response, so far, has been only promises that some kind of completely new funding plan, completely undefined though apparently not the tax proposed by mandate review, will eventually appear. Manley also has considerable say in the CRTC's direction. Not surprisingly, however, as Industry Minister he tends to view broadcasting as a business rather than a cultural force.

Whether or not the government moves, a number of developments suggest that broadcasters should themselves start rethinking their view of Canadian content out of self-interest. While it's unlikely that we'll ever have 500 channels to choose from, it's not unreasonable to expect that 100 might be around by the end of the decade, thus diluting current broadcasters' market share. Similarly, there are growing threats from abroad that could upset the current system, threats that can't be solved by more special deals from the CRTC or government. Entertainment is the second biggest U.S. export after aircraft. Mired in the U.S. administration's support for Nashville-based Country Music Television's ludicrous argument that it has a guaranteed spot on Canadian cable

was a message that Washington doesn't regard commercial broadcasting as a cultural industry exempt from trade action. More recently, the Clinton administration's hard-line attack on federal legislation blocking *Sports Illustrated*'s "Canadian" edition confirmed its attitude. Signal substitution may be Washington's next target.

Whatever happens in the future, the best long-term hope for Canadian private broadcasters is developing a distinct identity rather than just acting as American programming packagers. Their attempts so far have been exceptionally superficial. When John Cassaday left Campbell Soup early this decade to run CTV, he immediately began talking

about developing a brand identity. There's not been much to show for it beyond a proliferation of on-screen network logos. By contrast, high-quality drama made for and by Canadians can allow Canada's private networks to stand out from the growing crowd. What's more; good, overtly Canadian shows have shown their export sales potential in the past — even if they don't have Charles Bronson. It's time for Izzy to substantially rethink his dream. Asper may not care about his role in Canada's cultural future, but his own financial future may depend on developing it.

Ian Austen is a freelance journalist based in Ottawa.

Seven Myths About Canadian Culture

Debate of who we are, or should be, usually buried in popular myths

BY SUSAN RILEY

OTTAWA CITIZEN

Will the passionate, often abstruse and briefly revived debate over Canadian culture come alive again during the federal election?

It's hard to imagine culture shouldering aside more urgent issues: Jean Chrétien's credibility, Preston Manning's haircut, Jean Charest's overdue political resurrection.

If anything can, it's the full-blown passion of a federal election.

If the debate is reactivated, say, by another menacing gesture from the U.S. it would be helpful to clear away certain misleading but persistent myths.

These myths, brandished as weapons, only confuse what is already a complicated argument over how to best preserve a distinctive culture in English-speaking Canada: by nurturing it in a greenhouse of subsidies and tax incentives behind protective fences, or by sending it off to New York with only cab fare in its pocket.

MYTH ONE

■ **New, border-leaping technologies make Canadian content rules and other attempts to regulate the airways old-fashioned, even ridiculous.**

For all its promise, the Internet isn't going to replace books, magazines—even newspapers—any time soon.

While the information highway is an abundant and unregulated source of free information—everything from American lesbian glossies to the world's great books—StatsCan figures suggest that only 7 per cent of Canadian homes are wired.

Besides, says Keith Kelly of the Canadian Conference of the Arts: "It's hard to imagine snuggling up with a laptop to read *Alias Grace*."

As for direct-to-home television, there is already a significant gray market among rural and small-town dwellers beyond the reach of cable.

They buy satellite dishes that beam a nearly unlimited supply of American programming into their living rooms.

But the existence of this equipment doesn't mean Canada has to abandon dreams of making room for Canadian content, Kelly says.

What's required is a Canadian company obtaining its own satellite space, the capital and the political backing to offer gray-market subscribers a competing service featuring Canadian programming.

What's needed, in other words, is a combination of private enterprise and political will—not capitulation.

MYTH TWO

■ **The feeble measures intended to protect Canadian culture will be swept away by the immutable forces of globalization.**

There is nothing immutable about globalization, although Canada is particularly vulnerable, by virtue of geography, to its reach.

Toronto communications consultant Paul Audley says globalization is a fancy word for Americanization, describing the agenda of a group of U.S.-born multinational companies (Time Warner, Disney, Viacom), that perceive Canada only as an extension of the American market.

Audley prefers the term "internationalization," which suggests a world explosion of many cultures, rather than globalization, which leads to "centralization of decision-making and narrowing of choice."

While Canada is vulnerable to American cultural domination, it is not alone in trying to carve some space for its own culture.

Nations ranging from France to Australia to Saudi Arabia have devised barriers and incentives to offset the deluge of U.S. films, television shows and pop stars.

As Heritage Minister Sheila Copps points out, even the U.S. uses protectionist measures. Foreign ownership of American television licenses is restricted to 20 per cent.

Canada is not alone in trying to protect its culture. A variety of nations have laws aimed at warding off the American tide

And the Clinton administration has been castigating China for ignoring U.S. copyright law at the same time as its criticizes Canada's new copyright legislation for unfairly favoring Canadian artists.

MYTH THREE

■ **Cultural nationalists want us to pull a curtain around Canada and turn our backs on other cultures.**

Canada is, as Copps notes, "the most open market in the world" when it comes to culture.

Ninety-six per cent of the movies that appear in our cinemas are foreign, most of them American. Four out of five magazines sold at our newsstands are foreign, most of them American. Three-quarters of the television we watch every night is foreign, most of it American.

Seventy per cent of the content on Canadian radio stations is non-Canadian, most of it American.

Indeed, so overwhelming is the U.S. domination of our cultural market that author John Ralston Saul says we should not refer to tactics designed to preserve some small toehold for Canadian work as "protectionist," but rather as "anti-combines measures" aimed at

breaking monopoly control of the culture sector.

MYTH FOUR

■ **Canadian artists can compete with the best in the world without the benefit of state subsidy or support.**

Partly, true, but internationally acclaimed authors Margaret Atwood and Michael Ondaatje readily admit their literacy success couldn't have been achieved without early support from the Canada Council (which provides grants to aspiring writers) and from small, state-subsidized presses.

In the pop-music field, Alanis Morissette, Shania Twain and Céline Dion became stars thanks to energy, talent and good management—not Canadian content regulations. But they don't represent the norm.

Billboard's current Top 100 album list, for instance, includes only three Canadian names. Dion, Morissette and Twain. And a survey of the charts on both sides of the border in 1993, turned up only three Canadians on the U.S. Top 100 and only 15 on the analogous domestic charts.

The success of the three current megastars shouldn't overshadow the flowering of other home-grown talent (Jann Arden, Tragically Hip, Rankin Family) and hundreds of lesser-known artists who have benefited from Canada Council grants, Canadian content regulations and exposure on the CBC.

MYTH FIVE

■ **Nobody cares about culture these days.**

This is a hard myth to dispute in the face of polls that show scant public support for restoring funding to the embattled CBC. However, communications consultant Audley, a former Gallup pollster, says polls that ask Canadians to choose between spending on culture or hospitals are manipulated to produce a predictable response.

Such stark choices—enhanced child benefits or new military helicopters, for example—don't happen in real life, or at least not in real-life bureaucracies.

Meanwhile, there are other indications that Canadians do care about the fate of the CBC. A quarter of a million signed a petition this week to end cuts to the public broadcaster.

Significantly, Copps has been able to extract $10 million from tight-fisted Finance Minister Paul Martin for CBC-Radio—an inadequate gesture, but one prompted by pressure from Liberal MPs under siege by disappointed CBC supporters within their constituencies.

When it comes to other cultural products, Canadians vote with their wallets. Mega-bookstores have opened in several cities, stimulating sales (some 33 percent of them Canadian titles) and fuelling a boom in publishing.

Millions of people visit museums and art galleries, public libraries are busy, many theatres are prospering and CBC-TV's all-Canadian prime-time lineup is attracting rave reviews and large audiences.

The success of Morissette, Twain and Dion shouldn't overshadow the flowering of homegrown talent

MYTH SIX

■ **Like any product, culture only has value if you can export it.**

This notion underlies Art Egleton's controversial speech and isn't an unusual stance for a trade minister to adopt. But no less enthusiastic an entrepreneur than Robert Lantos—mercurial chairman of Alliance Communications Ltd., a leading exporter of TV shows and films to the U.S.—says his company would never have grown without a sound domestic base.

And while rare and special artists like Rohinton Mistry and Atom Egoyan produce work that transcends national borders and sounds universal themes, there are other cultural products and expressions peculiar to Canada—and no less valuable for it.

It is hard to imagine an export audience for the topical *This Hour Has 22 Minutes*, for instance, or for author Peter Newman's exhaustive accounts of Canadian history, but that doesn't mean they shouldn't be encouraged.

Culture isn't softwood lumber; it has more value at home than it does tied up in bundles and shipped to Japan.

MYTH SEVEN

■ **More government funding for the arts will solve everything.**

Wrong. More funding is more likely to enrich cultural bureaucrats, not an evil outcome in itself, but no guarantee of a strong indigenous culture.

As it happens, direct subsidies—such as those provided by the Canada Council and provincial arts councils—are allowed in most trading agreements. Their main drawback is that they drain the federal treasury and make finance ministers crazy.

Even if governments were willing and able to spend, say $100 million to replace lost advertising revenues to Canadian magazines now threatened with unrestricted American competition—the money alone wouldn't preserve our culture.

Audley argues that without laws that allow Canadians to distribute, market, and promote our own products, culture becomes a sort of "sheltered workshop."

That used to be the case with the National Film Board, which produced often-brilliant films that no one ever got to see.

(These days the NFB features and documentaries appear on specialty channels and such educational networks as TVOntario, but they are still essentially excluded from cinema screens.)

In his celebrated speech last February that put culture on the front pages for a short while, Eggleton complained of the "hodgepodge of Canadian content rules applied in a patchwork fashion, inconsistent from one sector to another and unclear in their goals."

There is an unstated yearning here, for a simple formula that can be applied to all cultural sectors—perhaps to all cross-border trade—to ensure that everything flows smoothly, forever.

Talk about myths.

Exporting Canadian culture

NOWHERE-LAND / *The sky—and policy walls—are falling. And Canadian cultural industries are getting the message: 'Internationalize, Internationalize, Internationalize.' Will we gain a global profile or lose our voice?*

BY DOUG SAUNDERS

The Globe and Mail

WHEN influential Toronto entertainment lawyer Michael Levine recently set out to produce a TV mini-series on a history of the Hudson's Bay Co. written by Peter C. Newman, the first thing he did was get on the phone with London, New York and Los Angeles to start making financing deals. When Canadian viewers watch the results of his labour unfold on their TV screens sometime in 1998, they will see a four-part documentary that has been carefully tailored to appeal to European and U.S. audiences.

"Now, we could take it and we could plant the entire story in Montreal and on Hudson's Bay and in Winnipeg, and we could tell it from a Canadian viewpoint in a way that I could guarantee that absolutely *nobody* would have bought it," says Levine, taking a break between conference calls in his small office on Yonge Street. "But the Hudson's Bay—that's a Canadian story like Terry Fox that has universal appeal. The way to do it is to focus on the Orkneys and the Scots and the money men in London and the British Royal Family, so you see it as an international story." When the cred-

its finally roll, they will include networks in the U.K. and the U.S., a major Canadian broadcaster and a hodgepodge of federal and provincial funding agencies, all of whom have had some say in its final form.

This is how culture is created in Canada today. Even a few years ago, the idea of exporting films, shows and books was something that arose *after* the creative work had been done here. Now, if directors, authors, journalists and musicians want to reach a Canadian audience, they very often must first demonstrate to local networks, movie producers, publishers and recording companies that their work has buyers in foreign markets. In some cases, this can mean "internationalizing" the content or focus of the work, adding themes and settings with broader appeal, or avoiding projects altogether that don't travel well—even if those projects could be important or appealing to Canadians.

The export-ification of Canadian culture became a public issue this week after the World Trade Organization ruled that Canada's policies protecting the magazine industry from U.S. competition are unacceptable and must be eliminated. Supporters of the WTO ruling argued

that magazines should follow other media and aim their products at the giant U.S. market. However, many magazine editors say this would mean eliminating content that appeals most to Canadians.

"I honestly don't believe that people in Des Moines or Bangor are going to be terribly interested in reading about Pamela Wallin and the everyday life of a woman in Saskatchewan," says Chatelaine editor Rona Maynard, sounding very much like many people in the film, television, book and music industries.

It is a transformation that seems to have happened almost overnight. "We never could have foreseen this a decade ago," observes Mark Starowicz, the CBC's head of documentaries. At that time, CBC News had 10 documentary teams whose assignments were geared to the network's news agenda; today there are none, and virtually all documentaries on the CBC (and all other Canadian broadcasters) are bought from independent producers who also have buyers in foreign markets. According to Starowicz, this means that important Canadian stories are not being told.

For six decades, until the late 1980s, the challenge faced by the Canadian media was to build local alternatives to the growing barrage of

U.S. voices. The era from 1936 onward was one of institution-building—the CBC, the private networks, the national magazine industry, the movie-production and distribution business, the publishing houses. But recently, seismic changes in Canadian society and international relations have created this second, unforeseen challenge, in which those very institutions are increasingly forced to balance their responsibility to Canadian audiences against the demands of lucrative foreign buyers.

Beginning in the early 1990s, everything began to change in ways that are just being felt now. On the one hand, the federal government very suddenly pulled out of funding culture. Direct expenditures began to fall, especially the huge amounts given to the CBC and the National Film Board. Perhaps more startling was the almost instant disappearance, between 1990 and 1992, of most indirect forms of support—tax credits and other incentives to attract investment in publishing, recording and filmmaking, which dropped from almost $1-billion in 1990 to the current level of almost zero. This very quickly drove many media organizations to begin seeking foreign partners for their endeavours.

At the same time, cracks began to appear in the trade and policy walls intended to protect Canadian culture industries from foreign domination. The flourishing of specialty cable channels was not matched by an increase in domestic TV and movie production, making Canadian content even rarer. Book publishers have begun to feel the effects of continent-wide distribution aimed at enormous bookstores, which make it much more desirable to produce books for an international market and avoid Canada-specific titles. And in the wake of last week's WTO ruling, executives in many cultural industries now say they are preparing to "go international" in anticipation of future rulings against cultural protection.

Many of those executives have had other reasons to look outward. The government agencies that finance broadcast media—Telefilm Canada, the Ontario and Quebec film-development offices and the Cable and Television Production Fund—now tend to act like banks, looking more favourably on projects with international partners. The Canadian advertising industry was almost entirely bought by U.S. firms in the early 1990s, making continent-wide "buys" more appealing. And many have been frightened into global marketing by the prospect of competition from enormous multinational culture companies such as Time Warner and Viacom.

For some, these conditions have created a grand opportunity for Canadians to have a strong voice in the international media. "I think we grow in stature as a nation and our culture is enriched and the quality is improved as we export," says Levine, who proudly describes himself as an "export nationalist." Indeed, his philosophy is reflected well in his work—he has been the deal-maker behind projects such as the 1986 mini-series *Anne of Green Gables* and *The Terry Fox Story* that have been both export-friendly and distinctly Canadian.

And, as Levine points out, an export orientation allows expansive-minded Canadians to free themselves from parochial limitations imposed by Canada's arbitrary borders and finally make films about so-called universal themes. His efforts helped make possible the television version of Michael Ignatieff's *Blood and Belonging* about tribalism and nationalism, and his Hudson's Bay story may well be a far better history for stepping outside Canada's physical and thematic boundaries. "Canadians are good at this dichotomy between your sense of identity as part of a tribe or part of a nation on one hand, and your sense of internationalism and your part of a greater world on the other," he said. "That's the dilemma of export, because the minute you export, by definition you are speaking to universals."

BUT the problems begin when directors and writers would rather not speak to universals, when they want to create something that would only make sense in Canada. "Nobody in the United States has to worry about anything like this," argues film producer John Kastner, who has produced dozens of documentaries including the recent award-winning *Hunting Bobby Oatway*, about the release of a sex offender into a small community. "They don't have to worry about foreign funding, they don't have to turn Manhattan into Moose Jaw." The opposite, Kastner says, has become all too common. In fact, he received enormous pressure from the producers of the PBS show *Frontline* to make *Oatway* more reflective of the U.S. penal system. Eventually, he convinced the CBC to produce it in-house at a much lower budget.

Many directors and producers don't bother fighting such battles. "In terms of documentaries it's a real problem," says Kastner. "What you're starting to see is a new generation of very gifted filmmakers doing things like *The Plague Monkeys* [a Canadian documentary about the African Ebola plague] as opposed to Canadian stories, because it's easier to get made, easier to sell."

The situation is even more dire in the world of book publishing, where many forms of government support have been eliminated or radically reduced and few forms of trade protection remain. In response, almost all publishers now look southward when they consider which books to publish. "We'd rather be publishing interesting books for a Canadian audience," says Anna Porter, founder of Toronto's Key Porter Books, which makes half its revenue from U.S. sales and plans to increase that to 60 per cent. "We've really had to cut back on things that I would really like to read while sitting back on a Sunday afternoon, things like books about Canadian politics."

She is not alone. Most book editors acknowledge privately that they now routinely reject book proposals that would be reasonably successful in Canada simply because they wouldn't find U.S. buyers. Or if they do accept the proposals, they often ask authors to modify their work to suit U.S. readers. In non-fiction books, references to Canadian incidents and locations are often removed and authors are asked to find examples from beyond our borders.

This is not limited to non-fiction. Toronto author Barbara Gowdy, for instance, had to change the ending of her novel *Falling Angels* for the U.S. edition in 1989, because New York editors told her that American readers want something more upbeat. Today, editors say that such a change would be less likely, for the simple reason that U.S. partnerships are often taken into consideration from the very beginning. Books may still be edited to satisfy the perceived tastes of the U.S. public, but now Canadian audiences have to read them that way too.

Some observers fear that this new export focus will create a bland, homogenized world on Canadian screens and pages, deliberately stripped of local references and character. Says Martyn Burke, a Canadian film producer who now does most of his work out of Los Angeles because of frustrations with the Canadian system: "If you go to New York and you say, 'I've got this great idea, it involves Kenora, Ontario,' they're going to look at you blankly and say, 'If you can add Peoria as well as Kenora then we'll be happy.' My question is, are we going to be able to do anything that's Canadian, or is it going to be this kind of nowhere-land?"

That particular nowhere-land is well known to Canadian movie producers. In the 1970s, the federal government tried to launch a film industry by creating a tax shelter for investments in export-oriented productions. The results were generally unwatchable films set in Canadian locales disguised as pseudo-American netherworlds. Similar products can now be seen in Europe, where attempts to make high-grossing films for a continent-wide market have resulted in a genre widely known as the "Euro-pudding," featuring actors from several countries and stateless, homogenous locations.

However, most of the Canadian culture being exported today is hardly stateless or homogenous. In fact, there appears to be a global appetite for many particularly Canadian stories, from the TV series *The Road to Avonlea* to Alice Munro's short stories to *The Boys of St. Vincent.* "That's just Shakespeare," says Starowicz. "There are some local stories that have such universal themes that they travel." But there is a great volume of Canadian culture that would lose everything in the translation—*This Hour Has 22 Minutes,* Maclean's magazine, Stevie Cameron's On the Take or the CBC's biography of Pierre Trudeau (which couldn't find a U.S. buyer).

People like Starowicz are more worried about what *isn't* getting produced—or in many cases, isn't even being thought about by writers and directors, who have altered their creative visions in anticipation of funding realities. They may approach a producer with 15 proposals, and have three of them accepted—none of which will be about the decline of fishing communities in Newfoundland. Or they might toss aside such ideas before they even knock on the door. "In documentaries, the decision-making point is at the buy-in. We don't change our stories, we murder them in the crib."

STAROWICZ knows this from personal experience. He is currently airing a seven-part history of international television news he directed (titled Dawn of the Eye, on CBC TV on Sunday nights), for which he had to travel to New York to pitch to U.S. networks. He tells of network producers cancelling appointments and asking him if the CBC is a Vancouver station. (Eventually the BBC and the U.S.-based History Channel joined the CBC as partners.) But he also found a novel way to keep local details in the series—by producing *three* distinct versions, one each for the Canadian, U.S. and British audiences. Few production companies have the resources to do this.

Ironically, the export boom has made Canadian film and television production a hugely successful industry. Our largest independent producers, such as Alliance and Atlantis, have offices around the world and impressive reputations in the global market. However, this expansion has led to criticisms that they make all their decisions from Los Angeles and are losing interest in their own country's stories. "In order to create Canadian films and documentaries, we have had to destroy them," says producer Martyn Burke. "Having to go to a half-dozen government agencies with different agendas, it just conspires against production companies doing anything Canadian." Just this month, the Ontario Film Development Corp. released a study which revealed that only a third of the money spent on films in the province went to indigenous Canadian productions.

Of course, people will argue endlessly about what constitutes a "Canadian" production. (Does it have to be set in Canada? Can it not involve other parties? How many Canadians does it take . . .) And Canadian audiences seem ambivalent: On one hand, shows such as *Hockey Night in Canada* and *Road to Avonlea* top the ratings, novels by Canadian authors are year-long bestsellers, and home-grown music tends to sell well. At the same time, Canadians have little taste for locally made movies, the top 20 TV shows each week rarely include more than four or five Canadian programs and Canadians are relatively indifferent to their own magazines, buying 500,000 copies of Maclean's every week, but 300,000 copies of Time. Nevertheless, there is a widely held sense that Canada should have more say in the contents of its media, since TV and film, in particular, still use billions of tax-payer dollars.

"Is the CBC turning into a gigantic production fund for independent producers who are making films more and more slanted at the United States?" Kastner asks. "Are Telefilm, the OFDC, all of these government-funded agencies really subsidizing independent producers who are making American-directed stories?"

This sense has long simmered under the surface. A 1994 survey by Ekos Research commissioned by the federal government described the industry's perceptions of federal film-development policy: "a predominant perception that the real goal is simply to increase the amount of production actually in Canada, without regard to whether that production reflects the work of Canadian creators or reflects Canadian society and contributes to Canadian identity."

People who watch the book-publishing and magazine industries have begun to express similar worries. "The price of entering the U.S. market is too high for most Canadian publishers to bother," said Patrick Walshe, who watches the media for the advertising industry. "If the government isn't going to step in and protect a distinctly Canadian culture, then we'll start seeing magazines collapsing pretty soon."

It is a quintessentially Canadian paradox: Just as Canada's cultural industries look better than ever from an international perspective, they are discovering that they still need state support to produce anything that they can actually call Canadian. "I'm waiting to see," said consultant Paul Audley, who had a hand in designing many of the federal culture policies that are now under threat. "Is the government still committed to ensuring there are Canadian-controlled productions and real Canadian content, content made by and for Canadians? We'll have to see if it matters to them."

Canadian culture policies pique U.S. interest

STRONG AND FREE / *Ottawa's support of culture industries draws fire from south of the border.*

BY DREW FAGAN

Washington Bureau

THE recent ruling by a World Trade Organization panel that Canadian magazine policies violate international trade rules has shaken Ottawa and the domestic cultural sector. This is a sector that employs close to one million Canadians.

The question now is, what next? Filmmakers, book publishers and other producers of cultural products are supported, just like the magazine industry, by Canadian government policies, which include protections of various forms and financial assistance. These policies were designed to boost Canadian cultural expression in a continental marketplace where U.S. entertainment giants dominate.

As well, these policies have long been a sore point with U.S. government officials, who are now examining the WTO decision to see if it provides advantages for future trade cases. Canadian officials, however, characterize the ruling as having been decided on narrow grounds that do not provide a sweeping precedent.

"The Canadian objective would be to limit the effect, and the longer-term objective of the United States would be to break open the Canadian regulatory system," said Dennis Browne, director of the Ottawa-based Centre for Trade Policy and Law.

A recent Canadian government survey of 26 nations, including most industrialized and major developing countries, found that all but three maintain some restrictions on foreign investment in their cultural sector.

A similar survey of 10 European nations found that all of them provide financial aid for domestic cultural production. But only Canada has both kinds of policies—restrictions and aid—for all four industries examined: broadcasting, publishing, filmmaking and sound recording.

Some of Ottawa's policies likely are immune from future attack by Washington because they were grandfathered under the North American free-trade agreement or exempted under terms of the WTO.

Most assistance programs receive little attention from Washington, partly because the overall amount of funding provided by Ottawa has been declining anyway in recent years. But the Clinton administration, in any case, probably will be looking anew at everything Canada does, as Washington seeks additional opportunities for a sector that represents the country's second-largest export.

"We haven't found many ways of setting up cultural protections... that make us happy," said a U.S. official last year. "We favour openness, and letting the choice go to the consumer. We have an economic interest in doing so."

When Washington turns its gaze toward Canada's cultural support mechanisms, this is what it sees:

	FILM	TELEVISION	RECORDINGS	MAGAZINES	BOOKS	NEWSPAPERS
FINANCING	Financial support for the Canadian film industry comes primarily from two federal agencies, the National Film Board and Telefilm Canada. Together, they provided about $200-million last year for the production and distribution of feature films that "interpret Canada to Canadians and other nations." Some of Telefilm Canada's budget supports television programming, and a new government fund for film and television production provides another $100-million annually. Two years ago, the federal government also revamped a tax credit, worth about $80-million annually, for investment in films produced by Canadian corporations.	In addition to subsidies from Telefilm Canada for television programming, a Cable Production Fund worth $40-million annually was established in 1995 to support TV production. The money, which comes from cable fees paid by Canadian households, is devoted to increasing domestic programming in areas particularly dominated by imports, such as children's shows and adult drama and comedy. The $100-million production fund announced by Heritage Minister Sheila Copps last fall also will go partly to television programming.	The only government subsidy received by the music industry is known as the Sound Recording Development Program. It provided about $4.2-million last year, but has been doubled for 1997. Ottawa has no significant tax-policy measures aimed at encouraging music recordings. Radio stations, however are required to provide funds to the Foundation to Aid Canadian Talent on Records (FACTOR), which helps underwrite Canadian recording efforts.	The World Trade Organization ruling last week found that a distribution subsidy provided to Canadian magazines, worth $58-million in 1996, is unfairly designed. The subsidy, which has existed for almost a century, is the largest government expenditure in support of the industry.	The Book Publishing Industry Development Program will provide $18-million this year to encourage the growth of Canadian-controlled publishing companies. The Canada Council also provides grants for the publication, promotion and translation of books.	The Publications Assistance Program subsidizes distribution of small, community newspapers and is worth about $3.5-million this year to that industry. (The program, which also assists magazine and book distribution, was not under direct attack in the WTO case although it is similar to the postal subsidy at issue in that dispute.)
PROTECTION	Ottawa maintains tough restrictions on foreign investment in the Canadian film-distribution business. Takeovers of Canadian-owned distribution operations are not allowed. The establishment of foreign-owned operations in Canada are only allowed for the marketing of their own films. Foreign takeovers of foreign-owned companies are contingent on a pledge to reinvest a portion of Canadian earnings in domestic film production. Despite these policies, foreign firms earn 83 per cent of the revenues from film distribution in Canada.	Licences for television broadcasters are granted only if 80 per cent of the shares, and all of the directors' positions, are held by Canadians. At least 60 per cent of all programming shown on Canadian TV stations must be domestic content, and at least 50 per cent of prime-time schedules must be Canadian-produced. Canadian cable companies must provide more Canadian channels than foreign. Foreign-owned specialty channels will be licenced for viewership in Canada only if they do not compete directly with a Canadian-owned service.	At least 30 per cent of recordings broadcast by most domestic radio stations must be produced by Canadian artists. The percentage is lower for stations that specialize in jazz or classical music. This policy, which has been criticized in the past for using a complicated formula to determine what qualifies as Canadian content, has been in place for about 25 years.	The WTO decision also struck down two Ottawa policies to combat split-run magazines. The two policies are: (1) a border restriction against the importation of split-run magazines that direct more than 5 per cent of their ads to a Canadian audience; (2) an 80-per-cent excise tax on the advertising revenue of any split-run magazine that evades the border barrier through publication in Canada. For the past 20 years, advertising expenditures have been tax-deductible in Canada only if the ads were placed in a Canadian publication. That law could potentially be attacked by Washington.	Under federal ownership rules, established in 1985 and revised in 1992, foreign companies cannot establish operations in Canada unless control is in Canadian hands. The acquisition of an existing Canadian-controlled business by non-Canadian interests is not permitted unless Ottawa concludes that the business is in financial trouble and no Canadian entity is interested in purchasing it.	Foreign companies are blocked from owning more than 25 per cent of Canadian newspapers.

	FILM	TELEVISION	RECORDINGS	MAGAZINES	BOOKS	NEWSPAPERS
THE FUTURE	Efforts by Polygram Filmed Entertainment, a subsidiary of the Netherlands-based Philips conglomerate, to establish operations in Canada split the Liberal government and have caused increased examination of the ownership restrictions established in 1988. Polygram is to abide by the existing rules until a government review is completed. But any opening of the market will be seized upon by international companies to make inroads into Canada at the expense of smaller Canadian-owned film distributors.	According to the Canadian Radio-television and Telecommunications Commission, foreign-owned specialty channels can be forced off the air in favour of Canadian-owned alternatives. A prolonged trade battle involving a U.S. country music network called CMT was resolved last year. But the issue is almost certain to come up again as the number of licenced cable channels in Canada grows. In the fast-growing field of direct-to-home satellite television, Ottawa-Washington negotiations over sharing facilities have broken down. U.S. concerns about Canadian content requirements are likely to be a future flash point.	Canada and the United States may have more battles over Canadian content in the growing field of specialty radio services. Pay audio, where subscribers receive commercial-free, digital-quality programming, is available in Canada. Canadian regulators have established content requirements, but Washington says the requirements make no sense when there is little Canadian-produced music of such styles as flamenco and polka. A trade case regarding specialty programming could provide the basis for a larger attack by the U.S. government on content rules in traditional radio.	The trade-panel decision may lead to a flood of split-run magazines into Canada. They would follow on the heels of Sports Illustrated's Canadian edition, which was the immediate cause of the trade case and has not been published since Ottawa imposed the 80 per cent tax on its advertising revenue.	Ottawa likely will continue to walk a fine line between angering the Canadian industry, which maintains a nationalist bent, and angering Washington. Canadian publishers were dismayed when the sale to U.S. interests of Ginn Canada Publishing, a textbook company, was approved by Ottawa in 1994. But Ottawa drew the Clinton administration's ire last year when a planned foray into Canada by Borders Inc., a U.S. book chain, was opposed by Industry Canada. The Borders dispute is likely to be cited in the 1997 edition of the U.S. government's annual list of foreign trade barriers.	The ownership restriction was not one of Washington's major concerns, at least compared to restrictions in other Canadian cultural industries. However, the limit is being questioned increasingly within Canada as ownership of newspapers nationwide becomes more and more concentrated.

Aboriginal Issues

As it has on many occasions in Canadian history, the question of aboriginal rights and the role of the aboriginal peoples in the Canadian political system has surfaced as a highly visible issue in Canadian politics in recent years. Since the Meech Lake Agreement, when aboriginal issues were specifically put on the agenda of social problems needing to be resolved, aboriginal leaders have continued to press their agenda on Canadian political leaders and the Canadian media. This section includes seven articles that cover the ever-increasingly visible issue of aboriginal rights and how this important social problem is being addressed.

In an article focusing on how Canada's Indian leaders are working together to decide strategy, Shafer Parker Jr. of the *Alberta Report* shows that the Indian leaders are divided on how to pursue greater autonomy without also incurring greater financial responsibilities. They recognize that some legal strategies leading to self-government may have the consequence of costing the Indian population a great deal in terms of government grants. The article describes the legal status of Canada's Indian populations and the strategies they have preferred for economic and political development.

A second article by Parker focuses on an interesting twist to the issue of the approaching division of the Northwest Territories. In an essay titled "Apartheid Has Its Attractions," Parker examines what will happen in 1999 when the Northwest Territories becomes two separate entities. His focus is on the part of the Territories called Nunavut, the eastern part of the Territories, which will have a population of approximately 22,000 people—17,500 of them Inuit. The problem is that some of the proposed Nunavut government institutions have been accused of leading to a system of race-based government there, and the minority population groups are protesting to the Canadian government that it has made a deal with the Inuit leaders that is not going to lead to a just social system.

The next article examines the Royal Commission on Aboriginal Peoples, which issued its final report in November of 1996. The commission was created to provide Canadians with the opportunity to include the aboriginal population in its national identity. When, in November 1996, the final report of the commission was handed down, the author of this essay suggests that the government of Prime Minister Jean Chrétien ignored it. This has led the aboriginal population to be disappointed with the record of the Chrétien government.

Rudy Platiel of *The Globe and Mail (Toronto)* describes three major issues affecting the future of Canada's native people in the next article. He suggests that these are increasing economic disparity within the native community, very modest political progress, and little advancement on native issues in the courts. In addition to the immediately obvious problems that are caused by these situations, they are going to be increasingly significant in future years and will require constant attention and energy to improve the future of Canada's native people.

In an article titled "An Unworkable Vision of Self-Government," Tom Flanagan discusses the final report of the Royal Commission on Aboriginal Peoples. He suggests that one of its major themes is that Canada's native people should move toward greater self-government because they are nations in the full sense of the term. This article discusses some of the implications of this general recommendation and concludes that the recommendations of the Royal Commission are far worse than the current status of the aboriginal peoples.

Joe Dion of *Policy Options* contributes an essay titled "Aboriginal Government: Alternative Outcomes." In it he discusses what is meant by "self government" as it affects aboriginal peoples, what the breadth of aboriginal jurisdiction would be, and how it would be financed. A First Nations Commission is discussed as a response to this problem, and the article includes discussion of several measures that could be agreed upon to move in the direction of establishing a First Nations Federation.

Finally, John Gray of *The Globe and Mail (Toronto)* examines the lack of attention during the 1997 federal election campaign to aboriginal issues and to the report of the Royal Commission on Aboriginal Peoples. The author concludes that aboriginal peoples are simply not significant on the Canadian political horizon and that much work has to be done before these issues will receive the attention that they deserve.

Looking Ahead: Challenge Questions

In how many different ways can we see the impact of native societies on contemporary Canadian society? Are the linkages visible in many different areas or in only a few?

UNIT 8

Has the government of Canada lived up to its obligations to the aboriginal peoples of Canada? What does the Report of the Royal Commission on Aboriginal Peoples suggest *should* be the role of aboriginal peoples in Canada?

Should the government of Canada support the claims of aboriginal leaders for native self-government? Are there any areas in which self-government should not be granted? What would be the financial implications of a self-governing aboriginal entity?

Do Canada's aboriginal peoples have the same type of claim to "distinct society" status as the people of Quebec? Are their claims stronger or weaker? Is there such a thing as an "inherent" right to self-government? Should there be a separate legal system for Canada's aboriginal peoples?

Apron-string sovereignty

Canada's native leaders want sweeping self-government—but without self-sufficiency

Perhaps no federal cabinet minister has ever been more sympathetic than Indian Affairs and Northern Development Minister Ron Irwin to the collectivist, special-status ideals that permeate contemporary Canada's Indian leadership. After all, while still a lawyer in private life, Mr. Irwin was himself a beneficiary of the country's state-funded Indian industry, representing a number of Ontario bands. And since assuming his portfolio in late 1993, he has tried openly to accommodate one of the most extravagant aims of native militants by operating as though the so-called "inherent right" of Indian self-government exists legally, even though Canadian voters rejected it in the 1992 constitutional referendum.

But even a man as accommodating as Mr. Irwin is discovering just how difficult it is to satisfy the contradictory demands of Indian leaders for more autonomy without attendant financial responsibility. Last month, in a move intended to assist bands in their stated aim to become more self-sufficient, the Liberal minister moved to extend modest powers to use reserve lands as collateral for raising investment capital. While the proposed Indian Act amendments fell far short of placing native individuals and businesses on an equal footing with other Canadians, Mr. Irwin was instantly pilloried by Assembly of First Nations (AFN) national chief Ovide Mercredi and other Indian leaders for allegedly undermining Ottawa's fiduciary responsibility to Indians. Given the Liberals' timidity and the chiefs' hostility, the economic ghettoization that blights reserve life seems likely to continue indefinitely.

Mr. Irwin unveiled his plans at the AFN's annual meeting in Winnipeg last month. "As a lawyer, I found the Act almost offensive," he told the assembly, adding that it was time to get rid of the "outdated, archaic, and paternalistic laws" that his audience found "offensive."

Judging from their reaction, however, it was the minister and his amendments that the chiefs found offensive. After listening to Mr.

Irwin explain that the amendment package was an interim measure designed to move forward the process of granting Indian bands total self-government and the economic freedom needed to compete successfully in a modern economy, the Indian leaders spent the next six hours telling him that because

Treaty 7 negotiations, 1877:
Since then, everything has changed except the idea of an Indian 'collectivity.'

they had not had an active part in drafting his proposals, they viewed the whole process as a betrayal of their interests. Furthermore, they stated in a resolution passed by the delegates, his amendments were offered "without regard to the priority issues of the First Nations with respect to the First Nations-Crown relationship" and were therefore irrelevant.

Before they left Winnipeg, the 800-plus delegates voted to reject Mr. Irwin's amendments package and to strike a committee to bypass him entirely and deliver their own legislative initiatives directly to Prime Minister Jean Chretien. That committee will hold closed-door sessions in Regina on October 17 and 18 to develop alternatives to Mr. Irwin's proposed amendments.

Those deliberations will be private, but the militant tone of the draft agenda hints at the likely direction. The agenda states that "the effect of [Mr. Irwin's] proposed amendments will be prejudicial to the rights and interests of the First Nations" and identifies ways to embarrass and pressure the Chretien government by taking the chiefs' case to the United Nations and other international tribunals.

True to his habit, Mr. Irwin signalled his willingness to bow to the native leaders' demands. He told the AFN delegates that he would change or delete any of the amendments they opposed and abandoned on the spot the most contentious ones allowing lending institutions to use leased land on reserves as security for loans. He also offered to alter his timetable for bringing forward the legislation, agreeing to wait until next year if necessary to hear the chiefs' recommendations.

But even though Mr. Irwin pledged to the chiefs that none of his amendments would alter the government's duty to hold reserve land in trust for Canada's native people, Mr. Mercredi nonetheless charged that the proposals would impose an alien property concept on an unwilling Indian populace. Lamented the AFN leader: "It means making our people into the people the Reform Party wants us to be—individuals with property for development or investment."

Other critics of the proposed amendments retort that their biggest flaw is precisely that they would fail to do that. In fact, most involve restructuring the powers of the minister and band governments to increase local control, repealing unused sections of the Act, and validating current practices not covered in the Indian Act.

Mr. Irwin is also proposing to enhance his own autonomy. Under his proposals, he and his successors would be able to grant management and control over reserve lands to band governments, to cede authority to manage and expend the revenues bands collect through on-reserve taxation and to set aside elections without securing cabinet approval through orders-in-council. Mr. Irwin argues that this would help reduce undue delays and lengthy bureaucratic processes, but it would also have the advantage of allowing him to confer additional privileges on his Indian charges with even less outside scrutiny than at present.

Provisions to be repealed include sections 32 and 33, which make it necessary for the minister to approve the disposal of agricultural products in the prairie provinces; section 34, which requires bands to comply with departmental instructions regarding the maintenance of roads and bridges; and section 71, whereby the minister authorizes the operation of farms on reserve lands. Other proposals include lengthening the term of office for chiefs and councillors from two years to three and requiring candidates for chief to be community members.

Most of this seemed palatable enough to the chiefs, but they balked at every change that might open the door to mainstreaming their property-holding arrangements and thereby enhance their band members' ability to engage in private business. Along with rejecting Mr. Irwin's offer of the power to use leased reserve property as security in financial transactions, the chiefs objected to his inclusion of a new section giving bands "the same rights, obligations and capacities as a person, *e.g.,* the right to sue and to be sued" and "the right to hold land." Also deemed offensive was a section that would regularize reserve lands with other land registry systems and provide greater security "to lending institutions and investors who would thus be more inclined to invest on reserve lands."

"It's obvious why the chiefs rejected Irwin's proposal to let reserve land be used as security for loans," says Reform party Indian affairs critic John Duncan. "Such moves upset the power of their collective governments by removing the need for a continued dependency on the federal government." Mr. Duncan maintains that the real reason the chiefs so stridently oppose any move toward private property arrangements is that such a move would help individual Indians escape the oppressive embrace of band bureaucracies. As Indians began building equity in their own homes and businesses, the authority of the chiefs and councils would necessarily be diluted. "It would definitely change things for existing aboriginal leadership," observes the Reform MP.

Russell Diabo, the AFN's coordinator for the Indian Act project, offers other explanations for the native leaders' displeasure. "Mr. Irwin told us that he made the change in the leasing regula-

tions so that bands could use reserve lands to generate more income," he says. "But the minister is really trying to coerce the First Nations to raise more of their own revenue, and we won't accept that." Mr. Diabo foresees that if Mr. Irwin has his way, a day will come when Ottawa will tell Indian bands it can reduce the size of their grants because they are now generating much of their own income.

Mr. Diabo further complains that Mr. Irwin's amendments to the Indian Act, while offered as a step toward self-government, are really part of a federal plan to "get out of its treaty responsibilities." And he accuses Mr. Irwin of trying to distract the chiefs with discussions about the Indian Act when the real issues are to protect Indians from the encroachment of provincial power and to grant statutory authority for band sovereignty.

"In the future Indian bands want to be a distinct order of government within Canadian federalism," Mr. Diabo says. "We want to be seen as an ongoing and permanent characteristic of the nation." This third order, he promises, "will be maintained in collectives." And echoing his boss's increasing militancy, Mr. Diabo hints ominously that Indians are prepared to use force in pursuing their goal of sovereignty. "The government had better take us seriously because the situation is becoming realtively de-stabilized. And there are definite implications from that."

Even more fundamental to the chiefs' opposition, Mr. Diabo continues, is that Mr. Irwin refused to grant them sole authority to decide how to rearrange their legislative status. Their right to this power, he claims, "was made clear by Canada's Supreme Court in the *Sparrow* decision of 1990. The court set out criteria for consulting with Indians and said that before legislation affecting them could be passed the government had to get Indian agreement that the legislation fulfilled a valid objective from the Indian point of view."

University of Calgary history professor Sarah Carter counters that some of Mr. Irwin's proposed amendments make good sense. For instance, Prof.

Carter, whose book *Lost Harvests* documents how federal policies prevented Indian bands from developing into viable farming communities after they settled on reserves in the late 1800s, argues the proposal to drop the sections of the Indian Act that require department approval before the barter or sale of livestock or farm produce are long overdue. Prof. Carter says those same Indian Act requirements drove many 19th-century Indians out of farming, an act of state-induced sabotage that triggered the slide into welfare dependency from which most western Canadian reserves have never escaped.

While he concurs with Ms. Carter in welcoming those of Mr. Irwin's proposed amendments which afford Indians more personal responsibility for their own welfare, B.C. constitutional lawyer Mel Smith says that the package is at best a half-measure. "It's a shame that the amendment I liked best, the one that allowed band assets to be held as security for loans, is the one the government dropped first," says Mr. Smith, author of *Our Home or Native Land?* "Reserves represent tremendous assets and anything that can get Indians to develop their property is a step in the right direction."

And whatever grandiose claims people like Mr. Diabo may make to sovereign powers, Mr. Smith asserts that "lawmaking rests in the hands of two orders of government only. The *Sparrow* decision had nothing to do with that. It only spoke to legislation that would abrogate enumerated aboriginal rights." Mr. Smith cites another recent ruling, *Howard,* as a precedent by which the Supreme Court of Canada made it plain that Indians had no right to joint decision-making.

Mr. Smith stresses that the whole idea of separate legal treatment has prevented the full and productive participation of natives in Canadian society. "We have to break the cycle where native people are forever the wards of the state," he says. "And that can only happen when Indian people are put on the same economic and legal footing as everybody else."

Shafer Parker, Jr.

Apartheid has its attractions

A draft constitution for the Western Arctic would enshrine race-based governance

As one of their last gasps in June 1993, the Mulroney Tories decreed the end of the Northwest Territories. Once described by former Prime Minister John Diefenbaker as "Canada's last great untouched inheritance," the NWT will become two separate entities on April 1, 1999. The split will create the eastern territory of Nunavut and a western territory that currently has to leave blank spaces where the name ought to go in some of its official documents. Internet humorists have suggested the Western Arctic might adopt the dyslexic-friendly moniker of "Bob", while other ways have begun referring to the region as "The-Rest-Of-It."

But critics warn that what Ottawa is in the processing of accomplishing in the north to the principle of equality is no joke. They contend that solely for reasons of political expedience, the vast territory and untapped mineral wealth of "Canada's inheritance" has been effectively given away to a tiny segment of Canada's population. Nunavut's 22,000 people, 17,500 of them Inuit, will gain a new government that possesses what amounts to provincial powers—including its own capital city, a legislature, a cabinet with a government leader dubbed "premier," powers of taxation and to establish and regulate services and resources, and a complete system of prisons and courts, including a appellate court and a Supreme Court of Nunavut.

And just two weeks ago, a Constitutional Working Group comprising the Western Arctic's representatives in the territorial legislature and aboriginal and federal-government representatives presented to "The-Rest-Of-It's" 36,000 people a draft constitution which, if approved by them and by Ottawa, will enshrine Nunavut-like powers and privileges. In fact, it will do even more: in a Canadian echo of South Africa's reviled and abandoned apartheid system, the territory would be governed by a pair of legislative assemblies that by law will be divided by race.

If allowed to stand, many observers think the changes in the NWT could also establish a dangerous race-based precedent for native land-claim settlements in the rest of Canada, particularly those still to be dealt with in British Columbia. It would also mean that Ottawa has taken a step towards enshrining a constitutionally-unwarranted "inherent right" of sovereign native self-government. Already, since Nunavut's Inu-

it land-claim agreement is constitutionally entrenched by section 35 of the Constitution Act, 1982, the territory may already have gained something approaching the sovereignty-association status that has been denied Quebec.

Moreover, in an echo of the Charlottetown Accord so resoundingly rejected at the polls, the Western Arctic's draft constitution attempts to enshrine a special right for a permanent veto power for a minority group. Unlike Nunavut's largely homogeneous Inuit population, the Western Arctic has a 53% non-native majority. Nevertheless, the draft constitution would lock in native domination of the territorial government for the foreseeable future.

With a land mass larger than Europe and a population density of about four people per 100 square miles, it is open to question whether the NWT is a good candidate for self-government. The problem is aggravated by a population that is by all objective standards the least prepared in Canada to handle its own affairs. When Nunavut is established, it will have the highest unemployment rate in Canada, the lowest literacy rate, the youngest and fastest-growing population, the most welfare recipients per capita, the highest cost of living and the most underdeveloped public infrastructure.

The Western Arctic runs a close second in the race for the bottom. While Nunavut has a birth rate three times the national average, the Western Arctic rate is 24.4 births per thousand population, nearly twice Canada's national rate of 13.2. The NWT's tiny population is for governing purposes made smaller by the huge percentage of people under 15 years of age. Nunavut's under-15 age-group totals 8,335, or 44% of the population, while the Western Arctic contains 10,560 youths under 15, about 56% of the total. And while welfare rolls may be growing faster in Nunavut, they are also climbing swiftly in the Western Arctic; in both territories, communities have recorded increases exceeding 250% over the past five years.

As for the expense involved in establishing the bureaucracy necessary for self-government, a report completed by management consultants Coopers & Lybrand in December 1992 estimates capital costs for new government buildings in Nunavut at $334 million. An estimated $520 million will be spent in operating costs between start-up in 1999 and the year

2008. After that, the report estimates that Nunavut will require $84 million a year more than it now costs to service the region from Yellowknife. The newly established bureaucracy will require 930 new jobs, along with 705 transferred from Yellowknife. Worse, virtually all these costs will have to be borne by taxpayers from elsewhere in Canada, since the consulting firm has projected that none of Nunavut's population will contribute any tax revenues for their new government in the foreseeable future.

The utter incapacity of Nunavut to pay for its grandiose array of legislative, administrative and judicial agencies has not dissuaded Western Arctic leaders from pressing for an equally elaborate system, with the alarming addition of legally-enshrined race-based rule. The draft package put together by the Constitutional Working Group proposes a bicameral legislative assembly, composed of a 14-member General Assembly based on population to "represent the general interests of all residents," and an eight-member Aboriginal Peoples Assembly representing each of the NWT's distinct bands. The General Assembly would be elected from the same ridings as now exist in the territorial legislature. Natives would be able to vote for representatives to both assemblies, but non-natives would be expressly disenfranchised from the Aboriginal People's Assembly. At present, 10 of the Western Arctic's 14 ridings are already held by natives.

The native representatives would exercise a *de jure* veto over all legislation. Proposed laws could not pass without a majority from both assemblies. If a law failed to gain passage on its first attempt, it could be brought back for a second vote which would require a two-thirds majority of the combined assembly. But since aboriginal representation is mandatory for at least eight of the 22 combined seats, the two-thirds threshold could never be met over a united native opposition. The guarantee of eight aboriginal-only seats also means that native representation could drop to as low as seven in the general assembly and still allow the racial group unimpeded domination, since it would retain a total of 15 in the combined houses, sufficient to override the veto provision.

The Constitutional Working Group will hold hearings across the Western Arctic on their proposed constitution until next March. Depending on what they learn in the hearing process, they will present a final proposal for public rat-

   From *Alberta Report*, November 4, 1996, pp. 19-21. © 1996 by United Western Communications, Ltd. Reprinted by permission.

ification a few months later. If the region's voters approve, it will then be sent to the federal government for passage in Parliament.

Dave Lovell, mayor of Yellowknife, the NWT's largest city and current capital, rejects the proposed constitution out of hand. "It isn't fair to the NWT's non-native population," he observes. "The aboriginals are starting with the deck stacked in their favour." Mr. Lovell points out that the western caucus in the territorial legislature is mostly aboriginal already, and that five of the eight cabinet members are also natives. "They do a good job," he says. "But if we try to lock in racial proportions it could become a contentious issue forever." Mayor Lovell maintains that "one man, one vote" is fundamental to democracy. "If Indians get two votes," he suggests, "why not give extra votes to other groups too?"

Mr. Lovell suggests that the draft constitution strongly favours natives because none of the Constitutional Working Group were from Yellowknife, the NWT's one cosmopolitan centre. "We're going to insist pretty strongly on the principle of one man, one vote," the mayor promises. "And a lot of Indians and Métis who feel the same way are going to join us."

But other leaders justify the rejection of the one man, one vote principle. For example, Métis Nation representative George Kurszewski, who served as co-chairman of the Constitutional Working Group, says the draft constitution's racist cast and quasi-territorial powers are warranted. "Aboriginal people have two kinds of guaranteed rights," he claims. "The right to self-government and the rights of a citizen of Canada." Therefore,

he says, a divided legislature is necessary to protect both kinds of rights.

Mr. Kurszewski also argues that a constitution guaranteeing special powers to native people is necessary because, unlike Nunavut, the Western Arctic is fractionalized between eight tribal groups and therefore can not "go the land claims course" to self-government. Such a course, he suggests, would merely result in a patchwork of governments and competing claims for lands and resources. A public government that gives native groups special status is the only way to avoid that problem while keeping crafting an arrangement attractive enough to make the tribal groups want to get involved.

"Besides," he argues, "the dual assembly doesn't really give native people a voting advantage" beyond what they currently enjoy. He explains that

Provinces by any other name

Concern has been expressed in some quarters that Canada's experiment in combining native self-government with new forms of territorial governments amounts to the creation of *de facto* provinces. But Kirk Cameron, director of northern political development for the Department of Indian Affairs and Northern Development (DIAND), does not see it that way. Mr. Cameron agrees that territorial governments have evolved to the point that they can hardly be distinguished from provincial governments. And he admits that "the Yukon and the Northwest Territories already have regimes for income tax and corporate taxes very similar to the provinces." Furthermore, the Yukon government, with its party politics, "looks very much like a province to me."

According to Mr. Cameron, however, this is a case "where it walks like a duck and quacks like a duck, but still isn't a duck." There remains one big difference between the territories and the provinces. "There are only 11 players in the constitution," he says, "the federal government and 10 provinces." But for Mr. Cameron, territories are limited only in the lack of a direct voice in federal constitutional discussions and the absence of legal resort to the "notwithstanding clause" to opt out of any Charter rights they oppose.

Mel Smith, who for nearly two decades was the senior advisor on constitutional matters to the province of British Columbia, has a different view. He argues that the new forms of government being put in place in Nunavut and the western Arctic, when combined with the powers given to various native groups as part of land-claim settlements, are resulting in territories that in some ways have *more* power than the provinces.

In Mr. Smith's 1995 book *Our Home or Native Land,* he states that the effort to establish a new government in Nunavut "may be unconstitutional because, since 1982, the Canadian Constitution requires that the establishment of new provinces requires the approval of not only Parliament but

also at least seven provincial legislatures having 50% of the population of Canada." Employing the identical metaphor as Mr. Cameron, Mr Smith adds, "If this new territory is not tantamount to establishing a new province . . . then I do not know what a new province would look like. If it looks like a duck, quacks like a duck and walks like a duck, chances are it's a duck."

Indeed, Mr. Smith suggests, the drafters of the Nunavut deal were aware they were according greater powers than held by the provinces. Subsection 2 of section 23 of the Nunavut Act reads: "(2) Nothing in subsection (1) shall be construed as giving the legislature (of Nunavut) greater power . . . than are given to the legislatures of the provinces." Mr. Smith posits the subsection was included "because the drafters of the legislation were so afraid that they might have given more legislative powers to the territory of Nunavut than were given under the Constitution to the provinces of Canada that there had to be a saving clause of this kind to ensure this didn't happen."

With a land-claim settlement agreement granting Nunavut's Inuit majority outright ownership of 350,000 square miles of land, mineral rights under 22,500 square miles, resource royalties forever, and an Inuit-dominated board to approve any development project, Mr. Smith contends that there is no doubt that Nunavut has more authority than the provinces. "Few Canadians may realize that the rights contained in land claim agreements such as this . . . cannot be changed in future—even by federal legislation—unless the aboriginal group which is party to such an agreement agrees to do so. The rights contained in the Nunavut land Claim Agreement are 'constitutionally entrenched' because section 35 of the Constitution Act, 1982 provides that the rights contained in future land claim agreements are constitutionally 'recognized and affirmed'."

—*S.P.*

they get two votes already as they vote for both their tribal leadership and their MLA. But when pressed, Mr. Kurszewski agrees that the Aboriginal Assembly will probably not be made up of elected band chiefs, meaning that by his admission native citizens "may actually end up having three votes."

Isn't all this indisputable evidence that the new system is grotesquely unfair for non-natives? No, the Métis leader replies, their representation will be ensured because Yellowknife's four ridings will always have non-aboriginal MLAs. But isn't one of those ridings filled by a native now? "Yes, but he got elected because of the quality of his work, not his ethnic status."

Despite the racial division promoted by the Western Arctic's draft constitution, Ottawa is refusing to condemn it. "We don't choose to react," says Kirk Cameron, director of northern political development for the Department of Indian Affairs and Northern Development (DIAND). "It's premature to jump on things that may not appear in the final document." Mr. Cameron, who was an observer in many of the working group's deliberations, suggests that eventually "we may see a massive shift in the working group's position." But ultimately, he retreats to the position that his ministry is looking for a "made in the north" constitution—irrespective of whether it violates Canada's own constitutional guarantees of individual equality. "It's not DIAND's business to

say if their proposal violates the Charter of Rights and Freedoms," he says. "The Department of Justice does that."

Mel Smith, former constitutional adviser to the province of British Columbia, and author of *Our Home or Native Land?*, says Ottawa trapped itself when it began championing an undefined view of self-government simply to appease Indian militants. "With this draft constitution DIAND's got itself in a box," he asserts, "But that comes from the undemocratic concepts they've been promoting for several years." He says DIAND is wrongheaded to encourage aboriginal groups to write their own laws and points out that nowhere else does the federal government ask for laws to come from outside its sovereign jurisdiction. Insists Mr. Smith: "Parliament has a perfect right to amend the Indian Act like every other act."

Furthermore, he argues, there will not be any real advance for Canada's aboriginals until "governments get the courage to insist on compliance with the laws created in Ottawa." Only then, Mr. Smith believes, can the "umbilical cord" which keeps natives chained to Ottawa in a destructive state of dependency be severed.

Mr. Smith reserves his greatest ire for former constitutional affairs minister Joe Clark, whom he credits with bringing native self-government to the fore in the failed Charlottetown Accord and who was hired by the NWT natives to chair a round of constitutional conferences in the north in 1994. "Joe Clark's a menace," Mr. Smith asserts. "At

Charlottetown he would have given away the store if the voters had let him."

Mr. Clark, on the other hand, rejects the apartheid description of the draft constitution. He says that having two assemblies—one of them explicitly race-based—merely "means the community recognizes that it is made up of different elements," adding that "you have to recognize the differences in order for the community to get together." When told that even the liberal-minded *Globe and Mail* had rejected race-based representation as undemocratic, Mr. Clark retorts that the Toronto paper does not understand "a genuine attempt to confront reality north of 60." "It's the difference between Bay Street and the back streets of Canada," he says.

Because of that sort of sympathy towards their extravagant aims, some of the north's native leaders are demanding even greater authority. For instance, Gerald Antoine, grand chief of the Deh Cho band, reports that his people will not cooperate with the Constitutional Working Group because they reject all forms of public government. "Before the treaties we took responsibility for ourselves," Chief Antoine notes. "And even when we made treaties, my people understood that we would continue to be self-governing."

But in rejecting the legal reach of public government, will the Deh Cho people also reject Ottawa's financial handouts? "That's an obligation the federal government took on when they signed the treaties," Chief Antoine responds. "Besides, the Inuit got continuing financial support in their land settlement."

—Shafer Parker, Jr.

ROYAL OMISSION

Aboriginal peoples and the inherent right to municipal government

by TONY HALL

In April 1992, a geographer named Jean Morisset from the Université du Québec à Montréal made a presentation to the Royal Commission on Aboriginal Peoples. "There can no longer be any possible future for the viability of Canada," Morisset told the Commissioners, "unless the Native component is included." He then predicted, "either this Royal Commission, because of forces which will escape its control, will hear the death knell of this country, or it will inaugurate its necessary new beginning, or, if one may say so, its real beginning."

Morisset is a Quebec nationalist who accuses many of his French-speaking compatriots of sabotaging the real integrity of their nation by advancing the lie that there is deep substance in a Québécois identity. For Morisset, the first Canada was the Métis Canada of the French and Aboriginal fur trade. "From a *canadien* viewpoint," he writes, "the fact that a country called Canada could exist was obviously less owing to France's effort than to the sociological and strategical alliance of the *canadiens* with the Indians....the *canadiens* as a people would have ceased to exist sometime in the 18th century if it had not been for the Indians. And this is precisely why the settlers of the English colonies referred to the wars that led to the Conquest of Canada as the French and Indian wars rather than as the Seven Years' War. This bespeaks the Indians' permanent geopolitical importance."

Morisset's "geopolitical" analysis was made plain to me during the summer of 1990, when I watched with dismay the televised images of angry Quebec commuters waving their fleur-de-lis and burning Mohawk Warriors in effigy before the Mercier bridge near Oka. The descendants of the original *canadiens* had apparently turned against their Indian relatives to exorcise the Métis strain from the family tree.

For Native peoples, news of Elijah Harper's stand against the Meech Lake Accord and pictures of the Canadian army's assault on Indian land were a call to action. Blockades sprung up in northern Ontario and British Columbia. Peace vigils were organized in Winnipeg and Toronto. In southern Alberta, Peigan Lonefighters used bulldozers to engineer their protest against the illegal construction of the Oldman Dam upriver from their reserve. I doubt if many know how close we came to civil war.

In 1991, Brian Mulroney's response to all of this was to set in motion the Royal Commission on Aboriginal Peoples. We had come too close to seeing the possible results of a direct collision between the sovereign assertions of Aboriginal peoples, the would-be Québécois nation and an internally divided Canadian state. Some bold alternatives were needed to place before the people of Canada.

The Royal Commission gave us a unique opportunity to orient ourselves to the ancient and recent history of this land. It held out the hope that we could approach the millennium with a deeper sense of where we have been and where we are headed on a continent, in a world, struggling to make sense of the many competing visions of sovereignty, self-determination and cultural integrity.

Last November, the Commissioners released their mammoth final report, entitled, *People to People, Nation to Nation.* By and large, news coverage of the Commission's broad-ranging findings, which centred on a proposal for a new Royal Proclamation to re-orient Canada towards the permanent geopolitical importance of the First Nations, was over in a couple of days. There were hints of Morisset's death knell in the apparent inability of the country's political and media elites to interpret the report as little more than a shopping list.

As with so many aspects of our national malaise, the sabotage began at the top. Prime Minister Chrétien studiously avoided saying a word about the report. On the day of its release, he rushed past reporters who were seeking a small sound bite and jetted off to the Orient. Several days later, he rewarded Chinese officials, whose own systematic human rights violations are too well known, with a $1.5 billion gift from Canadian taxpayers to buy our otherwise unsaleable nuclear technology.

Chrétien's very priorities demonstrate his gross inability to present Canadians with any bold vision of the country's future. In his early days as Pierre Trudeau's chief lieutenant, he simply implemented his boss's ideas and policies. Now, as PM, Chrétien has cynically shifted ground to deliver on plans first articulated by Brian Mulroney. His failure of leadership holds the potential to spark a very different kind of French and Indian war.

Just as Chrétien remains to many francophones in Quebec an embodiment of the Trudeau government's contemptuous decision to patriate the Constitution against the wishes of the National Assembly, so too does he carry heavy baggage in Indian Country. As Minister of Indian Affairs in

> *Prime Minister Chrétien studiously avoided saying a word about the report. On the day of its release, he rushed past reporters and jetted off to the Orient*

From *The Canadian Forum*, January/February 1997, pp. 5-6. © 1997 by Canadian Forum, Ltd. Reprinted by permission.

1969, it was Chrétien who tried to deliver Trudeau's White Paper aimed at the municipalization of reserves and the elimination of Indian treaties. Modern Indian politics took shape in rejecting this initiative, which was widely described at the time as "cultural genocide". Chrétien was also front and centre in the next major assault on Aboriginal and treaty rights in 1981, when he played a major role in the fateful Night of the Long Knives that excluded the Quebec government and Aboriginal peoples from the remaking of Confederation. Now his glib and contemptuous dismissal of the Royal Commission's report suggests a similar ignorance of the explosive potential in the Aboriginal file.

The federal decision to press ahead with major changes to the Indian Act several months before the release of the Royal Commission's report marks the extent of the Chrétien regime's disregard for the importance of the Commissioners' work. Rather than wait to see what the report recommended, Minister of Indian Affairs Ron Irwin plunged into the strategic legal core of Crown-First Nations relations to advance his agenda of municipalizing Indian reserves. In so doing, he is following the agenda set out by Chrétien in 1969 with his White Paper.

These cynical machinations lead directly away from an emphasis on treaties as the basis of Crown-Aboriginal relations, an emphasis whose importance is detailed at great length in the Royal Commission's report. The resignation of so many members of the Liberal Party's now defunct Aboriginal caucus came about because of the growing realization in Indian Country that the Chrétien government has nothing to offer Native people but new language for the same old institutional assimilation — i.e., the inherent right to municipal government.

But this is not 1969. Throughout the Western world, the right is affording new respectability to racist creeds. The way this racism is being played out in Canada is for politicians to posture themselves on the legitimate trepidation of middle-class taxpayers that they must carry the major financial burden of those most marginalized by the new economy. We saw a perfect instance of this at work in the official political responses to the Royal Commission's report.

The tragedy of this is that there has been no serious consideration given to the structural changes needed to shift the onus for economic revitalization of First Nations to the financial sector engaged in extracting natural resources. If a fair portion of those resources were deemed to be the Aboriginal share of Canada, then First Nations could largely escape the direct political control of the federal government. Similarly, middle-class taxpayers would be relieved of some of the enormous subsidies they now provide to corporations who export much of the country's resource wealth directly out of Canada.

By one calculation, every person born in Canada is immediately worth $960,000, based on our public assets and natural resources. In such a country, there is simply no excuse for the obscenely high rates of poverty, suicide, unemployment, incarceration and violence that characterize the lives of too many Native people. There is simply no escaping the direct connection between their marginalization and the immense metropolitan concentration of wealth in a country built on the theft and appropriation of the original peoples' resources. We have it in our power to transcend the original and continuing crime of Canada's genesis, but only if we face the future with a sense of optimism and justice — people to people, nation to nation.

Tony Hall teaches Native American Studies at the University of Lethbridge.

State of the Nations

The writing on the wall

*Canada's native people face the issues of wealth, power and rights
that will define their future*

BY RUDY PLATIEL

Native Affairs Reporter

FOR Canada's native people, the approaching millennium brings the promise of a brighter tomorrow and the prospect of some very dark times. Already, a general outline of aboriginal life in the next century is taking shape. By many accounts, it will be a future marked by three major factors:

♦ Increasing economic disparity within the native community.

♦ Modest, if any, political progress.

♦ Little advancement on native rights in the courts.

Let's look at these issues.

First, the economic disparity. It stems from a little-publicized trend over the past decade—the rapid growth of a free-enterprise economy among Canada's estimated one million aboriginal people, especially in the cities.

At first glance, that would seem to bode well for the future. However, as migration from the reserve to the city continues, there are ominous signs on the horizon. The fact that native newcomers, particularly in prairie centres, are unskilled and often impoverished raises the prospect of social fragmentation, greater unrest and increased crime.

"I see violence in the cities and a great deal more confrontation down the road if there is really no structural change," predicts Wallace Manyfingers, a staff worker at the Treaty Six organization in Edmonton.

"There is a growing underclass in Canada of First Nations people who are just really angry."

NATIVE anger, of course, is usually what grabs headlines and forms perceptions about the state of Canada's relationship with aboriginal people.

Consider the current decade. It began with the 78-day armed standoff between Mohawk militants and the Canadian military at Oka, Que. That confrontation was over land rights, as was the case five years later when violence broke out at Gustafsen Lake in the British Columbia interior and Ipperwash Provincial Park on the shores of Lake Huron.

Both showdowns attracted much more media attention than the quiet but substantial growth of an aboriginal business sector. (Not that it has gone totally unnoticed: banks have been scrambling to position themselves to take advantage of it.)

David Newhouse, a professor of native studies at Trent University in Peterborough, Ont., says the burgeoning of aboriginal enterprise is expected to signal a new phenomenon—the rise of an educated, well-off native middle class. A specialist on native business development, he says there are now 10,000 native-run enterprises across the country, many of them motivated by much more than simply a desire to make money.

"Aboriginal people have very much discovered the connection between wealth and power: If you create wealth, you begin to create power for yourself. With that power, you can begin to move toward self-government and a degree of control over one's own life."

However, he adds, this move "into the heart of capitalism" has a down side. Combined with the migration of unskilled people from reserves to the city, it's also likely to lead to a widening gap in the living standards enjoyed by segments within the native community.

The exodus from the reserves began three decades ago, so that now about 60 per cent of aboriginal people are urban dwellers. Their communities are already tasting the bitter fruits of economic disparity with problems that range from

Gang graffiti at Winnipeg grade school: Gap between middle-class and jobless natives could mean trouble.   (ROBERT TINKER/The Globe and Mail)

homelessness to the rise of the aboriginal street gang.

Such gangs have made a mark in Winnipeg, which has the nation's biggest native urban population, but Mr. Manyfingers says he expects to see the gangs spread to other cities, such as Regina, Saskatoon, Edmonton and Vancouver.

FURTHER complicating this blend of joblessness and homelessness is a sense of hopelessness rooted in the apparent lack of interest in doing anything about the situation.

Dan Bellegarde, co-chair of the Indian Claims Commission, is one observer who fears trouble. He points out two factors: festering native grievances about land claims and the long-awaited report from the Royal Commission on Aboriginal Peoples.

When it comes to settling land claims, the commission's report "has set out the template," explains Mr. Bellegarde, also a vice-chief of the

Saskatchewan Federation of Indian Nations. "I'm not saying it is all right or all wrong, but it has raised expectations tremendously in the Indian community.

"I'm afraid that unless these recommendations are taken seriously and given the time and consideration they deserve . . . we could be in for a very rough time. Pretty soon, the socioeconomic problem is going to be too much for municipal governments

to handle. It is going to create a serious problem—it already is."

As bad as city life can be, there is no compelling reason for the influx to subside because a dramatic turnaround in the grinding poverty found on some isolated reserves isn't exactly imminent. Informed observers look to the horizon and see no evidence that momentum is gathering for political change. In the courts, meanwhile, the legal ad-

About the Series

The Middle Kingdom is a daily feature of The Globe and Mail, Canada's National Newspaper, and is dedicated to examining "how and why things happen." The State of the Nations is one of The Middle Kingdom's series, and it ran from April 22–September 2, 1997.

For more data on this series: Send a fax to (416) 585-5085, E-mail to MidKing@GlobeAndMail.ca or

write c/o The Globe and Mail, 444 Front St., W., Toronto, Ont., M5V 2S9. (Be sure to include your name, address, and phone number.) On the Web: Links to the archive where State of the Nations installments will be kept as well as to the online discussion Native Canadians: What Next? may be found on the Middle Kingdom home page (http://www.TheGlobeAndMail.com/docs/webextra/middle_kingdom.—**Ed.**

The numbers

Nearly a million people in Canada claim aboriginal origin. They include 600,000 status Indians (see below) and about 57,000 Inuit. More than half the status Indians live in cities. Here's a population breakdown.

The regions	POPULATION	The top 10 cities	POPULATION
Ontario	134,160	Winnipeg	45,705
British Columbia	99,720	Montreal	45,230
Saskatchewan	92,325	Vancouver	43,440
Manitoba	91,565	Edmonton	43,355
Alberta	74,123	Toronto	40,555
Quebec	57,223	Ottawa-Hull	31,220
Atlantic provinces	23,225	Calgary	24,595
NWT	13,621	Saskatoon	14,530
Yukon	7,088	Regina	13,055
TOTAL	**593,050**	Hamilton	11,245

Sources: Statistics Canada – 1991 Census and Indian and Native Affairs Canada

vances that once fostered aboriginal rights seem to be stalled.

ON the political score, Prime Minister Jean Chrétien and Indian Affairs Minister Ron Irwin have made it clear that broad structural change—particularly anything connected with the Constitution—is simply not on the government's agenda.

This prompts Ovide Mercredi, national chief of the Assembly of First Nations, to describe the current administration as "the dark side" of native people's future. The Liberals, he says, are "a caretaker government waiting for things to happen.... This is not an interventionist government that is going to change the status quo."

Given that the polls suggest a Liberal return to power in the forthcoming general election, it's perhaps not surprising both that the prospect for political change is dim and that Mr. Mercredi has decided not to stand again when his AFN term ends this summer.

The political lull stems largely from the fact that all is quiet on the judicial front, contends lawyer and former university lecturer Mark Dockstator.

In the past, court decisions have always sparked political change, explains Mr. Dockstator, whose doctoral thesis on native self-government provided a historical basis for the royal commission's report.

For example, he says that the Supreme Court of Canada's reasoning in a 1973 decision on the Haida Indians led the federal government to establish a negotiating process to resolve land claims. In the same way, the court's 1984 Musqueam decision on federal fiduciary responsibility and its 1990 Sioui and Sparrow rulings that recognized other rights all triggered movement in the public arena.

"Every time the court expands the envelope, the government is forced, sometimes unwillingly ... to be at the table and try to define what the court says they have to."

BUT don't expect any new case law so dramatic and far-reaching. "I think the Supreme Court of Canada has signalled ... that the envelope is not expanding any more," says Mr. Dockstator. "They are not going to be the agent of change here; there is an upper limit and you've hit the glass ceiling, as it were."

In his view, the court feels that the broad outline to native rights has been defined—noiw it's up to governments and aboriginal people to do the rest.

All that said, what's the next step?

Mr. Dockstator sees a favourable omen in the realm of commerce. It may be that economic progress will replace legal precedent as the driving force behind a political agreement. After all, if they agree on anything, leaders on both sides generally feel that, to be meaningful, aboriginal self-government must be accompanied by economic development.

"Sometimes there is a debate on how to do that," he concedes, "but ... I think that could be one of the significant areas of positive change going into the next century."

About the author: For more than two decades, Globe and Mail readers saw native affairs largely through the eyes of Rudy Platiel. During that time, he, his notepad and camera were on hand at any pivotal event.

Before his recent retirement, Mr. Platiel reflected on the many changes he has seen in the native community and on what lies ahead for aboriginal people in the 21st century.

The fruit of his labours serves as an overview for State of the Nations, which will pit theory and stereotype against reality with a series of illuminating snapshots of native life across the country.

AN UNWORKABLE VISION OF SELF-GOVERNMENT

Les recommandations de la Commission au sujet de l'autonomie des Autochtones sont irréalistes et irréalisables. Elles vont à l'encontre de la nature humaine et des réalités économiques et politiques fondamentales. Selon l'auteur, elles ne devraient donc pas être mises à exécution.

by Tom Flanagan

The main theme of the report of the Royal Commission on Aboriginal Peoples is that Aboriginal peoples are nations in the full sense of the term. Thus Canada has to be refashioned from a nation-state (or perhaps a binational partnership) into a multinational confederacy. Somewhere between 60 and 80 Aboriginal nations (the Commission is unsure of the exact number), consisting of 2-3 percent of the present population of Canada, will be united with the rest by means of constitutionally entrenched treaties.

Aboriginal nations, enjoying an inherent right of self-government, will exercise powers comparable to, indeed greater than, those of the provinces. In time they will take over complete control of the health, education, welfare and economic development of their citizens. They will have nation-to-nation dealings with other governments, their own house of Parliament, a guaranteed seat on the Supreme Court and many other trappings of sovereignty. Their operations will be supported by revenues derived from land and natural resources, including existing Indian reserves and the Alberta Metis settlements plus lands derived from new and modernized treaties as well as other lands obtained as compensation for past surrenders and cutoffs.

However, this land and resource base will not make these governments self-supporting; the Commission's report contains literally dozens of suggestions for new Aboriginal programs to be funded in whole or in part by the federal and provincial governments.

Let me make four comments about this scenario:

1) As a bigger and better version of the Aboriginal provisions of the Charlottetown Accord, it seems politically unrealistic, to say the least. The Charlottetown Accord was soundly defeated, not just in a national referendum but also in localities where Aboriginal voters predominate. Of course, political feasibility is not fixed for all time, so I do not regard this observation of political infeasibility as a fundamental criticism.

The political-economic system proposed by the Royal Commission runs contrary to human nature.

2) Depending on how one counts, there may be about 900,000 Aboriginal people in Canada today. If there are 60 to 80 Aboriginal nations, that means the average nation will consist of about 10,000 to 15,000 people — many of them children, since the Aboriginal birth rate is much higher than the Canadian average. This high birth rate means that most Aboriginal nations will grow steadily, so that in a few decades they might average 20,000. Still, this is an extremely small number of people to support national governments that will carry out the range of functions envisioned in the Commission's Report. In practice, both funding and expertise will have to be imported from the outside, and most Aboriginal nations will be self-governing in name only. This is simply a consequence of size; I would make the same prediction about attempts to turn Grande Prairie, Alberta or Dauphin, Manitoba, into nations.

3) Implementation of the Commission's Report would make the 60 to 80 Aboriginal governments primarily responsible for economic development of their citizens. These governments would control the vast amounts of land and natural resources that are supposed to be transferred to Aboriginal nations. Unfortunately, this is a truly retrograde

 From *Policy Options*, March 1997, pp. 19-21. © 1997 by the Institute for Research on Public Policy. Reprinted by permission.

notion. At a time when governments all over the planet are trying to get out of business, when it has finally been recognized that only private ownership and the market generate economic efficiency, the Commission proposes to transfer billions of dollars of land and natural resources to what are essentially villages and rural municipalities masquerading as national governments.

The Commission espousal of notions, such as import substitution, that have had disastrous economic consequences in the Third World does not give me confidence in their economic wisdom. Much as I esteem lawyers, judges, academics and politicians, it would have been better to have put some economists and business leaders on a Commission whose mandate included designing a new economy for Aboriginal peoples.

Because Indians, Metis and Inuit respond to economic incentives in the same way as all other human beings, the perverse incentives of the Commission's proposal for a government-dominated Aboriginal economy will have predictable consequences:

• There will be inefficiency and bankruptcies as Aboriginal governments, like all governments, make irrational investment decisions.

• A small class of Aboriginal politicians, consultants and middlemen will do very well out of the system, while most Aboriginal people will fall even further behind the average Canadian standard of living.

• There will be massive corruption, nepotism and patronage as billions of dollars wash through dozens of tiny new national governments. The sheer number of these entities, their lack of experience and expertise, and the Aboriginal mystique will make public accountability impossible to achieve.

4) These new governments will be a menace to the individual freedom of Aboriginal people. In *Federalist 10*, James Madison made the classic argument for the so-called "extended republic." Small, homogeneous communities are easily taken over by majority factions bent on improving their position at the expense of the minority. The best protection of liberty is a large, diverse community where many overlapping interests can keep factionalism in check. These proposed Aboriginal national governments would be a perfect arena for the evils of factionalism that Madison described so brilliantly.

Moreover, the danger would be even worse because these governments would be endowed with a range of powers going far beyond those possessed by other Candian governments. Aboriginal governments, within their jurisdiction, would own land, housing and natural resources. They would control health, education, welfare, citizenship and economic development. They would have, on a small scale, almost the kind of control over individuals that used to be enjoyed by communist governments.

Of course, the situation would not be that bad, because people who did not like the way things were going could leave the jurisdiction of Aboriginal governments and live simply as Canadian citizens. Also, the Charter of Rights would apply to Aboriginal governments, and there might be recourse to the Canadian courts in some conflicts. Nonetheless, the situation would be bad enough for many individuals. The losers in the factional struggles endemic in all small, closely knit communities could easily be deprived of their homes, livelihood and social benefits. Politics would become not just the pursuit of power but a struggle for the means of life itself, at least for those unwilling to leave the community.

In short, the political-economic system proposed by the Royal Commission runs contrary to human nature. It puts too much power in the hands of governments and expects those governments to do what no government has ever been able to do, namely to run an efficient, growing economy that brings prosperity to more than a ruling elite. There are universal truths of politics and economics that apply everywhere in spite of cultural differences. We cannot expect Aboriginal peoples to thrive by ignoring or defying these truths.

None of what I have said is meant to defend the *status quo*. The bureaucratic tutelage and state socialism of the century-long Indian Affairs regime has been debilitating for Aboriginal peoples. But the Royal Commission's proposals, as far as I can see, would have even worse results. Fortunately, most of them seem unlikely to be implemented.

Tom Flanagan is a professor of Political Science at the University of Calgary. This paper is based on comments he gave at a Conference on the Report of the Royal Commission on Aboriginal Peoples hosted by the McGill Institute for the Study of Canada.

ABORIGINAL GOVERNMENT: ALTERNATIVE OUTCOMES

Il y a un vaste écart entre la conception concrète de l'autonomie que se font les peuples autochtones, d'une part, et celle qu'en ont le gouvernement fédéral et les provinces, d'autre part. L'auteur propose une fédération décentralisée, composée de nations délimitées suivant des critères territoriaux, chacune possédant sa propre sphère de pouvoirs, définie dans la constitution.

by Joe Dion

The impasse

There has never been agreement between Indians and federal authorities on any of the fundamentals that define what is really meant by self-government. For example, the kind of underpinnings that should support an Indian governance concept can only be determined by consensus on such key issues as the spirit and intent of historic treaties, and the contemporary relevance of pre-confederation protocols and Royal proclamations. Similarly, widely divergent views separate Indians and the federal government about such concepts as inherent sovereignty, jurisdiction, self-determination, citizenship, *etc.* Even the meaning of "peoples" and "aboriginal rights"

as used in Section 35 of the Constitution Act 1982 remains in dispute (for example, see Pelletier's article in this issue of *Policy Options*). When it comes to the application of international human rights conventions, some of which address the rights of indigenous peoples in universal terms, Indians and Ottawa maintain opposing positions.

Most Indians are concerned, with good reason, that Ottawa's current self-government initiatives are in the spirit of the assimilationist policy of the last century. Bill 79 calls for a revised and thoroughly gutted "Indian Act" as an interim step toward its early and final demise. This is to be accompanied by a phased dismantling of the Department of Indian Affairs. Bill 75 opens the door to a future Indian land regime that, by stages, will be divorced from Crown trusteeship and absorbed into each province's "fee simple" empire.

As far as most Indians are concerned, they never consented to the kind of humiliating wardship prescribed by the "Indian Act," nor to surrendering jurisdictional rights on their lands. At the same time, Indians are not prepared to see a statute abolished that is now as punishing to the government as it is to them. This is because most Indian people know that before they move out of the toxic relationship created by the "Indian Act," there will have to be agreement about where they will land in Canada's federal system.

There can be only one of two possible outcomes for the majority of Indians. The Indian Act can be a launching pad from a federal orbit into the black hole of provincial jurisdiction where, at best, Indians might retain some vestiges of an identity as scattered ethnic minorities. Alternatively, a number of distinct Indian nations that still survive within the borders of Canada can constitute, over time, a "First Nations Federation." According to linguistic, cultural and historic criteria that define nationhood, such a federation might consist of 10 to possibly 12 members. The ultimate aim of such a federation would be partnership within Canada's larger federal system, exercising a constitutionally defined sphere of sovereignty in their respective territories.

Canada currently consists of only two constitutionally defined sovereignties: a federal government capable of operating within its own exclusive sphere of powers; and 10 provincial governments, similarly endowed with the capacity to manage their internal affairs. Although the federal system permits an ebb and flow of fiscal and devolution

From *Policy Options*, March 1997, pp. 21-25. © 1997 by the Institute for Research on Public Policy. Reprinted by permission.

arrangements between federal and provincial governments, the essential autonomies represented in the enumerated powers of federal and provincial governments remains intact — short of constitutional amendments.

What is at stake for aboriginal Canadians is their right to survive as distinct, self-determining nations into the future.

All other governmental entities within the federal system are subordinate either to provincial or federal legislative authorities. At the provincial level, municipalities, townships and various other local administrations are dependent in large measure on funds provided by provinces and frequently, on program standards established by provincial authorities. As creatures of the provinces, these local governments can be abolished, amalgamated or taken under a form of trusteeship, depending on the political agendas of provincial legislatures.

Provinces are inherently assimilative. For an Indian nation, provincial jurisdiction amounts to a form of vivisection that cuts them off from members of their linguistic and cultural family in neighbouring provinces. At the same time, a provincial land regime would absorb what now are protected reserves as assets subject to the laws of the marketplace. Indians as individuals and families would find themselves dispersed, and ultimately submerged in each province's institutional and legal milieu.

Extinguishing Indians as distinct nations *via* provincial jurisdiction is being attempted concurrently with measures designed to see the northern territories eventually become full-fledged provinces. The Yukon and the Northwest Territories now have many of the legal and institutional trappings of provinces. These include elected legislatures, a public service and pending resource ownership as a prerequisite to becoming fully self-governing. When Nunavut appears on the scene as a separate entity in 1999, it is programmed to develop along the same lines as the other territories.

The fact that Inuit, in what is to become Nunavut, happen to be in the majority at present does not necessarily mean that they will have a significant role in its future legislature or public service. In the wake of extinguish-

ment settlements, the northern territories are being rapidly staked by the mining, petroleum and other resource extraction industries. The Northwest Territories, for example, is already affected throughout three-quarters of its land base. In addition, at least four diamond mines are also under development. Plans are in the works to drain lakes and divert rivers regardless of promises to set aside certain of those areas for hunters, trappers and fishers.

A significant influx of population from the south is likely to have two results: it will accelerate the transition of the three territories to full provincial status; and aboriginal peoples will be submerged in a tidal wave of nonnative migrants. As the scales are tipped in the longer run in favour of a non-indigenous majority, Aboriginal peoples are unlikely to have any more influence in northern government than they do in the south.

The texts of claims settlement accords and so-called self-government agreements in the northern territories leave no room for doubt about the future fate of Aboriginal peoples who live there. The agreements achieve "certainty" entirely in accordance with extinguishment terms spelled out in federal policy statements and publications. Aboriginal signatories surrender all their "Aboriginal claims, rights, titles and interests." In return, they get a fixed sum of money, "fee simple" land tenure in designated areas, temporary arrangements to sustain a traditional economy, and affirmation of their citizenship in Canada and the territory (that is, the emerging province) in which they live.

Because Section 35 of the Constitution Act of 1982 is regarded as an empty box by federal lawyers, northern extinguishment agreements become instruments that define Aboriginal and treaty rights in constitutional terms. So-called "modern treaties" have become a euphemism for extinguishment. In effect, signatories of extinguishment agreements foreclose any future hope they may have harboured to a place in Canada's federal system as nations in their own right.

Canada's indigenous peoples are no more willing to surrender their nationality to Durham's assimilation mill then is Quebec's French-speaking population. What is at stake with Aboriginal peoples is not their right to make bannock or to attend pow-wows. They were deeply rooted in this land as self-determining nations long before Europe's boat people arrived on their shores. In a much more fundamental way, what is at stake is their right to survive as distinct, self-determining nations into the future.

A people who define themselves in historic and legal terms as inherently sovereign are inclined to see their past and current treatment by Canada as something characteristic of an alien occupying power. As far as most Indians are concerned, occupation may suppress a people's national identity and rights but can never eliminate it. In their view moreover, inherent sovereignty, by definition, can be expressed either by separation from Canada, or by admission into confederation as distinct nations.

An Aboriginal balanced federation would recognize First Nations as founding peoples and make them full partners in Confederation.

To accommodate a position which the majority of Indians are not prepared to compromise, Canada would have to add a new dimension to its federal structure; one that makes room for distinct nations. In the end, there may be no alternative, aside from more active suppression, if the ongoing impasse about Aboriginal governance is to be resolved.

An Aboriginal balanced federation would recognize First Nations as founding peoples and make them full partners in Confederation. The principles on which a region-based federation would be balanced by a nation-based dimension are supported by international law and by Canada's own legal history.

The concept of a First Nations' autonomous entity functioning as a federation of Aboriginal nations in partnership with Canada's federated regions is not new. It has been discussed as a practical way of redressing the past for more than 20 years. Most recently, provincial-type status for Aboriginal nations was endorsed by the Royal Commission on Aboriginal Peoples. The Commission concluded that, contrary to the premise of federal policy makers, Indians are nations in the proper meaning of the word. In their view, this historical fact was sufficient grounds to seek an accommodation with Indian peoples as bodies-politic. Apparently, there is no statute of limitations on being a nation.

In the final analysis, it will be the responsibility of Indian peoples to foster the emergence of a First Nations Federation, as a prerequisite for partnership within Canada's political order.

A First Nations Commission, possibly established by an assembly of like-minded Chiefs and Elders, could lay the foundations of a First Nations Federation. The measures on which agreement is feasible, and which could be implemented entirely on the initiative of Indian people, could include:

• **An operational strategy:** At the outset, this would be based on the understanding that a First Nations Federation would have to grow over time. Moreover, the architects of such a federation would have to accept the fact that the process of reconstructing their nations would not necessarily restore them to their original state. Some Indian communities might have reason to hold back pending demonstrable results. Others may prefer to remain on the road to assimilation and have every right to make this choice. In contemporary terms therefore, an Indian nation would consist of those culturally and linguistically related communities who are willing to ally themselves with other similar survivors in pursuit of a common political goal.

• **Non-cooperation:** At present, the federal government is aggressively pursuing a number of initiatives intended to complete an extinguishment process begun in the last century. The fact that all these measures are in direct contradiction to principles spelled out by the Commission has not swayed Ottawa from its course. A federation of Indian peoples, which needs neither the approval of the federal government nor sanction by a Royal Commission, may be the only way of creating an exit ramp off the extinguishment track. To keep this option open, one of the first tasks of an Aboriginal federation on behalf of its members would be to put a freeze on all federally sponsored extinguishment agreements.

• **Political action:** A concurrent initiative by the First Nations Commission would be to launch an "Aboriginal Peoples Party." A convention would be necessary to pick a leader, to select and ratify the name of the new Party, and to build a wide consensus and constituency in support of the Party's platform.

• **Membership:** The constitution of the Party could conceivably provide for a broad-based membership, including non-native persons who support Aboriginal aims. On the other hand, it may choose to limit membership to Indian peoples exclusively. A membership policy would need to take into account voter make-up in electoral districts where candidates will be placed. One task of the Party leader would be to ensure that all eligible supporters are on the voters list. It has been estimated that anywhere from 12 to 21 ridings could be swung by an Indian vote.

• **Financing:** The Party would be financed through membership fees. A number of First

Nations corporations and resource-based reserves could be expected to make sizable contributions as well. Financial assistance from non-native enterprises who see the possibility of joint ventures with Indian companies might also want to be involved. Unlike more vulnerable Indian organizations which depend for their existence on federal funding, the Party would experience no such constraints in representing the interests of its membership.

The bottom line: recognition of the Federation of First Nations as an autonomous territorial entity operating under the aegis of its own government.

• **The platform:** The essential aim of an Aboriginal political initiative would be to create and, by stages, to enlarge a First Nations Federation under the auspices of a single provisional government. The federation likely would function in a decentralized way, given the large territory over which its nation members would be dispersed. Cohesion and a sense of purpose nevertheless could be maintained by means of satellite communication, both television and radio, as well as other available technologies.

Contrary to the specious and misleading statements of federal politicians, a new wing on Parliament Hill would not be needed for the representatives of 600 plus nations. Elected Aboriginal Members of Parliament would belong, for the most part, to one Party and would speak for the shared interests of one Federation. Before this happens, however, the Party would have to address itself to a number of priorities, including:

1) Selecting a suitable name and symbols for a federation whose starting point in any negotiations with Ottawa would be the inherent sovereignty of its member nations. The essential premise would be that inherent sovereignty equals eligibility for partnership with Canada in accordance with terms entrenched in the Constitution.

2) Consideration would be given to retiring an identity imposed originally by disoriented Europeans. The term "Indian" would fall into disuse. People would identify themselves by their citizenship in the Cree nation, the Dene nation, *etc*. For example, a term such as "Anasazi" could be selected to describe the federation (the word is associated with an ancient people who, according to some myths, migrated to the four corners of Turtle Island). Accordingly, a person could identify himself as a Cree or Dene national and a member of the Anasazi Federation.

3) The bottom line in any negotiations with the federal government would be an agreement that recognizes the Federation as an autonomous territorial entity operating under the aegis of its own government. This interim arrangement would allow time for a host of issues to be settled, including boundaries, resource ownership, original title, reparation payments, *etc*. Once these preliminaries have been resolved, the stage would be set for the emergence of a territorially based, autonomous federation of Aboriginal people, constitutionally mandated to look after their internal affairs and to participate as equal partners in shaping Canada's future.

4) It is becoming evident that Canada is more likely to be destabilized by regional and demographic dynamics than by the aspirations of First Nations. Demographic trends point to an evolving megalopolis stretching from Hamilton to Montreal and beyond. The west coast is becoming only the second region of significant population concentration. Linking these widely separated growth centres is a sort of Canadian outback that is actually losing people to economic opportunities on the western seaboard and the east. One can expect that an inevitable result will be an erosion of the confederation ties that have bound Canada together in the past. North-south and trans-ocean economic and cultural linkages could easily overwhelm a less profitable commitment to trans-Canada patriotism. Clearly, a new sort of glue will be needed if Canada is going to hang together. The answer could very well be an autonomous First Nations Federation, historically rooted in every region of Canada and integrated as an entity and an equal partner in confederation.

J. F. (Joe) Dion manages Vancouver-based Dion Resources Inc. He is President and Chief Executive Officer of the Indian Resource Council of Canada, and Founder and President of Indian Power Corporation.

Not a word about natives

Despite a royal commission's excoriation of governments for their shabby treatment of Canada's aboriginal peoples, the issue has played no part in the campaign. Perhaps, just perhaps, it has moved beyond the ken of politicians.

BY JOHN GRAY

The Globe and Mail
Toronto

FOR anyone who might idly wonder why there has been barely a mention of native people in the current election campaign, David Newhouse has an instructive story to tell.

For the past three years, Professor Newhouse has offered a simple question to first-year students enrolled in his native-studies program at Trent University in Peterborough, Ont.: What contribution have aboriginal people made to Canadian life? Over three years he has asked that of about 600 students, and not one of them has been able to think of a single example. "We don't have the political power to make people listen. And no economic power to get noticed," says Prof. Newhouse, an Onondaga who grew up on the Six Nations Reserve near Brantfore, Ont.

But his own personal experience may offer a different conclusion in the not-too-distant future. It reflects a remarkable change in the condition of native people in recent years.

When he enrolled at the University of Western Ontario in 1972, there were only 162 aboriginals in Canadian colleges and universities.

He was the first Indian to graduate from business administration. Last year more than 30,000 natives were enrolled in postsecondary institutions and more than 150,000 native people have graduated over the years. Beyond academe there are 10,000 native businesses, 50 native financial institutions, a native trust company and a native bank.

Little by little aboriginals are getting the political and economic power to be noticed. It will be a game of inches rather than of rapid movement, Prof. Newhouse says, but it will be at least a game of inches. "Those people are, one way or another, going to advance the agenda."

It was not a game of inches that was in the minds of the members of the Royal Commission on Aboriginal Peoples when they finally submitted their report to the federal government last autumn. Remember that report? It cost $58-million and took more than five years to complete, and they were advising all concerned on how Canada could—at least—resolve its disastrous relationship with its native peoples.

The members of RCAP (pronounced R-cap) entertained the fantasy that their efforts would be a matter of great moment. They were righting the wrongs of centuries,

and they were setting the political agenda of Canada, white and aboriginal, for the next decade, perhaps for the next generation.

So confident were they that they decreed the first ministers of the governments in Canada should sit down with the country's aboriginal leaders within six months. Together they would agree on a forum that would revolutionize the country and rectify the transgressions of too many generations.

Ah, well, David Newhouse could have told them a thing or two. Give or take a few days, we are at the six-month anniversary of the publication of the RCAP report. And what has been heard recently of it? Not a word. In the full flight of a federal election campaign, what has been heard about public policy and native people? Not a word. As for the first ministers getting together this month to rewrite history, there is no evidence they have even thought of it.

Within about 36 hours of its release, the 4,000-odd pages of the RCAP report disappeared from public view with barely a gurgle. Prime Minister Jean Chrétien, who first made a name for himself as minister of Indian Affairs and Northern Development, has said nothing. Ron Irwin, his Minister of Indian Affairs, said immediately after the report was made public that it would be crazy to spend so much money on it and shelve it. Then he shelved it.

Indeed, no political leader has had anything to say, for that is the nature of politics and the nature of Canada's aboriginal problem.

One bitter man is slowly learning that lesson. Ovide Mercredi, the national chief of the Assembly of First Nations, shakes his head: "The Indian agenda is not a priority in Canada."

Mr. Mercredi's analysis is that various governments have captured the national political agenda with talk of budget deficits and the need to downsize government and reduce spending. The result is a sense of fear in the public mind—fear about the future, fear about personal security. On that agenda there is no room for aboriginal people.

"When people are afraid about their job or losing their home, they're not going to think about the needs of other people," he says. "They're going to focus on their own personal agenda for their own family."

Mr. Mercredi is right, but there is more to it, far more.

For a start, if anyone wanted to change the national agenda, why choose to examine a report so massive that it is too heavy to carry?

Were the seven esteemed royal commissioners overcome by vanity or naiveté? The opening volume contains 732 pages and there are four more volumes. The size has made the report impossibly expensive. With the total document costing $250, the government can afford to send out only one copy to each of the country's 608 First Nation bands. Not even aboriginal people have easy access.

Its overwhelming weakness, and the one that has most certainly removed it from the current political agenda, is the nature of its central prescription—more money and more government. A lot more money and a lot more government.

The report advocates an increase of $2-billion a year in government spending—on top of combined governments' annual spending now of about $12-billion—over the next two decades. That is steep, and still rising. In an age when health care is being cut, education limited, public services obliterated and public pensions imperilled, the blood runs cold at the commissioners' casual explanation of projected cost estimates: "Figures rounded to the nearest $25-million."

David Cameron, a political scientist from the University of Toronto, pointed to RCAP's plans for "a whole new order of government, with its bureaucracies and civil servants, its councils and operating agencies, its legislatures and political leadership and staff." He said that, "for better or for worse, the Mike Harris Tories are more representative of the current mood and thinking of a majority of Canadians than are the aboriginal royal commissioners."

True, for most aboriginals, governments have always been the central fact of life. Government pays the cheques and writes the laws; government controls the resources and sets the rules even for hunting and fishing; sometimes government takes the land, and for a long time the government took native children and did its best to take their language; at the bottom end of the government chain, it's often the band governments that provide the only jobs available.

Still, the commissioners seem to be from another planet. Even for people who believe in the benign potential of government—and our numbers are dwindling at an astonishing rate—the history of what governments have done to Canada's aboriginal people must create some doubt as to whether governments can over be benign.

Still, RCAP has its virtues. Its recounting of aboriginal history is painstaking in its accumulation and devastating in its reading. For white and aboriginal alike, it is a history

we didn't know or didn't want to know, or a history we simply put aside because it was too unsettling to explore.

And there remains the condition of native people today. Life expectancy is lower. Illness is more common. Fewer children graduate from high school; fewer get past high school. Homes are flimsy and overcrowded; water and sanitation are often inadequate. Fewer aboriginals have jobs and more spend time in prison. And there is what the report calls an endless circle of disadvantage—family violence, educational failure, poverty, ill health, violence.

All this in a country deemed by the United Nations to be the best place in the world to live. Small wonder that in its annual survey a few months ago the U.S. State Department permitted itself a certain superior regard: "Canada's treatment of its aboriginal people continued to be one of the most important human-rights issues facing the country."

FOR people like Gary Williams, chief of the Curve Lake First Nation reserve north of Peterborough, the RCAP report has become a kind of primer. It is a guide to the history he never studied and an explanation of why he never learned the language of his Ojibwa ancestors.

The wretchedness of the native people and the failure of native policies are as old as the country, and there was nothing novel in the warning that "another failure could have dire consequences." The report actually cites the even more urgent warning of the Spicer commission on national unity of six years ago: "There is an anger, a rage, building in aboriginal communities that will not tolerate much longer the historic paternalism, the bureaucratic evasion and the widespread lack of respect for their concerns."

So what effect have these warnings had? By the measure of public-opinion polls, none whatsoever.

The view from the commissioners' chairs

◆ Estimated aboriginal population in Canada: Indian **624,000**; Métis **152,800**; Inuit **42,500**.

◆ Aboriginals as percentage of total Canadian population: **2.7**. Percentage of land mass south of Yukon/NWT dedicated to them: **less than 0.5**.

◆ U.S. aboriginals as percentage of total population in the United States, excluding Alaska: **less than 1**. Percentage of U.S. land mass dedicated to them: **3**.

◆ Native people in Canada as percentage of total population by region: Atlantic **1.3**; Quebec **1.0**; Ontario **1.4**; Manitoba **10.6**; Saskatchewan **10.5**; Alberta **4.9**; British Columbia **3.6**; Yukon **18.2**; Northwest Territories, **62**.

◆ Province with the largest aboriginal population: Ontario, with **160,000** people, about **20** per cent of the total native population.

◆ Percentage of aboriginals younger than 24: **56**. Percentage of all Canadians under 24: **34**.

◆ Number of aboriginals living in Canada's cities: **320,000**, about **45** per cent of the total aboriginal population.

◆ Number of reserve and native settlements in Canada: **11,000**.

◆ Number of aboriginal language families: **11**. Number of languages; **50**. Languages used most frequently: Micmac, Montagnais, Cree, Ojibwa, Inuktitut, some Dene.

◆ Percentage of aboriginals with Grade 9 education or less who have jobs: less than **50**. Percentage of aboriginals with university degrees who have jobs: **90**.

◆ Number of aboriginal physicians: about **50** (0.1 per cent of all physicians.) Number of registered nurses: about **300** (0.1 per cent of all RNs).

◆ Percentage of federal spending allotted to aboriginal programs in 1991–92: **3.7**. In 1995–96: **4.9**.

◆ Per capita amount spent by all governments on aboriginal people in 1992–93: **$15,714**. Per capita amount spent on all Canadians: **$10,026**.

◆ Amount spent by Ottawa in 1996 on remedial programs for social problems among aboriginal people: **$1.7-billion**.

◆ Percentage of aboriginal population over the age of 15 receiving social assistance in 1996: **28**.

◆ Rate of aboriginal incarceration in provincial jails: **11** times that of other Canadians. In federal penitentiaries: **5** times that of other Canadians.

◆ Average earning of employed aboriginal people in 1991: **$21,270**. Average earning of all Canadian: **$27,880**.

◆ Percentage of all Canadian men unemployed in 1990: **10.1**. Of aboriginal men: **27.2**.

◆ Percentage of all Canadian women unemployed in 1990: **10.2**. Of aboriginal women: **21.6**.

◆ Number of jobs required to raise the level of aboriginal employment to that of the general population: **80,000**.

Source: Royal Commission on Aboriginal Peoples.

Canadians don't really seem to care. Small wonder that the condition of native people has not been the core of the election campaign.

In July of 1991, a year after the Oka crisis, about the time the Spicer commission was reporting and just before the royal commission was created, an Angus Reid poll indicated that just 6 per cent of Canadians regarded native affairs as a matter of significant interest. A year later that had dropped to 4 per cent.

In the intervening years the Angus Reid polls have shown barely a flicker of interest in native affairs from respondents. By February this year, three months after the publication of the commission's report, native affairs were a matter of concern to a mere 1 per cent of the population.

One reflection of that indifference, albeit extreme, is an observation by Reform MP Garry Breitkreuz that the reaction of the average Canadian to the royal commission is: "You've got to be kidding. Are they really se-

rious thinking that this is possible in Canada today?"

The Yorkton-Melville MP, who says "some of my best friends are natives," wants no special benefits for Indians or anybody else. Special status for native people, he says, is just as bad an idea as a distinct society for Quebec.

People are protesting to him that they want no part of a public apology to the aboriginal people for past wrongs, such as was urged by the royal commission. Mr. Breitkreuz says they had nothing to do with that distant past. And besides, there is an abiding resentment toward native people because, "they can get by by doing sweet tweet."

Resentment is the basis of the white relationship. Bitterness about the loss of their land, in particular, haunts native people. More than two-thirds of native land promised by treaty has been lost, one way or another, since Confederation. There are proportionately far more aboriginals in Canada than in the U.S. but

they have proportionately a far smaller share of the land.

If they had got their fair share, the royal commissioners say "the position of aboriginal peoples in Canada today would be very different. They would be major land owners. Most aboriginal nations would be economically self-reliant. Some would be prosperous."

That kind of speculation is what political scientist Harold Laski called gambolling in the pluperfect. Native history is rich in what-ifs.

Even when there has been a settlement of sorts, it has frequently been an odd kind of settlement. Take, for example, the Crees of Northern Quebec. To permit Hydro-Québec to harness hydro power on their lands they got a packet of money, but did they really get justice?

Bill Namagoose, the executive director of the Grand Council of the Crees, recalls that the Crees were forced by federal policy to relinquish all rights to resources on their lands. So the Quebec government makes

$3.5-billion a year in hydro power from rivers on Cree lands, and $1.3-billion in forestry revenue from Cree lands. The Crees get nothing.

In some ways nothing has changed since the first European explorers arrived and decided the legal concept of *terra nullius* applied to the new land. Literally, it meant an empty land, devoid of people. In practice, it meant take whatever land you need and don't worry about those Indians.

Terra nullius is with us yet. The Oka crisis was about land that had been sacred to the Mohawks for hundreds of years. The more recent Ipperwash crisis was about Indian land "borrowed" for wartime use and then converted to recreational use for the Canadian army.

And now there is Voisey's Bay. Nobody, least of all the government of Newfoundland, disputed that the area around Voisey's Bay in Labrador was the traditional hunting and trapping ground of the Innu and Inuit. But when someone discovered what may be the world's largest nickel deposit there, things changed. Newfoundland will not guarantee the Innu and Inuit any royalties from a Voisey's Bay mine.

It is Mr. Irwin, the Minister of Indian Affairs, who explains the *realpolitik* of Voisey's Bay. Aside from the oil field at Hibernia, Newfoundland has only tourism as a source of revenue, he says, "so it's really important for the province to get this one."

There are stories like that across the country. *Terra nullius* dies hard.

People like Ovide Mercredi would have wished the election campaign to have been centred on native affairs. The RCAP report could have been debated every day. But, as even he acknowledges, "nobody wants to champion the issues affecting aboriginal people."

That includes the Minister of Northern Affairs. Although Mr. Irwin is leaving politics, he wants to

offend no one. A career in politics teaches you how to work both sides of the street: "There's not much in that report that I would say I'm opposed to. . . . But you have to live within the fiscal realities of what we're doing. So I would be misleading the aboriginal people to say I endorse this whole thing, *carte blanche.*"

Nobody had to explain to Mr. Irwin that Canadian voters are hardly ripe for revolution. And revolution it would be. There is no other way to describe a fundamental restructuring of the country's fiscal priorities and balance of legislative power. But the suspicion is that Garry Breitkreuz reflects the country better than the royal commissioners.

If recent history has proved anything, it is that the country is too complex to be seen through a single prism. There are too many peoples, too many histories, too many injustices, too many scores to settle. A single prism did not work for English-French relations, it will not work for the aboriginal peoples.

For one thing, the nature of the problem has changed; it may have moved beyond the ken of most politicians or royal commissioners. Any election debate on aboriginal affairs—if anyone had cared or dared—might simply have been yesterday's battle.

David Newhouse tells of a lot of effort to get urban aboriginals on the agenda of the royal commission. After all, 320,000 aboriginals, almost half the native people in the country, live in urban communities; there are more natives in Winnipeg than in all of the Northwest Territories. But the commissioners were more interested in traditional native life and problems. They agreed only reluctantly to study the phenomenon of urban natives.

Prof. Newhouse sees the aboriginal future very much in terms of those young people who were a trickle in colleges and universities

when he began, but who are now a flood. Sure, they want to maintain some sense of traditional values and social order, but they also want the urban and capitalist economy.

"The process of modernization and the adoption of capitalism as the dominant political-economic system within aboriginal society is well under way. It would be sheer folly to attempt to reverse the process or to attempt dramatic shifts in direction. I would argue that the forces of modernization are much too great to resist."

Aboriginal peoples have survived so far despite the pressures of governments to assimilate. But Prof. Newhouse is not convinced they can survive the pressures of capitalism.

"We will be absorbed one way or another. What we can do is mediate the worst effects of capitalism through the continued use of our values and the transformation of these values into institutional actions. The world that we used to live in no longer exists."

That may indeed be the wave of the future, and capitalism may transform the life of Canada's native people. But for most, the future is a long time away. Most of them remain where they have always been, most of them are young, and many of them are angry.

Bill Namagoose, the Quebec Cree, is worried about that anger and that blockades and violence are the only way native concerns get noticed. Certainly they aren't debated by politicians in election campaigns. "Poverty is such an issue in the communities. It's rampant. But the mood of the country is such that we can't address that issue. But how do we control the frustrations and reactions to that situation?"

In time Canada's native people may reap the bounties of the future, but before that happens the rest of the country may yet have to pay the costs of the past.

Foreign Policy and the Military

Canada's foreign policy has traditionally emphasized Canada's role as a peacekeeping nation and its support for the United Nations and other international bodies committed to the maintenance of international peace. Just as is true for other nations, however, Canada has developed a military defense policy, and it is a member of several defense-related organizations, such as the North Atlantic Treaty Organization. In this section five selections examine the current and future choices that Canada must make with regard to its foreign and military policy and some of the effort that is going into reexamination of these policies. Many of these articles relate to a post–cold war world and the implications of this new geopolitical situation for the Canadian armed forces.

The first selection analyzes Canada's foreign policy from the perspective of the period immediately preceding the 1997 federal election. Author Jeff Sallot suggests that the environment within which Canada's foreign policy is shaped has changed significantly in recent years. This article discusses several dimensions of Canadian foreign policy, including Canadian culture, security alliances, arms control, aid, and overseas economic relations.

Canadian strategic policy is put in a wider context in the second article in this unit. Brian MacDonald, in an article published in *Canadian Defence Quarterly*, discusses changes since the end of the cold war, Canada's peacebuilding initiative, whether it is necessary to maintain war-capable forces, and Canada's role in international military activity (such as the Gulf War). MacDonald concludes that it is time for a reexamination of the goals and the behavior of Canadian foreign policy.

Following a period of difficult and controversial military activity in Somalia and elsewhere in recent years, Canada's armed forces are reexamining their role in Canada and in the world. Allan Thompson in an article in *The Toronto Star* describes the "blueprint for the future" of the military presented by Canada's defense minister Doug Young.

The government's view of the future of the military is the focus of the next article, "Uncertainty about Future Undermines Forces," which describes some of the recent sources of tension and controversy that have plagued the Canadian armed forces. Author Paul Koring asks whether Canada in fact needs an army and suggests that problems of morale in the armed forces and social criticism can be resolved. Fundamentally, Koring asserts, a deep reservoir of support exists among the Canadian public for the military.

The final article in the section examines the broad question of the relationship between Canadian citizens and the Canadian armed forces. Paul Koring, of *The Globe and Mail (Toronto)*, asks whether there is a long-term "disconnection" between Canadians and the Canadian armed forces. He suggests that Canadian society is for the most part uninterested in the military and is not really inclined to support it actively, beyond a peacekeeping role. The needs of Canada's military are discussed here, and the article concludes that based upon its recent activities Canada's military may not be worth the amount of money spent on it.

Looking Ahead: Challenge Questions

What changes are likely to take place in the structure and identity of the Canadian military forces as a result of the end of the cold war?

Can Canada continue to play the role of international peacekeeper that it has so successfully developed in the past? With the ever-increasing demands for international peacekeeping forces in today's world, what is likely to happen to Canada's armed forces?

How does Canada's public respond to Canada's military today? Do events in which Canada's military becomes more visible to the public—such as its experiences in Somalia or in the Gulf War—affect the standing of the military? What is the likely future relationship between the public and the military?

UNIT 9

Neighbourhood watch

BY JEFF SALLOT

Parliamentary Bureau
Ottawa

L ET'S not mince words. Foreign policy is an exercise in self-interest that is rarely, if ever, marked by unfettered altruism. At best, a government and its people come to see that their own peace, security and wealth are linked to those of others, and that global politics and economics need not be a zero-sum game. Plainly, diplomacy is the art of convincing other countries they share your objectives.

This is an excellent time to rethink what Canada's foreign-policy should look like. For one thing, an election looms. For another, the world is changing: A post–Cold War Europe, the rise of Asian economic power and the global reach of data-transfer technologies present new opportunities for relations with the world beyond our borders.

Moreover, Canada is no longer restrained by the alliance politics that forced Ottawa to mute its criticism of Ronald Reagan's Star Wars scheme a decade ago and allowed the Mackenzie River Valley to be used by the U.S. Air Force as a test range for cruise missiles. There are new ways to project Canadian views and make Canadian voices heard beyond our borders.

While relations with the U.S. remain Canada's most intimate foreign affair, a revitalized Europe, the rising tide of Asian power and a wired world present new possibilities in a truly global village.

With this in mind, here is an optimal foreign-policy statement for Canada.

Maintain excellent relations with the U.S.

Every exercise in recalibrating Canadian foreign policy over the past 50 years has reached the same conclusion: The most important item on Canada's international agenda must be good economic and political relations with the United States.

Canadian politicians in the opposition parties succumb to the temptation to campaign using a subtle anti-American line—which is why

Jean Chrétien scolded the Tories during the 1993 campaign for being unseemly camp followers of the United States.

But that was election talk.

Only weeks after taking office, Mr. Chrétien agreed to endorse the North American freetrade agreement negotiated by the Tories in his first meeting with President Bill Clinton at a Seattle summit of Pacific Rim leaders. And despite concerns about the safety of Canadian ground troops in Bosnia, he renewed their assignment after an inconclusive Commons debate in January, 1994. Today there are about 1,200 Canadian soldiers working hand in glove, under a U.S. general, with about 10,000 U.S. counterparts in that troubled corner of Europe.

Similarly, the U.S. military was not at all interested in participating in a multinational force to assist Hutu refugees until Mr. Chrétien said Canada would organize the Central African refugee mission last November. With this gentle nudge from Ottawa, the U.S. came on board.

The Chrétien government also knows when to give way. Serious differences arose last year between Ottawa and Washington on the question of whether Boutros Boutros-Ghali should be given a second term as UN Secretary-General. The U.S. wanted to dump him. Canadian officials groused in private but publicly pulled their punches.

Our economic relationship is a big reason why. Two-way trade between Canada and just one state—California—equals all of Canada's trade with Japan. Our two-way trade in goods and services with the U.S. is more than $1.2-billion a day, and fully 65 per cent of foreign direct investment in Canada—some $110-billion a year—comes in the form of U.S. greenbacks.

Our trade disputes are persistent. But they are minor irritants when viewed in the context of the incredible size of our two-way trade. Our commercial relationship supports more than two million jobs in each country. In Canada it generates 28 per cent of our gross domestic product.

Economic intelligence gathering. There is one area where Canada should chart its own course, however: It should develop an intelligence-gathering capability. During the Cold War, Canada relied heavily on the U.S. and other allies to supply intelligence, which was largely defence-related. What is needed now is economic intelligence. As Alistair Hensler, a retired Canadian counter-intelligence officer says, yesterday's military allies are today's economic rivals.

Canadians could launch such a service and tuck it into the Department of Foreign Affairs and International Trade for about $10-million a year.

The U.S. would understand. Every other G-7 country has its own foreign intelligence service.

Multilateral organizations. The Canada-U.S. relationship is seen by others as a remarkable achievement considering our disparity in size. The Ukrainian government recently asked Canada for advice on how to help it develop better relations with its giant neighbour, Russia.

One of the tips is to keep the bigger power engaged in as many multilateral organizations as possible because they serve as an effective counterweight to the giant's unilateral impulses. These include the

North Atlantic Treaty Organization, the World Trade Organization and even the Organization for American States, which until recently was seen by Ottawa as Washington's private sandbox. Canada has always counted on multilateral organizations to reduce the impact of some of the go-it-alone policies that occasionally come out of Washington, including the most recent manifestation of its Cuba embargo, the Helms-Burton law.

Push for reform of UN secretariat. Ottawa regularly chides the U.S. for its late payments of UN dues, which are now about $1-billion in arrears. But to drive home the point Canada needs to be just as vigorous in its efforts to reform a cumbersome and sometimes corrupt UN secretariat, a favourite target of the U.S. Congress.

Foster economic relations with Asia

Let's get real about trade with Asia. It pales in comparison to our trade with the U.S. Almost 80 per cent of our exports go to the U.S., about $240-billion in 1995. Our exports to Asia were about $28-billion.

That said, the six fastest-growing markets in the world are in Asia: Hong Kong, Taiwan, China, Korea, Singapore and Japan. And our market share of exports to every one of them has declined over the years. In the case of China, Canada had a 5-per-cent market share in 1980; it was about 2.5 per cent in 1992.

Establish a presence. We have been slow to trade with the Pacific Rim: Canada has 2.3 million companies, yet fewer than 600 have offices in Asia.

Canadian sales in the Asian market account for only 1.6 per cent of all imports by Asian countries. Not only is our market share tiny, it has actually been shrinking in recent years, largely because of the increase in trade among the Asian countries themselves.

Canada's merchandise trade with Asia in 1995, the best year on record, was $17.5-billion (U.S.). This lagged behind all other G7 countries. Their figures were: United States, $179.9-billion; Germany, $54.1-billion; Britain, $27-billion; France, $26-billion; Italy, $22.6-billion. Japan, which remains the economic powerhouse of Asia, sold $193.4-billion worth of merchandise to its Asian neighbours. Australia, which like Canada must ship its goods across the ocean, sold $34.4-billion worth in 1995, more than twice as much as Canada.

"Team Canada" missions aren't enough. It takes time to develop the trust and personal relations—what the Chinese call *guanxi*—that generate business. It isn't enough for Ottawa to declare 1997 as the Year of the Pacific or for Vancouver to host a summit meeting this fall of heads of government from Pacific Rim countries.

Nobody knows this better than Raymond Chan, an MP from British Columbia with family ties to Hong Kong. He is the government's minister of state for Asian affairs and he's on the road continually to Asian markets. Representatives of about 25 Canadian companies were with him on his most recent foray last month to four regional centres in China. Dealing directly with local business contacts and regional officials may prove a far more effective approach than the three high-profile Team Canada photo ops that raise expectations that can't be met in the short term.

Look beyond China. Canada has a fixation with the Big Deal with China—think nuclear reactors—ignoring the possibility of niche markets in Japan, Thailand, South Korea and other Asian countries. Too few Canadian companies are following the lead of enterprises such as the B.C. snowboard manufacturer that is selling to Koreans or the Alberta patio-furniture maker whose tables and chairs were all the rage at the Tokyo home and garden show. The Chrétien government's preoccupation with China trade tends to obscure the fact that doing business

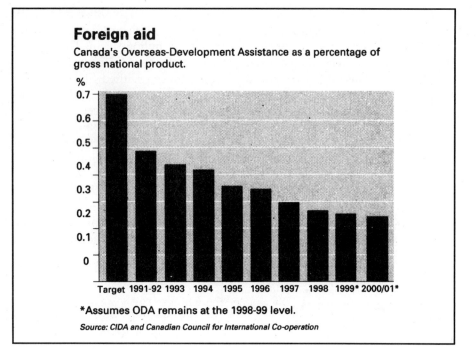

Foreign aid

Canada's Overseas-Development Assistance as a percentage of gross national product.

*Assumes ODA remains at the 1998-99 level.

Source: CIDA and Canadian Council for International Co-operation

with the one-party Communist regime is risky. The Conference Board of Canada documents 45 different risks for foreign firms operating in China. Two of the biggest are the fact the currency isn't fully convertable and it might be hard to bring profits home; and because the legal system is primitive, enforcing contracts is problematic.

Capitalize on our linguistic assets. Two million Canadians are of Asian origin and still have ties to the region. Many know Cantonese and other Asian languages. Yet Canadian school systems, with rare exceptions, are doing little to capitalize on these advantages and to teach Asian languages as a long-term national investment. School systems everywhere in Canada should emulate the Asian language programs pioneered in British Columbia.

Respect for human rights

Develop a coherent position. Canada's human-rights policy is all over the map. It has imposed sanctions on the murderous regime in Nigeria, including a ban on most defence sales. It has also been trying to organize escalating trade and eco-

nomic sanctions within the Commonwealth.

Yet in the case of China, which has one of the worst human-rights records, Canada has not only refused to lead, it won't even follow others in condemning Chinese abuses.

Ottawa recently said it would not co-sponsor a UN resolution fingering the Beijing regime, the first time since the Tiananmen Square massacre that Canada has not been a co-

sponsor of such a resolution. The Danes led the crusade this year at the UN conference in Geneva, with support from the United States, Britain and others, while Canada sat on the sidelines.

If a government doesn't respect the basic human rights of its own citizens we can't expect it to respect the contractual and other legal rights of foreign investors and business partners. That's why even an economics-driven foreign policy must promote human rights and the rule of law around the world. Authoritarian regimes should not be able to buy Canada's silence on human rights in exchange for commercial contracts.

Ultimately, democratic forces will succeed in supplanting authoritarian regimes in China, Indonesia, Burma and elsewhere in Asia as they are succeeding in Eastern and Central Europe and Latin America. The triumphant democrats will remember who their friends were and who kept faith with their cause. Canada does not want to be remembered for cozying up to dictators and turning a blind eye to human-rights abuses we would not tolerate at home.

There are creative ways Canadians can show solidarity with democrats without provoking direct confrontation with dictators. On his

International views of Canada

Foreign affairs and policy, 1992–97 % agree.

	WORLD LEADER: PEACE/RIGHTS		GENEROUS FOREIGN AID		DOES WHAT U.S. WANTS	
	1992	1997	1992	1997	1992	1997
CANADA	**90**	**94**	**94**	**94**	**77**	**69**
U.S.	62	75	38	55	48	53
Mexico	71	37	71	67	61	40
U.K.	51	51	38	38	35	40
France	52	84	42	66	39	56
Germany	44	61	40	62	51	68
Italy	59	63	42	49	54	56
Russia	43	39	61	28	36	50
Japan	47	59	47	52	63	66
South Korea	53	54	60	42	40	58
India	41	40	47	53	53	45
Australia	58	61	41	49	39	45

Source: Angus Reid Group surveyed 5,700 adults in 20 countries on a number of issues. The first line (Canada) shows what we think of ourselves; the second line indicates what Americans think of us. And so on.

WHAT THE OPPOSITION PARTIES EMPHASIZE

Progressive Conservatives would give priority to foreign-aid projects that respect human rights, promote self-sufficiency and development, especially those projects that call for "in-kind" assistance (supplying commodities) rather than infusions of cash. The Tories would develop a "rapid-reaction division" for the Canadian Forces to respond to trouble spots and would devise a system to procure military equipment at a lower price.

New Democrats call for Canada to show leadership within NATO on devising a defence strategy that does not depend on nuclear weapons. It supports ultimately eliminating them. The NDP would tighten controls on arms exports from Canada and would try to strengthen the UN so that the world body rather than NATO responds to military crises if they occur.

The Reform Party wants to make the Canadian International Development Agency more accountable for its spending by giving it a legislated mandate. Reform would try to amend NAFTA to strengthen Canadian protection of its fresh-water resources. It believes the Canadian Forces should include roughly equal numbers of reservists and regular members.

The Bloc Québécois wants an independent Quebec to have good relations with its North American neighbours and would want to join NAFTA. The BQ would also seek to reassure the United States on defence issues by continued participation in the NORAD continental air-defence alliance. The BQ has generally supported Canadian participation in international peacekeeping missions.

Canada's flow of trade

	EXPORTS (millions)	IMPORTS (millions)
All countries	258,418.4	232,937.2
United States	210,071.2	157,344.0
Total Asia	21,463.3	28,181.8
Total Europe	17,462.3	27,646.0
Japan	10,377.0	10,439.6
China	2,706.8	4,925.8
South Korea	2,676.3	2,727.6
Taiwan	1,362.4	2,863.1
Hong Kong	1,109.3	1,143.1
Indonesia	825.6	625.8
Singapore	529.3	1,190.9
Thailand	503.2	1,043.3
Malaysia	499.9	1,580.1
India	341.6	603.8

Source: Statistics Canada

Selling Canada overseas

Promoting Canadian culture abroad

	Per capita annum
France	$26.60
Germany	18.50
Britain	13.40
Japan	12.60
Canada	3.10

Source: Special Joint Committee of the Senate and the House of Commons on Canadian Foreign Policy, 1994

next trip to China, Mr. Chrétien might talk publicly about his own experience in democratic politics—both in government and opposition.

Imagine the impact if on his first trip to China he had introduced himself as a politician who was responsible for protecting the rights of the Canadian aboriginal minority and for the introduction of laws that enshrine the Charter of Rights in the Canadian Constitution. That sort of disarming introduction would send a powerful message.

Mr. Chrétien has said Canada cannot have much influence on human-rights issues with huge countries like China. But he sells us short. Until the government backed down on the UN resolution, the Liberals appeared to have changed their course on human-rights issues since Lloyd Axworthy became Foreign Affairs Minister last year. He has talked tough on such issues as the exploitation of Asian children as sex slaves and sweat-shop workers. And the government followed through with criminal code amendments that allow for the prosecution in Canada of men who visit the flesh pots of Asia and have sex with child prostitutes.

But we could do a lot more.

Set up import-certification program. We should consider human-rights standards for our imports just as we insist on safety standards. If a producer satisfied Ottawa that its goods weren't made in fire-trap factories, child-labour sweat shops or by political prisoners they would receive consumer certification. Imports without certification would not be banned. But Canadian consumers could at least make an informed choice about what kind of imports they want to buy.

Human-rights report cards. Ottawa should follow through with a promise made by the Liberals when they were in opposition to publish annual report cards on the human-rights performance of foreign governments, as the U.S. State Department does. Our foreign-affairs department complies human-rights evaluations, but refuses to publish them for fear of offending someone.

Sell Canadian culture

When we sell our culture successfully we can sell other things as well. Bryan Adams, Céline Dion, Margaret Atwood, Wayne Gretzky—we've got the goods. Hollywood sells America for the Americans. We shouldn't be shy about doing the same. Social commentator John Ralston Saul notes: "To put it crassly, American films sell America. They sell soft drinks, clothes, cars, tourism. They sell the myth. Nations which do not make every effort to export their cultures are naive and self-destructive."

We have a lot to build on with our own cultural industries. Moreover, other people like us and don't think we are pushy. Canada is one of the top 10 "most admired" countries in the world, according to a recent Angus Reid Group 20-country survey.

Mr. Saul, in a study for a parliamentary committee on foreign policy, says that our country is best known abroad for our artists, authors, musicians, film makers, dramatists and other cultural figures rather than for our domestic or international affairs. He relates his experiences in Europe three summers ago. Canadian books were reviewed in Le Monde, the French daily. The European, an English-language paper, devoted a full page to a Canadian musical about AIDS. Leonard Cohen was featured in a BBC radio interview. Seven or eight Canadian theatre companies popped up at the Edinburgh Festival. Everyone seemed to be talking about a new film on Glenn Gould. (He could have added that a fair chunk of the programming on TV Cinq, a French-language international television network, is Canadian.)

Spend money promoting culture. This can't be done by the private sector. Other countries recognize this. A parliamentary committee reported three years ago that France spends about $1.4-billion a year on international cultural activities, or about 18 times what Canada spends. On a per capita basis that's $26.60 in France versus just $3.10 in Canada.

It is probably more important for a country like Canada to promote its culture and values abroad than, say France, because we are so easily overshadowed by the United States. We have to make a greater effort to distinguish ourselves.

Exploit new technologies. In the past, much of the money we spent on promoting our culture abroad would have gone into mortars-and-bricks infrastructure such as a cultural centre in a foreign capital, or a library located in one of our embassies. Or we would have spent lavishly to put our theatre and dance companies on the road and to send our musicians on tour. The big budgets aren't there for this kind of promotion any more.

Arts and culture funding has been cut generally by the Liberals. The Canadian Conference of the Arts reports that direct federal support for arts and culture on a per capita basis has gone from $44.83 in 1993 to $35.29.

New technology might provide an answer. Within a few years, millions of people will be able to pull in digital satellite television broadcasts from anywhere else in the world—and we will be on an equal footing in the 500-channel universe. In the performing arts we should have no difficulty. Internet data-transfer technology will make our literature and visual arts accessible globally.

The challenge will be to restore an economic climate at home for Canadian artists to produce their best works about our country and ourselves.

Preserve security alliances Reduce defence spending.

Canada needs a cheap but effective defence policy. Our policy now is effective, but could be cheaper than the $10-billion a year we now spend. The basic defence policy is to deter an attack on Canada.

Its not easy to imagine who might want to—or could—attack Canada with the idea of seizing and holding territory. There is only one country with the necessary military capability but the possibility of an attack from our ally to the south is absurd.

Nevertheless, prudence dictates that we maintain some minimal deterrent force as insurance against a crackpot regime or outlaw force. We should be able to bloody the noses of bullies.

Maintaining a military capability is expensive. Even with the budget cuts of the past three years of $1.6-billion, we spend about 1.3 per cent of our gross domestic product on defence.

Develop a partnership with the U.S. Think of it as anti-war insurance. We pay an annual insurance premium of about $330 per capita so we don't have to worry about war. Can we buy the same protection at a lower premium? Yes, if we work out a realistic division of labour with our closest ally, the U.S., which already spends about $254-billion (U.S.) annually on defence. Converted to Canadian dollars and divided by the size of the U.S. population that works out to more than $1,300 per capita.

Canada could trim from the defence budget capital items like maritime helicopters and replacement submarines: 20 to 30 new helicopters could cost up to $1-billion depending how many gadgets are included. Four new submarines would cost between $600-million to $800-million, even at the "fire sale" prices the British are offering. These are costly pieces of kit whose main justification is to hunt down and destroy hostile submarines.

J. H. Taylor, one of Canada's most distinguished diplomats, says that though many Canadians find it hard to accept, we are "one of the most secure countries in the world . . . defended by the United States in the act of defending itself, whether we choose to defend ourselves or not."

What we bring to the defence partnership with the U.S. is our vast geography. Canada is a 4,000-kilometre-deep buffer along the northern flank of the United States. The Pentagon knows it would have to revamp its own military doctrine and spend much, much more money if Canada ever declared itself neutral.

Canada brings something else of great value to the partnership: its good name. With no colonial past and no aspirations to super powerdom, we represent a guarantee to other countries that there is no hidden U.S. agenda when we operate militarily abroad in a coalition with the U.S., as we did in the Gulf War in 1991.

Canada still has to be able to put some military assets on the table. But land forces—infantry, armour, signals, logistics and other army activities Canadians do well—are relatively inexpensive in comparison to fighter aircraft squadrons and maritime helicopters and submarines. And our land forces are greatly appreciated by the Pentagon, which is loath to commit its own ground troops to dangerous missions. On the other hand, the U.S. has the best air force and navy in the world and it is happy to oblige Canada through the NATO and NORAD partnership.

The Canadian Forces often try to compare Ottawa's spending on defence with that of our NATO allies expressed as a percentage of gross domestic product. Thus Canada's 1.3 per cent does not stand up to the 2.8 per cent in Britain, for example, or the 2 per cent in the Netherlands. But the fact is that most NATO countries are in Europe, where the threat of conflict is much greater.

Perhaps more valid comparisons can be made between Canada and other Western Hemisphere countries such as Brazil, which spends 1.1 per cent of GDP on defence, or Mexico, which spends 0.9 per cent. Japan is another country that ultimately depends on U.S. might for its security—and in a part of the world where the risks of conflict are much greater than in North America. Ja-pan spends about 1 per cent of GDP on defence.

Canada should move rapidly towards 1 per cent of GDP level for defence spending. In the current fiscal year this would save taxpayers more than $2-billion.

Champion arms control

Canadian policy is ambivalent in this area. We don't have any nuclear weapons, and have been content to let the U.S. defend us with theirs. Canadians have never dirtied their hands directly, though for 50 years we have had the materials and know-how to build nuclear weapons. Nor does Canada allow its superpower ally to base nuclear weapons on our territory.

Yet through the North Warning System of radar installations across the Canadian Arctic and our participation in NORAD, we are part of an alliance that depends on U.S. nuclear weapons to provide the ultimate deterrent. Thus, Canada provides important infrastructure for the Pentagon's nuclear force.

Russia and the U.S. have agreed in the Start II treaty to reduce their stockpiles by about two-thirds from Cold War days, and no longer keep their nuclear missiles aimed at each other. But even when Start II is fully implemented, the U.S. will still have 3,500 operational warheads and Russia will have 3,000—more than enough to blow us all to smithereens.

A World Court advisory ruling last year cast serious doubt on the legitimacy of ever using nuclear weapons in warfare. The Canberra Commission—a blue-ribbon international panel—reached the same conclusion.

Turn NATO into a non-nuclear alliance. But how do we ever put the genie back in the bottle? It will be a long process. Canada and non-nuclear partners in NATO, such as the Dutch, could make a good start by declaring their intention to turn NATO into a non-nuclear alliance.

We would find support from many Americans. The Washington-based Henry L. Stimson Center, a public-policy think tank, published a report recently from its special committee on eliminating weapons of mass destruction. It included several hard-eyed military realists, including former top generals from the Pentagon and a former defence secretary.

The panel said the ultimate objective of U.S. national-security policy should be "the elimination of all weapons of mass destruction from all states." Incentives will have to be found for the non-NATO nuclear states—Russia and China—to join a multilateral nuclear-disarmament process.

Severe penalties must be imposed on nuclear wannabe regimes that try to steal or buy nuclear-weapons technology and warhead material on the black market.

The toughest nuts may be Britain and France. Their own nuclear weapons guarantee them permanent seats at the UN Security Council. Without nukes they are simply two more members of the European Union.

We aren't going to eliminate the world's nuclear weapons in a decade, maybe not even in a generation. But we could make a start with a Canadian declaration that we do not want our allies to use their nuclear weapons to defend us.

Be generous with the poorest.

Foreign policy comes closest to altruism when we donate assistance to poor countries and peoples. Lester Pearson first set the target for Canadian Overseas Development Assistance at 0.7 per cent of our gross domestic product. It seemed like a reasonable amount for a generous and prosperous people. The current Liberal government, which is celebrating the 100th anniversary of Lester Pearson's birth this month (see D3), still espouses the 0.7 per cent target as its long-term goal. But that target has been decreasing. It has gone from a high of 0.5 per cent in the mid-1970s to just under 0.3 per cent in the current fiscal year.

Not only has the percentage dropped, but the total number of dollars has decreased. Finance Minister Paul Martin's deficit-fighting budgets have shrunk the size of the Official Development Assistance envelop from $3-billion to about $2.4-billion.

Combine defence and development budgets. In opposition, the Liberals had a different idea of how foreign aid should be structured. They suggested the defence budget—or at least a portion of it—and the Overseas Development Assistance budget might be combined into one international-security envelope. The Canadian foreign aid budget is about $2-billion a year. Military spending is currently five times that, or about $10-billion a year.

Putting the two into the same spending envelop is an acknowledgement that defence policy is a subset of foreign policy, and not the tail that wags the dog. It also recognizes that the ultimate objective is to make the world a better and thus safer place for everyone.

Many Third World problems eventually become international-security problems, as happened in Somalia in 1992 and Rwanda in 1994.

Combining part of the ODA and defence budgets would make it easier to direct resources toward Third World trouble spots before they explode into international security crises.

The defence budget has also taken a hit from Mr. Martin's deficit fighters. But the cuts in military spending have all gone to the bottom line. If, however, just half of those cuts to defence had been redirected toward the foreign-aid budget, Canada's ODA to GDP ratio would stabilize at 0.4 per cent. Canada would then be able to provide an additional $1-billion in development assistance this year.

CANADIAN STRATEGIC POLICY AND
THE CLASH OF CIVILIZATIONS

by Brian MacDonald

The Canadian Common Strategic Vision

In a recent op-ed piece, former Parliamentarian and long-standing senior columnist Douglas Fisher observed that "the federal Liberal party has members with attitudes ranging from: (1) enthusiasm for dismantling our armed services; (2) a highly-romantic conceit that Canada could become the top global peacekeeper, its personnel police and aid specialists, not infantry; (3) to those who believe

Does Canada require a modern main battle tank, such as this M1A2 *Abrams*?

General Dynamics Photo

the forces we have are about right; [and] (4) the military hawks who insist our forces should be tough, action-ready, and have top weapons and transport."[1]

These divisions are not new, either in the Liberal party or the Canadian population, but what *is* new is the change in the proportions between the groups. During the late Cold War any national opinion poll on the level of defence spending in Canada would yield similar results: about one-sixth of those polled thought we were spending too much; about one-third thought we were spending too little, and about half felt we were spending about the right amount — results which allowed successive governments to maintain the relatively skimpy defence budget status quo. Since the end of the Cold War the proportion of doves has increased and the defence budget has drifted downwards in Canada, as in other Western nations.

In Canada this has stemmed, in part, from the influence of a common strategic vision shared by all of the first three groups identified by Fisher. The 1994 Report of the Special Joint Committee on Canada's Defence Policy believed that "concepts of security are changing. Military security is but one element of a broader concept of national security that must reflect political, economic, social, environmental and even cultural factors."[2] While the 1994 Defence White Paper accepted that "we can expect pockets of chaos and instability that will threaten international peace and security" and "an unpredictable and fragmented world, one in which conflict, repression and upheaval exist alongside peace, democracy and relative prosperity,"[3] it

Brian MacDonald *is President, Strategic Insight Planning and Communications, Toronto, and author of* Military Spending in Developing Countries: How Much is Too Much? *(Carleton University Press, forthcoming).*

nonetheless concluded that "however horrendous the impact for the local population caught in the middle of civil wars, the absence today of adversarial relations among the world's great powers suggests that these conflicts are more likely to be contained."[4] The Foreign Minister observed in 1996 that the "end of the Cold War was hailed by some as the harbinger of global peace. But what it has brought us is not peace — but a new kind of war... The conflicts we face now are no longer military in nature, nor will they be resolved by military solutions alone. They occur within states, rather than between them, but they tend to spill over into surrounding regions."[5]

If this comparatively benign common strategic vision is an accurate assessment of the global strategic context both now and in the future, it is difficult to argue against the defence policy choices, force structures, equipment choices, and funding levels of the December 1994 White Paper and succeeding defence budget statements. Indeed, in an era of declining government budgets and competitive pubic sector policy choices, it may even be that we have provided too much for defence, and that there are other, better, cheaper ways of maintaining our stature in the world.

Such may be behind Foreign Affairs Minister Axworthy's October 1996 announcement of the Canadian Peacebuilding Initiative, which laid out the themes of his evolving foreign policy prescription in terms of "human security" and "peacebuilding,"[6] and his December 1996 address, "Foreign Policy in the Information Age," which added the concept of "soft power — the idea that knowledge and information confer international influence," and his belief that as "a middle power with limited military might...Canada is well-placed to wield 'soft power'."[7]

What comfort, then, for the "hawks"? While we may agree with Major-General Glen Younghusband's advice to the Special Joint Committee that "to believe that Canada will never require a greater military capability than peace-keeping is wishful thinking, and a defence policy based on wishful thinking would be dangerous indeed,"[8] it is equally wishful thinking to presume that the common strategic vision will go away by itself. If hawks are to successfully press their case for stable or enhanced funding, they will have to rebut the Canadian common strategic vision and posit an alternative strategic reality — one which requires the maintenance of war-capable, heavy forces.

The Huntington Thesis

Canada isn't alone in this dilemma. In the United States, for a brief period after the end of the Cold War, the seemingly seminal scholarly piece was Francis Fukuyama's "End of History" essay,[9] which argued that the Cold War was the last war, that the West had emerged triumphant, and that we were entering a peaceful era in which the entire world would gradually embrace the liberal values of the West. That vision ended in the United States with the outbreak of the 1990-1991 Gulf War; it has lasted longer in Canada.

It has since been replaced, in United States strategic circles, by Samuel Huntington's 1993 essay "The Clash of Civilizations,"[10] and his 1996 book *The Clash of Civilizations and the Remaking of World Order*.[11] The core of Huntington's thesis is that the conflict paradigm of the Westphalian system was of war between princes, that from the French revolution to World War I was of war between nation states, and that of World War II and the Cold War was of war between ideologies, but that the organizing paradigm of future wars will be of conflict between civilizations — and particularly that between, to use Kishore Mahbubani's phrase, "The West and the Rest."[12]

Huntington argues that civilizations "are defined by common objective elements, such as language, history, religion, customs, institutions, and by the subjective self-identification of people," and may include many individual states, or be limited to one, such as China. He argues that the future will be shaped by the interactions between "seven or eight major civilizations. These include Western, Confucian, Japanese, Islamic, Hindu, Slavic-Orthodox, Latin American and possibly African," and that the "fault lines between civilizations are replacing the political, ideological boundaries of the Cold War as the flash points for crisis and bloodshed." Within the Huntington paradigm the conflict in the former Yugoslavia can be understood

HMCS *St. John's:* Should naval and air programmes come at the expense of the Army?

as three-cornered between the Western, Slavic-Orthodox, and Islamic civilizations, and that of the Gulf War as between Western and Islamic civilizations — a portrayal which is common in Islam, regardless of the presence of Islamic client states among the Western-led coalition.

Huntington adds two other useful concepts. "Kin countries" share civilization membership and are drawn into conflicts not their own by appeals from other civilization members, as were first the Central Europeans and subsequently other Western countries on the side of the Croats; the Russians, Ukrainians, and Greeks on the side of the Serbs; and a variety of Islamic countries, including Iran, on the side of the Bosnian Muslims. "Torn" countries are divided over their loyalties. The prototype "torn" country, according to Huntington, is Turkey, which by history, culture, and tradition is Islamic, but which, since Kemal Ataturk, has had leadership elites who sought to define it as a modern, secular, Western state. A footnote cites Owen Harries as observing that Australia might be trying to become a torn state; though it has always been a full member of the West, "its current leadership [is], in effect, proposing that it defect from the West, redefine itself as an Asian country, and cultivate close ties with its neighbours."[13]

We, perhaps, might add a Canadian footnote by suggesting that the marginal role played by Canada in the Gulf War (which disappointed many among the American, British, and French who were expecting us to provide significant ground combat forces), and the thrusts of the 1994 Special Joint Committee report, the 1994 Defence White Paper, and the 1996 Ministerial statements, might be seen, like the Australian footnote, to represent a de facto proposal for Canada's defection from the West and embracing of "torn state" status — a collective policy judgment based upon the common strategic vision — one not synchronized with strategic reality.

Huntington posits (and he is not alone among American strategic analysts) that a de facto Confucian-Islamic coalition is evolving to challenge the hegemonic domination achieved by the West after its twin victories in the Cold and Gulf Wars. That coalition is seen as intent on increasing its military capacity by importing Western (and Slavic-Orthodox) military technology, developing indigenous arms industries, and acquiring nuclear, chemical, and biological weapons to counter superior Western conventional technology. A new arms race has begun in which the Islamic-Confucian coalition is building its arsenal, while the West is still focused on arms reduction vis-à-vis the Slavic-Orthodox civilization.

Can We Make a Case for the Huntington Thesis?

One way of testing the Huntington thesis is by a traditional strategic capabilities-intentions screen of his eight civilizations. Strategic potential, in the model of Bruce Bueno de Mesquita,[14] is a function of forces-in-being, population, and economic strength — with the latter two providing the mobilization base for the long war. On that basis, the African civilization could be excluded as a threat to the West because of its lack of either military or economic potential, or of any coherent central authority capable of forming the intention to collectively go to war. The four principal states of the South American civilization have been decreasing military expenditures for the last decade, have been increasing their economic and cultural relationships with the two North American members of the West, and would, arguably, be surprised and indignant that they were not considered to be part of Western civilization in the first place. Japan, as Huntington notes, is effectively an associate member of the West in economic matters, and while its military budget is large in real terms, it remains at about 1.0 percent of GNP. Further, Japan's forces have no true power projection capability at this point — and the Chinese have been conscious of the value of the United States-Japan military relationship in restraining the regrowth of Japanese military power.

The population of the Hindu civilization will amount to 80 percent of that of China by 2000, but its economic growth rate (5.0 percent annually from 1980-1993) has been slower than that of China (9.6 percent annually from 1980-1993).[15] Its 20-year space launch programme, however, now has a one ton into orbit capability, and a commercially available satellite imagery capability of six metres (i.e., better than SPOT imagery), suggesting that the 2,500 km., 500 kg. *Agni* intermediate-range ballistic missile[16] may not be its last development. Moreover, a recent CIA report[17] that the 75 percent finished Soviet aircraft carrier *Varyag* may be headed from the Ukraine to a breaker's yard in India, for "scrapping", is also interesting. Nonetheless, India's primary strategic concerns are more likely to remain focused on Islam and China, rather than the West.

Dr. Andrei Kortunov, Head of the Foreign Policy Department at the Institute of the United States and Canada, part of the Russian Academy of Sciences, observed, at the Spring 1992 seminar of the Atlantic Council of Canada, that the Russian analytic community agreed that the threat to Russia from the West was now of the past, that the current threat was from the South, and the future threat to Russia would be from the East.[18] Subsequent events add weight to the Huntington thesis, as Russian support of Armenia in the Armenia-Azerbaijan conflict is consistent with the "kinship" theory, and the Russian-Chechen war had a very heavy "clash of civilizations" dimension.

However, the striking decline in Russian economic and military capability, and the military's miserable performance in the Chechnya campaign, suggests that the Orthodox-Slav civilization may now be the "sick man" of the world island. An interesting question is whether Russia will lean East or West in its search for support during its strategic weakness. How will NATO expansion to include the middle European states, whose religious and cultural ties are far more inclined to the Catholic civilization of the West rather than to that of Orthodox-Slavic Eastern Europe, influence that dimension? A recent Interfax news agency report of Russian Defence Minister Igor Rodionov's statement that "Moscow would, as always, pursue the policy of developing a strategic partnership with China"[19] no doubt has caused some strategic dismay in Washington.

The spectre of an Islamic *jihad* is a popular element among the apocalyptic set. A major difficulty in arguing the case, however, is the reality that Islam includes four different major ethno-linguistic groups, the Arabs, the Turkic-speaking peoples, the Iranians, and the Malaysian-Indonesians, who are unified only by Islam — and not all by the same form. Nonetheless, the critical importance of Gulf oil supplies to the economies of the West (and to Japan, and increasingly to China) makes the capabilities and intentions of the Islamic states of the Gulf of vital strategic importance. The defeat of Iraq has suppressed one threat for the moment, but Iran remains hostile and supportive of fundamentalist forces dedicated to the overthrow of Arab governments allied to the West, though its own military capabilities remain limited, unless technology can be transferred from its strategic friends.

An examination of Chinese strategic behaviour, in the frame of the Huntington paradigm, is even more intriguing. The author was struck, during his 1987 discussions in Beijing with the Beijing Institute of International Strategic Studies and the reciprocal visit of a BIISS delegation to Canada in 1988, by the intense concentration by the

The evergreen M109 self-propelled howitzer: still credible with upgrades?

Canadian Forces Photo

Chinese participants on American strategic capabilities and intentions. It seemed clear that the Chinese saw the United States as their principal threat and security concern. The sweeping triumph of American technology during the Gulf War has added to Chinese disquiet as they have realized how large the gap is between American military technology and their own. And the appearance of two American carrier battle groups during the Taiwan crisis of 1996 certainly was seen as a blatant and heavy-handed intervention against one of the most basic and central of Chinese policy objectives — the reunification of China.

One Chinese response has been to secure its rear by reducing border tensions with the Hindu civilization. A second has been to play the Orthodox-Slavic card by taking steps to peacefully resolve boundary disputes in the Xinjiang-Central Asian Republics areas, and by massive purchases of Russian military technology — a strategy made palatable by the fact that the core of current PRC leadership was educated in Moscow in the 1950s.[20] Nor, as we have seen in the comments by Russian Defence Minister Rodionov, have the Russians been unwilling to play. Columnist Simon Beck reports that a 1995 visit by former intelligence chief and now Foreign Minister Yevgeny Primakov set up the April 1996 Beijing summit between Presidents Boris Yeltsin and Jiang Zemin, which was followed by the December 1996 visit to Moscow of Chinese Premier Li Peng.[21] That meeting saw an agreement to install an Su-27 production line in China as the next step after the initial purchase of Russian-built Su-27s, and the purchase of two Sovremenny-class destroyers equipped with SS-N-22 anti-ship missiles with the capability to attack Aegis-type warships.[22] Another response has been to provide technology and weapons to the Islamic civilization, including C-802 anti-ship missiles to Iran,[23] and nuclear technology to Pakistan[24] — developments which have led to sharp criticism from the Americans.

Huntington and Canadian Strategic Policy

In Canada, of course, we have the comforting 1994 White Paper statement that there is "the absence today of adversarial relations among the world's great powers," and the equally comforting 1996 Foreign Minister's statement that "the conflicts we face now…occur within states, rather than between them…"

Let us, as a thought experiment, suppose that Samuel Huntington is right, and that the 1994 White Paper, and the 1996 Foreign Minister, are wrong. Let us suppose that China and the United States are on a long-term collision course — not one leading to war in 1997, when China is far too militarily weak, but later when China's striking economic growth has given China the funds to finish the Fourth Modernization, achieve a true power projection capability and, as leadership elites of the People's Liberation Army have urged, be able to reunify China by military force, as well as exercise its declared sovereignty over the South China Sea. Let us suppose, as well, that there is an Iranian-supported coup against the Saudi royal family, intent on replacing it with a fundamentalist Wahabi-Islam administration in sympathy with Shi'i-Islam in Iran.

Then let us suppose that there is both a Gulf War II, and a simultaneous naval war in the South and East China Seas. Will we be able to sit them out? Is "torn state" status an achievable option for us? Can we afford the economic retribution from the trading partner which accounts for 80 percent of our international trade and 28 percent of our GNP?

If "torn state" status isn't an option for us — if we, as a "kin" country of the West, are not permitted to defect, if we have no choice but to pull our weight in the grand coalition of the West — then we might have to reconsider our current strategic posture and force structure decisions.

Which strategic theatre should we contribute to? If we are restricted to one because of budget constraints, and it is the Pacific theatre, then Vice-Admiral Thomas is correct, and the equipment renewal focus must be naval and air at the expense of the Army. If it is the Gulf theatre, and if the most effective war-fighting contribution to a coalition army group based upon current equipment holdings were selected, perhaps an artillery brigade of three M109 regiments and an ADATS regiment might be sent. But if a general-purpose army formation were to be our contribution, then the equipment renewal process might well have to include *Abrams* main battle tanks, *Bradley* infantry fighting vehicles, an MLRS (Multiple Launch Rocket System) regiment, a target acquisition battery, utility tactical transport and medium transport helicopters, attack helicopters, and strategic airlift — since, as former Chief of the Defence Staff Jean Boyle aptly pointed out, we are, at the moment, not capable of going to war.

Maybe we should be thinking about reorganizing our forces to give actual meaning to the 1994 White Paper's promise of being able to fight "alongside the best, against the best."

NOTES

1. *Toronto Sun*, 12 January 1997.
2. Canada, Special Joint Committee on Canada's Defence Policy, *Security in a Changing World*, (Ottawa: Canada Communication Group, 1994), p.5.
3. Canada, Department of National Defence, *1994 Defence White Paper*, (Ottawa: Canada Communication Group, 1994), p.3.
4. Ibid., p.6.
5. Canada, Department of Foreign Affairs and International Trade, Policy Statement 96/46, 1996.
6. Ibid.
7. Canada, Department of Foreign Affairs and International Trade, Policy Statement 96/53, 1996.
8. *Security in a Changing World*, p.14.
9. Francis Fukuyama, "The End of History", *The National Interest*, (Summer 1989), pp.3-18.
10. Samuel Huntington, "The Clash of Civilizations", *Foreign Affairs*, (Summer 1993).
11. Samuel Huntington, *The Clash of Civilizations and the Remaking of World Order*, (New York: Simon and Shuster, 1996).
12. Kishore Mahbubani, "The West and the Rest", *The National Interest*, Summer 1992.
13. Huntington (1993), p.45.
14. Bruce Bueno de Mesquita, *The War Trap*, (New Haven: Yale University Press, 1981).
15. *Human Development Report 1996*, (New York: Oxford University Press, 1996), pp.178-179.
16. *The Military Balance 1996/97*, (London: The International Institute of Strategic Studies, 1996), p.152. Also see Wyn Bowen, Tim McCarthy and Holly Porteous, "Ballistic Missile Shadow Lengthens", *IDR Extra*, (February 1997), p.7.
17. *The Washington Times*, 1 January 1997. Other sources point to the possible purchase of the Russian Navy's *Admiral Gorshkov*.
18. Personal recollection of the author.
19. *South China Morning Post*, 16 January 1997.
20. D. Shambaugh, "Containment or Engagement of China?", *International Security*, (Fall 1996).
21. *South China Morning Post*, 16 January 1997.
22. Ibid.
23. *Hong Kong Standard*, 19 December 1996.
24. *South China Morning Post*, 14 December 1996.

Blueprint for military's future

'Today, we begin the process of restoring the pride,' defence minister says

BY ALLAN THOMPSON
OTTAWA BUREAU

OTTAWA

SURROUNDED BY the historical memorabilia of Canada's military past, Defence Minister Doug Young yesterday strode into the auditorium of the Canadian War Museum to unveil his blueprint for the future.

To get there, Young had to pass down a long corridor lined with photos depicting the Canadian Airborne Regiment's mission to Somalia, a tour of duty that still haunts Canada's military.

And Somalia was virtually the first word out of Young's mouth when he introduced his reform package.

"Somalia, Bakovici, hazing, harassment, cover-up," he said. "We also have to think about the Somme, Hong Kong, Victoria Crosses, Normandy, Korea, Suez, Cyprus and courage."

Behind him the military organizers of the news conference had erected a banner: "Restoring the Pride."

"Today we begin the process of restoring the pride and sense of purpose to a vital national institution," Young said.

Young's prescription includes pay increases, an end to a ban on promotions, significant changes to the military justice system, creation of an ombudsman post, renewed emphasis on training and a package of administrative reforms.

Young said the measures outlined in his reports "represent the most comprehensive recommendations for change in the way the Canadian Forces function in a very long time."

But military analysts said that Young's package, while progressive, could hardly be classified as a radical departure from the status quo.

'This is not radical. But there is some innovation there'

"It's a step in the right direction but it's not the dramatic change that some people expected," said Stethem. "But it is enough to open the door to necessary evolutionary change."

"Young has attempted to seize the agenda, to take control of the argument and at least this provides a focus for the debate," Stethem said. "Now we can deal with things moving in a certain direction."

"This is not radical," said Alex Morrison, executive director of the Canadian Institute of Strategic Studies. "But I think there is some innovation there and people in the military will be pleased."

Based on the advice he received from the military and from a panel of historians and experts, Young submitted 65 recommendations to Prime Minister Jean Chrétien and forwarded, unchanged, another 35 recommendations for changes to the military justice system, compiled by a panel headed by for-

mer Supreme Court chief justice Brian Dickson.

The most substantive changes outlined yesterday were contained in the report submitted by Dickson along with retired general Charles Belzile and former MP Bud Bird.

Dickson's report cited one witness who said: "If you are going to trust the chain of command to lead the Canadian Forces into battle, surely you must also trust it to administer military justice appropriately."

Following from that lead, the Dickson panel recommended changes to reform the justice system from within—contrary to some recommendations that military justice be moved out of defence to the solicitor-general's department.

Perhaps most important, military police officers, like their civilian counterparts, will now have the power to lay charges. In the past, military police conducted investigations, but it was up to the commanding officer of the accused to decide whether or not to lay a charge and that process was open to command influence.

Summary trials, which handle relatively minor disciplinary matters, will be brought in line with the Charter of Rights. Maximum penalties will be 30 days confinement instead of 90 days and the convicted will have an avenue of appeal.

The death penalty, which remains on the military law books two decades after it was abolished in the civilian courts, will be scrapped.

The reform package recommends that the judge advocate-general's functions be codified and written into law in the National Defence Act.

And in order to keep the judge advocate at arm's length from prosecutions, an independent director of prosecutions will be appointed.

Improvements to military police training will include more co-operation with other police agencies, such as the RCMP. The head of the military police will be elevated to the new position of Canadian Forces Provost Marshall, a post that will have more command responsibility.

The three-year statute of limitations on charges connected to service offences—which prevented the laying of charges in connection with wrongdoing by Canadian peacekeepers at a Bosnian mental hospital, for example—will be eliminated.

And an independent office of complaint review and oversight, a sort of military police ombudsman, will be created.

"There has been far too much unnecessary secrecy surrounding the Canadian Forces and NDHQ (national defence headquarters) in particular," Young said. "When problems such as Somalia arose, Canadians saw a reluctance on the part of the organization to come clean."

Young promised to commit more resources to responding to requests for information from journalists and the public and to make the military justice system more accountable.

In terms of broad defence policy, Young said that he will stick by the blueprint outlined in the government's 1994 defence white paper, which soundly rejected calls for downsizing Canada's military to a specialized peacekeeping force.

The 1994 paper set out a policy, reiterated yesterday by Young, that Canada maintain a fully combat-capable fighting force that would, coincidentally, engage in peacekeeping work.

"The world we live in is more uncertain, and in some ways less safe, than at any time since 1945," Young said in defence of the need for a fully equipped armed force that costs about $10 billion a year.

Stethem said he was glad to see Young's endorsement of the existing defence policy of maintaining a combat-capable force.

'This blue ribbon panel was nicknamed the status quo gang'

"They're not constables, aid workers or Boy Scouts and that is critical," Stethem said.

Young stopped short of declaring a total ban on the use of alcohol on missions abroad—contrary to the advice of army commander Lt.-Gen. Maurice Baril, who favors a booze ban in the field. Instead, the existing policy of allowing commanders in the field to decide whether or not to allow troops to drink while off duty will remain, but with more input from headquarters and a provision for alcohol bans in emergency situations.

Young was sensitive to the criticism that much of the material he released yesterday had been generated in-house by the defence department.

And Belzile said that while the military justice panel was pressed for time and had to rely to a great extent on reports that were already being prepared by the defence department, there was no way he was part of any "rubber stamp" of defence policy.

"We have listened across the country to a lot of people other than the military and our recommendations and our findings really were based on our own opinions," Belzile said. "It is very much an independent report."

Young will continue the realignment of the ratio between officers and soldiers by moving to further reduce the number of people at the rank of general to fewer than 65 by 1998.

Specifically addressing the lessons learned from missions such as Bosnia and Somalia, Young said there will be more resources for training, particularly in the handling of prisoners and rules of engagement for using force.

But apart from calling for a clearer delineation of the roles of the military chief of defence and civilian deputy minister of the defence department,

Young did little to deal with what some analysts have called a two-headed beast atop Canada's military.

Critics were harsh in their judgment of Young's package.

"This is a political cover-up," said Reform MP Bob Mills (Red Deer), who suggested Young wanted to ram through his package before the federal election, which is expected in June.

"I think there is a real house-cleaning that is necessary and I think that house-cleaning should happen right from the top and if he did that he would start addressing the real problem, which is morale," Mills said.

"Now they're saying they're going to clear up the middle men but we're still going to keep the military answering to itself," said Scott Taylor, editor of *Esprit de Corps* magazine.

"This blue ribbon panel was nicknamed the status quo gang," Taylor said. "There are a few changes, some minor tinkering that is a step in the right direction."

Young made frequent references to what he called "intolerable" incidents in Somalia in early 1993, when Canadian peacekeepers tortured a Somali prisoner to death, shot another in the back and killed two other civilians.

"I think it would be a tragedy for Canadians to forget what happened in Somalia. As we will remember what happened in Vimy, you have to take the good with the bad," he said. "So I have no intention of trying to diminish the seriousness of what happened in Somalia."

Young was asked more than once to say how his package of changes, if it had been in place four years ago, would have prevented the incidents in Somalia. While reluctant to speculate, he said he hoped things would be different in future.

"But I don't think (the package of changes) buries the ghosts of Somalia," Stethem said. "The only possibility of burying the ghosts of Somalia lies in completing the investigation begun by the Somalia inquiry, probably now in the Senate committee."

Young said no amount of expertise and advice can get around human frailty.

"I don't think there are any recommendations that anybody can make," he said, "that can avoid errors in human judgment, that can deal with the foibles of humans and how they respond in certain circumstances."

Uncertainty about future undermines Forces

Ugly incidents overshadow the good and encourage critics

BY PAUL KORING
The Globe and Mail

AS the recruiting slogan promised: "There's no life like it." There's the ugly side of it: allegations of rape, torturing a teen-ager, blowing away a looter, punching out mental patients, hunting deer on an army range with machine guns, fiddling expense accounts, stuffing a cigar tube up the anus of a comatose guest. And just this week—revelations about tying up a woman infantry officer in the name of training.

To be sure, there is a larger reality. The airman dangling from a helicopter in a raging Atlantic gale to save the crew of a sinking freighter. The army officer walking through the blackness of a Bosnian night to rescue hostages from a sniper's nest. A sergeant abandoning the safety of his armoured personnel carrier to pull kids from a burst of gunfire.

And, more mundanely, there are 60,000 Canadian men and women doing a job few want in the full knowledge that the day may come when their government will send them into harm's way.

Do the Canadian Forces have problems only because of, as Defence Minister Doug Young claims, "a very limited number of people" whose disgusting, brutal and criminal conduct has besmirched a once-proud and still basically sound military?

Or is the "whole system rotten," which is the view of Jim Allen, a retired colonel who is among the harshest critics of the armed forces in general and the senior army brass in particular.

Cheerfully accepting that he is "one of the armchair pundits that [Mr. Young] denigrates," Mr. Allen said recently that he remains convinced that the "corruption is so widespread that the whole military needs to be torn apart and rebuilt."

It's a view increasingly heard, although both the government and the military itself seem wedded to the notion that a little tinkering here and there

can restore the lustre of the military's tarnished reputation.

"As always, the mind set is to rally round the flag and protect what is left," said Mr. Allen.

Another critic of the military is Michel Drapeau, who is also a retired colonel. Not surprisingly, Mr. Drapeau bluntly rejects the accusation that he's just a bitter ex-officer trying to tar the whole military as corrupt and venal. Rather, he argues that the institution that he loves and proudly served is sick and he, and others who recognize its faults, have a duty to try and force the government to fix it.

A third ex-officer, former major-general Lewis Mackenzie, is more supportive of the Canadian Forces, although he is very critical of the way in which the Liberal government has treated the military.

The man who is perhaps Canada's most famous soldier has no time for those who would disband the regular forces or who believe the system is corrupt to the core.

"Take a look at all the warts and, in fact, many of them are not terribly serious," Mr. Mackenzie said.

But he argues that the government should establish a clear role for the military and give it the resources to fulfill that role.

There is a general acceptance among critics of the armed forces that the hard questions simply aren't being asked. Does Canada need an army capable of actually fighting in a war? Former general Jean Boyle, with unprecedented frankness, as chief of defence staff admitted last year what most military analysts have long accepted as a given—that as currently equipped the Canadian army couldn't fight in the front line of a modern war.

Does Canada need scores of highly sophisticated jet fighters when no one can postulate any sort of credible airborne threat? What does the taxpayer want (and get) for the largest single chunk of discretionary federal spending that disappears every year into the army, navy and air force?

In looking at the current problems, Mr. Drapeau wants drastic action from the government and says bold measures, not three-month promotion freezes, are needed. On Dec. 31, Mr. Young announced a three-month freeze on promotions to the rank of lieutenant and higher while he prepares a report to the Prime Minister on his proposals for the future of the armed forces and their leadership.

But according to Mr. Drapeau, "The only way things can be fixed is if it is all torn apart. . . . We are in a crisis and the government needs to take bold steps."

He says armies normally are forced to examine their traditions and structure only "after a major defeat." But he suggests that the past few years have amounted to just that for the Canadian army.

However, he is doubtful that the current government has either the courage or the political inclination to undertake a radical rebuilding. "They're afraid to make real, major changes . . . afraid to break the mould of the old-boys club" that has fed the senior echelons for decades.

"So the same gang of bandits [will] be recycled again and again," Mr. Drapeau said.

Instead, and for starters, Mr. Drapeau said Mr. Young should look outside the current crop of senior serving generals for the next chief of defence staff and either select a police officer or one of the handful of retired military officers whom, he says, were never corrupted by the system.

The government believes Lieutenant-General Maurice Baril "is going to save them," Mr. Drapeau said of the current army commander who led the UN's aborted mission to Zaire late last year. Gen. Baril has been prominent in ordering investigations into various allegations of wrongdoing, notably the alleged abuse of patients at Bakovici mental hospital in Bosnia and the tying up of the country's first female infantry officer as part of a training exercise.

But with an officer corps little larger than a big-city high school, it is increasingly difficult to find anyone who hasn't been tainted, if only by proximity, in the recent scandals.

For instance, although Gen. Baril is widely regarded as the most likely next chief of defence staff, at least in part because he was untouched by the Somalia scandal, the general was the base commander at Canadian Forces Base Gagetown in New Brunswick when a young infantry officer, Captain Sandra Perron, was tied to a tree and allegedly left barefoot in the snow.

Critics will want to know what Gen. Baril did if he knew about the incident at the time he was base commander. And if he didn't know about the incident, the critics will ask why he did not.

Mr. Allen lampooned Mr. Young's promotion freeze and promise to recommend changes to the Prime Minster as "just another cop-out."

The Liberals' bandage approach "cannot work" and "[Prime Minister Jean] Chrétien isn't capable of the kind of leadership required," he said. Mr. Allen isn't alone in suggesting that the whole purpose and structure of the Canadian military needs to be examined and entirely rebuilt.

"It cannot be done from inside because you have a whole generation of generals who are sycophants" and a military that no longer bears any resemblance to the job it is supposed to be doing, the former colonel added.

He says the regular army should be scrapped, leaving only a few thousand officers and senior non-commissioned officers to provide training and staff work for any army built on massively revitalized reserves.

"Wipe out the regulars and start over . . . because the current decay is terminal," Mr. Allen said.

Even within the military, senor officers—preferring anonymity as always—are increasingly voicing disquiet about the gaping chasm between what the military is supposed to be and do and what it is actually capable of doing and is used for.

"What are they, Boy Scouts with guns," said a frustrated Mr. Chrétien during the darkest days of the Bosnian mission.

Too often, serving officers contend, the government wants them to be exactly that. Ministers simply don't understand that a combat-capable military needs good—and expensive—weapons and equipment.

Forces on defensive

The bad and the good
The ugly tales from Canada's embattled military have included allegations of rape, the torture of a teen-ager, the mishandling of mental patients and the infamous cigar-tube incident. But there are also stories of bravery and honour among the tens of thousands of men and women enlisted in the Canadian Forces.

The investigation
As Defence Minister Doug Young conducts a three-month investigation into the forces, a question is being asked: Is the military being tainted by a small number of people, as Mr. Young maintains, or is the system rotten to the core?

Proposed solutions
The government and military believe some tinkering can fix the problem and restore Canada's honour. Some critics think otherwise, believing that bolder action is warranted but that the government is too timid to launch such an exercise.

The criticisms
Critics also say the hard questions are not being asked. Does Canada need an army capable of fighting a war. Do we need high-tech jet fighters? And what does the taxpayer want for the biggest single chunk of discretionary federal spending that is pumped annually into the forces?

Allegations that former captain Sandra Perron was tied up have become the army's latest controversy. *(Canadian Press)*

Lewis Mackenzie, a retired major-general, complains about the government's treatment of the armed forces.

Corporal Michel Purnelle was arrested when he tried to turn information over to the Somalia inquiry.

Colonel Geoff Haswell faces a court-martial after implicating superiors in a plan to thwart access to information.

Lieutenant-General Maurice Baril is seen by many as the government's choice to be the next chief of defence staff.

Defence Minister Doug Young has promised to issue a report by March 31 on his plans for the Canadian Forces.

Former general Jean Boyle resigned as chief of defence staff under intense political pressure last October.

They say the ministers don't understand that preparing infantry officers for the kind of real-world hostage situation where a Canadian major gets chained to a pole next to a Serb ammunition dump means training using similar situations.

Mr. Mackenzie's support for the forces continues although his career ended early, at least in part because the top brass resented the media spotlight focused on him, his blunt-speaking manner, and his success as a UN commander whose performance in Sarajevo made him internationally famous.

However, he too wants the government to "clarify the role of the military."

"There is no relation between the [stated policy] and the reality of what the military is being asked to do. The disconnect is unbelievable," he said.

"By not sorting this out," the government is "sending a message of indifference, maybe even contempt," Mr. Mackenzie said. "What we are left with is an institution that is in danger of imploding."

"Maybe we don't need an army," said Jack Granatstein, a military historian and one of the co-authors of a special report to the liberal government on the future of the reserves.

"If there isn't any external threat, it's hard to justify spending $10-billion on a military that is falling apart and one where the leadership is corrupt," he said.

Although he doubts the current government will do so, Mr. Granatstein says what is needed is a full-blown royal commission to examine what kind of military Canada will need in the 21st century and how to build it. "A dispassionate look, not at what went wrong but what the future should be," Mr. Granatstein said.

There is a wide gulf among commentators on the future of the military. There are those, like Mr. Allen, who believe that the army, at least, is entirely disgraced and needs to be torn apart.

Then there are those, like Mr. Mackenzie, who argue that the structure is basically sound and what is needed is some clear leadership from the government. This would start with the immediate appointment of a new chief of defence staff with a clear mandate to defend the sullied reputation of the forces.

Despite this gulf, there is virtual unanimity that the Liberal government's inaction since it came to power has exacerbated, not eased the crisis.

"They keep hoping that if they ignore it, dump it on the Somalia inquiry, freeze promotions, play around here and there, the problems will vanish," said a disgruntled still-serving officer who worries that the best and the brightest are leaving the forces in droves.

Another officer, a reservist, who also asked not to be named, suggested the government was deliberately letting the military slide into public disrepute because it would make it an easier target for Draconian budget cuts.

Even Mr. Allen, who despairs of any bold action from Mr. Young, doubts that conspiracy theory. "There's nobody in the government or in the Defence ministry that is that Machiavellian enough to just let the [military] die of their own volition," he said.

The reserve officer said Mr. Young needs to do something now, not later, to restore confidence.

"A mechanism needs to be put in place to do two things, to restore the institution's confidence in itself and the public's faith in the institution." Otherwise, he added, the "pressure will keep ratcheting up until there is no one left. . . . Already the effect on day-to-day morale is almost immeasurable."

Mr. Young says he still believes the military—a few individuals excepted—are in fine shape.

While defending the Canadian Forces, Mr. Young has denounced those like Mr. Allen and Mr. Drapeau, whose sharp and sometimes caustic critiques of the Canadian military have become regular television news fare.

"Where were these guys when all this stuff was going on. Where were they posted. To the moon?" Mr. Young said scornfully.

In fact, former officers such as Mr. Allen and Mr. Drapeau spent decades serving in a military where speaking out was a sure route to a ruined and truncated career. Ever since the 1960s, when Liberal governments first started to slash and unify the Canadian Forces, senior officers who questioned the system were dumped.

Only in retirement have military officers had the freedom to publicly question the government's defence policy.

Even today, even after the Somalia scandal and the massive damage caused by the widespread belief that the military was engaged in a huge cover-up, whistle-blowers still find themselves in hot water.

Corporal Michel Purnelle, who tried to deliver material to the Somalia inquiry, was arrested. Days after Colonel Geoff Haswell went public with claims that the top brass and a deputy minister had approved a plan to deliberately thwart access to information, he was charged and now faces a court-martial.

So increasingly, officers and other ranks have turned to those, like Mr. Drapeau and the magazine Esprit de Corps, who have made a vocation out of exposing wrongdoing.

"I'm sick and tired of that crap," Mr. Young said in announcing his review of the future of the Canadian Forces and its leadership. But the hard fact remains that but for Mr. Drapeau and Esprit de Corps, and, to a lesser extent the mainstream media, much of the behaviour that Mr. Young finds so objectionable would never have come to light.

Within the armed forces, the morale has deteriorated to the point where some ordinary soldiers and junior officers privately admit to getting out of uniform as quickly as possible if they are off duty because the uniform is no longer something to be proud of wearing in public. Others are just waiting to get out of the armed forces.

Mr. Mackenzie, however, believes there remains a deep reservoir of support among the Canadian public for the military and an understanding that the misdeeds are confined to a few.

"I still find the easiest way to get an ovation is to praise the men and women doing a dirty job" on behalf of their country, he said.

But even he concedes that the support isn't limitless. "The Liberals almost seem to have a level of contempt . . . for those [in the military] who are doing an outstanding job."

Someone has to "go on the offence, to start standing up for these people. . . . The silence from the government is deafening," Mr. Mackenzie said.

THE MILITARY / *There is an enduring disconnection between Canadian society and its armed forces. If the average Canadian thinks about the military at all, it is mainly to misunderstand it. But the recent scandals have prompted inevitable questions about the nature of our peculiarly Canadian military culture.*

Warriors, weenies and worriers

BY PAUL KORING

The Globe and Mail

NOBODY understands, but I'm a warrior," exulted a Canadian naval officer, sitting in the wardroom of a destroyer patrolling the Persian Gulf. The wood fittings and pictures had been stripped from the walls in readiness for the impending war and the naval officer was heady with anticipation. "A warrior—not like those weenies back in Ottawa," said the naval officer.

As his shipmates outside blasted away at floating garbage, practicing for a war that for the Canadians would never really come, the portly weapons-system officer's proud boast of belonging to the warrior caste seemed faintly absurd.

But in late 1990, on the eve of the Gulf War, amid the massive buildup of allied military might, Canada's professional military could dare to speak about what in Canada has become the unspeakable: That being a soldier is all about being ready to kill and be killed. "It's about unlimited liability," says Lewis Mackenzie, the retired Canadian general who is perhaps Canada's best-known professional soldier.

But with the exception of an overzealous F-18 pilot who fired a hugely expensive missile in hopes of killing some Iraqis in an inflatable boat, Canada's soldiers, sailors and airmen saw no combat in the Gulf. At sea, the navy did sterling service shepherding unthreatened convoys of mainly U.S. supply ships feeding the massive allied war machine. In the air, the Canadian squadron of F-18s was held back by the Mulroney government until the air war was well and truly over. And on land, the handful of Canadian soldiers guarding a civilian airport in Qatar, a tiny Gulf emirate far from the action, never heard a shot.

The Gulf War drove home a brutal truth that in recent months has resonated louder than ever. Canadian society is largely uninterested in fighting (especially when the dispute is more about oil than Kuwaiti sovereignty). Moreover, we aren't prepared to do so. Asked by Britain and the United States to send a 5,000-soldier mechanized contingent to be part of the huge armoured thrust that would drive deep into Iraq—a real combat unit that Canada had told NATO was available—the senior brass admitted it wasn't possible. So Canada sent a field hospital to Saudi Arabia instead.

In the end, the "weenies" in Ottawa, both political and military, won. Between them they kept intact the odd, perhaps uniquely Canadian, military tradition. We go to great lengths to produce professional soldiers who are sidelined in war and in peacetime and relegated to building their reputations on distinctly unwarlike activities.

There is an enduring disconnection between Canadian society and its armed forces. If the average Canadian thinks about the military at all, it is to misunderstand it, to think of it engaged in noble efforts repairing schools in some far-off place or dangling beneath a helicopter, rescuing sailors. In fact, peacekeeping, search and rescue and even assistance to the civil authorities, such as at Oka, are secondary roles, useful but hardly worth the $10-billion cost of maintaining a war-ready military.

While the military wants to be seen as a capable combat force, its senior brass knows the only way to get new equipment is to exploit its unmilitaristic image.

The reality is that civilians have fought all of Canada's real wars, notably the First and Second World Wars, because those wars were too big to be fought by a tiny regular or professional force. And unlike its closest allies, France, the U.S. and especially Britain (the forebear of Canada's military traditions), Canada has had no little wars—no Falklands, no Chads, no Panamas—that allow the profession of arms to carve its way into the national psyche.

On a road north of Sarajevo, more than two years after Canadian troops had seized the city's airport in 1992 to begin a massive and largely futile peacekeeping effort, a Canadian army officer grumbled about how the Canadian military was perceived at home. "We want to be seen as soldiers by our peers in other armies and by Canadians. Instead, we are nothing but peacekeepers." He was bridling at the faintly derogatory label "CantBat," the name given by a British battalion to the Canadian peacekeeping forces

HMCS Halifax is one of Canada's newest fighting machines. Conceived during the Cold War, the anti-submarine frigate is capable of detecting and engaging 250 different underwater, surface or airborne targets simultaneously.

in Bosnia because the Canadians were hesitant about shooting back. It also irked him that successive Canadian governments, Conservative and Liberal, have been alone among NATO members in trying to block air strikes that ended up bringing warring parties to the negotiating table almost overnight.

In fact, Canada's proud history of peacekeeping (the Somalia blight excepted) is its military tradition. But that understandably sits uncomfortably on the shoulders of those who train for war.

In more than a dozen interviews with historians and military officers, both serving and retired there is widespread agreement that the "disconnect," as they call it, separating Canadian society and its military,

does exist. There was far less consensus on what, if anything, can be done about it.

What is clear is that the uneasy, almost deliberately distant relationship has its roots deep in Canada's history and geography. Not since the 1812–1814 war, long before Canada's birth, has the country faced serious foreign threat (except perhaps the Fenian raids). "We are quite unique in being a major nation that has faced no military threat and has no vital interest abroad," says a National Defence historian, who refused to be identified. In the late 19th century, the fledgling Canadian military actually prepared for war against the U.S. But it quickly became evident that such a plan was ludicrous.

Canada's professional military remained minuscule—regarded as primarily a group of instructors who would form the spine of an army should the need arise. And when it did, in both World Wars and to a lesser extent in Korea, it was civilians who became warriors. (At the outset of the Second World War, there were fewer than 10,000 officers and men in Canada's regular army, air force and navy.) Vimy, Dieppe and Normandy, and the liberation of the Netherlands, the strands on which Canada's military heritage is woven, were all fought by civilians enlisted "for the duration" of the hostilities.

There are almost no warriors who are revered in Canada. That may be cause for national pride. But it is no surprise that after the Second World War, the U.S. elected Dwight Eisenhower, a general, as president. In Canada, a diplomat named Lester Pearson became prime minister.

The lack of direct threat has isolated the professional Canadian military—the unloved regulars—from the larger society. And it has meant that, unlike almost every other Western nation, Canada has never imposed military service in peacetime.

As a result, the Canadian military has never had ordinary citizens rotating through its ranks, bringing with them the society's mores and values and taking away an understanding of the military ethos.

Although Britain and the U.S. have scrapped national service (and France has announced that it will), it remains the norm among Western militaries. Even in Britain and the U.S., a good chunk of the adult population is old enough to have direct knowledge of military service, and both countries maintain sizable reserves that guarantee the military remains a part of the lives of large numbers of the citizenry.

Canada's military has long distanced itself from the larger society. During the 1950s and 1960s, Canada's peacetime military was structured so it could actually fight a war that might need fighting tomorrow,

not six months or a year from now when the farmers and fishermen and factory workers have had time to get into uniform and journey overseas. The Cold War turned the Canadian military from instructors-in-waiting into a real fighting force. Decades of standing on guard in Europe added nothing to Canadian understanding of its professional warriors.

At home, the military has always been kept far from the mainstream on isolated bases—with its own schools, its own hospitals and its own social life. Such remoteness has fostered the kind of bonding considered essential to effective fighting forces, but it has also resulted in a distinctly military society. In a few scattered towns, the Canadian military is an integral part of life, but for Canada's urban population it is something called forth only to deal with real or imagined domestic emergencies, or more often sent to serve uneventful tours of duty in such faraway places as Cyprus under the United Nations' flag.

Canada's peacekeeping abroad is, of course, celebrated, especially if no shooting is involved. (No other nation has a military monument to peacekeeping like one recently erected in Ottawa.) In fact, when there has been shooting, the incidents have been glossed over, if not exactly hidden. Some serving and retired officers believe there has been an unspoken pact, stretching back decades between the high command and the government, to downplay violence.

For instance, the fierce fire fight in 1974 when Canadian troops battled the invading Turkish army at Nicosia airport in Cyprus is rarely mentioned in discussions of Canadian peacekeeping. Nor the 1994 battle between a Canadian battalion and Croatian forces in former Yugoslavia.

Both were dramatic examples of Canadian soldiers in combat that didn't conform to the notion that Pearsonian peacekeeping means never having to shoot. In fact, Pearsonian peacekeeping was really

about using military muscle to make peace—and fight if necessary—but that has largely been forgotten.

Then came Somalia. Suddenly the Boy Scout image of Canada's peacekeeping soldiers lay beaten and exposed by the reality of a teen-ager tortured to death by Canada's supposedly elite battalion. More than three years later, there are few answers. The big difference is that now the questions are being asked.

IF Canada needs a military, what shape should it take? Can a society that faces no real external threat afford the pretense that its puny military is ready to fight on land, in the air and at sea? And once its post-Cold War role is defined, how can that role be sold to both the professionals-at-arms and the broader society? In short, how can the distance between them be closed?

If historians point to a largely unthreatened nation as the source of Canada's current isolation from its military, those who wear or have worn the uniform tend to blame the 1960s' unification of the three branches of the armed forces, which they routinely and wrongly blame on former Prime Minister Pierre Trudeau. It was, in fact, his predecessor Lester B. Pearson's government that made the decision to unify the forces.

Although the three services, army, navy and air force, have won back their cherished green, blue and light-blue uniforms, the unification of the three into an integrated fighting force has never really been achieved. What remains is a messy compromise.

Far worse, at least in the minds of many senior officers, is the situation at National Defence headquarters, where civilian bureaucrats and career officers are thrown together in a hybrid that at once formulates policy and runs the military. It has created what one British staff officer has described as the inevitable tension between "warriors and worriers." It is found in all militaries in democracies, but in Canada the triumph of the worriers seems almost complete.

"Warriors don't get to be generals," says a general, who in fact was one. "And if they do, they either keep themselves or are kept as far as possible from NDHQ (National Defence Headquarters)."

Canada's practitioners of the profession of arms have had little opportunity to display their prowess and good reason to keep quiet about it if they aspire to a high rank. But at least top commanders are worried about the longstanding and increasing chasm between Canadian society and its military.

Several studies, going back at least two decades, have sought ways to bring the Canadian military closer to Canadian society.

National service is a non-starter, although it remains a popular notion in officers' messes. Shifting the emphasis and the spending from a small, professional military to a larger, part-time militia is a perennial favourite because it is seen as a relatively cheap means of building a bigger military while at the same time reducing the isolation of the regular forces.

However, the insurmountable obstacle remains: Mobilizing a well-trained and equipped militia takes too long. Modern crises, at home or abroad, tend to happen quickly and require immediate reaction. And even though reservists provided nearly a quarter of the manpower on some recent Canadian peacekeeping missions, there isn't a militia regiment in the country that could deploy quickly as a unit. It would be hugely expensive to get them and keep them in fighting shape for some future engagement.

In any event, the current government is committed to reducing, not increasing, the size of the militia.

There remains one alternative. That is to integrate the regular military into Canada's largely urban society. That is, move them off their bases and let them live like ordinary civilians. This model would increase interaction—and thus understanding—between civilians and the military through the myriad day-to-day contacts of neighbourhood and school.

The plain fact is that a small, highly technological military no longer needs to be isolated. True, if ordinary soldiers lived "on the market" rather than in massively subsidized military housing, they would need huge pay increases, as was made evident not long ago on the West Coast when sailors without military housing had to apply for welfare to make ends meet.

But the benefits—that the Canadian public and the military might get to know each other better—outweigh the costs.

More importantly, some clear reason for maintaining a professional military in Canada must be defined. The country faces no conceivable direct threat and the longstanding need to defend freedom in Europe seems irrelevant.

An army that occasionally goes peacekeeping on behalf of the UN, a navy that stands by ready to help the Mounties nab wayward Spanish fishermen or drug smugglers and an air force that hasn't intercepted even a curious intruder since the Soviet Union collapsed, isn't enough to justify $10-billion a year, the largest single discretionary spending item in the federal government's budget.

International Trade

In recent years, one of the most problematic issues in Canadian foreign policy has been the relationship between Canada and the United States. This has been articulated along a number of different policy dimensions, including foreign policy, military policy, and economic and cultural policy. Some of these questions were addressed in unit 7, in the context of cultural issues and the politics of culture in Canada. Canada wants to be seen as an independent state, one that makes its own foreign policy decisions and one that does not make decisions according to the desires of the United States.

It is clear that among the many policy areas that could have become subjects of tension, the biggest issues involving Canadian-American relations have been the Free Trade Agreement between Canada and the United States and later the North American Free Trade Agreement, involving the two actors and Mexico. Free trade was seen by many to have significant implications for cultural nationalism (something that was discussed earlier in this volume) as well as for the maintenance of a distinctly Canadian existence in Canada when the first agreement came into force in 1989, and it has continued to be seen in this way since that time. Many critics argued that with free trade the borders would be swept away and a continental (read: American) character would take over the entire North American marketplace. While this "worst case" scenario has not come to pass, there have clearly been some areas of the economy in which free trade has had a deleterious effect.

This section contains five articles that examine the problematic issue of Canadian foreign trade policy and its relationship with the United States. These works include discussion of issues related to the North American Free Trade Agreement (NAFTA). The industries of medicine, fisheries, culture, and farming are specifically examined in this collection.

The first article in the section explores the effect of the North American Free Trade Agreement on Canadian health care. The Canadian health care industry is one of the segments of public policy in which Canadians take most pride. Initial assumptions were that health care would not be affected by NAFTA, although at the time there were some critics of NAFTA who did not agree with this prediction. But more recent examinations suggest that the general purpose of the NAFTA, to open up all sectors of the economy to multinational interaction, may also apply to health delivery systems. The question is: How can Canada maintain its standards, much higher than those of the United States, and not go broke in the process?

An article titled "Darn Yankees!" explores fishing issues. The "salmon wars" have recently become a major irritant in Canadian-American relations, with actors on each side of the border claiming that the other side is inflicting major economic wounds on the fishing industry and possibly causing long-term damage to significant segments of the fishing industry. It is not easy to see where a solution acceptable to all parties will be found, but both sides are committed to working toward such a solution.

U.S. representative David Bonior, the minority leader of the U.S. House of Representatives, wrote a letter to *The New York Times* in July 1997 in which he argued that the first 3 years under the North American Free Trade Agreement have not brought the jobs promised, have not resulted in higher wages for Americans, and have not led to a cleaner environment, as promised by the pro-NAFTA forces when the agreement was being negotiated and ratified. He argues that NAFTA needs to be fixed.

The fourth article in this section focuses upon Canadian cultural industries. In this piece, titled "Yikes! They're Tipping the Cultural Balance," Sid Adilman of *The Toronto Star* focuses upon the preservation and survival of Canadian cultural industries. Adilman cites a recent World Trade Organization panel ruling that Ottawa cannot continue to engage in the "protectionist" actions it has followed in the past. The implications of this ruling for the Canadian television industry, publishing, movies, radio, and live performance arts are all discussed here.

The final selection in this section examines the grain trade in Canada's west. Darcy Henton of *The Toronto Star* examines the tensions of Canadian farmers over their right to sell grain on the open market rather than through the 53-year-old Canadian Wheat Board monopoly. Some farmers are hauling their grain across the border and selling directly to American markets. The article discusses the role of provincial governments in this area and the likelihood that a satisfactory resolution to the conflict will come soon.

Looking Ahead: Challenge Questions

What are the major arguments of those who seek increasingly free trade in the international marketplace? What arguments can be made against this kind of free trade?

Has Canada's experience with the North American Free Trade Agreement confirmed or refuted the arguments of those who predicted that the agreement would be disastrous for both the Canadian economy and Canadian culture?

How do the specific issues described here, such as the fisheries, the grain trade, or the medical industry, illustrate general tendencies of the marketplace? Do these specific cases show *different* patterns of behavior or simply specific illustrations of general rules? Explain.

Doctoring to NAFTA

Health care activists have won a significant battle for public health care. But the war is far from over

by COLLEEN FULLER

When Canadian actress Margot Kidder — famous for her 1970s role as Lois Lane in the Hollywood film *Superman* — was found disoriented and cowering in a Los Angeles backyard recently, newspaper accounts recalled that her decline began when her private health insurer refused to cover the bills from a car accident she suffered in the 1980s. Her co-star, Christopher Reeve, who portrayed Canada's expropriated superhero in the big movie, was recently paralyzed from the neck down in an accident. He requires 24-hour care, but he quickly learned that his private health insurance was capped at $1.5 million, a sum he is fast approaching. Both have been done in by the private-enterprise American health insurance system. The symbolism is almost too painful for Canadians to contemplate. For this is what the advocates of free trade are anxious to bring to Canada to replace our publicly funded non-profit health care system. If they succeed, even Superman and Lois Lane won't be able to help us.

Everything to allow this to happen was set up in the North American Free Trade Agreement (NAFTA), which came into effect on January 1, 1994. The negotiation and signing of the agreement were accompanied by ringing assurances that our government had protected our publicly funded health care system. This is the story of just how far that is from being true, and of how Canadians from across the country have had to struggle against governmental inertia and complacency to protect our health and social services from the aggressive global strategies of the corporate community.

First Brian Mulroney, free trade's main Canadian pimp, and then Jean Chrétien solemnly assured Canadians that health care was safe as they signed the massive trade agreement. Many Canadians were suspicious, of course. How could they not be when they read of the huge corporate campaign, the most expensive lobby in American history, to defeat the Clinton administration's modest attempts to introduce health care reform? To a considerable extent, the lobbying effort was designed to ensure that "Canadian-style health care" would never cross the international border. Sceptical Canadians working in health care couldn't help but wonder why these same corporations were such strong proponents of NAFTA, although this agreement — so our government said — accepted and protected the very same "Canadian-style health care".

That was a good question. Canadians had seen enough of the original Free Trade Agreement to know that while this huge and indigestible document seemed to protect, for instance, cultural industries in one chapter, the government gave up its right to regulate them in another chapter hundreds of pages further on.

They now discovered that the same was true of NAFTA, in relation to our health care system. The primary purpose of the agreement is to open up all sectors of the economy to multinational corporations. Nonetheless, Canadian health care activists who had been following the debates were shocked to find that Ottawa had failed to exempt the Canada Health Act when it signed NAFTA and had advised the provinces there was no need to shelter provincial health insurance. Consequently, not a single public health insurance plan was protected in the financial services chapter of NAFTA. Worried by this, the Canadian Health Coalition, an Ottawa-based group made up of unions and health care advocates, asked then-health minister Diane Marleau exactly which provisions of the trade deal shielded public health insurance and non-profit health care delivery from invasion by multinationals.

Marleau replied that her department had reviewed the relevant aspects of the agreement and had concluded that health care was protected. In particular, she pointed to an annex to Chapter 11 on investment and Chapter 12 on cross-border trade in services. This Annex II-C-9, as it is called, applies to national governments and says that Canada can introduce or maintain any measure regarding "social services established or maintained for a public purpose", including "health care". She concluded with a hope that this information would "put to rest your concerns as to the general misconception of the [negative] effect of NAFTA on insured health services" and encouraged the Coalition to spread the good news about the trade deal.

When they heard of these thin reassurances, British Columbia health care unions fired off their own letter asking Marleau exactly what was a "public purpose", and, for that matter, how did NAFTA define "health care"? It took the minister almost a year and a half to reply, and then she told them that Canada's NAFTA negotiating team had intentionally left the term "public purpose" undefined, because they believed that the vaguer the term, the better luck Canada would have when the armies of trade lawyers eventually sat down at NAFTA panels to decide what was permitted and what wasn't.

In those same Chapters (11 and 12), NAFTA appended another Annex — Annex I — which applied, not to national governments, but to provinces and U.S. and Mexican states. Under this Annex, provinces and states were given until the end of 1995 to list "measures" that would not be captured by the national governments within Annex II-C-9. The British Columbia Health Sciences Association, representing paramedical professionals, began lobbying their provincial government to list as exempt from NAFTA all measures protecting services in the health care sector (as well as their members' jobs). They quickly discovered that for the purposes of NAFTA such "measures" included not only legislation but all regulations, policies and procedures, and that, to be protected, each and every one had to be identified and listed by the province. To give an idea of the complexity of this, such things as the daily limit placed by the

B.C. Cancer Agency on the number of Pap smear slides examined by cytotechnologists to ensure accuracy in test results had to be listed, and the items to be listed ranged as far afield as legislation establishing preference for non-profit health providers. In short, a huge task. They began thinking they had plenty of time to do this, but, in view of its complexity, the deadline for provincial measures began to grow uncomfortably close.

In fact, the deadline had almost been reached when they received Marleau's reply revealing that there were, as yet, no definitions of "health care" or of "public purpose".

While this process was under way, and worried health care workers were lobbying the B.C. government for action under Annex I, Canada's lead NAFTA negotiator, John Weekes, advised the provinces that Canada intended to seek the "broadest possible interpretation of what constitutes a public purpose". He said the provinces needn't protect a long list of measures, because the provisions under Annex II-C-9 would be adequate presumably when "public purpose" was eventually defined. The implication was that this subtle but brilliant negotiating strategy would win over the Americans when the question finally made it to the appropriate NAFTA panel.

None of this, of course, was very reassuring to the people who were asking the questions, and it became even less so as it became clear that the subtleties of Canada's position either were not getting through to the U.S. trade representative, Mickey Kantor, or were leaving him cold. While Marleau was telling Canadian health care workers not to worry, Kantor was advising state governments that social services offered by the state, as well as by private providers "on a commercial basis", could not be reserved under NAFTA.

While Ottawa continued to insist its position was the correct one, health care activists were not so sure, in part because Canada's track record in front of various NAFTA panels was not encouraging. If the U.S. position were

correct, and obviously Kantor thought it was, NAFTA's "shield" was full of holes. The overwhelming majority of health services in Canada are not offered directly by provincial governments, but rather by the publicly funded nonprofit sector. In many areas such as rehab, diagnostic and X-ray services, for-profit companies compete with publicly funded providers for public health insurance dollars.

A few individuals in the British Columbia government were also worried. The state of Oregon, which had submitted some 600 measures for exemption, was surprised when the U.S. Trade Representative rejected all but 30 of them. Since Ottawa was advising the provinces not to submit an extensive list of provincial measures on the theory that the federal government's overarching protection was all that would be needed, it began to appear that Ottawa would follow Washington's lead and cut the provincial lists down, as they had two years earlier when submitting reservations to the financial services chapter.

At the same time, Ottawa seemed only vaguely aware that the United States might not agree with Canada's "broadest possible interpretation" of "public purpose". Canadian observers began to feel that if the U.S. definitions prevailed and the provinces (on Ottawa's advice) failed to protect their ability to regulate the activities of investors and service providers, then non-profit health care was in big trouble. In November 1995, the Canadian Health Coalition advised its members that they should urge their provincial governments to "list broadly" in Annex I, because of the ambiguities in the federal government's position.

Alberta nurses acted quickly. They were worried that the privatization policies of the Klein government would be writ in stone, permanently, unless laws that vested regulatory authority in the provincial government were protected. In B.C., the Health Sciences Association intensified their lobbying of provincial trade officials preparing Annex I reservations, and activists in P.E.I., Nova Scotia, Saskatchewan and Quebec demanded action from their own provincial governments. The deadline was drawing near, and it still wasn't even clear whether Ottawa would submit extensive provincial reservations to the appropriate NAFTA body.

By December, British Columbia and several American states were pushing for an extension of the December 31, 1995 deadline until there was clarification of some of the definitions, for these would decide what measures they should list.

The Canadian Health Coalition was working hard to draw the public into the debate but was frustrated by the cumbersome, complex language in NAFTA. Who cared? Well, certainly not newspaper publishers and broadcasters. As soon as mention was made of Annex-this or Annex-that, reporters' eyes would glaze over, and their mouths would twist into a suppressed yawn. Alberta's nurses succeeded in getting a news story on CBC Radio, and there was a short spurt of attention when a few reporters sniffed a potential scandal ("NAFTA slays Medicare, despite federal promises"), but very quickly the technical details turned them off.

Just before the deadline for Annex I reservations was reached, the U.S., Canada and Mexico agreed to an extension to March 31, 1996. The Coalition learned that only B.C. and Quebec were planning to submit an extensive list of reservations, though Ottawa said it was not necessary. Oregon had decided to submit what was called an "omnibus" reservation, meaning that everything that might conflict with NAFTA was protected. B.C. continued to compile its lengthy list but was looking at the Oregon example. Ottawa was non-committal about whether it would submit a general reservation for any province.

But now it was discovered that in the fall of 1995, federal officials, in a letter to the provinces, had acknowledged possible limitations on the scope of the federal Annex. Ottawa now took the position that whether a service was provided for a public purpose depended on how each country viewed the situation. In some cases, the public purpose nature of a service could be inferred from the circumstances. And,

in relation to health services, "the coverage of a service under a public health regime" would demonstrate a public purpose.

In other words, Canada was in quite a muddle.

All of this uncertainty convinced the Canadian Health Coalition of the need for an independent legal opinion, and, with the Canadian Union of Public Employees, it sought such an opinion from Dr. Bryan Schwartz, a constitutional expert at the University of Manitoba.

Released by the Coalition in mid-March, Schwartz's opinion confirmed that the protections given health care services under NAFTA were ambiguous at best. Canada's health care sector was rife with "grey areas", he wrote, and there were serious questions about whether hospitals and other publicly funded non-governmental institutions could be protected from competition with U.S. corporations. He said Canada did have a "broad" interpretation of Annex II-C-9, but "as the degree of government funding and regulation decreases, it becomes increasingly unclear whether a service is being provided 'for a public purpose' as defined by Ottawa." The U.S. Trade Representative, on the other hand, interpreted the Annex "narrowly", but Schwartz said the implications of this were not at all clear: "At its extreme it would mean that if any part of a sector is operated on a commercial basis, even the governmental part of the sector would be subject to the full force of NAFTA." Schwartz said it was "doubtful if the U.S. representative intended to make such extravagant claims", but some clarification would be useful.

Within days, Mickey Kantor obliged. In a letter to Oregon, he said that Annex II reservations could not include government services "if those services are supplied by a private firm, on a profit or not-for-profit basis". This made it clear, if it hadn't been before, that Canada's strategy of avoiding definitions and hoping for the best was not as clever as our trade negotiators had thought.

Now bells began to ring in provincial capitals. B.C.'s new premier, Glen Clark, told the federal government that he would exempt the entire health care sector unless there were stronger assurances from Can-

ada's NAFTA partners that health care was protected under Annex II-C-9. Activists in every province, coordinated by the Canadian Health Coalition, began a final push to convince their governments to list a "sectoral reservation" for health care. One by one, all except Alberta said they would follow B.C.'s lead and list a general reservation for health care and social services.

In the face of growing public concern, nervousness in the provincial capitals and a clear signal from the United States that Canada's non-profit health care sector was open to for-profit business, Ottawa began to scramble.

On March 25, just a few days before the final deadline, the Coalition met with the new federal health minister, David Dingwall. Since the Liberals had been elected, the Liberal caucus and, more importantly, the Cabinet had been dominated by free trade promoters in the Ministry of International Trade. Every public policy in the Liberal government has conformed to the trade agenda. Now that intense pressure questioning NAFTA's guaranteed health care shield was mounting, the Liberals found themselves vulnerable to charges that they were about to sell out Medicare. Sensitive to this accusation, Dingwall decided to challenge the policy dictates emanating from the trade people. This had never happened before and was therefore quite a significant event.

In his meeting with the Coalition, Dingwall maintained the party line that health care was safe under NAFTA. Nevertheless, he had taken Schwartz's opinion to the Prime Minister, who, in turn, had convened a Cabinet meeting. Schwartz, no opponent of free trade, is a strong believer in Canada's universal health care system. His opinion undoubtedly struck home within the Liberal government — especially his suggestions about what steps Ottawa might consider to improve the weak shield for health care in NAFTA.

Schwartz suggested that Ottawa take immediate steps to ensure Canada's definitions of "public purpose", "social services" and "health care" were acceptable to its NAFTA partners.

This could be done in a letter of understanding, something that would constitute an amendment to the trade deal by the parties. If Ottawa failed to do so, Schwartz said, the provinces must submit extensive lists of measures in case they could not be protected in Annex II-C-9.

A few days after Dingwall's meeting with the Coalition, Ottawa announced it had secured an agreement with the United States and Mexico that would eliminate any doubts about the NAFTA shield for health care. In fact, Canada had successfully sought and obtained an agreement with its NAFTA partners to reserve all measures in all sectors — except financial services — within the jurisdiction of sub-national governments that might conflict with many of the provisions of Chapters 11 and 12. The agreement represents a significant amendment to the trade deal, one that increases the ability of provincial governments to protect health and social services.

This was a major victory, not only for those on the health care front, but for everyone fighting to protect public services in Canada. It was a victory that was not won on the basis of a legal or technical argument, but because of the political pressure brought on the government by health care activists and some provinces.

Yet the struggle to protect Canada's health care sector from NAFTA is far from over. NAFTA is so vast and convoluted that few people, including many in government, understand how to interpret its manifold clauses. The victory in March strengthens the ability of Canadians to safeguard our unique system of public insurance and nonprofit delivery of services. But the gate that remains open is so wide that,

unless we are very careful, the horses-and-coaches of multinational corporatism could be driven into the heart of the system.

NAFTA was not so much designed to shield health care or other social services as to open up the economy to multinational corporations. The health care sector is not protected from the intellectual property provisions of NAFTA, and, consequently, escalating drug costs are threatening to bankrupt provincial drug plans and hospitals. Similarly, our public health insurance system was not shielded in the financial services chapter of the trade agreement, and many questions regarding its future remain unanswered by federal officials.

The public policy options open to all governments under NAFTA are visibly narrowing. Current negotiations among the provinces (with Ottawa pushing in the background) to extend the Agreement on Internal Trade (AIT) to the municipal, social services, education and health sectors could undo the broad reservation won in March. The AIT will force provincial governments to end practices that favour local service providers, including those in the health care sector. If the AIT is extended, it will require provinces to provide equal treatment to Canadian companies from other provinces when those companies want to invest or provide services. NAFTA, on the other hand, accords "national treatment" to U.S. and Mexican corporations. Therefore, a U.S. corporation is treated as if it were a Canadian company under NAFTA's rules, while under the rules of the AIT, provinces cannot discriminate against Canadian companies.

NAFTA poses other challenges to Canadian health care — the term "public purpose" is an example. The Annex I reservations apply to legislation that existed on January 1, 1994. Any new

laws, policies or procedures — or amendments to such existing measures — must conform to the rules of NAFTA. In addition, if Ottawa's public purpose definition is acceptable to our NAFTA partners, will the government be able to meet the criteria? The gutting of federal cash transfers to the provinces is ominous indeed – especially with NAFTA lurking in the background. Provincial delisting of services from public health plans in response to federal cuts exemplifies the ratchet effects built into NAFTA: once it's done, there's no turning back. Canadians may soon begin to ask where, exactly, is Ottawa headed, and why?

If, on the other hand, Ottawa is wrong and the U.S. definition prevails, then Canadians might just begin to mobilize around that dreaded word "abrogate".

This story re-affirms the old adage, "No defeat is final, no victory complete." Health care activists, jubilant about having won a battle, may be gearing up for the next round. But they can be sure that the devotees of free trade are right now closeted together, figuring out how best to protect NAFTA from Medicare, so that they can secure a toehold in Canada's health care sector for their U.S. corporate pals.

For if anything is clear, it is this: NAFTA and Medicare cannot co-exist in the same country. One of them's got to go.

Colleen Fuller is the Director of Communications with the Health Sciences Association of B.C. and has been involved in extensive discussions with government officials to ensure health services are protected in both NAFTA and the Agreement on Internal Trade. She works closely with the Canadian Health Coalition on a broad range of health policy issues.

DARN YANKEES!

Ottawa fashions a truce in the salmon war, but Victoria
sees only an empty gesture

BY CHRIS WOOD

The young day held an unmistakable air of anticipation. A fresh northwesterly breeze kicked up a
light chop on the silt-grey water of Canoe Passage. The low green banks of islands glowed in
the wind-washed morning light. At intervals of a few
hundred metres all along the channel, fish boats lay dead
in the water, engines idling, a long restless picket of
gillnetters that extended out to where only white dots
of sunlit hulls showed against the dark water of the
Strait of Georgia. On 500 decks, ears were cocked to
VHF radios.

At precisely 0800 hours, a neutral voice broke the radio silence, declaring: "The Area E gillnet fishery is
open." From New Westminster to Sand Heads, engines
roared, pink floats fell to the water and bows turned
across the current, as the boats drew curtains of nearly
invisible nylon gillnet mesh, some as long as three foot-
ball-fields, from bank to bank. Within seconds, the mouth
of British Columbia's Fraser River had become the
world's greatest salmon trap.

The fresh breeze and clockwork opening made a welcome antidote to the rancor and bluster that marked the
rest of last week's developments in Canada's—or, more
accurately, British Columbia's—salmon war with the
United States. Tensions remained high even after militant
members of the B.C. fishing industry released an American ferry, the Malaspina, which they had held captive

for three days in Prince Rupert. While the fishers returned to their nets, threats by some of them to escalate
confrontations this week kept the salmon dispute at the
top of Ottawa's diplomatic agenda. In Washington, the
Senate voted 81 to 19 for a resolution calling on President Bill Clinton to send the U.S. navy to protect Alaskan ferries' "right of innocent passage through
Canadian waters.

Prime Minister Jean Chrétien, returning from vaca-
tion, sent Foreign Affairs Minister Lloyd Axworthy to
Washington to mend fences. Emerging from a day of
bruising encounters with U.S. officials, though, Axworthy conceded that he had won little more from the
Americans than an agreement to consider new ways
to restart stalled discussions over the two countries'
differing interpretations of the failed 1985 Pacific
Salmon Treaty

In Victoria, pugnacious B.C. Premier Glen Clark made
it clear he did not consider that good enough. Negotiations between Canada and the United States aimed at
setting fishing targets have foundered for the past four
fishing seasons, scuttled by disputes over technical data
and even the meanings of key clauses in the treaty itself.
Giving Axworthy's deal no "reasonable possibility of being successful," Clark applauded the "courageous resis-
tance" of the Prince Rupert blockaders and even seemed
to urge them on to further confrontations. "We cannot

back down in the face of such minor progress," said the B.C. premier.

Clark's hard line reflected the frustration of British Columbia's roughly 6,000 salmon fishers. Gillnetter Kim Olsen, an unofficial spokesman for fellow militants, delivered a blunt ultimatum to federal Fisheries Minister David Anderson, the British Columbian who is also political minister for the province. "We basically told him that he has one week to come up with something for us," Olsen said after a meeting with the minister. If Anderson failed to resolve the dispute by the deadline? "Then we don't know what will happen," warned Olsen. Some of his colleagues were readier to speculate about possible courses of action. "The fleet was talking about blocking U.S. cruise ships and freighters," said John Stevens, a gillnetter from Ladner. Prince Rupert fisherman Des Nobels boiled the situation down to even more basic terms. Without some concessions from the U.S. side, said Nobles, "we're kicking American ass."

But other Prince Rupert residents were already adding up the cost of the fishers' initial action. While 200 Canadian fish boats kept the Malaspina blockaded at her dock, Alaskan officials announced they would break the lease that for 36 years has routed the state's Marine Highway System ferry through the B.C. port. Then, Alaska Gov. Tony Knowles announced that the state will sue the fishermen and the Canadian government for damages. Prince Rupert officials, already reeling from the loss of 700 jobs with an early-July pulp mill closure, estimated the loss of the ferry service, which attracted 70,000 passengers annually, would cost the town $12 million a year in tourism revenue. "The word is catastrophic," lamented Steve Smith, manager of Prince Rupert's Crest Hotel. "It's about 30 to 35 per cent of our business." In a related blow, a local fish-processing plant laid off 100 workers after Canadian fishers prevented salmon caught in Alaskan waters from reaching the Prince Rupert plant.

And while the men and women seemed well satisfied with the success of their protest ("We got our point across," said Olsen), many in Prince Rupert—and the tourism industry throughout the province—concluded that it was they, not the Americans, whose butts were feeling the pain. Pat Corbett, president of the B.C. Council of Tourism Associations, wrote to both Chrétien and Clark, praising the Prime Minister for Ottawa's "conciliatory approach" and warning the premier that salmon-war bluster could cost the $7-billion-a-year industry heavily. Anxiety over the impact of the ferry blockade found an echo at the local level in Prince Rupert. "I'm quite angry about it," said John Wood, whose Parry Place Bed and Breakfast, just two blocks from the ferry terminal, stands to be badly hurt if the ferry service does not resume. "I don't think you bully the Americans into doing something."

In fact, the U.S. administration reacted with unusual restraint to the seizure in a foreign port of a U.S.-flagship, to say nothing of the taking hostage of its 385 passengers. State department spokesman Nicholas Burns called the action "very unhelpful." And he characterized the burning of a U.S. flag by a man on a Canadian boat (he turned out to be a U.S. citizen named Rod Taylor) as "a great insult to the American people." But Burns expressed sympathy for the Canadians. "When people's livelihoods are at stake, emotions get high," said Burns, adding, "Canada is our greatest friend. Obviously, we are going to resolve this dispute peacefully."

Axworthy clearly shared that objective when he flew to the U.S. capital at midweek. After meeting separately with officials from the state department and Alaska's congressional caucus, Axworthy, looking exhausted, said he hoped to "lower the temperature" in the dispute. To that end, he said that Canada had given up trying to persuade the United States to submit the treaty dispute to binding arbitration. Instead, two "eminent persons"—retiring University of British Columbia president David Strangway and Seattle businessman William Ruckelshaus, a former U.S. cabinet official—will meet with the various interested parties in the salmon war and look for fresh ways to reopen negotiations. They will report by the end of this year directly to the President and the Prime Minister. At the same time, the two countries will establish what Axworthy called "an early warning communications system" to keep senior officials in touch on a daily basis and head off any future incidents like the one in Prince Rupert. Making the most of the slender agreement, Axworthy insisted: "This is now taken on by both the President and Prime Minister as a matter of high priority."

Clark promptly denounced the agreement. "The eminent persons will have no mandate to negotiate," the B.C. premier said. "No power to recommend a resolution and no deadline for completing their work." Clark, who had conferred earlier with Anderson and Defence Minister Arthur Eggleton, went on to say that "until and unless" those conditions were added to the eminent persons' mandate, British Columbia would stand by its threat to cancel a lease letting the U.S. navy test torpedoes at a submarine range in Canadian waters off Nanoose, on Vancouver Island's east coast. Victoria gave notice to Ottawa in June that it would cancel the lease in late August. Clark, declaring that "we have got to stand up to American overfishing," accused Ottawa of "appeasement" and added for good measure: "This may well be the first time—certainly in my memory—that the Canadian government doesn't stand on the side of Canadians." Clark, not invited to a Seattle meeting that Fisheries Minister Anderson is holding this week with the governors of Alaska and Washington state, cancelled a scheduled November conference in Vancouver with five U.S. state governors grouped with Alberta and British Columbia in the Pacific NorthWest Economic Region.

The clear morning sun dancing on the waves of Canoe Passage combined with the mystery and miracle of the salmon run itself to put the strong language and political manoeuvring into perspective. Veteran gillnetter Edgar Birch expressed reluctant support for the Prince Rupert blockade. "They had to do something like that," Birch said, keeping an eye on his net from the deck of his boat, the BevMark, "to get the Americans' attention." But most of the men and the few women setting nets on the river had more immediate concerns. "Three bloody fish!" Smokey Wilson, aboard Bleu Angel, complained to a visitor.

For Wilson and others in the commercial B.C. fishery, the endeavor may be less arduous than it was—and less chancy, thanks to such devices as electronic fish-finders. But it is far from an exact science. Success depends on keeping the net out of the way of sunken-log snags and the barges and deep-sea freighters that also use the fishing ranges. What comes out of the net is sometimes what is sought—last week, sockeye—sometimes not. Less valuable pink salmon may wind up in the nets. Or it may be valuable but endangered sturgeon, which, mostly, are pulled from the mesh and released. The fabled annual West Coast salmon run, in fact, is not a single event with clear rules or distinct borders, beginnings and ends. It does not even involve a single kind of fish. Five major species range from the short-lived pinks, about 2.2 kg, to the giant chinook, prized by sports fishers, that can grow to 30 kg over a lifespan of seven years. They have one characteristic in common, apart from being distant relations of landlocked trout: as they approach the end of a life spent roaming the trackless Pacific, an overwhelming compulsion drives them home to the west coast of North America. Each summer, millions of them find their way past fishnets, predators and turbulent river currents to reach the high inland headwaters, where they will continue their kind and then die.

That Sisyphean annual miracle of rebirth earned the salmon a central place in the mythology of British Columbia's First Nations, and it inspires contemporary artists and designers. The salmon's prodigious numbers earned it a key role in the province's economy. Salmon swim as deep in the British Columbia psyche as cod do in the Newfoundlander's identity. And that colors the hostilities between the Canadian and American fisherfolk on the coast as well as the three-sided political dispute among Victoria, Ottawa and Washington.

Much besides disputes and interventions can go wrong in the fishery. The sockeye that eluded the nets on the lower Fraser last week faced a perilous passage made more difficult by unusually high water in the river. At Hell's Gate, a particularly narrow defile in the Fraser Canyon north of Hope, the water boiled and coursed so violently that many fish failed to make it any farther. That created salmon jams in the eddies and backwaters downstream. "When you went up on the cliff and looked down, it was just black," said Rod Peters, one of an ex-

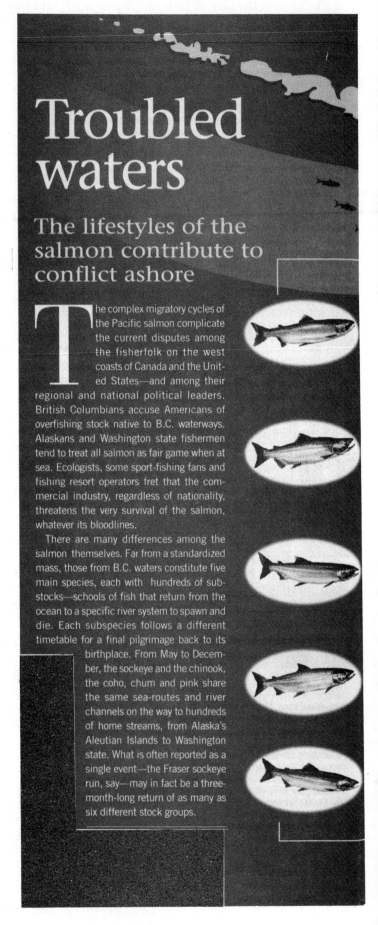

Troubled waters

The lifestyles of the salmon contribute to conflict ashore

The complex migratory cycles of the Pacific salmon complicate the current disputes among the fisherfolk on the west coasts of Canada and the United States—and among their regional and national political leaders. British Columbians accuse Americans of overfishing stock native to B.C. waterways. Alaskans and Washington state fishermen tend to treat all salmon as fair game when at sea. Ecologists, some sport-fishing fans and fishing resort operators fret that the commercial industry, regardless of nationality, threatens the very survival of the salmon, whatever its bloodlines.

There are many differences among the salmon themselves. Far from a standardized mass, those from B.C. waters constitute five main species, each with hundreds of substocks—schools of fish that return from the ocean to a specific river system to spawn and die. Each subspecies follows a different timetable for a final pilgrimage back to its birthplace. From May to December, the sockeye and the chinook, the coho, chum and pink share the same sea-routes and river channels on the way to hundreds of home streams, from Alaska's Aleutian Islands to Washington state. What is often reported as a single event—the Fraser sockeye run, say—may in fact be a three-month-long return of as many as six different stock groups.

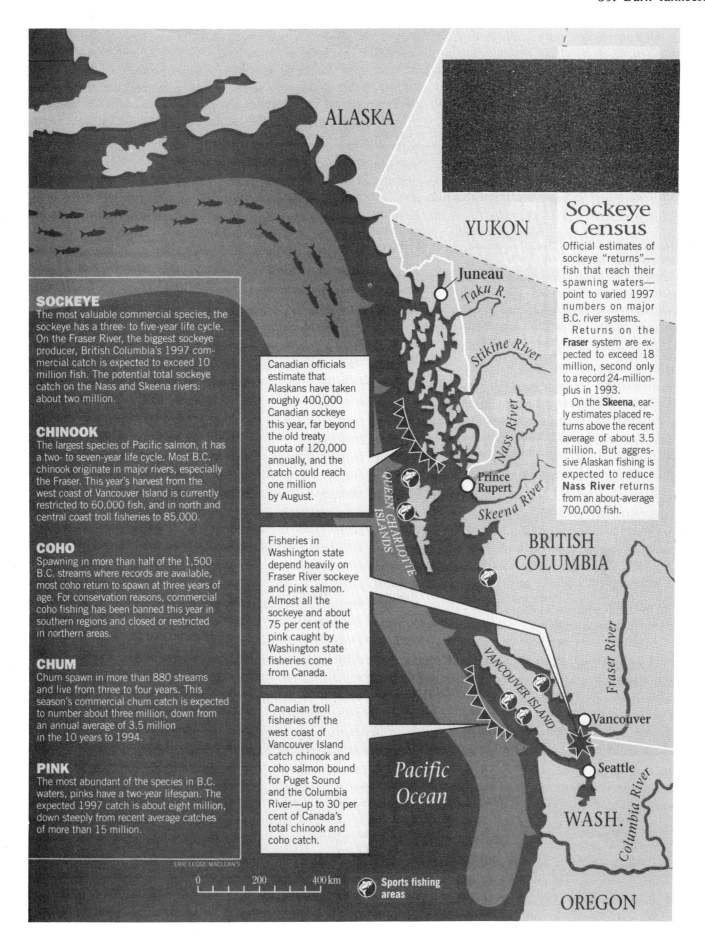

ALASKA

YUKON

Juneau

Taku R.

Stikine River

Nass River

Prince Rupert

Skeena River

BRITISH COLUMBIA

QUEEN CHARLOTTE ISLANDS

Fraser River

VANCOUVER ISLAND

Vancouver

Seattle

Columbia River

Pacific Ocean

WASH.

OREGON

Sockeye Census

Official estimates of sockeye "returns"— fish that reach their spawning waters— point to varied 1997 numbers on major B.C. river systems.

Returns on the **Fraser** system are expected to exceed 18 million, second only to a record 24-million-plus in 1993.

On the **Skeena**, early estimates placed returns above the recent average of about 3.5 million. But aggressive Alaskan fishing is expected to reduce **Nass River** returns from an about-average 700,000 fish.

SOCKEYE
The most valuable commercial species, the sockeye has a three- to five-year life cycle. On the Fraser River, the biggest sockeye producer, British Columbia's 1997 commercial catch is expected to exceed 10 million fish. The potential total sockeye catch on the Nass and Skeena rivers: about two million.

CHINOOK
The largest species of Pacific salmon, it has a two- to seven-year life cycle. Most B.C. chinook originate in major rivers, especially the Fraser. This year's harvest from the west coast of Vancouver Island is currently restricted to 60,000 fish, and in north and central coast troll fisheries to 85,000.

COHO
Spawning in more than half of the 1,500 B.C. streams where records are available, most coho return to spawn at three years of age. For conservation reasons, commercial coho fishing has been banned this year in southern regions and closed or restricted in northern areas.

CHUM
Chum spawn in more than 880 streams and live from three to four years. This season's commercial chum catch is expected to number about three million, down from an annual average of 3.5 million in the 10 years to 1994.

PINK
The most abundant of the species in B.C. waters, pinks have a two-year lifespan. The expected 1997 catch is about eight million, down steeply from recent average catches of more than 15 million.

Canadian officials estimate that Alaskans have taken roughly 400,000 Canadian sockeye this year, far beyond the old treaty quota of 120,000 annually, and the catch could reach one million by August.

Fisheries in Washington state depend heavily on Fraser River sockeye and pink salmon. Almost all the sockeye and about 75 per cent of the pink caught by Washington state fisheries come from Canada.

Canadian troll fisheries off the west coast of Vancouver Island catch chinook and coho salmon bound for Puget Sound and the Columbia River—up to 30 per cent of Canada's total chinook and coho catch.

ERIC I EGGE/MACLEAN'S

0   200   400 km

🌀 **Sports fishing areas**

tended family of Seabird band Stö-lo Indians camping last week a few miles south of Hell's Gate.

Family matriarch Berthie Peters holds an aboriginal permit to use the traditional fishing spot to catch salmon. Since the beginning of July, the clan's 12-m gillnets, strung out into the swirling current at the end of long cedar poles, had hauled in about 700 salmon—most destined for family larders, although a pilot federal program allows the family to sell some fish to commercial buyers.

Differing rules. Differing types of gear. Differing stocks, species and runs. The sheer complexity of the subject does much to bedevil salmon negotiations. Canadian and U.S. analysts disagree over everything, from the numbers of fish in different stocks to which side's negotiators most often walk out in a huff. Among fishers of the two nations, not even the names of all the fish are the same; Americans, for instance, call the chinook "king" salmon.

Disagreement is especially sharp over the terms of the 1985 Pacific Salmon Treaty Canadian officials insist that the key to the treaty lies in its first principle. That clause compels both countries to prevent overfishing and to manage their fisheries so as to ensure that "each party receives benefits equivalent to the production of salmon originating in its waters." Canada argues that Americans—mainly Alaskans—take as much as $70 million a year worth of salmon originating in Canadian waters to which they are not entitled under that so-called equity provision.

Most U.S. analysts insist the treaty—the result of two decades of negotiations—doesn't mean that at all. "I think the treaty was signed before it was ripe," says Dale Kelley, executive director of the Alaska Trollers Association. "The language is ambiguous. We have two sides that interpret what they think they signed in two tremendously different ways." In common with other Alaskans and the U.S. federal administration, Kelley favors a so-called abundance-based interpretation of the treaty, in which each side could take a fixed share of the harvest, with the number of fish varying according to the size of the salmon run. "As long as the Canadians want to bean-count," says Kelley, "and say, 'You have one of my fish so you owe me one,' I don't know if we're going to get anywhere.

Anderson says there is no chance of Canada forsaking its insistence on the equity principle. But the fisheries minister concedes that leaves him with few levers to swing Washington or Alaska to Ottawa's point of view. "The greatest card we have is the moral high ground," said Anderson. "We must appeal to the American national interest in showing moral leadership."

That may strike many B.C. fishers as a frail rod indeed. But Anderson and his colleagues in the federal cabinet have made it plain that they have no appetite for Clark's fish war. Even before Axworthy's pilgrimage last week, Canada's ambassador in Washington, Raymond Chrétien, carried that message to Alaska's congressional caucus in a series of telephone calls.

Another message may also have been intended for Victoria. Confided one Canadian official: "The difficulty will be finding a way for Clark to back down, because he is going to have to." But if the message had been heard, it was not evident by week's end. Clark offered to rescind the notice on the lease—but only if Ottawa first refused to make it available to the United States until the Americans come to terms on the salmon treaty.

That does not seem especially likely. Nor does any early agreement on the substance of the issues that have pitted British Columbia against its American neighbors over salmon. Actions such as the blockade of the Malaspina, said Kelley, "make it tough to get in the mood to negotiate."

Out on the water of Canoe Passage, gillnetter Birch was similarly gloomy, for different reasons. "Anderson's a yes-man," complained Birch. "I've got no optimism that he'll solve our problem." And with no change of attitude evident on either side, going fishing on Canada's West Coast seems likely to remain far from relaxing for seasons to come.

With JOHN DeMONT in Ottawa, RUTH ABRAMSON in Toronto and ANDREW PHILLIPS in Washington

I Told You So

By David E. Bonior

WASHINGTON

On Friday, the Clinton Administration released a report on the first three years of the North American Free Trade Agreement. The most the Administration could bring itself to say is that Nafta has had a "modest positive effect" on the American economy. That's a far cry from the extravagant promises made by the accord's proponents during the 1993 debate: "Hundreds of thousands of new jobs! Higher wages! A cleaner environment! Just you wait and see!"

They were wrong. The facts are in.

Three hundred thousand new jobs? No. The report, required by Congress, suggests that Nafta-related exports have created 90,000 to 160,000 new jobs. But those figures don't account for the 132,000 Americans who have lost their jobs as a result of the agreement. That's the number of Nafta-related job losses certified under the Labor Department's Nafta Trade Adjustment Assistance Program, set up to help displaced American workers.

Higher wages? No. Mexican wages along the border have dropped from $1 to 70 cents an hour, according to International Monetary Fund figures. A 1996 Cornell University study commissioned by the Labor Department found that 62 percent of U.S. companies surveyed

> ## Let's hear it for Nafta's 'modest positive effect'!

have used the threat of moving to Mexico to hold down wages here at home.

Environmental cleanup? No. Toxic sites along the border have continued to multiply. To date, only 1 percent of the $2 billion in cleanup funds promised under Nafta have been spent.

The Administration's report ignores these facts, trying to put the best face on an agreement that clearly hasn't delivered on its promises.

It is true that trade has risen between the United States and Mexico in the last three years, but it has been lopsided. Imports from Mexico have surged by 83 percent since 1993. What was a $2 billion trade surplus with Mexico before Nafta became a record $16 billion deficit last year.

Even the Nafta-generated exports are costing us jobs. More and more, multinationals are shipping components to Mexico, so they can be assembled by low-wage workers, then sent right back as finished products to the United States. According to an analysis by the University of California economist Harley Shaiken, these revolving-door exports have more than doubled, from $18 billion in 1993 to $42 billion last year.

So who does benefit from Nafta? Some of the big winners are the 28 core members of USA-Nafta, an industry group that lobbied for the agreement. Forty-two percent of these multinationals shipped jobs abroad once Nafta was adopted, an analysis of the Labor Department's trade adjustment assistance data shows. Their profits have increased by 296 percent, according to financial information published in Forbes.

Nafta's toll cannot be measured only in economic terms. The Administration's report also ignores real threats to our health and safety.

Imports of Mexican fruit have increased 45 percent since Nafta was enacted, and vegetable imports have gone up by 31 percent, the Florida Department of Agriculture and Consumer Services reported this year.

This produce rolls into the United States on 3.3 million trucks a year. Fewer than 2 percent of these trucks are inspected at the border, according to a May 1997 study by the General Accounting Office. That means parasites, pesticides and infectious diseases go undetected.

For example, the Environmental Working Group found that 18.4 percent of imported Mexican strawberries contain "very high rates of illegal pesticides."

Earlier this year in Michigan, 179 children became seriously ill after eating contaminated Mexican strawberries. Shouldn't such incidents argue for stiffer inspections of imported produce? Unbelievably, under Nafta, such inspections could be considered an unfair trade restriction.

This appalling lack of inspections is also encouraging the drug trade. The Drug Enforcement Agency says that 70 percent of the cocaine that enters the United States now comes across the U.S.-Mexican border.

Nafta has not delivered on its promises. Let's not repeat the errors of the past. Instead of rushing to expand it and putting other countries on the "fast track," let's concentrate on fixing Nafta first.

David E. Bonior, a Michigan Democrat, is the House minority whip.

Yikes! They're tipping the cultural balance

It's not just our magazines that are threatened. Mickey Mouse, Jack Valenti and the rest of American Culture Inc. want it all. Here's what Canada has put in their way

BY SID ADILMAN
ENTERTAINMENT COLUMNIST

Margaret Atwood ruminates in fiction about long-forgotten housekeeper Grace Marks convicted, maybe wrongly, of killing her Richmond Hill employer in 1843 and *Alias Grace* ignites readers in Canada and around the world.

Alanis Morissette exploits her break-up with a Toronto boyfriend in the song, "You Ought To Know" and jets to international fame.

Producer Kevin Sullivan gloms on to two of Lucy Maud Montgomery's orphan girls and attracts millions of TV viewers globally.

Maclean's exists as Canada's only newsweekly magazine.

Arguably, all these successes, and many more like them, have come because of Canadian content rules and/or other federal government support.

Canadian content thrives, and sells to audiences who are interested in being entertained or informed—certainly and appropriately not for the narrow, misguided reason of just supporting the home team.

Government protection of Canada's cultural industries is now threatened because of a World Trade Organization panel ruling that Ottawa has no right to ban split runs of American magazines such as *Sports Illustrated.*

Though specific to magazines, the ruling is widely considered just enough to propel powerful Hollywood lobbyist Jack Valenti into action again against government rules that bolster Canada's movies, TV programs, recording and publishing that collectively comprise the cultural industries.

Recent skirmishes include Ottawa's intention to keep out or restrict more foreign movie distributors for cinemas and satellite dish TV and thereby support Canadian distributors.

Valenti and U.S. publishing and recording industry lobbyists have no interest in getting control of Canada's theatre, ballet, dance or orchestra sectors—they're not money makers, not big commercial enterprises.

They argue that limits of any kind, no matter how small, by any foreign government is not only an outrage but a potential erosion of their profit making.

Strongly backed by Washington (no matter who is president), the lobbyists—in defiance of reality—paint American interests as being excluded from Canada by law.

In fact, American movies, TV programs, recordings, magazines and books have unfettered access to Canada and dominate annual sales by skywards of 95 per cent.

Valenti has even argued that Telefilm Canada investments for Canadian movies put the giant Hollywood studios at a *disadvantage*—and many U.S. politicians take his statement at face value.

For sure, though, a double standard operates: The very Canadian TV networks, distributors and publishers that Ottawa protects—and who now want more protection—depend largely on U.S. fare for their profits.

For example, CTV and CanWest Global, like all Canadian broadcasters, enjoy income tax rulings that keep most Canadian advertisers this side of the border. Yet those private broadcasters and others make their money on U.S. TV series they show.

Likewise, Alliance Communications, Canada's top TV and movie conglomerate, has secured more production investments from Telefilm Canada than any other private producer. Yet imported movies largely feed Alliance's distribution arm.

For all their pleas for more help, not one of the large commercial Canadian publishers stays in business by just publishing Canadian books.

Regularly pointing this out, American cultural industry lobbyists argue what's good for the U.S. (where no domestic content rules and no direct government investment support is needed or provided other than for PBS) is good for the world. Canada is just part of the U.S. "domestic" market.

There's nothing new about that, as *Dawn Of The Eye* (the CBC-TV series about movie theatre and TV news coverage) noted in last week's debut episode.

Perhaps anticipating further negative trade rulings, and coupled with across-the-board federal government budget cut-backs, Heritage Minister Sheila Copps has assembled a blue-ribbon committee from across the cultural industries that meets Feb. 9 and 10 in Ottawa to discuss and recommend new policies.

Today, The Star puts the current state of Canadian content and government assistance under the microscope: the policies, the changes to come and an assessment.

Canadian TV: It sells

"The best way to judge if Canadian content rules are working is this," says Robert Morrice, head of media and entertainment at Royal Bank: "Canada is the second largest exporter of TV programs in the world outside the U.S. To me if it's good enough to export, that tells us the industry is succeeding. Canadian content rules certainly helped."

Content rules: The Canadian Radio-television and Telecommunications Commission (CRTC), demands these *minimum* Canadian content regulations.

For private broadcasters, 50 per cent between 6 p.m. and midnight and 60 per cent overall for the broadcast year.

For CBC, a minimum 60 per cent Canadian content between 6 p.m. and midnight and 60 per cent overall for the broadcast year (CBC has now promised a minimum 90 per cent Canadian content.)

And there's between 40 and 50 per cent minimums for Canadian specialty channels and 30 per cent for pay-TV.

Foreign ownership of Canadian private broadcasting companies were amended last year to allow an increase to 33-⅓ per cent from 20 per cent. So, by blending owning and holding company interests, foreigners may now own as much as 43 per cent, but must leave effective control in Canadian hands.

Assessment: Canada may be a big exporter of TV programming but there's no better way to assess CanCon than by checking the ratings and they tell another story: Canadians love American programs best.

In the first 11 weeks of this season, not one Canadian prime-time series hit the Top 10. The big winners were all American—in order, *Seinfeld, ER, Millennium, Friends, X Files, Single Guy, Frasier, Spin City, Third Rock From The Sun* and *Caroline In The City.*

However, true national figures are impossible to calculate with accuracy. A. C. Nielsen compiles national figures only for CBC and CTV.

Baton Broadcasting and CanWest Global are designated as "systems"—neither is completely national, and neither qualifies as a network.

Ratings outside central Ontario—the largest, most influential TV viewing region in the country—are tallied by the BBM Bureau of Broadcast Measurement, which still uses the diary method.

Nielsen, in central Ontario, uses people meters, remotely controlled devices that electronically monitor, store and report what we watch.

The two measurement systems are incompatible—"like comparing apples and oranges," says one media consultant.

It's a different story in other parts of the country. Nielsen's season averages to date prove Quebeckers watch Canadian French- language shows in abundance, even to the exclusion of programs made in France. Quebec's Top 10 comprises only Canadian programs.

In British Columbia and Alberta, and the Maritime provinces, Canadian, particularly regional, shows fare far better than in southern Ontario, where viewers seem predisposed to American shows.

In addition, says Nielsen's Mike Leahy, "Southern Ontario is the most complex TV market in the world. We have systems within systems within networks (CTV-BBS-CFTO). We have a public broadcaster that survives on commercial revenue. We have an abundance of available and affordable specialty channels on the most sophisticated cable systems in the world, reaching about 90 per cent of the population. We have simulcasting, which allows Canadian broadcasters to air U.S. shows and to insert their own commercials, and to keep the revenue.

"And now we have U.S.-originated DTH satellite services. Penetration so far is small (between 1.5 and 5 per cent—as many as 200,000 homes across the country), which are illegal, but which offer incredible choices, virtually

inviting Canadians to become cultural immigrants to the U.S."

The result of this patchwork of competing services and regulations?

"Canadian programming loses money every time it's aired," says media consultant and author David Ellis.

"The cost of delivering a Canadian audience to one hour of Canadian programming is two to three times more expensive to broadcasters than to deliver Canadians to one hour of American programming."

One advertising rate card offers *Seinfeld* at $30,000 per-30-second commercial and *Traders,* which costs almost $1 million an hour to make, at $1,900.

"The CRTC is sending a deeply ambiguous message to private broadcasters," Ellis added. "Canadian content is a money loser, a loss-leader.

"But the future well-being of our TV culture depends on the number of programs they can develop, partially own, sell and distribute for profit."

More rules: There's more to protecting the Canadian TV industry than content quotas set by the CRTC. The quotas, in fact, really protect producers, particularly independents such as Alliance Communications Corp., which produces or co-produces *North Of 60* and *Black Harbour* for CBC and *Due South* for CTV.

What broadcasters get in return is the simulcast, the simultaneous substitution of their signals—and ads—over U.S. signals and ads. So, for example, on today's Superbowl simulcast, Canadian cable subscribers will get the Global version, not Fox's.

Thanks to simulcasting, which increases Canadian ratings of U.S. shows by 20 per cent or more, broadcasters here can charge more for commercials. That pours another $100 million into private network coffers every year. (It also helps explain why CBC-TV, which doesn't simulcast its prime-time schedule because it's all-Canadian, has smaller audience shares than CTV.)

Another way broadcasters benefit from the CRTC is through access rules and distribution and linkage requirements for cable companies.

These regulations limit the number of U.S. channels Canadian cable companies can carry and forces them to give priority to Canadian services.

Without these rules, cable operators might be tempted to run much cheaper (for them) American channels such as HBO and Comedy Central while never giving Canadian contenders a chance.

Radio

Like television, a foreigner can own up to 20 per cent of a radio station. A foreigner can, however, own 33⅓ per cent of a radio station's holding companies. The thinking here is to encourage foreign investment, but to control foreign influence on stations' content.

Policy (Music Radio): In guidelines changed little since their institution by the CRTC in 1970, 30 per cent of the music played must be Canadian according to the "MAPL System," which divides record-production into four categories:

■ **M** (Music must be composed entirely by a Canadian)
■ **A** (Artist—singing or performing instrumental music—is Canadian)
■ **P** (Performance, either for recording or live, is done in Canada)
■ **L** (Lyrics written by a Canadian).

To qualify as Canadian content, a piece of music must reflect at least *two* of the categories.

Policy (Talk Radio): None.

Audience Share (Music): Commercial: 30 per cent. CBC 50 per cent (pop), 30 to 40 per cent (classical).

Changes: Minor so far—significant ones possible. Modifications came in 1986 and 1991 and another in 1993 after Bryan Adams' complaints that songs co-written by him were Canadian enough. The CRTC now accepts the co-writing tag.

"But with the Americans' success with the *Sports Illustrated* split-run decision, they might take more aggressive action with the Canadian Content legislation," says Steve McLean, news editor of the music trade magazine, *The Record.*

Assessment: CRTC is likely to let FM radio play more top hits, says Brian Robertson, president of the Canadian Recording Industry Association. This won't alter radio's CanCon duties, what with international mega-success of Shania Twain, Celine Dion, Bryan Adams, Alanis Morissette. Should Canadians stop producing international hits, FM radio could pressure CRTC to "lighten up" on its CanCon demands.

Lively arts

Where the protection of Canadian culture in the performing arts is concerned, the Canada Council prefers carrots to sticks.

Though there was once a requirement of orchestras receiving council grants to program at least 10 per cent Canadian music, it was found to be ineffective and eventually dropped.

Nowadays, according to music officer, Russell Kelly, grant applicants in the opera and music theatre, orchestral and contemporary music programs are expected "to demonstrate a real commitment to Canadian work."

There are no specific regulations enforcing Canadian content in theatre.

Commercial producers are under no obligation to produce Canadian works or employ Canadian directors, actors, designers and so on.

Theatres in the not-for-profit sector, however, get grants based on their commitment to Canadian work. Special attention is paid to authorship.

Publishing

The problem: A small domestic market for books spread over a large geographic area, dominated by imported (mainly U.S.) product.

Only 12 per cent of Canada's English-language publishing firms are foreign controlled, but they account for 57 per cent of total sales in Canada—a re-

tail book market that currently takes in about $3.2 billion a year.

The U.S. exports $620 million U.S. worth of books to Canada a year—41 per cent of its total book exports.

The policies: The Baie Comeau policy on foreign ownership states that a Canadian publisher cannot sell out to a foreign owner and that no new majority

foreign-owned publishing house or book retailer can open shop here.

Foreign publishers established here before 1985, when the policy was put in place, were allowed to stay; nothing requires them to publish any Canadian books, though some like Random House, Penguin, HarperCollins and Little, Brown do.

Virtually all Canadian publishers are also importers, using proceeds from foreign books that they bring in and distribute here to finance publication of their own books.

At the provincial level, Quebec and Ontario require that all elementary and secondary school textbooks used in the province be Canadian produced.

Financial support is available to Canadian-owned publishers, though it is in steady decline. Grants are needed, publishers say, to help them compete against foreign-owned firms.

The Book Publishers Industrial Development Program (BPIDP) which the industry considers its most important support, dropped from $18.9 million in 1994–95 to $17 million in 96. In addition, translation grants and $6.7 million in block grants are supplied by the Canada Council to Canadian publishers (English and French) to support the publication of books of cultural value.

The results: The achievement of Canada's publishing industry has been spectacular—from Tokyo to Paris, readers know the names of Robertson Davies, Margaret Atwood, John Ralston Saul and Rohinton Mistry.

But the industry remains only marginally profitable after grants are factored in.

Movies

Policies: To qualify for an investment from Telefilm Canada or from virtually every provincial production investment agency, a Canadian movie must meet a minimum six-point Canadian scale, from lead actors to writer and director. Telefilm invests in script development and also gives distributors money for advertising and festival marketing. There is no Canadian content rule for movie theatres.

Assessment: Canadian movies represent, at the most, 2 per cent of all screen time. Their combined box office is even less. Few exceptions aside, Canadian moviegoers avoid Canadian movies—even those that receive rave reviews from the critics and other media attention.

What's wrong? Depends on who's talking.

Not enough money spent on advertising, says Robert Morrice, head of media and entertainment at Royal Bank, which invests heavily in interim movie financing. "There isn't enough money in the system for a marketing push. In the Canadian market you couldn't spend enough to get (profits) out of Canada. You'd have to go North American wide."

To Allen Karp, president of Cineplex Odeon, the theatre-owning company and Canadian movie distributor, the answer to what's wrong might be the Canadian content rules themselves. They're too strict, he thinks.

He cites *The English Patient*—not legally a Canadian content movie—"created by a Canadian (Michael Ondaatje) and about a Canadian nurse. To me, it *is* a Canadian story."

On the other hand, he notes, the acclaimed *Long Day's Journey Into Night* (distributed by his company, with a splash) was a Canadian-content film about a New England family based on a play by a U.S. writer.

Magazines

Policies: Bill C-103, passed in 1995, provides a strong disincentive against so-called "split-run" magazines, publications that insert a token amount of Canadian content in a mostly foreign-produced magazine in order to sell ads in Canada.

The law was passed after Time Warner Inc.'s *Sports Illustrated* did an end-run around 30 year-old customs rules barring the shipment of split-runs across the border.

SI found a loophole which allowed it to beam the magazine via satellite to a printing plant in Canada—while charging advertisers about half the rates it charged U.S. regional editions in similar sized markets. To head off the incursion of more split-runs, Bill C-103 imposed an 80 per cent excise tax on ad revenues they generate.

Customs Tariffs: In 1965, Customs Tariff Code 9958 was introduced to prevent split-run magazines from being shipped across the border—although other magazines could cross freely.

Postal Assistance Program: The federal government has provided for preferential postal rates for subscriber copies of Canadian magazines for more than a century.

The reduced rates range, depending on the magazine, from 20 to 85 per cent of what a U.S. magazine would have to pay. But, because of government cost-cutting, the postal subsidies have been drastically cut, from $229 million in 1989 to an estimated $47 million in 1998.

Canada Council Grants: The Canada Council provides for about $2 million in grants which go directly to magazines deemed to have sufficient arts and cultural content.

Tax Breaks: Section 19 of the Income Tax Act allows Canadian advertisers to deduct the cost of advertising in magazines that have at least 75 per cent Canadian ownership and 80 per cent Canadian editorial content.

Assessment: It was Canada's measures against U.S. split-runs that brought it up before the World Trade Organization. The Canadian magazine industry claims that barriers to split-runs allow it to survive, especially since 65 per cent of the industry's revenues come from ads.

Articles compiled by:
Sid Adilman, Peter Goddard, William Littler, Greg Quill, Judy Stoffman, Vit Wagner, Antonia Zerbisias

Against the grain

Prairie farmers face heavy fines and jail in bitter fight over future of Canada's wheat trade

By **Darcy Henton**
Western Canada Bureau

EDMONTON—One farmer is in jail, 150 more face charges and scores of farm trucks have been seized by customs officials in a modern- day range war over the western Canadian grain trade.

The emotion-charged dispute, which has pitted farmer against farmer and sparked a rash of demonstrations across the Prairies, is being waged over the need for the regulatory fences that control the grain market.

It's a philosophical dispute that touches on such issues as freedom, prosperity and Canadian sovereignty.

Self-described "freedom fighters" are risking jail and their farms to sell grain on the open market rather than through the 53-year-old Canadian Wheat Board monopoly, which sells grain to 60 countries around the world.

The renegade farmers are openly defying the wheat board and Canada Customs officials by hauling loads of grain in huge truck convoys across the border to American markets.

"Basically, I think it's just a right I should have," says Darren Winczura, 29, who has twice hauled grain from his 850-hectare farm in Viking, Alta., across the border without an export permit. "I want to market my grain to whomever I want. I want that freedom."

Dan Creighton says farmers can make more money marketing the grain themselves than through the board and for some of them, that might be the difference between making it or going bust.

Canadian farmers can generally get $1 to $2 more per bushel of wheat or barley in the U.S. than they receive from the wheat board—that's a difference of 15 to 30 per cent, says Jim Pallister, a member of a loosely based coalition of farmers who call themselves Farmers For Justice.

Depending on the size of the load, that can mean a difference of $1,000 to $2,000 per sale.

"It's a bit of a horror story," says Creighton, a Saskatoon businessman who is acting as an adviser to Farmers For Justice. "They're not getting the amount of money they need to survive in the system.

"Either they fight for it or they lose their farms."

The stakes rose this spring, when police and custom officials began a crackdown on the illegal grain exporters.

Several farmers who drove away with their trucks after being ordered to turn over the keys later had their vehicles seized from their farms.

Manitoba farmer Normal Desrochers says RCMP and customs officials hit his farm near Brandon in a predawn raid armed with search warrants, video cameras and tow trucks. He outraced an RCMP officer to one truck, grabbed the keys from it and then blockaded it with another piece of farm equipment. But the raiders towed away one truck loaded with $2,400 worth of barley.

"I guess they just picked on me to make an example of me to deter the rest of them from doing it," he says, adding that the strategy won't work.

"When prices increase, we'll all be just hauling like crazy unless they throw us all in jail. That's what they will have to do to stop us."

Andy McMechan, a Lyleton, Man., farmer, has been in jail. He was arrested July 7 for failing to hand over a tractor he used to haul loads of grain across the border just south of his farm.

Convicted of exporting grain without a permit, he was initially fined $2,000, then had his fines increased 10-fold. He has also been ordered to pay $55,000 in compensation to the wheat board.

Police had to escort the prosecutor through an angry mob of farmers following a court appearance by McMechan in Brandon when the farmers heard the federal government planned to seize his assets if he doesn't pay the fines. Yesterday, McMechan was returned to jail after a judge refused to accept a bond demanded for his release if it was posted by other accused farmers.

"It's sad when you consider that this guy who is in jail has four children," says friend Brad Harris. "It's very hard on his family.

"It's turned into a personal vendetta, and Andy McMechan won't give in to the tactics being used upon him. They're trying to take away his livelihood and that makes me mad."

Harris, 41, who farms on the other side of the Saskatchewan-Manitoba border, insists McMechan wasn't exporting grain for profit, but to bring pressure on the government to change a law that is currently under review.

Bill Cairns, who was convicted alongside McMechan, had his fine tripled to $1,000, but he told the judge he wasn't going to pay it.

Cairns, 53, who farms on the Saskatchewan-Manitoba border, 160 kilometres west of Brandon, is appealing his two convictions of exporting grain without a permit, but faces 60 days in jail if the conviction stands and he doesn't pay.

"I feel so strongly about it all that if they want to put us in jail for selling our own grain and trying to make a living, they can go ahead," he says. "I think they'll see a lot of other farmers taking the same stand."

The renegade farmers have the support of several groups that have long been lobbying for changes to the wheat board monopoly.

"Our opinion is that the status quo isn't acceptable when you have all these farmers running the border," says Sharon McKinnon of the 6,000-member Western Canadian Wheat Growers Association.

Clifton Foster of the Alberta Barley Commission says the commission doesn't condone breaking the law, but it sympathizes with the renegades.

The commission has launched court action challenging the monopoly under the Canadian Charter of Rights and Freedoms.

But farmers on the other side of the issue say the renegades are throwing the wheat out with the chafe and have accused them of short-sightedness and greed.

"I think these 'Farmers for Just Us' would like to have their own self-interest legislated at the expense of the collective interest of the majority," says Cory Ollikka, 26, who farms 110 kilometres northeast of Edmonton.

"It just seems to me that the majority of individual farmers would not benefit from an eroded or destroyed wheat board.

"You will wind up with a select few farmers maybe making more money while the rest of the farmers are left twisting in the wind in the open market."

Ollikka claims that American farmers "would kill for a system of grain marketing such as ours."

Saskatchewan farmer Arnold Korte says most Saskatchewan farmers support the board, but their voices are being drowned out by noisy activists.

"They are definitely the minority, but for some reason they get a lot of public attention," says Korte, 61, who farms 125 kilometres east of Saskatoon.

The Alberta government has waded into the fray with two court actions challenging the wheat board monopoly and a plan, which if approved by the courts, will allow farmers an opportunity to market their own grain.

In a controversial 1995 Alberta plebiscite on the issue, 16,000 farmers voted almost 2 to 1 in support of more freedom in marketing their grain.

That action, in the federal court and Alberta court of appeal, has incensed the Saskatchewan government, which says farmers would lose more than $300 million annually if court action killed the board's monopoly.

"The Alberta government's motion to end the Canadian Wheat Board's monopoly is based on a misleading philosophical argument that ignores economic reality," complains Saskatchewan Agriculture Minister Eric Upshall.

Wheat board officials contend a dual market that would allow farmers to market their wheat and barley either through the board or elsewhere would spell doom for the federal board.

"The dual market is the slippery slope to an open market, and farmers should understand that before they make their decision," says board spokesperson Bob Roehle. "The price of grain will inevitably go down because they will have more farmers selling the same product to the big buyers who will very quickly play one farmer off against the other."

A panel set up by federal Agriculture Minister Ralph Goodale has recommended changes to the wheat board that would give farmers more opportunity to sell to their own markets, but some farmers fear the divisiveness over the issue will be used as an excuse by the minister to procrastinate. Goodale has given 130,000 prairie farmers until the end of the month to make their views known.

The National Farmers Union has led the campaign to retain the board.

President Nettie Wiebe says the issue boils down to farmers choosing whether to collectively market grain through their own board or through brokers and trans-national grain trading companies.

Roehle concedes there is no simple solution. He says farmers on both sides of the issue have dug in their heels.

"It's a thorny, thorny issue the federal government is facing because it is so divisive. Trying to find some middle ground is a tough challenge.

"Mr. Goodale will have to figure out how to walk that line and somehow bring peace back on to the Prairie."

KEITH MORRISON/BRANDON SUN FILE PHOTO
HANDCUFFED: Farmer Andy McMechan is taken into court in Brandon. Convicted of exporting grain without a permit, he was jailed and fined.

Index

fish catch, Canadian, 215
foreign policy, Canadian: and altruism, 191; and Canadian Peacebuilding Initiative, 193; economic intelligence in, 187; and export of culture, 190; foreign intelligence in, 187; and human rights in China, 188–189; and import certification program, 189; partnership with U.S. in, 190; and teaching of Asian languages, 188
foreign trade, Canadian: and niche markets, 187; with Asia, 187; with U.S., 187
fragmentation, cultural and territorial, 94, 95
French, minority status of, in Canada, 12
funding, in arts and culture, 190

global economy, education and, 110
government fiscal policy, sustainability of, 75
grain exports, legality of some, 223–224; and Charter of Rights and Freedoms, 224; and wheat board monopoly, 223–224
gross domestic product, percent of exports of, 13

"have" provinces, of Ontario, Alberta, and British Columbia, 76
health, education, and welfare, financing of, 75, 79
House of Commons, women in, 35–43; and cynicism, 36; and financial insecurity, 37; and fund-raising, 36; minority women in, 38–43
Huntington thesis, 194–195

imports, Canadian, 189; of grain, 223–224
income, per capita, of Canadians, 11
income security programs, 75
Indian self-government, "inherent right" of, 164
institution building, era of, 156
insurance, public, and NAFTA, 208–211
international law, and secession, 84, 85
internationalization, versus globalization, 152
interprovincial decision making, 79
Inuit, 97, 173, 177, 183

Japan, 187, 195

"knowledge corridors," 110

language families, aboriginal, 182
language policy: and bilingualism, 81, 83; and Charter of Rights and Freedoms, 82; and geographical separation of languages, 81; and potential for collapse of minority language, 82; and rate of assimilation, 82–83; and territorially based language rights, 81–83
language rights: as human rights, 81; question of, 10, 81–83
Laurier, Sir Wilfrid, 59
Leak of the Week campaign, 103
Liberal Opposition Party, 53
Liberal Party of Canada, 8, 56, 57, 58, 112, 118, 119, 120, 121, 122, 123, 127, 131, 164, 173, 190, 192
linguistic trends in Canada: costs of training in a second language, 137; French–English bilingualism, 136, 137; and French speaking outside Quebec, 136; within Quebec, 136, 137

Madison, James, 175
magazine industry: and disincentive for "split runs," 222; and grants, 222; postal

subsidies in, 222; and tax breaks, 222; trade protection policies in, 156, 159, 160
markets, Canadian foreign, 187
Maritime Union, case for: and aboriginal self-government, 111; and exports, 110; and the global economy, 109, 111; and international context of sovereignty, 109; and "knowledge corridors," 110; and Quebec's separatism, 109; and resource-dependent economy, limitations of, 111, and sustainable development, 109
Meech Lake Accord, 51, 52, 53, 169; draft of, 9; unraveling of, 10; agreement on wording of, 9, 20, 21
metric measurements, 45
military, future of Canadian: administrative reforms in, 197, 198; and Canadian disinterest in fighting, 202; cost of, 198, 203; and Defense White Paper, 1994, 148; and the death penalty, 197; and isolation of military from Canadian society, 205; and military justice system, 197; and morale, 198; and need for dismantling and rebuilding, 201; and need for leadership from government, 201; peacekeeping role of, 203, 204; and training, 197, 198; and U.N., 205
military, professional: and civilians, 204, distinctly military society of, 204; instructors as, 204; and isolation from Canadian society, 205
military, scandals in, 199, 200, 201, 203, 204
Montreal, 95
Morissette, Alanis, 153, 219
Mulroney, Brian, 8, 169, 170

National Film Board, 146, 154, 156, 160
national unity, 101
nations, distinct, as new part of federal structure, 178
native peoples, marginalization of, 170; and natural resources, 170
New Democratic Party (NDP) 119, 123, 130, 189
Newfoundland, 52, 87, 88, 97; joining Confederation of Canada, 87, 90
newspaper industry, subsidy in, 160; trade protection policies in, 160
niche markets, 187
North American Free Trade Agreement (NAFTA): and Agreement on International Trade (AIT), 211; health care sector and, 211; imports and, 218; and incompatibility with Medicare, 211; and multinational corporations, 211; new jobs and, 217; and pesticides in produce, 218; and U.S. corporations, 211; and U.S. job losses, 217; and wages, 217
North Atlantic Treaty Organization (NATO), 187, 189
Northwest Territories: birthrate of, 166; new self-government of, 166; race-based governance of, 166–168; splitup of, 166
Nunavut, 166, 177

Official Languages Act, 13, 136, 137, 138
Official Opposition, 112
Our Home or Native Land (Smith) 165, 167, 168
overspending, in Canadian government sector, 75

Parizeau, Jacques, 91

Parliament: and actual representation of voters, 46; and democracy, 44–47; and democratic accountability, 48; demographic makeup of, 34; and desires of Canadian population, 30–33; and gag motions, 45; intent of, 45; and "keeping in touch" function, 31; and local service, 31; and one-on-one problem solving, 32; and riding advocacy, 31; women in, 35–43
Parliament, 35th, social diversity of: and active community involvement, 43; and comparison with earlier parliaments, 41–42; and discrimination, 42; and methodology of determining personal origin, 39–40; and mixed heritage, 42; and double-token value of minority women, 43
Pearson, Lester B., 13
People to People, Nation to Nation (Royal Commission on Aboriginal Peoples), 169, 180, 181, 183
performing arts, 221
Persian Gulf War, 191, 194, 196, 202
polling, federal election: and designs of surveys, 117; and election coverage, 117; and margins of error, 116; and regional polls, 117; and sampling, 116; and telephone surveys, 117
premiers, provincial and federal role of: and 80 percent solution, 99; and equalization program, 98; rebalancing agenda and, 99; and youth programs, 98
Progressive Conservative Party, 52, 56, 112, 189
provinces, emerging, 177
provincial government, closeness to the people of, 25
provincial jurisdiction, and federal norms, 79; and interprovincial decision making, 79
provincial responsibility, 79
public health services, nonprofit delivery of, and NAFTA, 208–211
publishing industry; 158; and Baie Comeau policy on foreign ownership, 221; dominance of imported products in, 221, exports of books in, 221; future of, 161; tax credits in, 156, 160; trade protection in, 156, 160

Quebec: aboriginal peoples of, and secession, 85; and borders, modification of, 91; budgetary status of, 128; Charter of Rights of, 83; constitutional amendment for secession of, 22; and diversity, 97; and election of 1997, 125; as ethnic entity, 96; and French speaking, 136, 137; and Maritime Union, 109; pro-separatist government of, 15–17; and recognition of differences, 21; and referendum on sovereignty, 16; separatism of, 8, 109; separation referenda on, 14, 54, 56; unilingualism within, 137

radio: and Canadian content, 221; foreign ownership of, 221; and policy, 221
rebalancing, of federalism, 79, 80
recording industry, 158; future of, 161; tax credits in, 156; trade protection in, 156, 160
redistribution, 75, 76, 78
Reform Party, 112, 118, 119, 120, 122, 123, 124, 125, 128, 130, 131, 138, 189

Credits/Acknowledgments

Cover design by Charles Vitelli

1. The Constitution and Canadian Federalism
Facing overview—Industry, Science & Technology (ISTC) photo.

2. The Parliamentary System
Facing overview—Industry, Science & Technology (ISTC)

3. The Supreme Court and Its Role in Canadian Politics
Facing overview—Industry, Science & Technology (ISTC) photo.

4. Quebec
Facing overview—AP/Wide World photo by Tom Hanson.

5. The Provinces in the Canadian Federation
Facing overview—Le Château Frontenac photo.

6. Political Parties and Elections
Facing overview—AP/Wide World photo by Fred Chartrand.

7. The Politics of Culture
Facing overview—Industry, Science & Technology (ISTC) photo.

8. Aboriginal Issues
Facing overview—Museum of the American Indian, Heye Foundation photo by M. R. Harrington.

9. Foreign Policy and the Military
Facing overview—U.S. Air Force photo by Sargeant R. Barry Johnson. 200—*Globe and Mail* photo by Kevin Whitfield (top left), Canadian Press photo (top middle, bottom left, bottom right), Reuters Standard Life Centre photo (top right, bottom middle). 203—*Globe and Mail* photo by Kevin Whitfield.

10. International Trade
Facing overview—AP/Wide World photo.

ANNUAL EDITIONS ARTICLE REVIEW FORM

■ NAME: _____ DATE: _____

■ TITLE AND NUMBER OF ARTICLE: _____

■ BRIEFLY STATE THE MAIN IDEA OF THIS ARTICLE: _____

_____

■ LIST THREE IMPORTANT FACTS THAT THE AUTHOR USES TO SUPPORT THE MAIN IDEA:

_____

_____

_____

_____

■ WHAT INFORMATION OR IDEAS DISCUSSED IN THIS ARTICLE ARE ALSO DISCUSSED IN YOUR TEXTBOOK OR OTHER READINGS THAT YOU HAVE DONE? LIST THE TEXTBOOK CHAPTERS AND PAGE NUMBERS:

_____

_____

_____

_____

_____

■ LIST ANY EXAMPLES OF BIAS OR FAULTY REASONING THAT YOU FOUND IN THE ARTICLE:

_____

_____

_____

_____

■ LIST ANY NEW TERMS/CONCEPTS THAT WERE DISCUSSED IN THE ARTICLE, AND WRITE A SHORT DEFINITION:

_____

_____

_____

_____

_____

*Your instructor may require you to use this ANNUAL EDITIONS Article Review Form in any number of ways: for articles that are assigned, for extra credit, as a tool to assist in developing assigned papers, or simply for your own reference. Even if it is not required, we encourage you to photocopy and use this page; you will find that reflecting on the articles will greatly enhance the information from your text.

We Want Your Advice

ANNUAL EDITIONS revisions depend on two major opinion sources: one is our Advisory Board, listed in the front of this volume, which works with us in scanning the thousands of articles published in the public press each year; the other is you—the person actually using the book. Please help us and the users of the next edition by completing the prepaid article rating form on this page and returning it to us. Thank you for your help!

ANNUAL EDITIONS:
CANADIAN POLITICS Fourth Edition
Article Rating Form

Here is an opportunity for you to have direct input into the next revision of this volume. We would like you to rate each of the 62 articles listed below, using the following scale:

1. **Excellent: should definitely be retained**
2. **Above average: should probably be retained**
3. **Below average: should probably be deleted**
4. **Poor: should definitely be deleted**

Your ratings will play a vital part in the next revision. So please mail this prepaid form to us just as soon as you complete it.
Thanks for your help!

Rating	Article	Rating	Article
	1. How Meech Changed History		29. The Stolen Revolution
	2. Canada's Challenge: Uniting Hearts and Minds for a Federal Future		30. Renewing the Case for Maritime Union
			31. Suppose Your Vote Counted
	3. Separate Sovereignty—Québec and Canada: Equal Partners		32. Counting the Votes so All Votes Count
			33. Elections Bring Polls and the Question: Can the Numbers Lie?
	4. A Constitutional Solution: The Evolution of Canadian Federalism		34. The Fickle Finger of Folk
	5. The Case for Strengthening Federal Powers		35. Distinct Societies
	6. What Kind of Representatives Do Canadians Want?		36. Sovereignty's Stumbling Bloc
	7. Educated, Middle-Aged Males Dominate Parliament		37. Unheeded Warnings
	8. Women: Why the House Is Not a Home		38. Canada Talks the Talk
	9. Minority Women in the 35th Parliament		39. Open to Interpretation
	10. The Elected Dictatorship: Can Parliament Be Made an Adequate Instrument of Democracy? Easily		40. CRTC Abandons Cultural Red Flag
			41. The Juneau Report and the Gordian Knot of the CBC
	11. Lines in the Political Sand		42. Culture between Commercials
	12. Is Senate Reform a Dead Issue?		43. Seven Myths about Canadian Culture
	13. Is He Up to the Job?		44. Exporting Canadian Culture
	14. Politicians Defer to High Court		45. Canadian Culture Policies Pique U.S. Interest
	15. Needed: A Better Way to Make Supreme Court Appointments		46. Apron-String Sovereignty
			47. Apartheid Has Its Attractions
	16. Order in the Supreme Court! Ad-Hockery Is Running Wild		48. Royal Omission
			49. The Writing on the Wall
	17. Clerks Labor to Keep Justice in Balance		50. An Unworkable Vision of Self-Government
	18. Court Backlog Crisis Looming Again		51. Aboriginal Government: Alternative Outcomes
	19. Fiscal Federalism and Quebec Separatism		52. Not a Word about Natives
	20. Interprovincial Role—Quebec: Looking for Change		53. Neighbourhood Watch
	21. Arrêt! You Are Entering a French-Speaking Area		54. Canadian Strategic Policy and *The Clash of Civilizations*
	22. Stéphane Dion: 'These Grave Questions Cannot Be Avoided'		55. Blueprint for Military's Future
			56. Uncertainty about Future Undermines Forces
	23. Bernard Landry: Ottawa's Line Is Anti-Democratic		57. Warriors, Weenies and Worriers
	24. Stéphane Dion: 'I Am Entitled to Insist on a Process That Is Clear'		58. Doctoring to NAFTA
			59. Darn Yankees!
	25. Not "Distinct Society" but "Distinctive Societies"		60. I Told You So
	26. Provinces Muscling in on Federal Territory		61. Yikes! They're Tipping the Cultural Balance
	27. Ottawa Plays Tough Guy with Provinces		62. Against the Grain
	28. Alberta Reopens the Big Spending Tap		

(Continued on next page)

ABOUT YOU

Name _____ Date _____

Are you a teacher? ❑ Or a student? ❑

Your school name _____

Department _____

Address _____

City _____ State _____ Zip _____

School telephone # _____

YOUR COMMENTS ARE IMPORTANT TO US !

Please fill in the following information:

For which course did you use this book? _____

Did you use a text with this *ANNUAL EDITION*? ❑ yes ❑ no

What was the title of the text? _____

What are your general reactions to the *Annual Editions* concept?

Have you read any particular articles recently that you think should be included in the next edition?

Are there any articles you feel should be replaced in the next edition? Why?

Are there any World Wide Web sites you feel should be included in the next edition? Please annotate.

May we contact you for editorial input?

May we quote your comments?

ANNUAL EDITIONS: CANADIAN POLITICS, Fourth Edition